ECONOMIC INTEGRATION
BETWEEN UNEQUAL PARTNERS

New Dimensions in Political Economy
General Editor: Ingrid H. Rima, Professor of Economics, Temple University, US

This ambitious new series is designed to bridge the gap between received economic theory and the real world that it seeks to explain. The dramatic events in Eastern Europe, the resurgence of an invigorated market capitalism and the prospects of integrated trading and financial communities have created new interest in the term political economy, which will be a dominant theme of titles included in this series.

The Political Economy of Global Restructuring
Volume I   Economic Organization and Production
Volume II   Trade and Finance
Edited by Ingrid H. Rima

Economic Integration between Unequal Partners
Edited by Theodore Georgakopoulos, Christos C. Paraskevopoulos and John Smithin

Economic Integration between Unequal Partners

Edited by

Theodore Georgakopoulos,
Athens University of Economics and Business, Greece

Christos C. Paraskevopoulos
York University, Canada

and John Smithin
York University, Canada

NEW DIMENSIONS IN POLITICAL ECONOMY

Edward Elgar

© Theodore Georgakopoulos, Christos C. Paraskevopoulos, John Smithin 1994

All rights reserved. No part of this publication may be reproduced, stored in a retrieval system, or transmitted in any form by any means, electronic, mechanical, photocopying, recording, or otherwise without the prior permission of the publisher.

Published by
Edward Elgar Publishing Limited
Gower House
Croft Road
Aldershot
Hants GU11 3HR
England

Edward Elgar Publishing Company
Old Post Road
Brookfield
Vermont 05036
USA

British Library Cataloguing in Publication Data
Economic Integration Between Unequal
Partners. – (New Dimensions in Political Economy Series)
  I. Georgakopoulos, Theodore   II. Series.
  337

Library of Congress Cataloguing in Publication Data
Economic integration between unequal partners/ edited by Theodore
  Georgakopoulos, Christos C. Paraskevopoulos, and John Smithin.
      p.   cm. — (New dimensions in political economy)
  "Most of the papers [included] were originally presented at an international conference, held in Athens, Greece in August 1992, sponsored by York University (Toronto) and the Athens University of Economics and Business" — Introd.
  1. European Economic Community—Congresses.   2. Europe—Economic integration—Congresses.   3. European Economic Community countries--Economic conditions—Regional disparities—Congresses.   4. North America—Economic integration—Congresses. 5. North America--Economic conditions—Regional disparities—Congresses.
6. International economic integration—Congresses.   7. Regional economic disparities—Congresses. I. Geōrgakopoulos, Theodōros A.
II. Paraskevopoulos, Christos C.   III. Smithin, John N. IV. Series.
  HC241.2.E2926 1994
  337.1'42—dc20   93-38385
                                                                                                      CIP

ISBN 185278 878 X

Printed and Bound in Great Britain by
Hartnolls Limited, Bodmin, Cornwall.

Contents

List of Illustrations	viii
List of Tables	ix
List of Contributors	xii
Foreword	xiii
Richard S. Eckaus	
Acknowledgements	xv
Introduction	xvii
Theodore Georgakopoulos, Christos C. Paraskevopoulos and John Smithin	

PART I THE PROCESS OF ECONOMIC INTEGRATION IN NORTH AMERICA

1. NAFTA: A Brief Assessment — 3
   Gary C. Hufbauer
2. Restructuring North America: The Impact of Unequal Integration — 23
   Ricardo Grinspun and Maxwell A. Cameron
3. Competitiveness and Productivity between Canadian and US Manufacturing Industries — 35
   Christos C. Paraskevopoulos
4. Labour Markets, Productivity and Trade Unions in the NAFTA Countries — 56
   Edur Velasco Arregui
5. Caribbean Economic Integration (CARICOM) — 65
   George E. Eaton

PART II INTEGRATION AND UNEQUAL DEVELOPMENT IN THE EUROPEAN COMMUNITY

6. Internalization and externalization of EC Trade — 83
   Evrard Claessens
7. Economic Integration and Unequal Development: The Experience of Greece — 98
   Theodore Georgakopoulos

vi   *Economic integration between unequal partners*

8. The Common Agricultural Policy in the Process of European Integration and Convergence   110
    George P. Zanias
9. Regional Imbalances and National or Federal Social Protection   122
    Jozef Pacolet and Erik Gos
10. Health Expenditure and Market Integration in the European Community   135
    Theo Hitiris
11. An Approach to Economic Integration of a Small Country   143
    George K. Zestos

PART III   THE POLITICAL ECONOMY OF ECONOMIC INTEGRATION

12. Trade Among Partners Who Differ in Their Economic Development   161
    Ingrid H. Rima
13. Triple 'A' Trade: Asymmetry, Access and Adjustment, The Inflexible Limits of Trade Blocs   170
    Daniel Drache
14. Economic Integration: 'Gobble-ization' or Partnership? The Case of Southern Europe   186
    O.F. Hamouda
15. Peripherality and Divergence in the EC: The Need for Industrial Policy   201
    Philip Arestis and Eleni Paliginis
16. The 'Sensitive Issues' of the EC-1992 Programme and US Business   210
    Mike Pournarakis

PART IV   MONETARY AND FINANCIAL ASPECTS OF THE INTEGRATION PROCESS

17. Financial Integration in the EC: Conceptual Approach and Implications   223
    Sotirios Kollias
18. Monetary Union and Economic Integration: The Less Developed Areas of the European Community   235
    A.J. Kondonassis and A.G. Malliaris

19. The Macroeconomic and Microeconomic Consequences of
    Alternative Exchange Rate Regimes: Implications for European
    Monetary Union   243
    John Smithin and Bernard M. Wolf
20. The Greek Financial System: Strategies for Convergence   252
    Themis D. Pantos and Christos C. Paraskevopoulos

PART V   LESSONS FROM THE UNIFICATION OF GERMANY

21. Unequal Integration: The Case of German Re-unification   273
    Horst Tomann
22. Restructuring the East German Economy   282
    Jürgen Müller

Index   297

Illustrations

9.1	'Behavioural' characteristics of the labour market	123
9.2	Reasons for regional divergence and EC policies	124
9.3	Relation between national income, social protection and regional cohesion	127
9.4	Trade off between GDP and social expenditure, 1987	127
9.5	Trade off between GDP and GDP dispersion, 1987	128
9.6	Trade off between social expenditure and GDP dispersion, 1987	129
11.1	Annual percent growth of Y, Y/L and TFP, total GDP, Greece	149
11.2	Annual percent growth of output, total GDP	150
11.3	Annual growth of labour productivity, total GDP	150
11.4	Annual percent change in TFP, total GDP	151

Box

9.1	Decomposition of regional fiscal capacity and needs	125

Tables

1.1	Mexico: selected balance of payments accounts, 1980–90 and projected 1991–95	4
1.2	United States and Mexico bilateral merchandise trade, 1980–92	5
1.3	Value of United States trade with Mexico, 1991	6
1.4	United States and Mexico: trade in automobiles and parts, 1986 and 1991	9
1.5	Mexico: vehicle production and exports by manufacturer, 1989	10
1.6	United States: global trade in textiles and apparel, 1978–91	11
1.7	United States: agricultural trade with Mexico, 1980 and 1991	13
1.8	US jobs supported by exports to Mexico and dislocated by imports from Mexico, 1990, and future scenario resulting from the impact of NAFTA and related reforms	17
2.1	Social democratic criteria for economic integration: comparing North America and the European Community	29
3.1	Annual growth rates of output, capital and labour in selected Canadian manufacturing industries	39
3.2	Annual growth rates of output and sources of growth in selected Canadian manufacturing industries	41
3.3	Annual growth rates of total factor productivity and sources of growth in selected Canadian manufacturing industries	42
3.4	Annual growth rates of labour productivity and sources of growth in selected Canadian manufacturing industries	43
3.5	Annual growth rates of capital productivity and sources of growth in selected Canadian manufacturing industries	46
3.6	Annual growth rates of output, capital and labour in selected US manufacturing industries	47
3.7	Annual growth rates of output and sources of growth in selected US manufacturing industries	48
3.8	Annual growth rates of total factor productivity and sources of growth in selected US manufacturing industries	49
3.9	Annual growth rates of labour productivity and sources of growth in selected US manufacturing industries	50

x *Economic integration between unequal partners*

3.10	Annual growth rates of capital productivity and sources of growth in selected US manufacturing industries	51
3.11	Annual rates of local technical progress and returns to scale for Canadian (Ontario, Quebec, British Columbia) and US total manufacturing	52
5.1	Statistical profile	67
6.1	Import and trade volumes of the European Community	84
6.2	Comparative growth (%) of EC imports (only EUR-9)	85
6.3a	Example of the 'Monnet index' 1976–80	86
6.3b	Product proportional shifts with 'Monnet index'	87
6.4	Monnet index (1988–91) with import-value indicator	88
6.5a	Export value indicator with EURO DIVIDEND INDICATOR	89
6.5b	MVI-value indicator	90
6.6	German proportional shifts and Euro Dividend	90
6.7	The Spanish Euro Dividend indicator	92
6.8	Country statistics of Euro Dividend indicators	93
6.9	National % shares in intra-EC value trade	95
6.10	(Exhibit) Trade dividend graph	96
7.1	Greece's budgetary receipts and payments 1981–1993	99
7.2	Some indices of the trade and welfare effects of Greece's entry	102
7.3	The impact of accession on trade in agricultural and manufactured products	103
8.1	Expenditure and revenue under the CAP	111
8.2	Net budgetary transfers in the European Community (average 1986–90)	113
8.3	Magnitude of CAP benefits (1984/85 and 1985/86)	116
8.4	Distribution of CAP benefits (ECU) by income class and farm size (1984/85–1985/86)	117
8.5	Net farm value added at factor cost per AWU in the EC	118
9.1	Results of the various simulations	130
10.1	Health care expenditure in EC member states, 1988	137
10.2	Health expenditure in EC countries	140
11.1	Sources of growth of output for three EC countries' Gross Domestic Product, GDP	146
11.2	Factor input growth and factor substitution percentage changes (annual rates)	147
11.3	Productivity, output and input growth average percentage change (annual rates)	148
11.4	Labour productivity, total factor productivity and factor substitution, GDP	152

11.A.1	Greece: exports, imports and trade openness	154
11.A.2	Greece: geographic distribution of trade, 1980–87 (exports)	155
11.A.3	Greece: geographic distribution of trade, 1980–87 (imports)	155
13.1	Trade dependence of core industrial economies	181
14.1	Decisive group	194
16.1	Cross-border mergers and acquisitions in the Economic Community 1988–1989	217
17.1	Exports of goods and services, 1991 (by major areas)	224
17.2	Use of currencies in international financial transactions	225
17.3	Stockmarket capitalization, 1991	225
17.4	Programme of financial integration	226
17.5	Harmonization of prudential rules	227
17.6	Financial integration: main EC directives	228
17.7	Taxation on interest from deposits	233

List of contributors

Philip Arestis, University of East London, UK
Maxwell A. Cameron, Carleton University, Canada
Evrard Claessens, University of Antwerp, Belgium
Daniel Drache, York University, Canada
George E. Eaton, York University, Canada
Richard S. Eckaus, Massachusetts Institute of Technology, USA
Theodore Georgakopoulos, Athens University of Economics and Business, Greece
Ricardo Grinspun, York University, Canada
Erik Gos, Catholic University of Leuven, Belgium
O.F. Hamouda, York University, Canada
Theo Hitiris, University of York, UK
Gary C. Hufbauer, Institute for International Economics, USA
Sotirios Kollias, Commission of the European Communities, Greece
A.J. Kondonassis, University of Oklahoma, USA
A.G. Malliaris, Loyola University of Chicago, USA
Jürgen Müller, DIW Berlin, Germany
Jozef Pacolet, Catholic University of Leuven, Belgium
Eleni Paliginis, Middlesex University, UK
Themis D. Pantos, University of Toronto, Canada
Christos C. Paraskevopoulos, York University, Canada
Mike Pournarakis, Athens University of Economics and Business, Greece
Ingrid H. Rima, Temple University, USA
John Smithin, York University, Canada
Horst Tomann, Free University of Berlin, Germany
Edur Velasco Arregui, Autonomous Metropolitan University, Mexico
Bernard M. Wolf, York University, Canada
George P. Zanias, Agricultural University of Athens, Greece
George K. Zestos, Ball State University, USA

Foreword
Richard S. Eckaus

This book is an important step in broadening and deepening the discussion of the implications of economic integration among nations. There are oceans of literature on economic integration, but most of that has been journalistic hyperbole. By comparison, there are only small ponds of informed and economically sophisticated analysis and too little of that has found its way into political and public awareness.

There is, for example, little evidence in most of the public discussion of the considerable scepticism within the economics profession with respect to the magnitude of the benefits of the extension of the economic integration in Europe in 1992 and 1993 and the merits of a common European monetary system. The neglect is unfortunate for many reasons. Not the least of these is that public perceptions of these benefits have encouraged nearly every geographical region to consider forming its own free trade community.

Putting aside the common overstatement of the potential gains in the European case, there are two main sources of misgivings. The first comes from proponents of free trade who argue that its scope should be worldwide, if its benefits are to be captured. For these free traders, the gains from increased intra-regional trade made possible by a common market are more than offset by the dangers of intra-regional preferences that create handicaps for outsiders trying to export to the region.

The second type of apprehension focuses on the implications of important economies of scale for the relocation and concentration of industry. In the past the trade barriers in Europe promoted a higher degree of industrial diversity within its countries than is typically found within the states in the US in order to satisfy a wide range of demands in each protected market. The removal of the trade barriers means that one or a few plants large enough to achieve all the potential economies of scale in production can serve the entire market. Production costs will fall, but there will also be major dislocations and rearrangements of industry and employment, with associated private and social costs that are customarily overlooked.

On the financial and monetary side, much of that part of the economics profession that studies such things has also been highly sceptical of the proposal for a common European currency. A common currency for Europe would deprive its countries of the modest but still important potential for an independent monetary policy that remains after adherence to the European Monetary System. The breakdown of that system has demonstrated more dramatically the importance attached to such independence than have the economics journal articles.

There are, in turn, two possible explanations for the popular and political neglect of these apprehensions. The first is that they are simply not understood. Perhaps only the first basic economics textbook chapter on free trade has been explained to policy-makers and the qualifying footnotes, advanced chapters and more recent commentaries have been neglected. The other possibility is that, for many policy-makers, the basic agenda in the expansion of the European Common Market and the European Monetary System is not economic, but political. There may have been some willingness to make sacrifices in the former area in the hope of creating conditions for political unity. Perhaps that is a good bargain, but, if so, why conceal it, unless there is a suspicion that voters would not buy it.

In the end, of course, it has been impossible to fool all of the people all of the time, and the strong misgivings of voters finally emerged. That happened in Denmark's first rejection of the Maastricht treaty, in the large protest votes in other countries in which a public referendum has been held and in the angry parliamentary debates.

One of the lessons of the dramatic economic and political events in Europe of the past year or so must be that economic integration should be debated thoroughly. This book is a significant step in applying that lesson. A still more significant step would be the regularization of this discussion: a re-creation of the ancient Greek forum in which the issues are discussed in front of the public on a regular basis.

Acknowledgements

Most of the contributions in this volume were originally presented at an international conference, held in Athens, Greece, in August 1992, sponsored by York University and the Athens University of Economics and Business. The Athens conference was the first major joint activity between the two institutions under an Exchange Agreement signed in April 1991. We would like to thank, at the outset, the two sponsoring universities, but particularly the Athens University of Economics and Business for the superb organization and publicity in hosting the Athens conference, and all participants.

Special thanks go to former Rector Andreas Kintis for embracing the idea of establishing the exchange – an idea conceived on the island of Spetses in the summer of 1989 – and for making it a reality.

In addition to the editors of these volumes a number of other colleagues served on the organizing committee of the conference, or helped in other ways, and would like to thank G. Christou (Chair), G. Alogoskouphis, A. Andrikopoulos, N. Baltas, N. Christodoulakis, K. Gatsios, R. Grinspun, N. Karamouzis, F. Lazar, and K. Vaitsos.

We received excellent secretarial support from Eleftheria Apostolidou (Athens University of Economics and Business) and Agnes Fraser and Dawn Freeman (York University).

We appreciate the financial support of the following non-academic sponsors: Alpha Finance, A.N.Z. Grindlays Bank, City Bank N.A., Credit Bank S.A., the Jean Monnet Programme of the European Community, the Greek Ministry of Culture and National Westminster Bank Ltd.

We would like to thank the series editor, Ingrid H. Rima, and the publisher, Edward Elgar, for their support and encouragement of this project.

Finally, thanks are due to Julie Leppard and other members of the staff of Edward Elgar Publishing Limited, both at Aldershot and Cheltenham, for their customary high quality work on this volume.

Introduction
*Theodore Georgakopoulos, Christos C.
Paraskevopoulos and John Smithin*

The papers collected in this volume deal with various aspects of the contemporary phenomenon of the rise of the major trading blocs, such as the European Community (EC) and the potential Canada–US–Mexico free trade area under the North American Free Trade Agreement (NAFTA). The rise of these trading blocs has profound implications, in both socio-economic and geopolitical terms, for the future of the international economic system as we have known it.

Most of the papers were originally presented at an international conference, held in Athens, Greece in August 1992, sponsored by York University (Toronto) and the Athens University of Economics and Business. The aim of the conference was to bring together perspectives from both sides of the Atlantic, with particular emphasis on the contentious issues which arise in a process of economic integration in which unequal partners are involved. In addition to participants from both Greece and Canada, whose economies are, of course, at very different stages of economic development, but whose citizens nonetheless share the common feeling that their nations are among the smaller players in their respective blocs, there are contributors from Belgium, Germany, Mexico, the USA and the UK.

The key issue for debate is the question of whether the apparently irreversible trend towards mega trading blocs will lead, as their proponents claim, to a higher overall rate of economic growth, a reduction of economic disparities and convergence between unequal partners, or whether the process is a 'zero sum game' where one partner's gain can only come at the expense of another. Perhaps nor surprisingly, there is no consensus on this basic question among the contributors, and the reader must come to an individual judgement as to which of the several arguments presented here are the most persuasive. Broadly speaking, opinion is divided between a relatively optimistic and a relatively pessimistic assessment. The former would rely not only on traditional economic arguments about comparative advantage and the static 'gains from trade', but also on the 'dynamic' benefits of economic integration which have been identified in the more recent literature. The latter, however, stresses the loss of sovereignty on the part of the national governments, and hence of their ability to pursue both macroeconomic and microeconomic policies appropriate to local conditions. It is also suggested that the integration process is changing, and will change, the balance of power between capital and labour, in favour of the former.

The volume is divided into five parts. Part I, with contributions by Gary Hufbauer, Ricardo Grinspun and Maxwell Cameron, Christos Paraskevopoulos, and Edur Velasco Arregui, deals primarily with issues arising from the NAFTA. This section also contains a paper by George Eaton on the CARICOM integration process in the Caribbean. Similarly, Part II concentrates on the EC, with chapters by Evrard Claessens, Theodore Georgakopoulos, George Zanias, Erik Gos and Jozef Pacolet, Theo Hitiris, and George Zestos.

Part III raises a number of contentious issues in the political economy of trading blocs. Contributions by Ingrid Rima, Daniel Drache, Omar Hamouda, Philip Arestis and Eleni Paliginis, and Mike Pournarakis collectively attempt to answer the vital question of who will ultimately be the winners and who will be the losers in the economic integration process.

The monetary and financial aspects of economic integration are dealt with as a separate topic in Part IV, including papers by Sotirios Kollias, A.J. Kondonassis and A.G. Malliaris, John Smithin and Bernard Wolf, and Themis Pantos and Christos Paraskevopoulos. These contributions deal with matters which have become particularly controversial since the crisis in the ERM in 1992 and 1993, and the difficulties this raises for the EC's drive towards an eventual common currency.

Finally, Part V, containing chapters by Horst Tomann and Jürgen Müller, focuses on a very prominent recent example of a rapid integration process between two obviously unequal partners, the unification of Germany. This provides a dramatic case-study of precisely what is involved in the effort to fuse into one the economies of two partners at very different stage of economic development.

This volume will obviously not settle the debates about either the desirability or the viability of the trend towards mega trading blocs, particularly in the changed circumstances which have arisen following the collapse of communism and the restructuring of the Central and Eastern European economies. However, it is to be hoped that the reader will at least gain a greater appreciation of the complexity of the questions that are involved.

It should be noted that since the ratification of the Maastricht Treaty in November 1993 the European Community (EC) is now frequently referred to as the European Union (EU). However, as most of the contributions here were written before that change the older style (EC) is retained throughout.

PART I

THE PROCESS OF ECONOMIC INTEGRATION IN NORTH AMERICA

1 NAFTA: A Brief Assessment
Gary C. Hufbauer[1]

Background and implications for the members

On 17 December 1992, the United States, Canada, and Mexico signed a historic trade accord. The North American Free Trade Agreement (NAFTA) is the most comprehensive free trade pact (short of a common market) ever negotiated between regional trading partners, and the first reciprocal free trade pact between a developing country and two industrial countries. The NAFTA is scheduled to enter into force on 1 January 1994, after ratification by the three legislatures.

For Mexico, the NAFTA reinforces the extensive market-oriented policy reforms implemented since 1985. These reforms have promoted real annual growth of 3 to 4 per cent in recent years, and a falling rate of inflation, now approaching single digits. The NAFTA portends continuation of the fast pace of change in the Mexican economy by extending the reform process to sectors such as autos, textiles and apparel, finance, telecommunications, and land transportation. Mexican exporters will also benefit in two distinct ways: the relatively unfettered access to the US market that they already enjoy under various unilateral US programmes will be sustained; and the few remaining US trade barriers will be liberalized.

The prospect of NAFTA implementation has already generated strong expectational effects, with capital inflows to Mexico estimated at about $27 billion in 1993 (of which about $6 billion will likely be foreign direct investment; see Table 1.1).[2] These large inflows are the financial counterpart to the growing Mexican current account deficit generated by imports of machinery, equipment and other capital goods, all essential ingredients for the sustained development of the Mexican economy.

For the United States, the NAFTA reforms should enhance an already important export market. US exports to Mexico have grown rapidly since 1986, and in 1992 reached an annual rate of about $43 billion (see Tables 1.2 and 1.3). US suppliers of intermediates, capital goods and high technology products should continue to reap large benefits as prime suppliers of the growing Mexican market. Over time, the NAFTA should impel industrial reorganization along regional lines, with firms taking best advantage of each country's ability to produce components and assembled products and thus enhancing North American competitiveness in the global marketplace.

Table 1.1 Mexico: selected balance of payments accounts, 1980–90 and projected 1991–95[a] (millions dollars)

Account	1989	1990	1991	1992	1993	1994	1995	1996	1997
Current account	(6 085)	(7 114)	(13 283)	(22 001)	(25 381)	(29 034)	(29 291)	(29 827)	(28 968)
Trade	(2 596)	(4 434)	(11 064)	(20 177)	(23 489)	(26 807)	(26 627)	(27 357)	(27 098)
Nonfactor services	2 477	1 571	2 405	2 200	3 100	4 248	5 465	7 148	9 087
Factor services	(8 042)	(7 716)	(6 866)	(6 302)	(7 295)	(8 823)	(10 519)	(12 054)	(13 443)
Transfers	2 075	3 465	2 242	2 277	2 303	2 347	2 390	2 436	2 485
Capital account (net)	3 176	8 164	20 179	20 362	26 893	28 761	28 553	29 682	28 683
Foreign Investment	3 557	4 628	12 302	14 837	14 241	17 250	17 047	17 453	17 732
Direct	3 175	2 633	4 761	5 813	6 213	7 956	8 122	8 656	9 820
Portfolio	493	1 995	7 540	9 024	8 028	9 294	8 925	8 796	7 912
Special drawing rights and other	124	(181)	315	(478)	382	(526)	(548)	(248)	(288)
Errors and omissions	3 305	2 183	1 241	1 975	(342)	1 505	1 836	1 365	1 330
Addenda									
Change in gross reserves	272	3 414	7 822	815	787	1 757	1 645	1 468	1 332
Total accumulated FDI[b]	26 587	29 220	33 981	39 794	46 007	53 963	62 085	70 741	80 561

Notes:
[a] Discrepancies are in the original data.
[b] Total accumulated Foreign Direct Investment (FDI) for 1989 was obtained from Banco de Mexico, 'The Mexican Economy', May 1992, p. 264.

Sources: CIEMEX-WEFA, 'Perspectives Economicas de Mexico,' March 1993, p. 109 and 112.

Table 1.2 United States and Mexico bilateral merchandise trade, 1980–92

Year	US exports to Mexico Billions of dollars	Per cent of total US exports	Per cent of total Mexican imports	Per cent of US GDP	US imports from Mexico Billions of dollars	Per cent of total US imports	Per cent of total Mexican exports[a]	Per cent of Mexican GDP[a]	Bilateral balance ($ bill.)
1980	15.1	6.9	69.7	0.6	12.8	5.0	69.3	6.9	2.3
1981	17.8	7.6	66.5	0.6	14.0	5.1	60.4	5.8	3.8
1982	11.8	5.6	67.0	0.4	15.0	6.2	62.5	9.0	-3.2
1983	9.1	4.5	72.1	0.3	17.0	6.3	62.0	11.9	-7.9
1984	12.0	5.5	74.8	0.3	18.3	5.4	61.3	10.7	-6.3
1985	13.6	6.4	73.7	0.3	19.4	5.4	66.7	11.0	-5.8
1986	12.4	5.7	73.6	0.3	17.6	4.5	72.4	13.5	-5.2
1987	14.6	5.8	74.0	0.3	20.5	4.8	69.2	14.6	-5.9
1988	20.5	6.5	75.6	0.4	23.5	5.1	73.4	13.5	-3.0
1989	25.0	6.9	73.4	0.5	27.6	5.6	74.7	13.7	-2.6
1990	28.4	7.2	74.8	0.5	30.8	6.0	78.6	13.1	-2.4
1991	33.3	7.9	71.8	0.6	31.9	6.3	82.0	11.3	1.4
1992	43.2	9.6	n.a.	0.7	36.4	6.6	n.a.	12.5	6.8

Notes:
n.a.: no available.
[a] These figures somewhat overstate the importance of Mexican exports to the United States because they include total shipments from maquiladora plants, and most maquiladora inputs originate in the United States.

Source: International Monetary Fund, 'Direction of Trade Statistics', Yearbook. 1987 and 1992; International Monetary Fund, 'International Financial Statistical', Yearbook 1990; World Bank, 'World Debt Tables', 1989–1990 and 1990–1991; US Department of Commerce, Office of Mexico, 'Data Sheet', January 1991; Banco de Mexico, 'The Mexican Economy', 1991. International Monetary Fund data reprinted with permission.

Table 1.3 Value of United States trade with Mexico, 1991 ($ millions)

Sector	US exports to Mexico	US imports from Mexico
Energy[a]		
Crude Petroleum and Natural Gas	41	4 822
Refined Products	567	210
Automotive		
Motor vehicles	300	2 800
Parts	5 400	4 900
Steel[b]		
Iron and Steel Products	879	303
Textiles & Apparel[c]	1 016	879
Textiles	536	206
Apparel	480	673
Agriculture[d]	2 998	2 527

Notes:
[a] 1990 figures.
[b] Figures are for SITC 67.
[c] Includes MFA products only.
[d] Total agricultural products.

Sources: US Department of Commerce, 'US Industrial Outlook, 1993'; American Textile Manufacturers Institute; and US Department of Agriculture.

In addition, the NAFTA meets key US foreign policy objectives. The US debate often ignores the foreign policy dimension, blithely taking for granted that Mexican steps towards economic reform and political pluralism are irreversible. But Mexico's economic reforms are still vulnerable to political and financial shocks, and democratic reforms are still in their infancy. The NAFTA should anchor achievements already made in Mexico and point towards a more prosperous and democratic southern neighbour. Over a period of decades, Mexican prosperity should sharply reduce illegal immigration into the United States, now running at about one million persons annually, of whom perhaps 100,000 become new permanent residents each year.

For Canada, the NAFTA reinforces, and in some cases strengthens, its FTA preferences in the US market. Canada achieved many of its specific objectives in the negotiations, such as clarifying the method used to calculate the regional content for autos and retaining the Canada–US FTA provision that exempts Canadian cultural industries from external competition. In addition, the NAFTA improves Canada's access to the Mexican market. Although Mexico is a relatively small export market for Canada (under $2 billion but growing fast), the NAFTA will expand export opportunities for Canadian firms in several key sectors, such as financial services, automobiles, and government procurement.

In the next ten years or so, the biggest consequence of NAFTA will be a surge in US–Mexican trade, led by a wave of new investment in Mexico. Over the long term, the main impact of larger US–Mexican trade will be higher incomes made possible by greater efficiency and faster growth. Efficiency in both economies will be boosted by the tendency of each country to export those goods and services in which it has a comparative advantage. Faster growth will result from more intense competition among a larger number of firms in each segment of the market, and from an expanded North American market that will enable each firm to realize economies of scale. In turn, this could result in an improved trade balance for North America with the rest of the world, or better terms of trade for North America.[3]

In round numbers, if two-way US–Mexico trade in the intermediate term expands by $25 billion on account of NAFTA, and if classic comparative advantage benefits realized by both countries amount to just 7.5 per cent of expanded trade, the annual efficiency gains would be about $1.9 billion. In addition, the growth gains from enhanced competition and larger markets might benefit the Mexican economy by as much as $12.5 billion annually.[4] To an unknown extent, the larger and more competitive North American market would also confer dynamic gains on US producers.

Together, the efficiency benefits and growth stimulus of NAFTA could exceed $15 billion annually. Over the long term this figure, rather than jobs gained or lost, is the true measure of the economic gain from the NAFTA agreement. Annual gains of $15 billion are equivalent to making an addition to the combined capital stock of the two nations of about $75 billion – not bad for government work.[5]

Specific NAFTA provisions
In essence, the NAFTA is a new, improved, and expanded version of the Canada–US Free Trade Agreement (FTA). In large part, the agreement involves commitments by Mexico to implement the degree of trade and investment liberalization promised between its northern neighbours in 1988. However, the NAFTA goes further by addressing unfinished business from the

8   Economic integration between unequal partners

FTA, including protection of intellectual property rights, rules against distortions to investment (local content and export performance requirements), and coverage of transportation services.

The NAFTA provides for the phased elimination of tariff and most non-tariff barriers on regional trade within ten years, although a few import-sensitive products will have a 15-year transition period. US–Canada bilateral tariffs will continue to be phased out according to the FTA schedule, i.e., by January 1998. In addition, the NAFTA extends the innovative dispute settlement procedures of the FTA to Mexico; it contains precedent-setting rights and obligations regarding services and investment; and it takes an important first step in addressing cross-border environmental issues.

Following is a sector-by-sector summary of the key provisions of the NAFTA text, including an assessment of the agreement's main achievements and shortcomings.

Energy

The NAFTA negotiations offered an opportunity to integrate Mexico's abundant oil reserves with US and Canadian financial capital and technological expertise. But Mexico's historic commitment to oil as a symbol of national sovereignty prevented a sweeping liberalization of the energy sector. The agreement failed to break the Pemex monopoly over Mexico's energy sector. The NAFTA does not ensure foreign investment in oil exploration, production, or refining; it does not provide for risk-sharing contracts; and it does not permit US and Canadian firms to enter Mexico's retail gasoline market. Moreover, Mexican energy trade remains subject to a far wider range of contingent restrictions than US or Canadian energy trade. (For US–Mexico energy trade see Table 1.3.)

Despite these shortcomings, the NAFTA does make modest progress in opening Mexico's energy market. Most notably, the agreement gradually opens Pemex and CFE (the State Electricity Commission) contracts to foreign participation. In addition, Mexico will allow performance contracts, under which US and Canadian oil and gas field service companies operating in Mexico can be paid a bonus for exceeding contract targets. Finally, the NAFTA substantially increases US and Canadian access to Mexican electricity, petrochemical, gas and energy services.

Automobiles

A key US and Canadian objective in the NAFTA negotiations was to open Mexico's highly protected automotive market. This goal was achieved. Mexico has the fastest-growing major auto market in the world, and improved US access to this market was critical to the endorsement of the NAFTA by the Big Three (General Motors, Ford and Chrysler).[6] (For US-Mexico trade in

Table 1.4 *United States and Mexico: trade in automobiles and parts, 1986 and 1991*

	US imports from Mexico			US exports to Mexico		
		As a percentage of:			As a percentage of:	
Year	Billions of Dollars	Total US manufactured imports from Mexico	Total US auto and parts imports	Billions of dollars	Total US manufactured exports to Mexico	Total US auto and parts exports
1986	2.7	25.7	4.0	1.7	16.8	9.0
1989	4.9	25.0	6.3	3.4	16.5	12.3
1990	6.9	35.2	7.9	4.8	21.7	13.0
1991	7.7	n.a.	9.1	5.7	n.a.	13.9

Note: n.a.: not available.

Sources: US Department of Commerce data sheets: US Foreign Trade Highlights 1989; US International Trade Commission data sheets; 'Review of Investment Liberalization Measures by Mexico and Prospects for Future United States – Mexico Relations' (USITC Publication 2326), October 1990; US Department of Commerce, 'Industrial Outlook 1993', pp. 35–9 and 35–20; and GATT, 'International Trade 1990–91'.

Table 1.5   Mexico: vehicle production and exports by manufacturer, 1989

	Total production (units)	Exports as a percentage of production	Exports to the US as a percentage of total exports
Chrysler	161 446	42	91
Ford	126 271	31	100
General Motors	112 786	36	100
Nissan	120 880	21	0
Volkswagen	108 374	20	92
Total	641 132	30	83

Source: Automotive Parts Manufacturers' Association, 'The Mexican Auto Industry: A Competitor for 1990's', Toronto: Automotive Parts Manufacturers' Association, September 1990, pp. 27 and 37.

the Auto sector and Mexican vehicle production and exports by manufacturer, see Tables 1.4 and 1.5.)

The NAFTA will eliminate all of Mexico's automotive tariffs and most of its non-tariff barriers over a transition period lasting five to ten years. Mexico's tariff on autos and light trucks (20 per cent) will be cut in half immediately, and then phased out either over 10 years (autos) or 5 years (light trucks). Mexico will eliminate its domestic content and trade balancing requirements within 10 years and will immediately eliminate its quota on imports of new vehicles. Despite the NAFTA's considerable success in liberalizing Mexico's auto market, the agreement falls short by embracing a restrictive rule of origin for autos: the ultimate figure will be 62.5 per cent, compared to the current FTA figure of 50 per cent.

As a consequence of NAFTA, within ten years an integrated auto market will exist in North America. By world standards, the regional industry should be highly competitive. In fact, drawing on economies of scale and a variety of labour skills, North America could become the world's low cost producer of autos and trucks, and a major net exporter of these products.

Textiles and apparel
The textiles and apparel chapter is notable for its speedy elimination of virtually all quotas on North American trade in textiles and apparel, and its fast phase out of tariffs. The agreement will eliminate all tariffs on North American textile and apparel trade within ten years. In addition, the United States will immediately lift its import quotas on Mexican textile and apparel

products that meet the new rule of origin, and will gradually phase out quotas on Mexican goods that do not qualify for preferential treatment. However, the benefits of liberalization will be limited by the NAFTA's ultra-strict rule of origin that determines which textiles and apparel will be eligible for tariff and quota elimination. Moreover, the NAFTA rules of origin will likely divert textile and apparel trade from other suppliers; the Caribbean nations may be especially hard hit in this area. (For US–Mexico trade in textiles and apparel see Table 1.3, and for total US trade in textiles and apparel see Table 1.6.)

Table 1.6 United States: global trade in textiles and apparel, 1978–91 (millions of dollars)[a]

	Textiles		Apparel	
Year	Imports	Exports	Imports	Exports
1978	2 400	2 225	6 108	677
1979	2 399	3 189	6 291	931
1980	2 676	3 632	6 849	1 202
1981	3 250	3 619	8 008	1 232
1982	3 000	2 784	8 703	953
1983	3 460	2 368	10 292	818
1984	4 874	2 382	14 513	807
1985	5 274	2 366	16 056	755
1986	6 151	2 570	18 554	900
1987	6 918	2 900	21 960	1 132
1988	6 748	3 651	22 877	1 575
1989	6 417	3 897	26 026	2 087
1990	6 800	3 700	24 740	2 240
1991[b]	7 132	4 108	23 034	2 881

Notes:
[a] Values are for Standard International Trade Classifications 65 (textiles) and 84 (apparel). Imports are stated on a c.i.f. basis, exports on a f.a.s. basis. Import volumes are in millions of square-yard equivalents.
[b] Values are for SIC 22 (textiles) and SIC 231–238 (apparel).

Source: William R. Cline, *The Future of World Trade in Textiles and Apparel* 'Washington: Institute for International Economics, 1990', table 12.1; US Department of Commerce, 'U.S. Industrial Outlook 1993', pp. 9–3 and 32–7.

Agriculture

Agriculture is the only area where the NAFTA does not involve a trilateral agreement between the three countries. Instead, two separate bilateral agreements were negotiated: one between the United States and Mexico, and another between Mexico and Canada. For US–Canada agricultural trade, the provisions of the Canada–US FTA continue in force.

In the US–Mexico bilateral agreement, the NAFTA largely incorporates a bargain on agriculture linking Mexican liberalization of field crops to US horticultural reforms. The bargain provides for the elimination of US trade barriers on a large variety of horticultural products, cotton and sugar, in exchange for the phase-out of Mexican import restrictions on some field crops, dry beans, pork, potatoes, apples, and nonfat dry milk.[7]

The US–Mexico farm trade agreement makes laudable progress in the liberalization of agricultural trade barriers. While the liberalization of the most sensitive farm products will be gradual and phased in over a longer time period than most products covered by the NAFTA, trade barriers will be eliminated on bilateral US–Mexico farm trade within 15 years – a notable achievement compared to the snail's pace of GATT negotiations. (For US–Mexican agriculture trade, see Table 1.7.) However, the NAFTA failed to build on the limited results of the FTA with regard to US–Canadian bilateral farm trade. As a result, US–Canada farm trade will continue to face important constraints.

Financial services

In time, the NAFTA will dramatically improve investment access for US and Canadian financial firms doing business in the Mexican market.[8] However, the right to establish a business presence in Mexico is phased in at a measured pace, with interim caps placed on the market share that can be controlled by foreign financial firms.[9] Nonetheless, by January 2000, virtually all Mexican restrictions on entry into the financial services market and individual firm size will be eliminated. After that, temporary safeguard measures may be applied in the banking and securities sectors, but not beyond January 2007, and only if foreign market shares reach high levels. However, for individual foreign banks, a cap on growth through acquisition will still be applied even after the transition period.

Transportation

In the transportation sector, the NAFTA negotiators accomplished far more than expected. Within a few years, the United States and Mexico will be connected by a common network of trucking, rail, and other transportation services.

Table 1.7 United Stated: agricultural trade with Mexico, 1980 and 1991 (millions of dollars)

	1980 US exports	1980 US imports	1991 US exports	1991 US imports
Animals and animal products	277	99	1 123	391
Animals, live	18	89	184	362
Meats and meat products	39	1	415	2
Poultry and poultry products	23	0	131	0
Dairy products	48	1	121	1
Fats, oils, and greases	65	0	97	1
Other	84	8	174	24
Grains and feeds	1 222	10	739	40
Feed grains and products	1 042	5	550	negl.
Corn	678	0	148	negl.
Grain sorghums	319	0	372	negl.
Other feed grains and products	45	5	31	negl.
Other	180	5	189	40
Fruits, fruit juices, and nuts	20	125	86	445
Fresh and frozen fruits	9	102	45	293
Prepared or preserved fruits	3	16	11	38
Fruit juices	1	7	4	63
Nuts	7	0	26	51
Vegetables	239	347	123	902
Fresh and frozen vegetables	7	303	29	790
Prepared and preserved vegetables	226	44	24	112
Dried beans	220	0	22	n.a.
Other vegetables	6	0	70	0
Oilseeds and products	502	27	524	43
Soybeans	259	n.a.	344	n.a.
Other oilseeds and products	243	n.a.	180	n.a.
Sugar and coffee	n.a.	332	117	366
Sugar and related products	n.a.	21	114	33
Coffee	n.a.	311	2	333
Other agricultural products	208	119	285	340
Total agricultural products	2 468	1 059	2 998	2 527

Notes: n.a. = not available.

Source: U.S. Department of Agriculture, 'Foreign Agricultural Trade of the United States', 1991.

The NAFTA permits US, Mexican, and Canadian trucking companies to carry international cargo to and from the contiguous US and Mexican states by the end of 1995, and to have cross-border access to all the United States and Mexico by the end of 1999 (current laws prevent US truckers from carrying cargo across the border, even though 85 to 90 per cent of US–Mexican trade moves by land). In addition, the NAFTA allows US and Canadian investment in Mexico's bus and trucking firms, and harmonizes many of the technical and safety standards for truck and rail operations. The remaining major barriers in the transportation sector, including differences in truck weights and sizes and the highly restrictive cabotage laws, might be liberalized in later talks under NAFTA auspices. The major task ahead is to build large amounts of road and bridge infrastructure.

Telecommunications
The NAFTA makes substantial and rapid progress in opening up access for North American firms to Mexico's telecommunications market for enhanced or value-added services, and should accelerate both cross-border investment in telecommunications facilities and enhanced telecommunications services. US and Canadian exporters should benefit both from the immediate elimination of most Mexican tariffs and non-tariff barriers on telecommunications equipment, and from the rapidly growing Mexican demand for telecommunications services and equipment. Mexico will benefit by the rapid conversion of its third world telecommunications system to first world performance levels. As a result, North American producers of all kinds of goods and services should find it easier to do business in Mexico.

Investment
The NAFTA negotiators produced a landmark agreement on investment, with the notable exception of obligations relating to the primary energy sector. The NAFTA commits all three countries to provide national treatment to investors from NAFTA partners, and contains a most-favoured-nation (MFN) obligation ensuring that NAFTA investors are treated as well as any other foreign investor in the country. In addition, the agreement will phase out over ten years all requirements relating to export performance, domestic content, domestic sourcing, trade balancing, product mandating, and technology transfer. Mexico has stated that its liberalization measures will be extended to investors from all countries.

The three countries also agreed to permit private investors to seek binding arbitral rulings directly against the host government in an international forum. In parallel, the United States and Mexico negotiated a tax treaty that reduces the high statutory withholding rates charged on interest, dividends, and royalties flowing in both directions. In short, the NAFTA agreement on investment is far superior to that produced in the Uruguay Round on trade-related investment measures (TRIMS).

Intellectual property rights
In the intellectual property area, the NAFTA stands as a model for resolving outstanding disputes and for locking in reforms previously enacted. The agreement locks in and strengthens Mexico's protection for patents, copyrights, trademarks, and trade secrets. The two major shortcomings are the cultural exemption maintained by Canada and the exclusion from patentability for biotechnology inventions.

The NAFTA's accomplishments relating to intellectual property were so striking that it has quickly become the preferred benchmark for evaluating the accomplishments of GATT and other trade agreements. Still, the value of NAFTA provisions on intellectual property rights will clearly depend on the effectiveness of enforcement, and this is largely a matter of practice in each partner country. My expectation is that, within five years, Mexico will protect intellectual property as well as the United States or Canada.

Environment
The NAFTA stands as a landmark accord for handling environmental issues in a trade agreement. However, the solutions reached by the Bush Administration fell behind the rising curve of environmental concerns. By contrast with goals advocated by environmental groups, the NAFTA provisions appear 'mild in terms of obligations on Mexico, and vague in terms of substance'.[10] In recent years Mexico has unilaterally raised its standards and will probably continue to do so. While the NAFTA attempts to ensure that existing standards are maintained, it does not contain provisions to upgrade the enforcement of existing standards or to adopt enhanced standards.

The NAFTA allows each country to maintain and enforce existing federal and sub-federal health, safety, and environmental standards and allows a partner to prohibit the entry of goods that do not meet its product standards. The agreement explicitly states that parties, including their sub-federal entities, may enact still tougher standards. However, while the NAFTA attempts to ensure that existing standards are maintained and encourages countries to 'harmonize up' their process standards, it does not provide an explicit plan for countries to achieve this goal, nor does it provide a mechanism to prevent countries from relaxing standards or enforcement measures to attract investment.

The NAFTA dispute settlement procedures are environmentally friendly in various ways. First, to promote cooperation and harmonization, the agreement establishes a Committee on Sanitary and Phytosanitary Measures and a Committee on Standards-Related Measures, both of which will play a role in dispute resolution proceedings. Second, while the NAFTA allows a government to challenge any environmental measure, it explicitly places the burden of proof on the challenging party. Third, the Dispute Settlement chapter gives the complaining party the right to have a dispute resolved either through the NAFTA dispute mechanism or through the GATT.[11] To the extent that NAFTA environmental standards are higher than the GATT standards, the complaining party will thereby have a better chance of achieving its objectives.[12]

In February 1992, the United States and Mexico released a 'Border Plan' that commits the two countries to cooperate in addressing the serious pollution and other environmental conditions along their 2000-mile border. The Border Plan, while an important first step, does not commit the parties to specific projects and lacks a long-term funding strategy.

To reinforce and improve upon existing agreements and programmes, President Clinton has proposed the negotiation of a supplementary agreement which would create a North American Commission for the Environment (NACE). Clinton's proposal essentially would give more funding and more enforcement power to the Bush Administration's Commission. According to Clinton, his Commission would have 'substantial powers and resources to prevent and clean up water pollution', and would 'encourage the enforcement of the country's own environmental laws through education, training and commitment of resources, and provide a forum to hear complaints'.[13]

The precise powers of NACE are the centrepiece of trinational negotiations now underway (April 1993). In my view, the NACE's success (or failure) in providing a forum for consultation and convergence of environmental standards will be far more consequential than its role in applying trade remedies or other sanctions against badly-behaving firms or industries.

Labour adjustment
Schott and I estimate that the NAFTA will exert a modest but *positive* effect on the US labour market. By our estimates, the agreement – in conjunction with Mexican domestic economic reforms – will create about 170,000 *net* new US jobs in the foreseeable future (this figure should be reached by 1995, five years after the NAFTA talks were first proposed) by comparison with the 1990 position (see Table 1.8).[14] Indeed, with surging US exports to Mexico ($43 billion in 1992, compared with $28 billion in 1990), and a slower rate of expansion of US imports from Mexico ($36 billion in 1992, against $31 billion in 1990), many new US jobs have *already* been created. If the NAFTA is rejected, we would expect the United States to experience *job losses* by comparison with the situation in 1992. The reason is that a rejection of NAFTA will probably cause capital to leave Mexico, in turn forcing Mexico to contract its imports and expand its exports, thereby slashing the US trade surplus with Mexico.

Table 1.8 US jobs supported by exports to Mexico and dislocated by imports from Mexico, 1990, and future scenario resulting from the impact of NAFTA and related reforms[a]

	Median weekly wage	Base level (1990) Exports	Base level (1990) Imports	Scenario for the foreseeable future Exports	Scenario for the foreseeable future Imports	Net job change vs. 1990	Percent of total US jobs
Merchandise trade (billions)		$28.4	$30.8	$45.1	$38.5		
Average weekly wage		$420	$424	$420	$424		
Total jobs supported/ displaced (thousands)		538.0	579.9	854.4	724.9	171.4	
Jobs, by type (thousands)							
Executive administrative, & managerial	$620	59.1	67.3	93.9	84.1	17.9	0.12
Professional specialty	$634	29.6	33.8	47.0	42.2	9.0	0.06
Technicians & related support	$508	12.8	15.5	20.3	19.4	3.7	0.10
Sales	$418	75.6	80.4	120.1	100.5	24.4	0.17

Table 1.8 continued

	Median weekly wage	Base level (1990) Exports	Base level (1990) Imports	Scenario for the foreseeable future Exports	Scenario for the foreseeable future Imports	Net job change vs. 1990	Percent of total US jobs
Administrative support, including clerical	$365	61.1	67.5	97.0	84.4	19.1	0.10
Service	$280	34.6	37.0	54.9	46.3	11.1	0.07
Precision, production, craft, & repair	$483	83.5	94.1	132.6	117.6	25.6	0.19
Machine operators, assemblers, & inspectors	$336	85.7	76.9	136.1	96.1	31.2	0.41
Transportation & material moving	$419	30.6	35.9	48.6	44.9	9.0	0.18
Handlers, equipment cleaners, helpers, & labourers	$305	31.3	32.0	49.7	40.0	10.4	0.23
Farming, forestry, & fishing	$263	34.1	39.3	54.2	49.1	10.2	0.30

Note to Table 8: The assumptions behind the scenario for the foreseeable future are spelled out in Gary Clyde Hufbauer and Jeffrey Schott, *NAFTA: An Assessment*, 1993. Basically it was assumed that NAFTA and related Mexican reforms will boost US exports to Mexico by $16.7 billion over the levels otherwise obtained, and boost US imports from Mexico by $7.7 billion. In this scenario, no allowance is made for normal trade growth in the absence of NAFTA and related reforms.

To obtain figures for jobs by occupational category supported by exports to Mexico in 1990, the Department of Commerce figures for direct and indirect jobs supported by exports to Mexico in 1990, by industry, were multiplied by coefficients representing the ratio of specific occupations within an industry to total jobs within that industry for the United States at large. For example, the figure for sales jobs supported by agricultural exports to Mexico was obtained by multiplying the total number of jobs (direct and indirect) supported by agricultural exports to Mexico by the ratio of sales jobs to total jobs in US agriculture as a whole.

To obtain figures for jobs by occupational category displaced by imports from Mexico in 1990, a parallel method was used. Department of Commerce figures for direct and indirect jobs in each industry supported by exports were multiplied by the ratio between US imports from Mexico and US exports to Mexico for the products of that particular industry. To make the calculation manageable, only the top 100 imports and exports were used in calculating these ratios. The top 100 imports and exports account for 96.8 per cent of total US imports and 96.7 per cent of total US exports to Mexico in 1990.

Numbers for total jobs by occupation supported by exports, or displaced by imports, in 1990 were obtained by summing the figures for each industry.

The average weekly wage for jobs supported by exports to Mexico in 1990 was obtained by taking a weighted average of the median wage for each occupational category, where the weights are the proportion of each occupational category supported by exports to the total number of jobs supported by exports. The same procedure was used to obtain the average wage associated with jobs displaced by imports. In these calculations, 1991 median wage figures were used.

The figures for jobs by occupation supported by exports or displaced by imports in the future scenario was obtained by multiplying the respective 1990 figures by the ratio of scenario exports (or scenario imports) to base year exports (or base year imports). Average wages were calculated in the same way as those for 1990. This methodology does not allow for productivity growth either in terms of jobs or in terms of wages.

Sources: Data for total jobs, by industry, supported by exports to Mexico in 1990 was obtained from the Office of the Chief Economist, Economics and Statistics Administration, US Department of Commerce, 'U.S. Jobs Supported by U.S. Merchandise Exports to Mexico: Supplemental Report,' May 1992. The coefficients representing the ratio of specific occupational categories within an industry to total jobs within that industry for the United States at large are derived from unpublished data for the year 1991, collected by the Bureau of Labor Statistics. The data for average weekly wages for the year 1991 for each occupation were obtained from Bureau of Labor Statistics, US Department of Labor.

Nevertheless, in the United States, opposition to the NAFTA has focused on potential job losses and downward pressure on American wages. The Bush Administration tried to address these concerns through three mechanisms: explicit NAFTA provisions, a formal binational cooperation programme with Mexico, and President Bush's new job training programme.

Several explicit NAFTA provisions will smooth the transition for US workers, including 15-year transition periods for the most sensitive sectors and improved safeguard mechanisms to protect sensitive industries against a flood of imports. The second mechanism to meet labour concerns – binational cooperation – has resulted in a series of bilateral agreements to promote closer cooperation and joint action on a variety of labour issues.

The third, and most critical, mechanism to address US labour adjustment issues came in August 1992 when President Bush proposed a new worker adjustment programme – Advancing Skills Through Education and Training (ASETS). ASETS would have spent $10 billion in new funding over five years on training and adjustment assistance for displaced workers, of which $1.67 billion, or $335 million annually for five years, was to be earmarked (if needed) for workers displaced by the NAFTA.[15] Most importantly, the Bush plan subsumed NAFTA adjustment in the larger context of retraining workers, whatever the cause of dislocation.

Not surprisingly, President Clinton has promised a bigger and better approach to labour adjustment. In his October 1992 campaign speech, Clinton first pledged that he would negotiate a supplemental agreement to reinforce worker standards and safety. While specific objectives for such a pact have not yet been spelled out, the supplemental negotiations are likely to seek to establish commitments to the aggressive enforcement of national labour laws and regulations, monitoring of labour markets by a trinational commission, and dispute settlement provisions to encourage compliance. Such an agreement would significantly expand the responsibilities of the nascent US–Mexico Binational Commission, particularly with regard to enforcement mechanisms. In terms of labour training, President Clinton may use Bush's plan as a point of departure for an even more ambitious programme. However, the Administration has yet to spell out the details of its own programme for assisting US workers dislocated by increased imports from Mexico.

Dispute settlements
The NAFTA extends the dispute settlement provisions of the Canada–US FTA to Mexico and establishes a trilateral North American Free Trade Commission to administer the agreement and adjudicate disputes over the interpretation and application of NAFTA rules. Further, the NAFTA includes new provisions to ensure that parties comply with panel procedures and rulings, and strengthens existing extraordinary challenge procedures of the Canada–

US FTA. In addition, Mexico agreed to undertake significant legal and judicial reforms to provide due process guarantees and effective judicial review for disputing parties.

The dispute settlement provisions represent one of the most noteworthy accomplishments of the NAFTA negotiations. In return for significant reform of its judicial and administrative practices in the application of its trade laws, Mexico gains full rights under the innovative dispute mechanism for reviewing anti-dumping and countervailing duty cases. In addition, the NAFTA fine-tunes the FTA by adopting compliance provisions to insure that the panel procedures are not impeded, and by strengthening the extraordinary challenge process.

Accession to the NAFTA

The NAFTA contains an accession clause, modelled after similar provisions in the GATT, but without the GATT's procedural underpinnings. While membership is open to all countries, application procedures for joining the club and membership criteria remain to be worked out by the three countries. At this point, the NAFTA only requires that new members be accepted by all member countries and approved by their respective legislature (i.e., any country can veto new members).

The absence of geographic limitations on the accession clause is perhaps its most notable feature. The scope of potential partners was deliberately left open to forestall accusations that NAFTA was seeking to build a hemispheric 'fortress'. *In principle*, accession is open to all countries, including important Asian trading countries such as Japan and Korea. *In practice*, the US Congress is unlikely to provide the US President with the authority to negotiate FTAs with such powerful competitors.

Indeed, the near-term prospects for the enlargement of NAFTA are limited. Few countries are ready to undertake and sustain obligations of a reciprocal FTA with the United States (including intrusive environmental and labour obligations), and the United States is not ready to negotiate new FTAs with major (nor perhaps minor) trading nations. Given the extensive domestic agenda that President Clinton plans to enact in his first-term, the Administration may not want to spend large amounts of political capital in a domestic fight over the enlargement of NAFTA.

Notes
1. Material in this chapter is taken from Gary Clyde Hufbauer and Jeffrey J. Schott, *NAFTA: An Assessment*, Washington, DC: Institute for International Economics, February 1993. Copyright © 1993 by the Institute for International Economics. All rights reserved. Diana Clark provided research assistance. The views herein are those of the author, and do not necessarily reflect the views of the Institute staff, Advisory Committee or Board of Directors.

22   Economic integration between unequal partners

2. Investment has anticipated trade reforms in Mexico just as it did in Europe after passage, in 1986, of the Single European Act, which presaged the internal market reforms of the EC 1992 process.
3. Whether a more competitive North America translates into an improved trade balance or an appreciated currency (and hence better terms of trade) will depend on macroeconomic conditions in North America and other regions of the global economy.
4. In an unpublished study, the authors of this assessment have calculated that, for Latin America taken as a whole, a scenario of broad policy liberalization, including dramatic trade reform, could boost the region's GDP by $385 billion over a decade, while increasing its two-way trade by $235 billion. The suggested ratio between GDP gains and trade expansion resulting from sweeping policy reforms is an astonishing 1.65. This figure, of course, is subject to estimation errors and assumes dramatic policy reforms. Even making liberal allowance for modelling errors and less-than-sweeping policy reforms, it seems plausible that trade liberalization could yield dynamic gains of at least 50 per cent of the resulting two-way trade expansion for the Mexican economy, which was highly protected in the late 1980s. The figure cited in the text for dynamic gains, $12.5 billion, is calculated as 50 per cent of our projection of NAFTA-induced two-way trade expansion of $25 billion.
5. The $75 billion figure assumes that capital invested in the US and Mexican economies yields a real social return of 20 per cent per year.
6. Automobile unit sales in Mexico are expected to reach 1 million by 1995, up from 740 000 in 1992 (*Financial Times*, 18 June 1992, p. 6). US–Mexico two-way trade in automotive goods could easily double or triple under NAFTA auspices, growing from $8.3 billion in 1990 to $20–$25 billion by 1995.
7. In 1991, Mexico's exports of horticultural products to the US amounted to $1.3 billion; US field crops exports to Mexico totalled $740 million, of which sorghum represented $371 million and corn $147 million. With liberalization, two-way agricultural trade will soon double and, within ten years, quadruple. *Report of the Agricultural Policy Advisory Committee for Trade on the North American Free Trade Agreement*, September 1992, pp. 14 and 17.
8. The agreement covers both traditional financial service providers (banking, securities, and insurance firms), and non-traditional providers such as non-bank banks and financial affiliates of commercial entities (e.g. GE credit, AT&T credit).
9. The interim caps apply to the number and size of foreign firms permitted access to the Mexican market, but do not constrain the scope of their operations.
10. Peter Uimonen and John Whalley, 'Trade and Environment: Setting the Rules,' Washington, DC: Institute for International Economics, July 1992, manuscript, p. 113.
11. While parties are free to make the initial choice of forum (GATT or NAFTA), once dispute settlement procedures are initiated in one forum, they cannot be switched to another. NAFTA Article 2005.
12. Since NAFTA does not cover process issues, it appears that cases in that realm would be resolved in the GATT. See Steve Charnovitz, 'Environmental and Labour Standards in Trade', *The World Economy*, May 1992, pp. 335–356; 'GATT and the Environment: Examining the Issues,' *International Environmental Affairs*, 4(3), Summer 1992.
13. 'Expanding Trade and Creating American Jobs,' Remarks by Governor Bill Clinton, North Carolina State University, Raleigh, NC, 4 October 1992.
14. By our calculations, a gross total of 316,000 US jobs will be created by the NAFTA, while a gross total of 145,000 US jobs will be dislocated. Our estimate that 145,000 US jobs will be displaced works out to under 2 per cent of total displacements in the American economy over a five year period. We start the clock from a 1990 base because the prospect of the NAFTA generated expectational effects that resulted in sharp increases in bilateral trade and investment.
15. Under ASETS, up to an additional $335 million annually could be drawn from a discretionary fund, if required. The reserve fund contingency implied an upper level job loss figure of about 300,000 workers over ten years.

2 Restructuring North America: the impact of unequal integration

Ricardo Grinspun and Maxwell A. Cameron[1]

Introduction: Free trade as a restructuring programme

The conclusion of North American Free Trade Agreement (NAFTA) negotiations on 12 August 1992, and the ongoing ratification and implementation process, raise major political and economic issues in Mexico, Canada, and the United States. Observers in many other countries – in particular in Japan and the nations of Europe, Latin America, and the Caribbean – have also focused their attention on the process of North American integration and the prospect of the entire hemisphere becoming a free trade zone. The NAFTA negotiations have stimulated a lively debate regarding the feasibility and desirability of alternative paths of economic integration, and the likely implications for each of the three countries involved.

The belief that a free trade area like NAFTA will provide significant benefits to each one of the countries involved, and in particular to the smaller Canadian and Mexican economies, is based on well-known propositions on the gains from trade. In this traditional analysis enhanced access to the huge US market will provide impetus for export-oriented industrialization for the smaller economy. Recent neoclassical analysis on imperfectly competitive markets and the gains derived from economies of scale rates the benefits from liberalized trade still higher.[2] These benefits are estimated using highly abstract, computable general equilibrium models that are presumed to be 'objective'. Optimistic forecasts – based on such models – regarding the job, export, and production gains Canada would reap from the implementation of the Canada–US Free Trade Agreement (CUFTA) played an important role in the Canadian public debate before ratification of that agreement.

The economic arguments for free trade are seriously flawed. Most econometric models do not incorporate intrafirm trade – trade between affiliates of transnational corporations (TNCs) – which accounts for much of the commerce between Canada, the United States, and Mexico. TNCs enjoy a growing ability to move capital and restructure production on a global basis in order to lower unit costs of production and maximize returns. The effects of 'free trade' on movements of capital and investment diversion are more important – and less understood – than the effects on commodity trade. A key outcome of CUFTA and NAFTA is likely to be a significant shift of economic and political power toward US- and Canadian-based TNCs. This must be recognized and studied for its diverse and far-reaching implications.

Government intervention crucially affects the structure of markets and the pattern of international trade. Mexican and Canadian exports are often affected by the application of US trade-remedy law. Contrary to expectations, CUFTA has not protected Canada from the political use of US trade laws. Ongoing disputes over regional content in automobiles under CUFTA suggest that even the threat of US harassment can inhibit foreign investment. Similarly, NAFTA leaves potent US trade-remedy laws intact, while significantly restricting Canadian and Mexican policy options (Sinclair, 1993). NAFTA, like similar agreements, is another instrument to manage and shape trade and investment flows across North America. NAFTA shifts the decision-making in these areas to big corporate capital, which is primarily based in the United States.

Recent Canadian experience suggests that neoclassical trade theory is poorly suited to predict the outcome of economic integration. Optimistic claims regarding the benefits of free trade that are derived from these theories must be treated with caution, since they understate key aspects of the integration process. Econometric models discount the role of governments in economic activity as well as the role of intrafirm trade. They also tend to disregard other elements of economic integration such as (a) changes in income distribution; (b) the effects of investment flows and increased capital mobility; (c) macroeconomic imbalances; (d) differences between countries and regions in the level of economic development and productivity; (e) differences between countries in the nature of institutional, social, and political structures; (f) the role of domestic markets, 'human capital', and technological change in economic growth; (g) urban-rural and other regional links; and (h) the environmental impact.

Our intention is to go beyond the narrow view of free trade presented by neoclassical economics and to explore the implications of free trade from a political economy perspective. Without denying that free trade will affect trade and investment flows, we focus on the impact of free trade on economic and societal restructuring. The main argument is that free trade either directly encourages this transformation or contributes to consolidate past restructuring. In particular, free trade is likely to: (a) promote domestic restructuring, so that the private sector – a euphemism for large corporations and transnational capital – plays the leading role in economic activity; (b) redefine the relationship between the state and civil society, weakening government intervention at all levels; (c) impose a neo-conservative economic programme of monetarist macroeconomic policies, privatization, and deregulation, in place of such Keynesian goals as full employment; (d) harmonize downward labour, occupational, social, and environmental standards (social dumping); (e) promote regressive, post-Fordist restructuring and weaken trade unionism; and, lastly,

(f) weaken the provision of public services in the three countries. In essence, then, free trade can be seen as a component in a neo-conservative structural adjustment programme for North America (Campbell, 1993).

Bruce Campbell has argued that CUFTA is an effective multipurpose device for advancing this neo-conservative agenda in Canada. It has been used by the United States in tandem with the General Agreement on Trade and Tariffs (GATT) as a whipsaw to weaken interventionist Canadian laws and regulations. CUFTA thus served the Conservative government as a key lever to facilitate the implementation of its policy programme. Canada's experience should be taken seriously by other countries considering free trade arrangements with the United States.

Free trade can also play a role in consolidating the neo-conservative restructuring model imposed on highly indebted countries such as Mexico. Judith Teichman (1993) analysed the dramatic restructuring that Mexico underwent prior to NAFTA. Central to the new economic strategy has been a concerted effort to reduce the state's role through privatization of public enterprises. Teichman's research suggests that domestic conglomerates and transnational corporations have been the major beneficiaries of both privatization and export incentives. This new economic model has resulted in a new political alliance between big business and the Mexican state.

NAFTA and economic development

NAFTA will significantly affect economic development in each of the three countries involved. The importance of the development question for Mexico and the rest of Latin America is obvious. However, this is also a serious question for Canada and the United States. Canada's industrial heartland, as well as certain regions of the United States, have undergone a process of deindustrialization in the post-free trade era due to the relocation of industrial production to lower-wage areas.

Indirect pressures that CUFTA has created to shape public policies have become a major issue in Canada. Opponents of free trade argue that CUFTA and NAFTA constitute much more than trade agreements. They are an industrial strategy that forces an outward-oriented, natural resource-based, and TNC-driven model of development (Watkins, 1993). Free trade affects a whole spectrum of economic and social policies. Important examples are regional development programmes, which are vulnerable to challenges from the United States as so-called unfair trade practices.

On the question of Mexican economic development, proponents usually assume that there will be massive economic gains for Mexico from NAFTA. They take the optimistic position that NAFTA will attract capital to Mexico, reverse capital flight, and provide jobs (Hart, 1990). This view leaves crucial questions unanswered:

26 Economic integration between unequal partners

(a) How much capital will be attracted to Mexico? How much will be directed to productive investment, and how much will go to speculation, financial intermediation, and to the purchase of existing assets? Are capital inflows going to reverse the debt-related outflow of resources that is crippling Mexico?

(b) What kind of jobs are going to be created in Mexico? Will these be more *maquiladora*-type jobs – without backward linkages to the rest of the economy, based on low wages, and producing social and environmental disruption? To what extent will this job creation compensate for the loss of the traditional industrial base that was the inevitable result of trade liberalization without adequate safeguards?

(c) What will happen to real wages and income inequality in a context of tremendous pressure to maintain 'international competitiveness' (which in the case of Mexico is achieved mainly by compressing wages, coercing independent trade unions and avoiding environmental regulations)? How will the democratic process and labour rights be affected?

(d) What will happen to food self-sufficiency and to the quality of life in rural Mexico as a result of expanded agroexport operations?

(e) What effects will there be on 'human capital': education, health, living conditions, training programmes, occupational rights, occupational safety, and unemployment insurance?

(f) How will the Mexican economic and political system be affected by the increased capital mobility and heightened power of the economic elite and TNCs?

(g) What will be the results of NAFTA's restricting the ability of the Mexican government to apply independent domestic policies (regional and sectoral development policies; income redistribution policies; social programmes; energy policy; and so on)?

There are no easy – and few pleasant – answers to most of these questions. Although there is no doubt that NAFTA will promote rapid economic growth in certain regions of North America (in particular, on both sides of the Mexican–U.S. border), the nature of economic and social development implied by this growth is still unclear. Kathryn Kopinak (1993) raises the concern that the current phase of Mexican development is characterized by extremely unequal, enclave-type growth in the *maquiladora* sector, with no prospect for a broader modernization of the economy and society. In fact, the 'boom' of the Mexican economy in the early 1990s has strong components of financial and speculative growth, which may not be stable in the long term. There are already signs that the current industrialization strategy – which is intended to insert Mexico into the worldwide production strategies of TNCs – may be short-lived and subject to boom and bust cycles.

As Jeff Faux and Thea Lee (1993) point out, the danger for the United States is that NAFTA commits the country to a faulty response to the competitive threat arising from Japan and from a unified European common market. In particular, they see NAFTA as harmful to the long-term competitiveness of the United States, arguing it will encourage lower wages and make it more difficult for governments at all levels to invest in infrastructure, training and education. Robert Kreklewich (1993) foresees similar worrisome tendencies. He argues that Canadian and U.S. TNCs are shortsightedly taking advantage of CUFTA and NAFTA to accelerate a poorly conceived restructuring from Fordism to flexible manufacturing systems. This restructuring is characterized by regressive working conditions and increased social tension.

Environmental concerns have emerged in the course of the NAFTA negotiations. These negotiations were marked by intense opposition from environmental groups. There are good reasons for this, given the environmental disaster created by the *maquiladora* industry. Steven Shrybman (1993) insists on the necessity of designing trade and economic policies that are environmentally sound and at the same time provide a fast and energetic response to the development needs of Mexico and other underdeveloped countries. Unfortunately, the August 1992 NAFTA (like the GATT) limits the use of trade policy to maintain environmental standards.

Asymmetries of power
NAFTA reinforces the regional dominance of the United States – not only economically, but also culturally, militarily, and politically. Asymmetries of power, wealth, technology, and cultural influence among Mexico, the United States, and Canada, guarantee that the short and long-term benefits and adjustment costs will be distributed unequally within and between the member countries. Moreover, these asymmetries transform NAFTA from a narrow trade and investment treaty into one that affects, directly and indirectly, the whole pattern of life in the smaller societies.

As Gerald Helleiner argues (1993), if a small country is bargaining for an agreement in which it will gain more market access than its more powerful partner, that stronger partner will inevitably attempt to extract some compensating concession. Mexico's national product represents about 3 per cent of the total North American economy; it will gain far more market access through trade liberalization than will Canada or the United States. Mexico made major concessions to sweeten the deal for the United States, including new legislation on intellectual property and investment. In the energy sector Mexico neither privatized PEMEX nor provided guaranteed supplies to the United States. Nevertheless, US firms can bid for contracts and PEMEX will be restructured to facilitate greater foreign investment. Petroleum has enormous political and symbolic value in Mexico, for it is a major power resource that had been used to strengthen Mexico's bargaining position in relation to the United States in the past. Thus, as John Dillon argues (1993), future control over energy resources has potent implications for Mexico's bargaining power in bilateral relations with the United States.

Finally, asymmetries in power affect how the legal text of an agreement is translated into actual policy at the implementation stage (Drache, 1993). A major lesson of CUFTA's implementation is that bilateral trade agreements do not insulate smaller countries from the political use of US trade-remedy law. Harassment of Canadian exporters continues, discouraging third-country investors from investing in Canada as an export platform to the United States. Canada can threaten to retaliate, but will think twice before escalating a trade war with the country that absorbs most Canadian exports.

Conclusion: Shaping economic integration to satisfy societal needs

Economic integration – both regional and global – is driven by deep structural transformations in the nature of world capitalist competition. Should this trend toward economic integration be opposed by political parties and social forces concerned with social agendas in the North and in the South? Opposition to economic integration is neither necessary nor realistic. *How* economic integration is institutionalized, however, is crucially important.

It is useful to design general criteria to evaluate economic integration from a social democratic perspective. The first column in Table 2.1 presents a suggested, partial list of questions to ask. Whether the process of integration will fulfil these criteria depends on the particular actors and the institutional setting put in place to promote integration. The second column in Table 2.1 asks how well the August 1992 NAFTA agreement measures up to these criteria. A glimpse at the table shows that NAFTA gets a very low mark in this evaluation. Even in those areas where the negotiators made an explicit effort to respond to criticism – such as worker retraining and environment – the outcome is partial and likely to be insufficient (this does not include the Clinton side agreements on labour and environmental standards being negotiated at the time of writing this chapter). The NAFTA performs poorly because the objectives of the negotiating governments were dictated by the geopolitical interests of each administration as well as by a deep commitment to a neo-conservative agenda. This agenda, clearly, is largely inconsistent with an alternative social democratic one. It remains to be seen whether the Clinton administration represents change in this regard.

It is most illuminating to compare NAFTA with the process of economic integration in Europe. Advocates of NAFTA frequently point to the European Community (EC) as a precedent for a NAFTA, and argue that a free trade agreement with Mexico would create the world's largest and richest trading

Table 2.1 Social democratic criteria for economic integration: comparing North America and the European Community

A: Criteria	B: How does the NAFTA measure up?	C: How does the EC measure up?
(a) Are significant redistributive mechanisms to be implemented to bridge the gap between countries at different levels of development?	At the national level, the major issue is the lower level of Mexican development and the negative transfer of resources through debt-servicing. NAFTA does *not* incorporate compensatory financing or debt relief. Moreover, there are serious doubts whether the current 'trickle down' model of economic growth, supported by NAFTA, can provide a decent standard of living for most Mexicans.	The difference in levels of development between the three countries in NAFTA is more dramatic than the economic disparities within the EC, where the major issue is the lower level of economic development in southern countries such as Portugal and Greece (but also Ireland in the north). The EC recognizes the developmental needs of these regions and has established compensatory funds to shift resources. The effectiveness of these measures remains to be seen.
(b) Are significant redistributive mechanisms to be implemented within each country to compensate displaced workers and communities?	NAFTA does not specify or require the implementation of programmes such as worker retraining and relocation. Each country must decide separately on this important issue. In Mexico, the country with the largest social deficit, the recent trend has been to trim social expenditures. In Canada, the Mulroney administration is not planning new programmes. The reasons raised in (e) below also constrain Mexico's and Canada's ability to implement new programmes. The United States under the Clinton administration has promised to implement new initiatives in areas such as labour retraining.	In the EC there is an ongoing concern over the distribution of economic benefits within and between member nations. Labour mobility between countries diminishes the adjustment costs for workers. These costs are also lessened by a stronger commitment to maintain the welfare state, at least in some member countries (for example, through a social charter). There is recognition of the need for high levels of taxation and government social expenditure, in sharp contrast to North American trends. Views on whether costs and benefits of integration are distributed fairly among different social groups are divided.

Table 2.1 continued

A: Criteria	B: How does the NAFTA measure up?	C: How does the EC measure up?
(c) Is economic integration tied to a deepening of participatory democratic institutions?	The contrary seems to be the rule. NAFTA has all the characteristics of an elite-driven process, both at the economic and political levels. Key promoters are TNCs, for which NAFTA represents a 'continental bill of economic rights.' NAFTA implies a shift in the balance of power away from the state and toward TNCs. Trade unions are also weakened by unfettered capital mobility. NAFTA helps perpetuate an undemocratic political regime in Mexico, which continues to practice repressive policies toward independent labour unions and to manipulate electoral outcomes.	Democracy is a condition of membership in the EC. A country with an authoritarian political system like Mexico could probably not become a member. There is some effort to promote democratic participation at all levels of the EC, for example through the 'subsidiarity' concept. European TNCs are key promoters of integration, but there is an effort to share some of the benefits and to distribute power to other sectors of society, in particular labour. Views on the effectiveness of these measures are divided. Decision-making is based more on relatively open and participatory institutions (such as the Commission and the Parliament) than on secretive committees. Nevertheless, there is a 'democratic deficit' – more power is transferred to supra-national bureaucracies than to the European parliament.
(d) Are substantial mechanisms implemented to promote *upward* harmonization of social, labour, and environmental standards?	The likely effect is some harmonization *downward* as a result of social dumping. NAFTA does not set standards for social programmes, occupational safety, or labour rights (Clinton-initiated talks on side-agreements will address some of these issues). NAFTA promotes deregulation, privatization and increased capital mobility, creating pressures that may erode existing social programmes and make	There is an ongoing concern over the impact of economic integration on social, labour, and environmental standards, and an effort to set minimum standards so as to avoid social dumping. There is a clear recognition that harmonization of standards will happen as a result of integration. The Maastricht Treaty includes a social charter, which was signed by most EC members. Trade unions

the implementation of new ones more difficult. Trade unions may see their bargaining power weakened as a result of labour segmentation, restructuring of production, and increased capital mobility. The treatment of environmental issues is declaratory and lacks significant implementation powers.

(e) Is the ability of the regional and national governments to engage in developmental policies recognized and protected?

NAFTA is likely to hinder the ability of governments in Canada and in Mexico to promote economic development. NAFTA creates a new framework for public policy that is market-oriented and emphasizes conservative macroeconomic policies. Fiscal, monetary, industrial or trade policies – all are affected by this policy framework. The lack of agreement on a common definition of allowable trade subsidies constrains the use of policies targeted to specific regions or sectors, since these can be challenged as 'unfair' measures. For example, Canadian regional development programmes are often challenged by the United States. Of particular concern in Mexico are constraints on the ability to implement programmes for rural development. Increased financial deregulation creates further constraints on domestic policies (in particular those that are not 'business-friendly'), by increasing the threat of capital flight.

NAFTA does not create these democratic institutions. As a consequence, there is a shift of power to the major national player. At the same time, the

have been weakened as a result of integration, but probably less than in North America on a comparative basis. Although countries with very high environmental standards will be affected, there is an effort to avoid downgrading to the lowest common denominator.

In the EC there is no analogy to the hegemonic power of the US and its dominant influence over policies in Mexico and Canada. Nor is there an analogue to the strong impact of invasive US trade law, which is legitimized by NAFTA, and which shapes policy in the other countries. In the EC, intra-community trade is driven by EC rules, not by national rules of a specific national actor. Moreover, the concept of subsidiarity is opposed to the spirit of NAFTA, which is to strip power from national and regional governments. There is a strong sense of protection in the EC for regulatory and interventionist policies, such as the CAP. Also, the concept of regional development funds is respected and encouraged.

(f) Is the unavoidable loss of political and economic autonomy and

European integration is based on the assumption that economic integration entails a loss of political and economic sovereignty – through, for example,

Table 2.1 continued

A: Criteria	B: How does the NAFTA measure up?	C: How does the EC measure up?
sovereignty at the state and regional level compensated by the creation of truly representative supranational institutions?	myth is propagated that trade agreements can be separated from sovereignty and social standards. There is also a major shift in economic and political decision-making to unelected, unrepresentative corporate and 'technical' bureaucracies. (An example of technical bureaucracies are those that handle the dispute settlement mechanism.)	monetary union. The loss of autonomy and sovereignty at the national level is compensated by the creation of institutions like the European Commission and the European Parliament. These represent efforts to create supranational institutions that will be somewhat representative, democratic and accountable. There is no national actor that plays an overwhelmingly dominant role, although there is concern regarding German predominance. There is relatively less reliance on undemocratic 'dispute-settlement' mechanisms and 'technical' bureaucracies.
(g) Is integration based on increased mobility for capital *and* labour?	Increased mobility is created only for capital, thus promoting a shift of power to corporations. The only labour mobility included in NAFTA is for business representatives.	Labour gains mobility between different countries, counterbalancing the shift of power to capital. Labour mobility from outside the EC (immigration) has been reduced.

Note: The table does not incorporate the NAFTA side agreements on labour and environmental standards being negotiated at the time of preparation of this chapter.

Source: Columns A and B adapted from Grinspun and Cameron (1993b, Table 1.1).

bloc. In sharp contrast to NAFTA, the European Community has developed a complex institutional framework to deal with issues such as decentralization (subsidiarity); labour mobility; compensatory arrangements; social, labour, and environmental standards; and supranational institutions. Even so, many Europeans are worried that these institutions are not adequately fulfilling their objectives. Without trying to ignore the significant problems that the EC confronts, there are fundamental contrasts between the European and North American integration efforts, as the third column in Table 1 details.

The European example demonstrates that the proper question to ask about economic integration is not whether it should or should not be implemented, but rather *how* it is implemented. Cuauhtémoc Cárdenas, leader of the Mexican Party of the Democratic Revolution (PRD), has called for an alternative Trade and Development Pact in North America (1992). In sharp contrast to NAFTA, the pact would utilize managed trade as a tool of development, and would include some labour mobility, compensatory financing for less developed regions, and a social charter that would promote harmonization of social, labour, and environmental standards to the *highest* common denominator. Although such a pact does not appear to be likely in the near future, it is useful as a critical standard by which to evaluate NAFTA.

Notes

1. Authors' note: Many of the arguments in this paper are developed in different chapters of Grinspun and Cameron (1993a). This chapter draws heavily on Grinspun and Cameron (1993b). Funding was provided by the Government of Ontario, the Centre for Research on Latin America and the Caribbean (CERLAC) at York University, and research grants for Max Cameron from the Social Sciences and Humanities Research Council of Canada and Carleton University and for Ricardo Grinspun from York University.
2. There is a broad literature on these issues. A simple introduction is provided in Krugman & Obstfeld (1991, chapter 6).

References

Campbell, B. (1993), 'Restructuring the economy: Canada into the free trade era', in Grinspun and Cameron (eds.).
Cárdenas, C. (1992), 'The continental development and trade initiative' in Cavanagh, J., Gershman, J., Baker, K. and Helmke, G. (eds), *Trading Freedom: How Free Trade Affects Our Lives, Work and Environment*, San Francisco: Institute for Food and Development Policy.
Dillon, J. (1993), 'The petroleum sector under continental integration' in Grinspun and Cameron (eds).
Drache, D. (1993), 'Assessing the benefits of free trade' in Grinspun and Cameron (eds).
Faux, J. and Lee, T. (1993), 'Implications of NAFTA for the United States: Investment, jobs, and productivity' in Grinspun and Cameron (eds).
Grinspun, R. and Cameron, M.A. (eds) (1993a), *The Political Economy of a North American Free Trade Area*, Montreal: McGill-Queen's; New York: St. Martin's Press, and Macmillan, UK.
Grinspun, R. and Cameron, M.A. (1993b), 'The political economy of North American integration: Diverse perspectives, converging criticisms' in Grinspun and Cameron (eds).

Hart, M. (1990), *A North American Free Trade Agreement: The Strategic Implications for Canada*, Ottawa and Halifax: Institute for Research on Public Policy.

Helleiner, G. (1993), 'Considering U.S.–Mexico free trade' in Grinspun and Cameron (eds).

Kopinak, K. (1993), 'The maquiladorization of the Mexican economy' in Grinspun and Cameron (eds).

Kreklewich, R. (1993), 'North American integration and industrial relations: Neo-conservatism and neo-Fordism?' in Grinspun and Cameron (eds).

Krugman, P.R., and Obstfeld, M. (1991), *International Economics: Theory and Policy*, (2nd ed.), New York: HarperCollins.

Sinclair, S. (1993), 'NAFTA and U.S. trade policy: Implications for Canada and Mexico' in Grinspun and Cameron (eds).

Shrybman, S. (1993), 'Trading away the environment' in Grinspun and Cameron (eds).

Teichman, J. (1993), 'Dismantling the Mexican state and the role of the private sector' in Grinspun and Cameron (eds).

Watkins, M. (1993), 'An alternative trade and development model for Canada' in Grinspun and Cameron (eds).

3 Competitiveness and productivity between Canadian and US manufacturing industries

Christos C. Paraskevopoulos[1]

I Introduction

Canada and the United States not only are the world's largest trading partners – albeit unequal – they are also among the wealthiest and most prosperous countries. In fact, the real per capita income, in both countries, ranks among the top two or three nations in the world but the *growth* in real incomes has declined dramatically in the last 20 years or so. In their most recent reports, the Economic Council of Canada (1992) and the Conference Board (Freedman, 1989) both agree that, given population trends and the economic stresses of the last decade (i.e., fiscal and trade deficits), both countries need substantial improvement in productivity in order to avert a decline in their living standards. However, per capita improvements can only be attained by population and productivity increases, that is, by increases in the amount of work being done (more people working, and working longer hours) and by increases in productivity. Growth in labour productivity, in turn, is determined by two factors, namely, improvement in the overall efficiency of the production process – total factor productivity – and increased capital per employed person – capital accumulation. In short, the goal of improving living standards is inextricably linked to productivity growth as the key factor. This study is attempting to address this question for selected Canadian and US manufacturing industries.

Total Factor Productivity Growth – a broad measurement of overall efficiency for all inputs – and individual input productivity growth are measured, estimated, compared and analysed through the use of both a non-parametric and a parametric methodological approach.

The non-parametric framework is based on Solow's general index of disembodied technological change (1957). The parametric framework, however, is utilizing a version of the translog production frontier with biased technological change which is a straightforward adoption of the methodology of Boskin and Lau (1990). Accordingly, Section II discusses the accounting framework of analysis and the theoretical specification of the model. Section III deals with data used in the study. The empirical findings are discussed in Section IV. The concluding remarks are summarized in the last section.

II Methodology

There are various methods of identifying and measuring economic growth and technical progress. In this section we outline the methodology used to: (1) calculate and theoretically analyse the indices of growth, including growth of industrial output of 'total factor productivity'; and (2) develop a relatively new theoretical model reflecting the industrial production function and the input substitution possibilities.

A Indices of growth and productivity measures

a Rate of growth of output Our production function relates the flow of output, Y, to the stock of capital, K, and labour, L. To this production function we impose the assumptions of constant returns to scale, neutral technological change, and perfect competition in both the output and factor input markets. Under these three restrictive assumptions we can calculate the rate of growth of output, Y, and its sources of growth as follows:

$$\dot{Y} = \sum_{i}^{2} \overline{S}_i \dot{I}_i + \dot{T}, \ i = K, L \ldots \qquad (3.1)$$

where, $\dot{Y}$ = rate of growth of output, $\overline{S}_i$ = average share of factor inputs, $\dot{I}_i$ = rate of growth of factor inputs, and $\dot{T}$ = rate of growth of total factor productivity.

Equation (3.1) gives the contribution of factor inputs and technology to the rate of growth of output where the input effects are measured by the rates of growth of input quantities, I_i weighted by the corresponding average factor shares (S_i).

b. Total Factor Productivity Index In an accounting framework, the Total Factor Productivity Index, $\dot{T}$, is obtained directly from equation (3.1) as a 'residual'. That is,

$$\dot{T} = \dot{Y} - \sum_{i}^{2} \overline{S}_i \dot{I}_i \ldots \qquad (3.2)$$

Equation (3.2) defines the rate of growth in the rate of total factor productivity as the difference in the rate of growth in output less the percentage change in the share-weighted sum of the inputs. The index of equation (3.2) is the well known Solow's general index of disembodied technological change (1957).

c. *Factor Input Productivity Indices* The rate of growth of the average productivity for a factor input may be obtained as follows:

$$API_i = \overline{S}_i \sum_i^2 (\dot{I}_j - \dot{I}_i) + \dot{T} \ldots \quad (3.3)$$

B. Model specification

We adopt the model of Boskin and Lau (1990) which formally parameterizes the potential differences in inputs across regions. The origin of their approach can be traced to the concept of meta-production function introduced by Hayami and Ruttan (1970, 1985). Our model is derived in the following steps:

(1) All the regions are assumed to have the same underlying time-invariant production function. The production function, however, applies to 'efficiency-equivalent' quantities of output and inputs. An interpretation of identical underlying production function is that the same fundamental knowledge is available to all regions.

(2) The production function is assumed to be a Cobb–Douglas function of the efficiency-equivalent capital and labour inputs (see equation (1.7) in Boskin and Lau (1990). The value of the production function gives the efficiency-equivalent quantity of output. There is no restriction on the sum of the input coefficients of the Cobb–Douglas function. Hence, the degree of returns to scale is a free parameter which can be estimated from the data.

(3) The observable output and inputs are converted into efficiency-equivalent units by multiplying each commodity by its 'augmentation factor'. Each augmentation factor is regional-specific and time-varying. Technical progress is represented by these augmentation factors. Following Boskin and Lau (1990), we parametrize the augmentation factor for the *i*th region and the *i*th commodity ($j = K$ for capital, or L, for labour) with the exponential form: $\exp(c_{ij}t)$, where t is time and c_{ij} is a constant which will be called the *augmentation rate parameter*. Empirically, we expect the augmentation factors to account for the differences across regions in such factors as: climate, topography and infrastructure, quality of inputs and composition of outputs. In particular, any regional difference in the rate of technological progress for each input will be reflected in the different values of the augmentation rate parameters.

(4) Given the Cobb–Dougals specification in step (2), it is shown in Lau (1980) that only a single augmentation factor can be identified. We, therefore, set $c_iL = 0$, for all i.

38 *Economic integration between unequal partners*

(5) Given steps (1) to (4), which together form a special case of Boskin and Lau (1990), the estimable production function of the *i*th industry is given by:[2]

$$\ln Y_{it} = \ln Y_0 + a_K \ln K_{it} + a_L \ln L_{it} + a_K c_{iK} t \dots \qquad (3.4)$$

where Y_{it}, K_{it}, L_{it} and t are respectively quantity of output, capital input, labour input and time trend. The rest of the symbols in the equation are parameters (augmentation rate parameters and parameters in the Cobb–Douglas production function) to be estimated.

The parameters in each production function appear in a nonlinear way although it is clearly linear-in-parameter after a suitable reparametrization. Also, some of the parameters (the *a*'s) are common to the production function of each province. Hence, all the production functions are estimated jointly by seemingly unrelated regression.

III Data sources and estimation procedures

Time-series data on prices and quantities of output and inputs of capital and labour employed in this study are derived from the following sources:

A. Canada:
Time-series data on prices and quantities of output, wages, labour input, and capital stock employed in the estimation of productivity and output growth rates were obtained from the following government sources: *Manufacturing Industries of Canada* published by Statistics Canada; *Industry Price Indexes* published by Statistics Canada and *Fixed Capital Flows and Stocks, Canada* published by Statistics Canada.

B. United States:
Time-series data for the corresponding US variables were obtained from: Bureau of Labor Statistics, US Department of Labor, November 1991.

Using the aforementioned data and the methodology described in Section II we proceed as follows: First: the indices of growth and productivity measures for all the selected Canadian and US manufacturing industries of equations (3.1) to (3.3) have been calculated and are reported in Tables 3.1 to 3.10). Second: at this stage the parametric portion of the research is still in progress. The empirical estimates obtained, so far, are quite preliminary, reflecting the work-in-progress nature of this project. Meanwhile, some preliminary results and the results of an earlier study of the three largest Canadian provinces (see Ma and Paraskevopoulos, 1992) will be briefly discussed.

Table 3.1 Annual growth rates of output, capital and labour in selected Canadian manufacturing industries (percentages)

Period	Growth Rate of Output Y	Growth Rate of Capital K	Capital Rate of Labour L
Food and Beverages			
1962–1969	3.87	3.78	1.03
1969–1979	1.02	2.73	1.06
1979–1989	0.30	2.69	−1.09
Paper and Paper Products			
1962–1969	4.40	6.17	2.47
1969–1979	3.03	3.08	0.24
1979–1989	1.20	4.92	−0.49
Primary Metals			
1962–1969	4.59	4.79	2.22
1969–1979	1.33	3.68	1.45
1979–1989	1.70	2.65	−1.45
Transportation Equipment			
1962–1969	12.5	6.38	5.8
1969–1979	4.6	3.03	2.0
1979–1989	4.8	7.99	2.9
Chemical and Chemical Products			
1962–1969	7.13	6.48	3.34
1969–1979	3.57	6.82	1.17
1979–1989	4.22	3.63	1.44

Notes:
(a) The symbols in Tables 3.1 to 3.10 read as follows:
$Y = (\partial Y/\partial t)(1/Y)$
$K = (\partial K/\partial t)(1/K)$
$L = (\partial L/\partial t)(1/L)$
$T = (\partial T/\partial t)(1/T)$
$S_K = 0.5\ (S_K^t + S_K^{t-1})$
$S_L = 0.5\ (S_L^t + S_L^{t-1})$
(b) The numbers in parenthesis represent percentage distribution.

40   Economic integration between unequal partners

IV   Statistical results

A.   Factor-input productivity analysis

a.   Growth patterns of output   Table 3.1 reports the annual rates of growth for five Canadian manufacturing industries, and Table 3.6 for their US counterparts.

Among the Canadian industries, and for all three sample periods, the highest growth rate is recorded in *Transportation Equipment* followed by *Chemicals*, and the lowest rate in the *Food and Beverages* manufacturing industries. Among the US industries *Chemicals* exhibit the highest rates in the 1960s and the 1970s but not in the 1980s where it suffered a substantial reduction. *Paper* recorded the highest rate in the 1980s while *Primary Metals* recorded the lowest rate in the last two decades. By comparison we observe higher rates of growth in the Canadian industries of *Transportation Equipment*, *Primary Metals*, and *Chemicals* than in their US counterparts while the US *Food* and *Paper Products* industries recorded higher rates than in Canada.

b.   Sources of output growth   The observed patterns of output growth can be evaluated in terms of input used, their productivities and technological factors per se. Table 3.2 and Table 3.7 summarize the contribution of each factor-input and technology on output growth for selected Canadian and US manufacturing industries respectively. In all Canadian industries, with the exception of *Transportation Equipment*, the 'total factor productivity' effect was negative and the major contributor to the decline in the output growth. On the other hand the 'capital effect' was positive while labour's influence was mixed. In *Transportation Equipment*, TFP was positive and the major contributor to output growth followed by capital. The *Chemicals* industry high growth is attributed almost entirely to capital formation. The patterns of growth in the US counterpart industries are similar to the Canadian but the rates are lower.

c.   Total factor productivity   Table 3.3 reports the sources of growth in total factor productivity for the Canadian Manufacturing Industries and Table 3.8 for the US. These tables show that in both countries a negative or small growth performance in total factor productivity was recorded in all industries except *Transportation Equipment*. The dominant source of total factor productivity in all industries except *Transportation* is labour, suggesting that these industries are subject to *labour-induced* efficiency. This means that as the relative price of labour increases, other things being equal, labour quantities decline which, in turn, increases labour productivity and, subsequently, total factor productivity. On the other hand, and for the same industries

Table 3.2 Annual growth rates of output and sources of growth in selected Canadian manufacturing industries (percentages)

Period	Rate of Growth of Output Y	Labour Effect $S_L L$	Capital Effect $S_K K$	Total Factor Productivity T
Food and Beverages				
1962–1969	3.87(100)	0.25(6)	3.20(83)	0.42(11)
1969–1979	1.02(100)	0.28(17)	1.98(194)	−1.24(−121)
1979–1989	0.30(100)	−0.32(−106)	2.14(713)	−1.52(−507)
Paper and Paper Products				
1962–1969	4.40(100)	0.87(20)	10.22(232)	−6.69(−152)
1969–1979	3.30(100)	0.08(3)	4.69(155)	−1.74(−58)
1979–1989	1.20(100)	−0.15(−19)	8.19(683)	−6.84(−570)
Primary Metals				
1962–1969	4.6(100)	0.83(18)	6.22(135)	−2.45(−53)
1969–1979	1.3(100)	0.51(39)	4.42(340)	−3.63(−279)
1979–1989	1.7(100)	−0.49(−29)	3.18(187)	−0.99(−58)
Transportation Equipment				
1962–1969	12.5(100)	2.20(18)	1.13(9)	9.17(73)
1969–1979	4.6(100)	0.74(16)	0.59(13)	3.27(71)
1979–1989	4.8(100)	1.10(23)	1.31(27)	2.39(50)
Chemical and Chemical Products				
1962–1969	7.13(100)	0.60(8)	5.63(79)	0.90(13)
1969–1979	3.57(100)	0.20(6)	7.91(271)	−4.54(−127)
1979–1989	4.22(100)	0.22(5)	3.44(82)	0.56(13)

Note: See note in Table 3.1

Table 3.3 Annual growth rates of total factor productivity and sources of growth in selected Canadian manufacturing industries (percentages)

Period	Growth Rate of Total Factor Productivity T	Sources of Growth Productivity of Labour $S_L(Y-L)$	Productivity of Capital $S_K(Y-K)$
\multicolumn{4}{c}{Food and Beverages}
1962–1969	0.42(100)	0.69(164)	–0.27(–64)
1969–1979	–1.24(–100)	–0.01(0)	–1.23(–100)
1979–1989	–1.52(–100)	0.41(27)	–1.93(–127)
\multicolumn{4}{c}{Paper and Paper Products}
1962–1969	–6.69(–100)	0.68(10)	–7.37(–110)
1969–1979	–1.74(–100)	0.93(53)	–2.67(–153)
1979–1989	–6.84(–100)	0.52(8)	–7.36(–108)
\multicolumn{4}{c}{Primary Metals}
1962–1969	2.45(–100)	0.89(36)	–3.34(–136)
1969–1979	–3.63(–100)	–0.04(–1)	–3.59(–99)
1979–1989	–0.99(–100)	1.64(166)	–2.63(–266)
\multicolumn{4}{c}{Transportation Equipment}
1962–1969	9.17(100)	2.35(37)	6.82(74)
1969–1979	3.27(100)	0.96(29)	2.31(71)
1979–1989	2.39(100)	0.73(31)	1.66(69)
\multicolumn{4}{c}{Chemical and Chemical Products}
1962–1969	0.90(100)	0.68(76)	0.22(24)
1969–1979	–4.54(–100)	0.41(9)	–4.95(–109)
1979–1989	0.56(100)	0.42(75)	0.14(25)

Note: See note in Table 3.1

Table 3.4 Annual growth rates of labour productivity and sources of growth in selected Canadian manufacturing industries (percentages)

Period	Growth Rate of Labour Productivity $Y-L$	Capital Effect $S_K(K-L)$	Total Factor Productivity T
\multicolumn{4}{c}{Food and Beverages}
1962–1969	2.84(100)	2.42(85)	0.42(35)
1969–1979	−0.04(−100)	1.20(3000)	−1.24(−3100)
1979–1989	1.39(100)	2.91(209)	−1.52(−109)
\multicolumn{4}{c}{Paper and Paper Products}
1962–1969	1.93(100)	8.62(447)	−6.69(−347)
1969–1979	2.79(100)	4.53(162)	−1.74(−62)
1979–1989	1.69(100)	8.53(505)	−6.84(−405)
\multicolumn{4}{c}{Primary Metals}
1962–1969	2.37(100)	4.82(203)	−2.45(−103)
1969–1979	−0.12(−100)	3.51(2925)	−3.63(−3025)
1979–1989	3.15(100)	4.14(131)	−0.99(−31)
\multicolumn{4}{c}{Transportation Equipment}
1962–1969	6.7(100)	−1.97(−37)	9.17(137)
1969–1979	2.6(100)	−0.67(−26)	3.27(126)
1979–1989	1.9(100)	−1.49(−26)	2.39(126)
\multicolumn{4}{c}{Chemical and Chemical Products}
1962–1969	3.79(100)	2.89(76)	0.90(24)
1969–1979	2.40(100)	6.94(289)	−4.54(−189)
1979–1989	2.78(100)	2.22(80)	0.56(20)

Note: See note in Table 3.1.

44   *Economic integration between unequal partners*

capital-induced efficiency was negative throughout. This means that technology is *not neutral but capital-embodied* technology which is affecting negatively multifactor productivity. This is so because, as the price of capital rises, relative to other inputs, capital-induced technology is reduced. This reduction, given output, will reduce total factor productivity. In short, the overall productivity of the production process (TFP) with the exception of the Canadian *Transportation* is adversely affected.

d. Labour productivity   Table 3.4 reports the sources of growth of labour productivity for the Canadian Manufacturing Industries and Table 3.9 that for their US counterparts.

Among the Canadian industries *Transportation Equipment*, and *Chemicals*, and to a lesser extent *Paper* exhibit high rates of growth in the 1960s and the 1970s but in the 1980s the highest growth rate is recorded in *Primary Metals* followed by *Chemicals*. On the other hand, *Food and Beverages* exhibit, over the entire sampling period, the lowest growth rate. Among the US industries, *Chemicals* exhibit the highest growth rates in the 1960s and the 1970s followed by *Paper* in the 1960s and *Transportation Equipment* in the 1970s. In the 1980s *Paper* recorded the highest growth rate followed by *Food Products*. Through the entire period *Primary Metals* recorded the lowest rate of growth in labour productivity.

By comparison, we observe higher rates of growth in the Canadian industries of *Transportation Equipment, Primary Metals* and *Chemicals* than in their US counterparts, while the US *Food* and *Paper Products* industries recorded higher rates than in Canada. It should be noted that the growth pattern of labour productivity as discussed in the preceding section, (*a*), mirrors that of output growth.

As noted earlier the growth of labour productivity is influenced by two key factors, namely, the overall efficiency of the production process (TFP) and capital accumulation (K/L). Table 3.4 reports the sources of growth of labour productivity in the Canadian manufacturing industries. In *Food* and *Paper Products*, total factor productivity was negative and the major contributor to the decline in productivity growth. The contribution of capital accumulation was positive and significant but not large enough to avert the historic slowdown. The effect of capital accumulation is mainly the source of high productivity rates in *Chemicals* and for the 1980s in the *Primary Metals* industries. The observed high rates in *Transportation Equipment* are entirely explained by total factor productivity and not by capital accumulation. As far as the US manufacturing industries are concerned (Table 3.9), the growth of labour productivity in *Food*, *Paper Products* and *Chemicals* is almost entirely explained by the influence of capital accumulation whereas in *Transportation Equipment* the influence is equally divided. In *Primary Metals* the situation is mixed. In short, as far as labour productivity is concerned, the Canadian manufacturing industries have an overall competitive advantage over their US counterparts. Canadian industries in *Transportation Equipment*, *Primary Metals* and *Chemicals* recorded higher rates than their US counterparts while *Food* and *Paper and Paper Products* industries recorded higher rates than in Canada.

e. Capital productivity   Table 3.5 reports the sources of growth of capital productivity for the Canadian manufacturing industries and Table 3.10 that for their US manufacturing industries respectively. In all Canadian industries, except for *Transportation Equipment* (1960s and 1970s), *Paper Products* (1970s and 1980s), *Primary Metals* (1980s), *Transportation Equipment* (1980s) and *Chemicals* (1980s), capital productivity has been *negative*. The implication of this is: (a) All these industries are, clearly, overcapitalized, and capital accumulation is growing at a faster rate than the industrial output. In addition, the Canadian industries appear to be more overcapitalized than their US counterparts. (b) The observed negative total factor productivity was the major contributor to the decline (negative) in capital productivity growth. (c) These industries utilize *capital-using* technologies. This means, as noted earlier, the technology is *not neutral but capital-embodied*, and, as such, has a negative effect on the total factor productivity. This is so because: (1) As the price of capital relative to the prices of the other inputs increases, capital use declines. (2) As the quantity of capital declines, other things being equal, capital-induced technology is reduced. (3) The reduction in capital-induced technology, given output, will reduce total factor productivity.

The findings in Table 3.3, as we noted earlier, support this argument. It should be noted, however, that the increase in total factor productivity, as a result of *labour-saving* technology is not large enough to offset the decrease in total factor productivity resulting from *capital-using* technologies.

In conclusion, the manufacturing industries in North America are overcapitalized over time, as shown by the significant number of them with negative capital productivity. This results from data showing capital accumulation in these industries as growing at a faster rate than industry output. The Canadian industries appear to be more overcapitalized than their US counterparts. This suggests that many of these industries may benefit from a larger and expanded potential market, other things being equal. These other things, however, include, among others, the skills of workforce, R & D activities, corporate decision-making power and infrastructure in the country. On the other hand, overcapitalization is expected to accelerate the process of industrial restructuring. This is a major problem in Canada as most of the recently closed manufacturing activities were relocated to the US. Furthermore, on the plus side, overcapitalization could – for a smaller country like Canada –

Table 3.5 Annual growth rates of capital productivity and sources of growth in selected Canadian manufacturing industries (percentages)

Period	Growth Rate of Capital Productivity $Y-K$	Labour Effect $S_L(L-K)$	Total Factor Productivity T
Food and Beverages			
1962–1969	0.09(100)	–0.33(–367)	0.42(467)
1969–1979	–1.71(–100)	–0.47(–27)	–1.24(–73)
1979–1989	–2.39(–100)	–0.87(–36)	–1.52(–64)
Paper and Paper Products			
1962–1969	–1.77(–100)	4.92(278)	–6.69(–378)
1969–1979	–0.05(–100)	1.69(3380)	–1.74(–3480)
1979–1989	–3.72(–100)	3.12(84)	–6.84(–184)
Primary Metals			
1962–1969	–0.2(–100)	2.25(1125)	–2.45(–1225)
1969–1979	–2.35(–100)	1.28(54)	–3.63(–154)
1979–1989	–0.95(–100)	0.04(4)	–0.99(–104)
Transportation Equipment			
1962–1969	6.12(100)	–3.05(–50)	9.17(150)
1969–1979	1.59(100)	–1.68(–105)	3.27(205)
1979–1989	–3.19(–100)	–6.58(–175)	2.39(75)
Chemical and Chemical Products			
1962–1969	0.65(100)	–0.25(–38)	0.90(138)
1969–1979	–3.25(–100)	1.29(40)	–4.54(–140)
1979–1989	0.59(100)	0.03(5)	0.56(95)

Note: See note in Table 3.1.

Table 3.6 Annual growth rates of output, capital, and labour in selected US manufacturing industries (percentages)

Period	Growth Rate of Output Y	Growth Rate of Capital K	Capital Rate of Labour L
Food Products			
1962–1969	3.05	5.53	0.16
1969–1979	2.02	4.55	−0.48
1979–1986	1.20	0.31	−0.67
Paper and Allied Products			
1962–1969	5.34	1.98	2.16
1969–1979	2.59	2.95	−0.11
1979–1986	2.33	2.94	−0.47
Primary Metals			
1962–1969	4.57	2.28	2.71
1969–1979	0.90	−0.90	−0.50
1979–1986	−6.14	1.14	−7.14
Transportation Equipment			
1962–1969	6.24	2.90	3.38
1969–1979	2.31	2.00	−0.46
1979–1986	0.88	2.28	0
Chemical and Allied Products			
1962–1969	6.96	7.28	3.04
1969–1979	3.77	3.60	0.52
1979–1986	0.44	3.00	−1.07

Note: See note in Table 3.1

48 Economic integration between unequal partners

Table 3.7 Annual growth rates of output and sources of growth in selected US manufacturing industries (percentages)

		Sources of Growth		
Period	Rate of Growth of Output Y	Labour Effect $S_L L$	Capital Effect $S_K K$	Total Factor Productivity T
Food Products				
1962–1969	3.05(100)	0.03(1)	6.19(203)	–3.17(–104)
1969–1979	2.05(100)	–0.08(–2)	5.09(248)	–2.99(–146)
1979–1986	1.20(100)	–0.12(–10)	0.39(33)	0.93(77)
Paper and Allied Products				
1962–1969	5.34(100)	0.78(15)	2.02(38)	2.54(47)
1969–1979	2.59(100)	–0.04(–2)	2.62(101)	0.01(1)
1979–1986	2.33(100)	–0.15(–6)	2.45(105)	0.03(1)
Primary Metals				
1962–1969	4.57(100)	0.99(22)	2.96(64)	0.62(14)
1969–1979	0.90(100)	–0.17(–19)	–0.87(–97)	1.94(216)
1979–1986	–6.14(–100)	–2.28(–37)	0.96(16)	–4.82(–79)
Transportation Equipment				
1962–1969	6.24(100)	1.22(20)	3.54(57)	1.48(23)
1969–1979	2.31(100)	–0.16(–7)	1.05(46)	1.42(61)
1979–1986	0.88(100)	0 (0)	0.76(86)	0.12(14)
Chemical and Allied Products				
1962–1969	6.96(100)	0.97(14)	11.68(168)	–5.69(–82)
1969–1979	3.77(100)	–0.15(–4)	4.68(124)	–1.06(–28)
1979–1986	0.44(100)	–0.28(–64)	3.01(684)	–2.29(–520)

Note: See note in Table 3.1

Table 3.8 Annual growth rates of total factor productivity and sources of growth in selected US manufacturing industries (percentages)

Period	Growth Rate of Total Factor Productivity T	Sources of Growth Productivity of Labour $S_L(Y-L)$	Productivity of Capital $S_K(Y-K)$
	Food Products		
1962–1969	–3.17(–100)	0.54(17)	–3.71(–117)
1969–1979	–2.99(–100)	0.41(14)	–3.40(–114)
1979–1986	0.93(100)	0.33(35)	0.60(65)
	Paper and Allied Products		
1962–1969	2.54(100)	1.15(45)	1.39(55)
1969–1979	0.01(100)	0.98(980)	–0.97(–870)
1979–1986	0.03(100)	0.89(2967)	–0.86(–2867)
	Primary Metals		
1962–1969	0.62(100)	0.65(105)	–0.03(–5)
1969–1979	1.94(100)	0.48(25)	1.46(75)
1979–1986	–4.82(–100)	0.32(6)	–5.14(–106)
	Transportation Equipment		
1962–1969	1.48(100)	1.03(70)	0.45(30)
1969–1979	1.42(100)	0.97(68)	0.45(32)
1979–1986	0.12(100)	0.31(258)	–0.19(–158)
	Chemical and Allied Products		
1962–1969	–5.69(100)	1.25(22)	–6.94(–122)
1969–1979	–1.06(100)	0.94(89)	–2.00(–189)
1979–1986	–2.29(–100)	0.40(17)	–2.69(–117)

Note: See note in Table 3.1

Table 3.9 Annual growth rates of labour productivity and sources of growth in selected US manufacturing industries (percentages)

Period	Growth Rate of Labour Productivity $Y-L$	Capital Effect $S_K(K-L)$	Total Factor Productivity T
\multicolumn{4}{c}{Food Products}
1962–1969	2.89(–100)	6.06(210)	–3.17(–110)
1969–1979	2.50(–100)	5.49(220)	–2.99(–120)
1979–1986	1.87(100)	0.94(50)	0.93(50)
\multicolumn{4}{c}{Paper and Allied Products}
1962–1969	3.18(100)	0.64(20)	2.54(80)
1969–1979	2.79(100)	2.69(100)	0.01(0)
1979–1986	2.80(100)	2.77(99)	0.03(1)
\multicolumn{4}{c}{Primary Metals}
1962–1969	1.86(100)	1.24(67)	0.62(33)
1969–1979	1.40(100)	–0.54(–39)	1.94(139)
1979–1986	1.00(100)	5.82(582)	–4.82(–482)
\multicolumn{4}{c}{Transportation Equipment}
1962–1969	2.86(100)	1.38(48)	1.48(52)
1969–1979	2.77(100)	1.35(49)	1.42(51)
1979–1986	0.88(100)	0.76(51)	0.12(14)
\multicolumn{4}{c}{Chemical and Allied Products}
1962–1969	3.92(100)	9.61(245)	–5.69(–145)
1969–1979	3.25(100)	4.31(133)	–1.06(–33)
1979–1986	1.51(100)	3.80(252)	–2.29(–152)

Note: See note in Table 3.1

Table 3.10 Annual growth rates of capital productivity and sources of growth in selected US manufacturing industries (percentages)

		Sources of Growth	
Period	Growth Rate of Capital Productivity $Y-K$	Capital Effect $S_K(L-K)$	Total Factor Productivity T

	Food Products		
1962–1969	−2.48(100)	0.69(28)	−3.17(−1.28)
1969–1979	−2.53(100)	0.46(18)	−2.99(−1.18)
1979–1986	0.89(100)	−0.04(−4)	0.93(104)

	Paper and Allied Products		
1962–1969	3.36(100)	0.82(20)	2.54(76)
1969–1979	−0.36(−100)	−0.37(−103)	0.01(3)
1979–1986	−0.61(−100)	−0.64(−105)	0.03(5)

	Primary Metals		
1962–1969	2.29(100)	1.67(73)	0.62(27)
1969–1979	1.80(100)	−0.14(−8)	1.94(108)
1979–1986	−7.28(−100)	−2.46(−34)	−4.82(−66)

	Transportation Equipment		
1962–1969	3.34(100)	1.86(56)	1.48(44)
1969–1979	0.31(100)	−1.11(−358)	1.42(458)
1979–1986	−1.40(100)	−1.52(−129)	0.12(9)

	Chemical and Allied Products		
1962–1969	0.32(−100)	5.37(1678)	−5.69(−1778)
1969–1979	0.17(100)	1.23(724)	−1.06(−624)
1979–1986	−2.61(−100)	−0.27(−11)	−2.29(−89)

Note: See note in Table 3.1

52   Economic integration between unequal partners

lead to a recapitalization and retooling for high value added industries specializing in high quality and special production runs catering to different market segments.

B.   Econometric modelling analysis

As noted earlier, the parametric portion of the research is still in progress and the empirical results obtained so far are preliminary, as the estimates at *the industry level*, in many instances, were statistically insignificant.[3] Meanwhile, we report here some results for US total manufacturing and similar results of an earlier study by Ma and Paraskevopoulos (1992) for the total manufacturing of the three largest Canadian provinces.

Following Boskin and Lau (1990) we estimate the parameters of the first-differenced-form of equation (1) for US total manufacturing, and report the results in Table 3.11. From Table 3.11 we obtain for US total manufacturing returns to scale estimate of 1.13 and an estimate for the rate of local technical progress of 2.3 per cent respectively. It is interesting to compare the US results with that of Ma and Paraskevopoulos (1992), also reported in Table 3.11, for the three largest provinces in Canada. They report a returns to scale

Table 3.11   Annual rates of local technical progress and returns to scale for Canadian (Ontario, Quebec, British Columbia) and US total manufacturing

	Returns to Scale	Annual Rate of Local Technical Progress (Percentages)
CANADA		
Ontario	1.188	0.91
Quebec	1.188	1.50
British Columbia	1.188	1.56
UNITED STATES	1.130	2.30

Note: We derive returns to scale (*RS*), and the annual rate of local technical progress (*RTP*) from the estimated parameters of equation (4) as follows: $RS = a_L + a_K$ and $RTP = \partial \ln Y/\partial t$.

Source: (a) Canada:
From Ma and Paraskevopoulos (1992).
(b) United States:
Derived from the following estimated parameters of equation (4):
$\ln Y = -0.757 + 0.046 \ln K + 1.084 \ln L + 0.023t$;
   (−1.54)   (0.44)   (16.57)   (5.81)
$\bar{R}^2 = 0.99; D - W = 0.72; F = 3.013$

estimate of 1.188 and an estimated rate of local technical progress of 0.91 per cent, 1.5 per cent and 1.56 per cent for Ontario, Quebec, and British Columbia respectively. Hence, we have obtained a lower returns to scale estimate and a higher estimate of the role of technical progress for US total manufacturing than for its Canadian counterpart. While these differences may be due to real differences in the structures of the two economies, it appears, for the most part, to be consistent with the productivity trends revealed earlier in our accounting framework.

These findings, however, clearly indicate:

(a) There is some evidence in support of the view that the production technology, in both countries, exhibits increasing returns to scale in the total manufacturing but the returns to scale are higher in the Canadian than in the US. This, coupled with the observed overcapitalization, clearly suggests that expansion of the volume of economic activity is more cost efficient in Canada than in US manufacturing. In short, other things being equal, trade liberalization may be more beneficial to Canadian than to US manufacturing in the long run.

(b) The higher rate of technical progress estimated for US total manufacturing is partly due to the fact that US firms are larger in size, spend more on R&D, and tend to be more innovative than their Canadian counterparts.

V Concluding remarks

This analysis provides some insights and empirical evidence about the relationship between industrial factor-input efficiency and productivity growth for five Canadian, and US manufacturing industries. Based on historical trends relevant to the selected manufacturing industries and utilizing two alternative frameworks, we: (1) calculated and critically analysed factor-input-productivity trends and identified the sources of growth of these input productivities; (2) calculated the multi-factor productivity index and measured and assessed each factor's contribution to overall efficiency; (3) identified and analysed the character of technological progress in Canadian and US manufacturing.

The major findings of the preceding analysis are as follows:

(a) As far as labour productivity is concerned, the Canadian manufacturing industries have an overall competitive advantage over their US counterparts. Canadian industries in *Transportation Equipment, Primary Metals* and *Chemicals* recorded higher rates than their US counterparts while the *Foods* and *Paper and Paper Products* industries recorded higher rates than in Canada.

(b) The manufacturing industries in North America are overcapitalized over time, as shown by the significant number of them with negative capital productivity. The Canadian industries appear to be more overcapitalized than their US counterparts. This suggests that many of these industries may benefit from *a larger and expanded potential market*, other things being equal. On the other hand, overcapitalization is expected to accelerate the process of industrial restructuring. This is a major problem in Canada as most of the recently closed manufacturing activities were relocated to the US. Furthermore, on the plus side, overcapitalization could – for a smaller country like Canada – lead to a recapitalization and retooling for high value added industries specializing in high quality and special production runs catering to different market segments.

(c) There is some evidence in support of the view that the production technology, in both countries, exhibits increasing returns to scale in total manufacturing but the returns to scale are higher in Canada than in the US. This, coupled with the observed overcapitalization, clearly suggests that expansion of the volume of economic activity is more cost efficient in Canada than in US manufacturing. In short, other things being equal, trade liberalization may be more beneficial to Canadian than to US manufacturing in the long run.

(d) The higher rate of technical progress estimated for US total manufacturing is partly due to the fact that US firms are larger in size, spend more on R & D, and tend to be more innovative than their Canadian counterparts.

Although this study provides important insights, more research is required for a complete understanding of the relationship between factor-input efficiency and productivity growth in order to evaluate the relative competitiveness of the Canadian and US manufacturing industries.

Notes

1. I wish to thank York University (Atkinson College, Atkinson Grant in Aid of Research) and SSHRC (travel) for partial financial support; and Nichol Ma for his contribution throughout this project.
2. Boskin and Lau (1990) have employed the translog functional form which includes the Cobb–Douglas form as a special case. Equation (3.4) is obtained by setting the coefficients of the second-order terms in the translog, and the labour augmentation rate parameter equal to zero. We have also imposed the restriction that the augmentation level parameters in Boskin and Lau (1990) are all identically equal to one.
3. Some of the proposed revisions are: (1) the data used need to be re-examined with attention to the measurement of capital and its utilization, and (2) potential statistical estimation problems such as identifying and correcting for the stochastic processes of the error terms and the simultaneity of the regressors should be addressed.

Bibliography

Abramovitz, M. (1962), 'Economic Growth in the United States,' *The American Economic Review*, **52**(4), 762–82.

Andrikopoulos, A.A. and C.C. Paraskevopoulos (1989), 'Energy Efficiency and Productivity Growth in Canadian, Japanese, and US Manufacturing,' mimeo.

Auer, L. (1979), *Regional Disparities of Productivity and Growth in Canada*, Economic Council of Canada.

Baltagi, B.H. and J.M. Griffith (1988), 'A General Index of Technical Change', *Journal of Political Economy*, **98**(1), 20–40.

Berndt, E.R. and L.R. Christensen (1973), 'The Translog Functions and the Substitution of Equipment, Structures and Labor in US Manufacturing 1929–68', *Journal of Econometrics*, **1**, 85–113.

Berndt, E.R. and M.S. Khaled (1979), 'Parametric Productivity Measurement and Choice Among Flexible Functional Forms', *Journal of Political Economy*, **87**, 1220–46.

Boskin, M.J. and L.J. Lau (1990), 'Post-War Economic Growth in the Group-of-Five Countries: A New Analysis,' Center for Economic Policy Research Publication No. 217, Stanford, California: Stanford University.

Christensen, L.R., D.W. Jorgenson and L.J. Lau (1973), 'Transcendental Logarithmic Production Frontiers,' *Review of Economics and Statistics*, **55**, 28–45.

Economic Council of Canada (1992), 'Pulling Together Productivity, Innovation and Trade', EC22-180/1992E.

Freedman, A. (1989), 'Productivity Needs of the United States,' Research Report No. 934, The Conference Board.

Gallant, A.R. and D.W. Jorgenson (1979), 'Statistical Inference for a System of Simultaneous, Nonlinear, Implicit Equations in the Context of Instrumental Variables Estimation', *Journal of Econometrics*, **113**, 272–302.

Hayami, Y. and V.W. Ruttan (1970), 'Agricultural Productivity Differences Among Countries', *American Economic Review*, **60**, 895–911.

Hayami, Y. and V.W. Ruttan (1985), *Agricultural Development: An International Perspective*, revised and expanded ed., Baltimore: Johns Hopkins University Press.

Lau, L.J. (1980), 'On the Uniqueness of the Representation of Commodity-Augmenting Technical Change', in L.R. Klein, M. Nerlove, and S.C. Tsiang (eds), *Quantitative Economics and Development: Essays in Memory of Ta-Chung Liu*, New York: Academic Press, 281–90.

Lau, L.J. (1986), *Lecture Notes on Price and Allocation Theory*, Stanford, California: Department of Economics, Stanford University.

Norsworthy, J.R. and D.H. Malmquist (1983), 'Input Measurement and Productivity Growth in Japanese and US Manufacturing', *American Economic Review*, December, 947–67.

Ma, B.K. and C.C. Paraskevopoulos (1992), 'Economic Growth of Canadian Total Manufacturing By Regions: An Econometric Analysis', mimeo.

Raynauld, J. (1988), 'Canadian Regional Cycles: the Quebec–Ontario Case Revisited', *Canadian Journal of Economics*, **XXI**, (1), 115–28.

Solow, R.M. (1957), 'Technical Change and the Aggregate Production Function', *Review of Economics and Statistics*, **39**, 312–20.

4 Labour markets, productivity and trade unions in the NAFTA countries
Edur Velasco Arregui[1]

Introduction
In this chapter I shall reconstruct basic trends in labour markets, productivity and trade union activity in the countries that have signed the potential North American Free Trade Agreement (NAFTA). In the first section I show the rapid growth of the labour force in the North American Bloc (NAB) and compare it to the slowdown in productivity. In the second section I show the internal movements of the labour force in the economic area of North America. In the third section I reconstruct the divergent trajectories in union organization within the three participating countries, Canada, the United States and Mexico. The basic hypothesis of this paper is that the main objective of the NAFTA is not trade. The real target of NAFTA is to transform labour relations; that is, through the regulation of an enlarged space for accumulation NAFTA will transform the power relationship between labour and capital.

Employment and productivity in the North American Bloc
One of the outstanding features of the economic region of he North American Bloc (NAB), comprised of Canada, Mexico and the United States, is that, compared to Japan and the European Community (EC), the labour force has grown rapidly since 1978. While Japan added six million workers to its labour force, reaching 63 million in 1990, and the core of the EC, that is, Germany, France, UK, Netherlands and Italy, together, increased their labour force to 111 million in 1990 (from 103.4 million in 1978), the NAB countries expanded their work force by 37 million to reach a level of 167.1 million in 1990 (BLS, 1992, p. 96). In relative terms, this means that the average growth rate of the labour force, in the NAFTA countries, during the period between 1978 and 1990, was 2.1 per cent per year, double the Japanese rate and triple that of the EC.

Despite the combination of a slow economic growth and a rapid increase in the number of job seekers, the NAB countries have experienced a relatively low increase in their rate of unemployment. During the current period of stagnation in the United States and Canadian economies, the unemployment rate for the NAFTA countries, 8.5 in 1991, is below the average rate for the EC countries, but above the Japanese unemployment rate, according to

IMF figures (IMF, 1991, p. 135). The United States and Canada have created 18 million jobs since the 1981–1982 recession, thus stabilizing the labour market until the present period of stagnation. This successful stabilization of the labour market in the US explains to a large extent why the American people have been willing to support the economic policies developed by the Republican Administrations during the last 12 years. The Mexican experience has been quite different because Mexico suffered a deep slump throughout most of the 1980s. The recent ephemeral recovery, however, has created a compensating force just when Canada and the United States began their extended recession (INEGI, 1992).

Between 1975 and 1988, 29 million new jobs were created in the United States economy. Of these new jobs 5.9 million were created in trade, 8.8 in services, and 4.1 in health services and in the education system. If we sum the increases in these sectors the total would represent 61 per cent of the new jobs created during this 13 year period. But all of these activities were in sectors with productivity rates below the average, and with slow historical growth trends. This relative shift-share of employment from activities with a dynamic productivity trend, like manufactures or transport and communications, to activities with a reduced level of efficiency explains the convergence of slow growth, expanded employment, and stagnant productivity in the United States.

The impressive employment growth has a dark side, a low rate of productivity growth in the North American Bloc compared to relatively fast advances in the EC and Japan. The IMF demonstrates that labour productivity in the EC increased by two per cent during the period from 1982 to 1991. In Japan, gains made in the efficiency of daily work were impressive: an average of 3 per cent each year during the dame period (IMF, 1991, p. 132).

In contrast, inside the NAB, average productivity growth in the period 1978–1991, despite the remarkable recovery of productivity in some branches of United States manufactures, was only 0.8 per cent. Since the Gross Domestic Product (GDP) for the whole region increased at a moderate average rate of 2.6 per cent, during the twelve years since 1978, and as employment increased at a 1.8 percentage rate, the small difference indicates limited productivity growth, representing only two-fifths and one-quarter of the annual productivity increases in the EC and Japan, respectively.

There are, however, some significant differences among the North American Bloc countries. Canada was the country with the best performance in the last decade, with an annual increase in productivity of 1%. In contrast, the efficiency of the US and Mexican economies only advanced at 0.6 per cent and 0.5 per cent, respectively. This structural knot in the US and Mexican economies created other restrictions in the accumulation process. In both countries the ratio of investment to GDP dropped during the last twelve years. In the United States it was only 15.2 per cent in 1990, while in Mexico it was 16.5 per cent. In Canada, on the other hand, the investment ratio increased dramatically, representing 22.3 per cent of GDP in 1990. In 1978 it had only been 18.1 percent. But, in the region as a whole, the level of capital resources per worker allocated to introduce new technologies in the different economic activities has been reduced by almost one tenth of one per cent since 1978.

Three labour markets and one working class
The working class in the North American Bloc moved from one country to the other, as if they were in the same nation, long before the governments decided to create customs and border patrols. In the early part of the twentieth century, thousands of American workers laboured in Mexican oil fields, mines and railroads. In search of better wages and running away from the civil war, large numbers of Mexicans left their country after 1910 for the southern states of the United States. Between the Canadian and the American labour markets, for many decades, there was mobility between the workforce located in the twin industrial districts of both countries, and the labour markets were relatively homogeneous. Fewer differences exist among the Golden Horseshoe cities on both sides of the border than between the Great Lakes and the Southern regions within the United States (Davis, 1986, p. 193).

After the end of World War II, the US Government decided to preserve the internal labour market as a closed haven for American workers. Less so on the northern border and more so in the south, policing increased throughout the next decades to prevent movements of undocumented labour.

In Mexico, the vigorous economic growth of the 1950–1970 period created conditions which decreased the rate of emigration to the United States. In the countryside, however, the presence of thousands of landless peasants created a small but constant movement to the US. During the 1970s one million Mexican workers emigrated to the United States, most of them through hidden roads, and not through customs. Since the late 1970s, the particular conditions of the Mexican labour market began to create tremendous pressures on the labour market of the North American Bloc, with large movements of Mexican workers to the sunbelt in the United States.

The Mexican baby-boom of the 1960s was followed by an incredible expansion of the labour force during the 1980s; this expansion was strengthened by two other processes: the urbanization of the population and the incorporation of young educated females into the labour market. But, at the very moment at which one million young Mexicans were ready to enter the labour market each year, the Mexican economy began a prolonged and deep recession for the following seven years: a biblical punishment. If a revolution has not occurred it is only because the Mexican regime has an escape valve: emigration to the United States. If we compare the data of the 1980 and 1990 censuses of population in both countries, we can estimate the permanent emigration of Mexicans to the United States at three million. Seasonal emigration has increased from 1.8 million in 1980 to eight million in 1992 (US Statistical Abstract, 1984, p. 95 and *El Financiero*, agosto 4 de 1992). This means that a huge proportion of the unemployed Mexicans and a significant part of the impoverished peasants and informal traders attempt to cross the two thousand mile border between the first and the third world at least once a year. One-third of the Mexican labour force participates in the United States labour market for at least a few months every year.

On the other side, a not so well known story, is the important presence of American workers in the Mexican labour market. Mexico has the largest population of American citizens outside the United States with 500,000 US citizens living within its territory. This is double the number of American citizens in Canada. With the NAFTA negotiations, the managerial and administrative jobs in many Mexican companies are taken up more and more by US professionals.

The immense presence of the Mexican workers in the southern United States encountered the development of a dynamic service sector, employing cheap immigrant labour as a decisive source of profits. The presence of an inexpensive source of labour, such as that of Mexican immigrants, has also contributed to the relocation of many American industries to the west. In 1963, for example, California had 1.4 million industrial workers, which represented 8.2 per cent of all manufacturing employment. In 1990, the 2.2 million manufacturing workers in California represented 11.5 per cent of US employment in manufacturing (California Statistical Abstract, 1990, p. 23). These workers produce 120 billion dollars (US) in industrial goods each year. The absence of the trade union organizations in the Mexican labour force has changed the income distribution in States like California. In this state, for example, the share of wages of the Gross State Product fell from 64 per cent in 1970 to 59 per cent in 1990.

According to the 1990 US Census of Population, in 1991 3.5 million workers of Mexican and Latin American origin (Hispanic workers in the terminology of the Census) participated in industrial activities in manufactures, construction and mining. In those activities Mexican workers represented 13 per cent of those employed. In terms of the Mexican community itself, 56 per cent of the males and 18.2 per cent of females laboured in industrial activities. Overall, while only 29 per cent of the white labour force participated in industrial activities, 41 per cent of the Mexican labour force in the United States participated as industrial workers. The ethnic division of the labour market, in which Mexicans hold the lower paid and difficult jobs on the shop floor, while the white employees are concentrated in managerial and administrative positions, will be reinforced with the potential destruction of the small and medium-sized factories in Mexico: their productivity is only one-eleventh of the average industrial productivity in the United States (Velasco, 1991, p. 12).

The flow of Mexican workers was encouraged not only for the regional restructuring of the United States economy, in an attempt by American corporations to escape from industrial districts with a high trade union density, but also as a consequence of the erosion of wages caused by the structural incapacity of the Mexican economy to absorb the masses of young workers (Bortz, 1991, p. 64). The wage share of GDP in the Mexican economy was 40% in 1976. But with the economic crisis and growing inflation, the wage share decreased to 24.5% of GDP in 1990 (INEGI, 1991). The huge unemployment rate forced labour to accept just about any wage which was offered in exchange for their daily effort. Official trade unions also played a decisive role in this process, as we will see below. The accumulated losses of Mexican labour during the last 15 years reached the extraordinary figure of 325 billion, if we sum the wage participation in the GDP during this period, and subtract it from the income that they could have received if wage participation in the GDP had been maintained at the 1976 level.

In 1991, the real wage of an average Mexican worker had decreased to a level that represented only 65 per cent of the real wage 15 years earlier. With a virtual stagnation of the product per employee in the entire economy, the accumulation process continues to squeeze income out of the wage earners. As we can see, this wage drop in the Mexican labour market has encouraged millions of people to risk their lives crossing the border in search of an income six times that which they could receive in their own country (Hufbauer and Schott, 1992, p. 127).

Despite the drop (by three points) of the wage share in the US southern region in the last 20 years, Mexican emigration has created limited pressure on the US labour market. During the last ten years the wage share of GDP only dropped one point from 60.7 to 59.7 in 1991. The reason is that the pressure of Mexican immigrant workers is on low-wage activities; they only have a limited impact on other segments of the labour market (Hufbauer and Schott, 1992, pp. 112–13). We estimate the net effect of immigration as half a point in the wage share lost.

In Canada, a combination of a strong social safety net for unemployed workers, the bargaining power of the trade unions, and an increase in labour productivity created the conditions for successive increases in the wage share of GDP. In 1960 Canadian workers took 51 per cent of the GDP; 30 years later they obtained 57 per cent, a share which began to converge with that held by US labour.

After the end of the Cold War, US corporations did not need to endorse the implicit pact with the United States working class, and they did not receive the international support to maintain it either. Now, only the ferocious forces of the market will prevail. The capital–labour compromise is over. The North American Free Trade Agreement is just a part of the overall strategy to recover the competitiveness of American corporations. And the role of NAFTA is to convert the illegal threat of the undocumented migrant workers into a legal one with the possibility of installing American factories in Mexico and employing cheap labour. The real goal of NAFTA is not to increase commerce with a poor economy. The real aim of NAFTA is to break the confidence, in both mind and soul, of the American workers, to take away their confidence that sooner or later they can find a job. If NAFTA is ratified, the 11 million Mexican workers that could compete directly and indirectly in the United States labour market, are going to play on the same field without any restrictions. With the current continental level of unemployment, NAFTA will create a deep downswing in the historic wage trend in the United States and Canada. That is the hope of some corporations to revitalize capital accumulation in the North American Bloc. But to be successful in this attempt they need to confront the trade union challenge to NAFTA.

The trade union challenge to the Free Trade Agreement
The North American Free Trade Agreement is going to reinforce some current trends within the countries of the North America Bloc. First, it will cause a decline in manufacturing jobs and a concurrent growth in employment in the service, financial, and information sectors in the three countries. Secondly, it will increase capital mobility among the industrial districts of the potential new free trade area. Third, a larger share of the labour force will be comprised of minorities and women, as a part-time and contingent workforce. Fourth, it will weaken the bargaining power of local unions. NAFTA is the spatial mechanism to reorganize work on the shop floor and the rules of labour relations. It is an essential measure to redefine the participation of workers in the social product (Hecker and Hallock, 1991, p. 3).

This real threat to the social and working conditions of workers has generated a movement within the AFL-CIO and the Canadian Labour Congress to block the approval of NAFTA. In Mexico the government-controlled unions have limited the capacity of labour to resist and to mobilize. Trade unions have approached this decisive moment with diverse social organizational capacities in each of the three countries.

During the past 25 years we find divergent trends in union density within the three countries. The Canadian trade unions experienced a non-linear increase in their capacity to organize reaching a 36 per cent unionization rate among non-agricultural paid workers in 1990 (Statistics Canada, 1992, p. 159).

In absolute terms unionized workers grew to 4.1 million in 1990 from 1.6 million in 1965. In the United States in 1965, unions represented 24.8 per cent of the civilian labour force and had 18.5 million members. In 1988, union density was only 16.9 per cent and the membership had decreased to 17 million. In Mexico, the union rate has remained at a steady level of 16 per cent since 1970.

Historically Canada has had a high rate of unionism in the industrial core industries of manufacturing, construction and transport. In 1990, 1.5 million workers were unionized in these economic activities, with an average union density of 44 per cent. Another particular feature of Canadian trade unionism is the relatively homogeneous geographical presence of the industrial unions across the provinces (Statistics Canada, 1992, p. 49). In contrast, rates of unionization have had great regional variation in the United States and Mexico (Curme, 1990, pp. 22–6). In part, the national presence of industrial unions within the Canadian Labour Congress encouraged the expansion of unions to other economic sectors, such as trade and services. Moreover, the presence of industrial unions within the New Democratic Party (NDP) introduced working class issues into the broader arena of national and provincial politics.

In contrast, the relative inability of the Mexican and US trade unions to create solid bases in these industrial activities debilitated labour movement structures. In Mexico, attempts to overcome a narrow sense of trade unionism resulted in the building of popular fronts between unions and community organizations in the 1970s. The state thwarted democratic unionism by repressing the railroad and energy workers' unions, and then allowing the registration of opposition parties in the electoral process; thus limiting any expression of community-based concerns to narrow electoralism. Subsequent attempts to link trade union and community based politics met with repression (Salinas and Imaz, 1984, Volume II, pp. 175ff). Even the state social programmes covered by the umbrella programme named 'Solidaridad' during the 1990s follows the same idea in maintaining a separation between the community and unions. This new territorial social base of the state is used to weaken the bargaining power of the working class inside the Mexican political structure (Pradilla Cobos, 1993, pp. 61–2).

If we conduct an international comparison we find that trade unions in the NAFTA countries had a total membership of only 24 million workers, that is, 14.4 per cent of their labour force. In Western Europe, trade union membership has reached 43.4 million workers, and the union density is 36 per cent (Visser, 1989). In order to explain this divergence we would need to reconstruct some processes that determine union density, such as differences in labour laws, different levels of employer resistance and union avoidance, structural shifts in labour markets and union organizing strategies (Hecker and Hallock, 1991, p. 3). But the latest figures show how the NAFTA project will develop conditions that will dramatically increase the bargaining power of corporations and weaken the capacity of workers to resist.

In the last two years, the situation of unions has worsened notably. The Canadian trade unions have been weakened in the goods producing industries. In this sector, 700,000 jobs have been lost and union membership has been reduced by 250,000. As a result, union density has been reduced (Statistics Canada, 1992, Canadian Observer, 5.26). In the United States the current recession has also decreased union membership. In Mexico plant closures in central Mexico coincide with an escape to the non-union areas near the border.

The strategic options for unions fall into three categories as defined by Hecker and Hallock: 1) restrict the mobility of capital so that it cannot shop for cheaper labour in the non-unionized industrial districts within countries, or outside in the lower-wage industrial nations like Mexico, 2) raise the cost of doing business in other nations through international organizing, international labour standards, and multinational bargaining campaigns, 3) accept the mobility of capital, and choose to compete in the world economy on some basis other than wages – for example, a 'high wage/high performance' industrial policy – and deal with the adjustment side through domestic labour market policies.

Note
1. I would like to thank Teresa Healy, from Carleton University, and Martin Valadez, a doctoral candidate in history at Stanford University, for their valuable comments and suggestions on earlier drafts of this paper. This work would not have been possible without their help. I, however, take responsibility for any imperfections which may remain.

References
Bortz, Jeffrey (1991), 'La Industrialización y el Mercado de Trabajo en México' in *Revista Investigación Económica*, 195, Volume L, Universidad Nacional Autónoma de México, 43–69.
Bureau of Labor Statistics (1992), 'Current Labor Statistics', *Monthly Labor Review*, 4,115, United States Department of Labor, Washington, DC.
California Department of Finance (1990), *California Statistical Abstract*, State of California, Sacramento.
Curme, Michael (1990), 'Union Membership and Contract Coverage in the United States', *Industrial and Labor Relations Review*, 1(44) 10–45.
David, Mike (1986), *Prisoners of the American Dream: Politics and Economy of the United States Working Class*, London: Verso.
Hecker and Hallock (1991), *Labor in a Global Economy: Perspectives from the United States and Canada*, Eugene, Oregon: University of Oregon Books.
Hufbauer, Gary and Jeffrey Schott (1992), *North American Free Trade: Issues and Recomendations*, Washington, DC: Institute for International Economics.
International Monetary Found (1991), *World Economic Outlook*, Washington, DC.
Instituto Nacional de Estadística Geografía e Informática, INEGI, (1991), *Cuentas Nacionales 1980–1990*, México.
Instituto Nacional de Estadística Geografía e Informática, INEGI, (1992), *Cuadernos de Información Oportuna*, México.

Pradilla Cobos, Enrique (1993), *Políticas Territoriales: Un Balance Inconcluso hasta 1994*, Revista Coyuntura, **32**, 61–70.
Salinas, Samuel and Carlos Imaz (1984), *Maestros y Estado*, Serie Estado y Educación, Universidad Autónoma de Guerrero, México.
Statistics Canada (1992), *Labour Unions 1989*, Ministry of Industry, Science and Technology, Ottawa.
United States Bureau of Census (1984), *United States Statistical Abstract*, US Department of Commerce, Washington.
United States Bureau of Census (1991), *United States Statistical Abstract*, US Department of Commerce, Washington.
Velasco Arregui, Edur (1991), *De las especialización por los costos a los costos de la especialización*, Ponencia al Congreso de la UAM-Azcapotzalco, El TLC y sus Perspectivas, November 12, México.
Visser, Jelle (1989), *European Trade Unions in Figures*, New York: Deventer Editions.

5 Caribbean economic integration (CARICOM)

George E. Eaton

The West Indies Federation 1958–1961 may be cited as a modern example where political integration was seen as the precondition for regional economic cooperation and integration, rather than the other way around, and the federation foundered when the fiscal implications, both political and economic, of closer economic cooperation/integration became apparent.

In a sense, the cart had been put before the horse, a lesson which was not lost on West Indian political and intellectual leaders. A fresh start was made, with priority being given to economic cooperation, in 1965 when Antigua, Barbados and Guyana formed the Caribbean Free Trade Association (CARIFTA). It did not, however, start functioning until May 1968, when other Commonwealth Caribbean countries joined. Belize joined in 1972. CARIFTA was deepened into the Caribbean Common Market (CARICOM) in July 1973 as a result of the signing of the Treaty of Chaguaramas in Trinidad.

As it stands CARICOM is made up of two concurrent integration movements with overlapping membership. The Bahamas, Barbados, Belize, Jamaica, Guyana and Trinidad and Tobago are members of CARICOM, but not of the Organization of Eastern Caribbean States (OECS), while there are eight countries/territories which have membership, full or associate, in both CARICOM and the OECS. The OECS came into existence on June 18 1991 when seven Eastern Caribbean countries, Antigua and Barbuda, St. Kitts-Nevis and Montserrat (the Leeward Islands group) and Dominica, Grenada, St. Lucia and St. Vincent and the Grenadines (the Windward Islands group), signed the Treaty of Basseterre. The purposes of the Treaty, to which the British Virgin Islands more recently acceded, are to promote cooperation among member states among themselves as well as at the regional and international levels, to promote economic integration, unity and solidarity, common defence of their sovereignty, territorial integrity and independence, and to the fullest extent possible, harmonization of their foreign policies. The OECS, it may be noted, had been preceded by the Leeward Islands Federation (ended in 1956), the West Indies Federation (1958–61), the West Indies Associated States (WIAS) Council of Ministers, and the East Caribbean Common Market (ECCM), both inaugurated in 1968.

Under the Treaty the acronym 'CARICOM' may be used to refer to the narrower Caribbean Common Market having to do only with economic integration or to the broader Caribbean Community, involving non-economic dimensions.

The three main areas of activity of the Caribbean Community are:[1]

1. the pursuit of *Economic Integration* as set out in the *Common Market* Annex to the Treaty;
2. *Functional* (non-economic) *Cooperation* which covers areas ranging from common services such as the University of the West Indies (UWI), to cooperation in culture and radio and television broadcasting;
3. the coordination of foreign policies of member States (both in trade and economic and other general areas).

Let me deal first with Economic Integration. The main policy instruments are:

1. market integration;
2. coordinated or joint actions in production;
3. joint actions in extra-regional trade and other economic transactions, and
4. a special regime for the Lesser Developed Countries (LDCs).

Market integration
This consists of the establishment of free trade between the Member States and a common external tariff and protective policy. These make for the integrated market. There are however additional measures designed to facilitate market integration which fall under the heading of monetary and financial cooperation such as exchange rates, clearing arrangements for trade and other intra-regional transactions and payments or exchange control practices.

Coordinated or Joint Actions in production are of the very essence of integration. The joint actions envisaged are regional industrial programming, rationalization of agriculture, joint development of the region's natural resource and cooperation in tourism.

Joint Action in Extra-Regional Trade and other transactions such as cooperation and coordination in export production and obtaining new or expanded markets abroad. What is envisaged here is the progressive coordination of external trade relations.

Statistical profile
While the Caribbean communities may be described as a collection of ministates (population of 5.5 million) there are still sizable discrepancies between them. Jamaica, the largest of the Caribbean communities and 90 miles from

Table 5.1 Statistical profile

	Area (sq. km)	Population*	GNP at Market Prices US $000's*	Per capita GNP US$*	Real Growth Rate % 1980–90*
Antigua & Barbuda	440	79 000	363	4 600	5.2
Bahamas**	13 939	253 000	2 811**	11 096**	n.a.
Barbados	431	257 000	1 680	6 540	1.7
Belize	22 960	189 000	373	1 970	5.3
British Virgin Islands	153	14 900	133**	8 667**	n.a.
Dominica	750	82 000	160	1 940	4.3
Grenada	344	94 000	199	2 210	5.8
Guyana	214 970	798 000	293	370	2.7
Jamaica	11 424	2 390 000	3 606	1 510	0.7
Montserrat**	102	12 000	n.a.	n.a.	n.a.
St. Kitts & Nevis (337)	269	40 000	133	3 330	4.8
St. Lucia	616	150 000	286	1 900	6.3
St. Vincent & Grenadines	388	114 000	184	1 610	6.9
Trinidad & Tobago	5128	1 283 000	4 458	3 470	4.3
TOTAL	271 914	5 755 900	14 753		

Notes:
* Data for 1990 unless otherwise indicated
** GDP rather than GNP. Real growth rate 1980–1987. Montserrat.

Source: World Bank, *World Atlas* (Statistics on 185 Countries & Territories).

Cuba in the West, has a population of 2.39 million inhabiting 11,424 sq. km, while Trinidad and Tobago, 1200 miles east of Jamaica has a population of 1.28 million inhabiting 5128 sq. km.

The seven smaller islands of the Eastern Caribbean which make up the Windward and Leeward chain of islands, along with the British Virgin Islands and Barbados, have a combined population of about 843,000 and land masses ranging from 102 sq. km to 750 sq. km, while Belize in Central America (22,960 sq. km) and Guyana in South America (214,970 sq. km) have populations of 189,000 and 798,000 respectively.

In recognition of the fact that market integration by itself was not likely to immediately benefit the LDCs, special concessions and special development opportunities were provided for the LDCs in the CARICOM Treaty.

The rationale or case for integration

The most important arguments cited in favour of Caribbean integration are:

1. *Overcoming constraints of small size*, by enlarging the size of the internal/regional markets. Even the largest of the CARICOM states as noted above are still relatively tiny as compared with most other countries of the world, to say nothing of the Caribbean itself, where there are several neighbouring countries which individually have larger populations, as for example Cuba (population 10 million), Dominican Republic (6 million), Haiti (6 million), than all the CARICOM states combined (5.5 million). Some of the economic consequences of small size are spare productive capacity and high unit costs, because of inability of national markets to provide scope for sustaining plants of critical minimum size.

   The Island Developing Communities (IDCs) are also mountainous, making for reduced arable land and difficult conditions for mechanization of major export crops, sugar and bananas, and for inland transportation. Population and geography have thus served to strain the carrying capacity for sustainable development. The two mainland countries Belize (Central America) and Guyana (South America) are exceptions in that both have relatively large amounts of usable but unused and under-utilized land space.

   Other resources in the CARICOM region are limited to bauxite (Jamaica and Guyana), oil and natural gas (Trinidad and Tobago) and more generally, sand, sea and sun for tourism and marginal fishing.

   Finally, the CARICOM communities lie in the path of natural disasters, and from time to time crops, housing and infrastructure are destroyed or severely damaged by floods, hurricanes, volcanoes and earthquakes.

Regional integration presumptively offers prospects of extending production possibilities internally through joint efforts. Externally also there is the presumed advantage of increased bargaining power especially in dealing with other regional trading blocs and major industrial countries.
2. *Functional cooperation* can also provide economies of scale through development of common services in areas of education, health, meteorology, industrial relations, communication, transportation, coping with natural disasters, food production.
3. *Enhancing cultural identity and unity.* Externally the West Indies has been viewed as a collectivity for centuries, and internally the quest for an identity has been a recurring theme and ideal in the Caribbean ethos and aspirations.

Achievements and shortcomings

Liberalization of trade through removal of trade barriers was set back during the 1970s by balance of payments crises in Jamaica and Guyana which forced them to impose quantitative restrictions on imports from other CARICOM countries. While Jamaica was able to remove all of its restrictions in 1979, Guyana continued to experience difficulties and was joined by Trinidad and Tobago during the 1980s. Intra-regional trade as a percentage of total trade which had risen from 5 per cent in 1967 (EC $97.5m) to 10 per cent in 1981 (EC $1.6 billion) fell between 1982 and 1986 to less than one-third of the 1981 figure. By 1991 it had recovered to EC $1.3 billion.

The Treaty also envisaged a full common external tariff by August 1981. This called for the harmonization of tariffs with due allowance being made for phasing in over a longer period as far as the LDCs are concerned. New rules of origin, intended to give encouragement to the use of domestic and regional raw materials, have however proved controversial, but this is by no means unique to the Caribbean.

Decision-making in the Caribbean community

One of the main reasons why progress in realizing the modest objectives of CARICOM has been slow is that the Treaty of Chaguaramas contained no real mechanism to enforce implementation either of the Treaty or of the decisions made by organizations and institutions of the Community. Indeed the Treaty requires unanimity in decision-making. Unlike the EC, which created a Commission which could make proposals on policy to the Council of Ministers and make regulations which have the force of law, CARICOM has had no organizations or institutions with supra-national powers. The result is that the timetable of implementation of the decade of the 1980s has lurched forward to become the timetable of the 1990s.

The Europeans on the other hand, established a European Court of Justice to deal with treaty violations as well as a European Parliament, which initially had deliberative powers only, but was later given the power to approve the budget of the Commission.

As far as CARICOM is concerned, its greatest success has been in the area of Common Services such as the maintenance of the University of the West Indies (UWI) as a regional institution with three main campuses in Jamaica, Barbados and Trinidad and in other areas of functional cooperation such as health care, meteorology, library services, and agricultural research.

The current mood and situation

CARICOM Heads of Government at their tenth meeting held in Grenada in July 1989 issued a declaration (the Grand Anse Declaration) setting a new timetable for advancement of the Integration Movement. The year 1991 was targeted as the date to put in place:

- a common external tariff, rules of origins and a harmonized scheme of fiscal incentives and the removal of all remaining trade barriers;[2]
- free movement of skilled and professional personnel, and free flow of capital. The Kingston Declaration of July 1990 focused on the link between human development and economic growth and development and called for expanded output of trained personnel from the UWI. The challenge faced by the UWI to meet the skilled manpower needs of the region has been compounded by a significant and ongoing 'brain drain', from the member states, but particularly so from Jamaica, Guyana, and Trinidad and Tobago.

A West Indian Commission was established under a mandate from the CARICOM Heads of Government in 1989, to further the cause of both economic and political integration through a process of widespread public consultation both in the region and among the West Indian diaspora. Its final report was released in July 1992. The new sense of urgency reflects recognition of new global realities and trends including:

1. *The globalization of production and internationalization of capital* under the hegemony of transnational corporations which is leading the major industrial countries of the world to coordinate economic policy so that they can achieve a greater degree of stability.
2. *The emergence of mega-blocs in the field of trade*:
   - the USA and Canada Free Trade agreement (1989) which may be expanded into the USA, Canada and Mexico Free Trade Agreement (NAFTA).

- the establishment of the European Single Market in 1992. Traditional Caribbean exports of bananas, sugar and rum could be adversely affected as in the long run it may be difficult to preserve preferential commodity agreements intact.
- The Pacific Rim – encompassing Japan, China, Taiwan, Hong Kong, North and South Korea.
- The ASEAN countries including among others Singapore, Thailand and Malaysia which may also be expanded to accommodate linkages with Australia and New Zealand.
- Similar regional groupings are making progress in Latin America such as The Central American Common Market, the ANDEAN Group and the Southern Cone Common Market.

3. *International (Bretton Woods) Development Agencies Trusteeship*
Since the late 1970s the ability of the CARICOM communications to independently chart or pursue unconventional or radical solutions aimed at overcoming perceived structural disadvantages has been severely curtailed by economic and fiscal crises and loss of control of their economies to external systems.

Due to balance of payments deficits and the need for hard currency accommodation, CARICOM countries have effectively been placed under IMF and World Bank trusteeship to secure adherence to structural adjustment programmes. These programmes are being used to enforce in the most extreme form a specific ideological model of economic management which reflects the current preoccupation of the major industrial countries which control the multilateral institutions. IMF and World Bank technocrats have virtually been writing budgets, setting interest rates and deciding fiscal and monetary policy, enforcing ideological shifts to market driven development, deregulation and privatization and determining eligibility of individual CARICOM countries for other forms of development aid (commercial loans, technical assistance).

4. *World realignments in the realm of geopolitics* could also lead to a major redistribution of donor aid and international lending resources. The break-up and collapse of the Soviet Empire and Eastern European countries already has initiated a massive transfer of financial resources from Western countries and international institutions such as the IMF and the World Bank.

In the US hemispheric sphere of influence, the US Government in pursuit of its various regional development initiatives – the Caribbean Basin Initiative of President Reagan and the Enterprise Initiative of President Bush – has indicated that it wishes to proceed on a group basis rather than a single country basis. The Caribbean Basin Initiative (CBI) was a legislative package, inaugurated in 1984, which contained three provisions, the centrepiece of which was one-way duty free access to the US market for certain Caribbean products. The other two provisions included a $350 million supplemental aid appropriation for close to 30 Caribbean and Latin American countries which met 'beneficiary' criteria and status, and a provision that permitted US firms to claim tax deductibility for business convention expenses in CBI beneficiary countries. The Enterprise for Americas Initiative (EAI), the precursor for NAFTA announced by President Bush in June 1991, encompassed trade, investment, and debt relief policy measures directed at the countries of Latin America and the Caribbean. This trade initiative was aimed, among other things, at creating a Western hemisphere multilateral free-trade zone. The main thrust of the new investment sector lending programme under the aegis of the IDB (IADB) was to promote privatization and the liberalization of investment regimes, while the debt relief policy involved the forgiveness of some US development (soft) loans in order to bolster an effort to reduce commercial bank debt – in other words tying debt relief to private US investment.

The trends, noted above, towards globalization and regional trading blocs, externally imposed structural adjustment programmes and world realignments in hemispheric geopolitics have all served to highlight the degree of vulnerability of the individually small and very small CARICOM countries and have led to a more persistent call for the deepening of regional (CARICOM) integration.

Deepening of CARICOM

It is now being urged that the Caribbean Community become more self reliant by mobilizing to take advantage of the region's economic advantages and opportunities, which are:

- natural resources endowment – suitable for export agriculture for food, livestock and fisheries products; minerals such as bauxite, oil and natural gas, tourism;
- large amounts of usable but unused and under-utilized land space (Guyana, Belize);
- geographical location at the junction of the three Americas (North, Central and South);
- unique preferential access to three major world markets – USA (CBI and EAI), Canada (through CARIBCAN, the CANADA/CARICOM Agreement), the EC (through the Lomé Convention), plus the possibilities of the ALADI (Latin American Integration Association).

The steps/developments associated with deepening are (a) the establishment of a fuller range of regional legislative, executive, and judicial institutions to facilitate both policy-making and implementation, (b) the extension of the OECS physical security pact to all CARICOM countries so as to combat the dangers of the narcotics trade, arms and smuggling and mercenary attacks, intra - as well as inter - country, and (c) the creation of an integrated regional air link through the merger of existing national and regional carriers as well as the efficient operation of a regional shipping service.

Performance capacity
As noted earlier, the non-implementation of decisions taken by CARICOM Heads of Government and other organs and institutions of the Community has been one of the major shortcomings of the CARICOM experience.

The West Indian Commission in its Final Report proposed a revision of the Chaguaramas Treaty to provide for a comprehensive set of Regional (Unity) Institutions and structures including:

1)	Conference of Heads of Government	Supreme Legislative (existing)
2)	Council of Ministers	(Political Executives)
3)	CARICOM Assembly	(Deliberative)
4)	CARICOM Commission	(Central Administrative Authority)
5)	CARICOM charter of civil liberty	(Charter of Rights and Freedoms)
6)	CARICOM Supreme Court	(final Court of Appeal)
7)	CARICOM Secretariat	(existing but to service the proposed CARICOM Commission)

At their meeting in Trinidad in October 1992, the Heads of Government agreed to the proposed structure with the exception of the CARICOM Commission. In its place will be an executive (implementing) agency, the Bureau of Heads of Government, including the Outgoing, Current and Incoming Chairs of the Conference of Heads of Government, with the Secretary General of the CARICOM Secretariat as the Chief Executive Officer.

Economic strategies to further the deepening of Caribbean (CARICOM) economic integration
Economists tend to focus on two approaches to economic integration, namely the market liberalization approach and the cooperation in production approach.

The market liberalization approach espouses the removal of barriers to trade among countries, including barriers to trade in goods and services, money and capital flows, and progressive liberalization of movement of human resources and, as the ultimate step, monetary union with a common currency.

The EC, for instance, has relied primarily on the principles of market liberalization, but this has not precluded coordination of macroeconomic policies, science and technology policy, cooperation in industrial policy, energy policy and above all joint agricultural policies and programmes.

The cooperation in production approach logically reinforces market liberalization by actually promoting production between member countries. This approach involves both resource combination and programmed allocation of production in sectors and subsectors as between countries/members to create linkages in production regionally or sub-regionally and thereby accrue the advantages of economies of scale. As a general proposition, the cooperation in production approach tends to be combined with market liberalization to a lesser or greater degree in third world economic groupings. The CARICOM (Chaguaramas) Treaty envisaged reliance on both approaches. Under market liberalization, there is formal provision for freedom of movement of goods between the constituent countries, a common external tariff (CET) and a common protective policy. On the other hand no member state is obligated to allow freedom of movement of persons, whatever their levels of skills or attainments. The same holds true for the establishment or movement of services. In fact, the treaty specifically provides for 'the regulated movement of capital among the member states of the region'. The overall result therefore has been rather hesitant and gradual attempts at liberalization policies, and very limited progress if any at all on cooperation in production.

The West Indian Commission both in its Progress Report and in its Final Report sought to give a push to the integration movement by calling for immediate action on travelling in the region by providing easier travel, using simple and easily available forms of identification; free movement of skills beginning with graduates of the UWI and other recognized regional educational institutions and all duly accredited media workers; the creation of a common currency, which would have the effect of eliminating transactions costs of national currency conversions as well as exchange rate uncertainties in trade and investment decisions; enlarging investments, by creating flexible financial instruments to facilitate investment by the very sizable Caribbean diaspora, as well as the establishment of a Caribbean Investment Fund; creating a CARICOM Single Market which means coming to grips with the three major common market instruments – the common external tariff, rules of origin and a harmonized scheme of fiscal incentives.

The political economy of integration
If it is accepted that closer economic integration or economic union offers the best prospect of ensuring the long-run survival of the CARICOM communities, what is the most appropriate political economy or path of least resistance? We must first begin with an appreciation of what is involved in the different levels or stages of economic integration.

A free trade agreement (FTA) may be considered the first stage. In pursuit of freer trade (rather than free trade since not all trade barriers are subject to elimination and non-tariff barriers may remain intact), the members undertake to levy no tariffs and to impose no quantitative restrictions against the imports of participating countries within the FTA. Goods move freely, but services and capital and labour may not. Participants are also under no obligation to coordinate economic and monetary policy, far less fix exchange rates among themselves. In the absence of free movement of services and of factors of production, FTA is not presumptively more optimal than scenarios of protection. At best the FTA may serve as a restraint against sudden changes in trade policies that may result in increased discrimination against the trading interests of trading partners and the imposition of irritating new protectionist measures. This is the '*insurance or we cannot afford not to*' argument being relied upon for example by the Government of Canada to answer criticisms about the adverse effects of the FTA on employment and investment in Canada.

The second stage of integration should involve coordination of production and free movement of capital, supported by coordinated macroeconomic and other structural policies. The objective here is to develop common policies for the union as a whole.

The third and final stage is full monetary integration and a common currency. Monetary integration may itself take a variety of forms ranging from a common currency and common unit of account, responsive to a single monetary policy, to separate currencies linked by irrevocably fixed exchange rates which are fully convertible into each other. It is possible also to have a unit of account different from national currencies or a parallel common currency circulating freely with national currencies.[3]

Monetary integration may also be preceded by a system of policy coordination where central banks and fiscal regimes agree to coordinate their policies, within limits, so as to achieve predetermined objectives. Another variation may involve an exchange rate mechanism where separate national currencies are linked together but still permit exchange rates to vary within specified limits.[4] Monetary integration may also be accompanied by financial integration (mobility of financial assets) but this is not necessarily dependent upon monetary integration.

Gradualism vs acceleration

Two schools of thought have emerged in the Commonwealth (CARICOM) Caribbean as the most appropriate political strategy. One, inspired by EC experience, espouses a gradualist approach as being consistent with the narrowing of disparities in economic regimes and performance. As far as monetary integration is concerned the gradualists argue for a fairly loose exchange rate mechanism which links currencies but allows for variations of some magnitude. As central banks gain experience in policy coordination and develop a stabilization fund, the currencies can be linked more tightly and a central monetary authority established, in effect creating a regional currency as a unit of account. The final step would be currencies which are rigidly tied to each other.

Farrell observes[5] that the gradualist-stages approach has much to commend it – a more or less uniform performance *vis-à-vis* inflation and resource utilization among participating countries, and working towards the narrowing of disparities, economic and administrative.

The second school of thought, also citing European experience, argues that the gradualist approach tends to be long drawn out and requires institutional support which may not be available and that the accelerated approach – going straight for a common currency, though not necessarily for monetary integration – is the preferable approach. There is already an Eastern Caribbean Central Bank which has provided a stable inflation-moderating currency for the OECS states and which has been a contributory factor in the creditable economic performance of the OECS countries during the 1970s and 1980s. We should note that between 1980 and 1990, per capita income growth averaged 5.4 per cent across the OECS countries.

Integration among unequal partners

'Economic unions are rarely successful without the glue of intra-regional subsidies, as the European experience amply demonstrates.'[6] Unfortunately, the stark reality is that the more developed member states of CARICOM, Jamaica, Barbados, Guyana and Trinidad and Tobago, are currently in no shape to facilitate the transfer of compensatory payments/subsidies/resources to the LDCs. The MDCs have experienced grave external debt problems, some from the 1970s, others from the 1980s, which have put economic pressures on their balance of payments and their fiscal regimes. Negative growth or inhibited growth and recovery have been the end result. For example in 1988 the external debt for Guyana and Jamaica was 465 per cent and 144 per cent of GDP respectively. Currently around 60 per cent of export earnings in Guyana and 40 per cent in Jamaica are being used for debt servicing. In once oil rich Trinidad and Tobago, debt as a percentage of GDP rose from 15 per cent in 1984 to 57 per cent in 1988. The MDCs are still suffering the trauma of stabilization and structural adjustment programmes imposed under the trusteeship of the IMF–World Bank.

Among the eight member Organization of East Caribbean States (Antigua, British Virgin Islands, Dominica, Grenada, St. Kitts, St. Lucia, Montserrat and St. Vincent) Antigua's debt rose from 34 per cent of GDP in 1984 to 83 per cent in 1988. But it is to be noted that during the decade of the 1980s the OECS countries made significant gains in the standards of living of their citizens despite being extremely vulnerable to unfavourable external circumstances. They managed to maintain positive per capita income growth with low indebtedness. Continued concessionary external finance and conservative fiscal and monetary policies provided the base for tourism and construction booms and a strong banana market. Nevertheless the current profile of the LDCs reflects their historical development as plantation economies compounded by the other constraints of mini-island states. Of note are:

- reliance on *agricultural exports* (sugar and bananas) produced in most cases at costs that are higher than world prices and which survive only through preferential marketing arrangements.
- economies that are relatively undiversified and which do not have sufficient linkages between the various production sectors at national and regional levels. In other words, they have very small and virtually non-existent manufacturing sectors, not really geared to exporting to both regional and extra-regional markets.
- economies that are extremely open and vulnerable to external shocks and that extends even to the life saving tourism/hospitality industry.
- the ratio of exports to GDP is between 65 per cent and 73 per cent in 5 countries, between 54 per cent and 58 per cent in 3 countries and between 32 per cent and 46 per cent in 3 countries. The average ratio for all middle income developing countries is 18 per cent.
- high import propensities aggravated by inability to provide even moderate self sufficiency at national and regional levels in providing food, including livestock and fish products or at developing agro-industries based on domestic inputs.
- high levels of urban and rural unemployment.

The CARICOM treaty, not surprisingly, therefore provided for the LDCs a special concessionary regime which includes, inter alia.

- a longer period for freeing intra-regional trade;
- a longer period for phasing in the common external tariff (17 years);
- the right to impose protective tariffs and quantity restrictions in both

78 Economic integration between unequal partners

- agricultural and manufactured products already being produced by the MDCs
- more competitive fiscal incentives for both local and foreign capital and technical assistance.

Whatever impetus external threats or challenges posed by mega blocs and global competitiveness may give to a rapid deepening of Caribbean integration, CARICOM will have to face up to the criticisms made by LDCs that the common external tariff is likely to impact adversely on their economies, especially if the MDCs, which are being reoriented under IMF–World Bank imperatives to liberalized market driven economies, agree to a common external protective tariff which may be more compatible with their higher competitive threshold, but more threatening to the smaller agricultural commodity based economies.

Widening of CARICOM

The discussion about the deepening of CARICOM – that is to say, creating greater interdependence among member countries – has also led to discussion about the desirability and feasibility of the widening of CARICOM – that is to say, extending Caribbean Community trade linkages beyond the West Indies to the Caribbean Archipelago. Under this scenario the Caribbean would encompass the West Indies plus all islands of the archipelago plus Belize and the Guyanas. The final scenario, which presently may be considered a utopian ideal, would be the inclusion of the West Indies and the Caribbean Archipelago in the Caribbean Basin – which would include all the mainland shores washed by the Caribbean, Venezuela,[7] Colombia, Central America and Mexico. While this broad umbrella may be appropriate for US hemispheric economic policy, it certainly would aggravate the problems and difficulties of integration between unequal and culturally diverse partners.[8]

Concluding observations

As the reshaping of the economic and geopolitical configurations of the 20th century world continues, many nations face the prospect of being relegated to the periphery or becoming appendages or client states of more powerful patrons or overlords. The English-speaking Caribbean has grown accustomed to economic relations which have arisen out of their geopolitical circumstances and historical past. These relations have had both advantages and disadvantages. The advantages have been guaranteed markets and prices for what may be considered the political commodities (sugar and bananas) and to some extent bauxite (strategic stockpiling). The disadvantages have been dependent and vulnerable economies, subject to fluctuations in commodity export earnings, unfavourable terms of trade and dualistic and often skewed economies. To overcome perceived structural disadvantages, successive countries of the region have struggled to effect transformation of structures of production and/or modernization; by experimenting with every conceivable socio-economic and political model or system. In the English-speaking Caribbean, we have witnessed first industrialization by invitation or dependent capitalism, then democratic socialism and now market liberalization in Jamaica; revolutionary socialism in Grenada, cooperative socialism in Guyana, state-led or public enterprise oriented development in Trinidad and Tobago and other territories.

The CARICOM countries are now faced with a number of options. According to William Demas (*Towards West Indian Survival*, 1990) there is firstly the status quo – with CARICOM not being much deeper than it currently is but with probably a higher level of functional cooperation and closer unity among the members of OECS. Under this scenario the CARICOM (West Indies) would merely or marginally survive, survival being defined as 'continuing material improvement, especially for lower income groups, and the creation of productive and reasonably well-paid jobs for the unemployed' (Demas).

Secondly, there is a worse case scenario of heightened external dependence and semi-colonial clientalism involving *de jure* or *de facto* absorption into a big and powerful country or group of countries. Survival as defined above might be assured for some but not all of the CARICOM communities. Thirdly, there is the demanding but still feasible option of deepening the Caribbean community into a regional economy and creation through export led growth of a collective niche to compete internationally.

Small size and limited resources point to the desirability of mobility of capital and its corollary of currency convertibility, and also of labour to enable firms of the region to undertake joint ventures in production as well as marketing. The solution to small size may well be emphasis on quality rather than quantity and accordingly the establishment and maintenance of the highest quality infrastructure and human resources becomes a primary consideration.

There is, however, the reality that the deepening of CARICOM integration will require a transfer of resources both to the region and among member countries to overcome the economic costs of the deepening of interdependence, more so among unequal partners. Within economic union, the call will become more strident to address disparities between member states and lagging units may have to be compensated by incentives or increased economic activity. Freer markets and increased competition may drive hitherto protected small- and medium-sized firms to the wall. In recent years the manufacturing component of intra-regional trade has been a significant proportion of CARICOM exports: for Jamaica the 65–78 per cent range, Trinidad and Tobago 61–69 per cent, Barbados 69–80 per cent, and Guyana 34–77 per cent. During the 1980s few of the LDCs recorded less than 50 per cent of total manufacturing exports to CARICOM and in some cases it was 75 per cent. In 1990, manufacturing accounted for 66 per cent of Antigua's exports to CARICOM, while the figure for St. Vincent was 32 per cent and for St. Lucia 18 per cent.

The additional layers of public administration and defence and security requirements are likely to result in greater public expenditure. But, on the credit side of the integration balance sheet there is the prospect of uniform fiscal and budgetary discipline which may reverse the past two decades of budgetary and inflationary deficit financing which has led to dissipation of foreign exchange reserves, balance of payment crises, and prolonged and painful stabilization and structural adjustment programmes, the price exacted by the IMF and World Bank for providing hard currency accommodation and development loans.

Notes

1. Caribbean Community Secretariat (1981).
2. So far eight member states representing 92 per cent of the Common Market have introduced a CET package. Likewise ten of twelve member states have introduced the rules of origin drawn up in 1981.
3. See Farrell (1991).
4. Farrell (1991).
5. Farrell (1991).
6. Hufbauer and Schott (1992).
7. It is interesting to note that pursuant to the 'Principles for a Multilateral Agreement' between the Caribbean Community and Venezuela signed in St. Kitts on July 1, 1991, CARICOM and Venezuela have signed an Agreement under which, on a phased basis beginning January 1, 1993 and January, 1996, Caribbean products will gain duty-free access to the Venezuela Market. The Agreement will be administered by a CARICOM/ Venezuela Joint Council on Trade and Investment which will meet at least annually. CARICOM in turn will grant most-favoured nation treatment in the application of the customs tariff in respect of all imports from Venezuela.
8. The West Indian Commission's Final Report 1992 recommends that CARICOM should remain the inner core of the region and that an Association of Caribbean States be created as the vehicle for promotion of other special arrangements with NAFTA, and Latin America in general.

Bibliography

Caribbean Community Secretariat, (1981), *The Caribbean Community in the 1980's. Report by a Group of Experts*, Georgetown, Guyana.
Demas, William, (1990), *Towards West Indian Survival* (Occasional Paper No.1), West Indian Commission.
Eaton, George, (1988), 'The Jamaican Labour Movement and Caribbean Integration', *Caribbean Integration and the Labour Movement Part II*, Caribbean Labour Series, November, Curaçao: Caribbean Institute of Social Formation (CARISFORM).
Farrell, Terrence, (1991), 'The Political Economy of Caribbean Monetary and Financial Integration', *Caribbean Affairs*, 4(4), October–December Trinidad Express Newspaper Ltd.
Hufbauer, Gary and Jeffrey Schott, (1992), *North American Free Trade, Issues and Recommendations*, Washington, DC: Institute of International Economics.
The West Indian Commission, (1991), *Towards a Vision of the Future*, Progress Report.
World Bank, (1991), *World Atlas*, Washington.

PART II

INTEGRATION AND UNEQUAL DEVELOPMENT IN THE EUROPEAN COMMUNITY

6 Internalization and externalization of EC trade

Evrard Claessens

The topic of economic integration raises questions of both public and scientific interest. Among the major issues relating to representative indicators of economic integration are the old questions of mutually comparative strength (Mill, 1861) and a variety of other approaches to integration (Hitiris, 1988, p. 35). Among these, economic measures have some advantages since they appear to be better quantifiable than, say, cultural and political arguments. Among the economic measures static indicators of strength are standard, such as GDP, population, GDP per capita and more advanced indicators. Other measures are more dynamic and address changing trade patterns and trade balance within the 'group' which is supposed to be integrated, and the growth of 'internal' exchanges relative to those with the 'outside world'. Among these are visible trade, services and capital flows.

This chapter addresses the recent evolution of product trade within the European community and with the rest of the world. Because the analysis compares import and export flows, some services are implicitly included in the analysis, for example, those which are directly related to the inward processing or upgrading of products. The direct trade of 'pure services' (those not related to the 'value added' of products) are not considered here since the related statistics have about a three-year delay compared to the rather rapid availability of product statistics. Capital flows are omitted too because of the dominant measurement problem relative to both the registration of the flow and to the definition of true origin and destination (EC, 1990, 1991, 1992). Thus, product trade is perhaps only the 'tip-of-the-iceberg,' but it is a visible tip which offers the quickest registration.

1. The basic trends

The period of investigation (1976–91) allows special attention to the most recent years (1988–91), i.e., after the 'deadline 1992' decision of the Single European Act. The starting year 1976 is not only the beginning of the last quarter of the century, it also constitutes the first 'normal' year after the turbulent first oil shock (1973), a transition year of pending orders (1974), and an oversensitive reaction in 1975. In 1976 EC trade globalizes in new and wider directions. China's exports to the EC rose from 600,000 tons to

84 *Economic integration between unequal partners*

more than 10 million tons. In 1979, the second oil crisis was real, and 'oil dependency' became a significant variable (Claessens, 1984). On the European continent the year 1980 initiated a period of savings, viz. import substitution. The UK became the major European integrator by progressively spending its oil-pounds on the Continent and accelerating intra-European trade. After 1984 economic growth consolidates into a positive cycle (1988–91) which is now fading away. Table 6.1 presents some statistics relating to these events, with total and non-mineral EC imports, including the intra-EC share of the latter. The main trend is that EC mineral imports drop from three-quarters down to less than two-thirds, and the intra-EC share of non-mineral imports rises from 50 to 60 per cent.

This trend of 'de-mineralization' and 'communitarization' is further clarified in Table 6.2 by a number of characteristic growth figures. Thus columns 'a' and 'b' give some characteristic growth numbers relating to total and non-oil imports, of which 'd' is the difference. This difference between the total and characteristic numbers follows from a procedure which is known as

Table 6.1 Import and trade volumes of the European Community

Year EUR9	total European world imports			Intra-EC trade	
	millions of tons	Mineral %	Non-min	in %	in millions of tons
1976	1 378	74.24	25.76	49	175
1977	1 351	73.75	26.25	51	180
1978	1 225	69.23	30.77	51	193
1979	1 500	73.03	26.97	51	208
1980	1 443	71.75	28.25	52	210
1981	1 325	71.03	28.97	54	207
1982	1 277	69.19	30.81	54	212
1983	1 254	67.87	32.13	55	222
1984	1 339	68.34	31.66	56	238
1985	1 396	67.77	32.23	57	255
1986	1 427	66.41	33.59	58	276
1987	1 452	64.71	35.29	57	290
1988	1 509	64.61	35.39	59	315
1989	1 574	64.42	35.58	60	334
1990	1 635	64.04	35.96	59	346
EUR12	1 817	64.17	35.83	58	378
1991	1 722	64.64	35.36	59	362
EUR12	1 919	64.73	35.27	59	401

Table 6.2 Comparative growth (%) of EC imports (only EUR-9)

Period	mineral. (a)	non-miner. (b)	difference (d) = (b)–(a)	intra-EC (c)	'Monnet index' (m) = (c)–(b)
1976–80	4.66	14.77	10.11	19.87	5.10
1980–84	–7.15	4.01	11.22	13.24	9.23
1984–87	8.42	20.84	12.42	22.23	1.39
1988–90	12.60	14.84	2.24	9.84	–5.00
1988–91	14.12	13.90	–0.22	15.10	1.20

Notes: 1988–90 is repeated in 1988–91 to account for trend irregularities (German unification & opening to the 'East').

Source: Eurostat data NIMEXE up to 1987, CN since 1988 and E. Claessens; 'Monnet' module 90-30566.

'shift-share analysis' (Isard, 1976, and Claessens, 1990a). Likewise the difference between the non-mineral imports (column b) and the intra-EC non-mineral trade is called the 'Monnet index' (m), which is given in the last column. This index indicates integrating intra-trade when m > 1.

Table 6.2 also shows that non-mineral imports accelerated until 1987 (together with their share of intra-EC trade, up to 60 per cent). The acceleration of this intra-EC share compared to global EC world imports (the Monnet index 'm') is highest in the 1980–84 economic crisis and decreases afterwards. The period 1988–90 produces a negative index, but in 1988–91 there is a positive number.

2. Growth patterns in product trade and the 'Euro Dividend'

Table 6.2 defines the 'Monnet index' (m) as an acceleration of intra-EC trade relative to the EC world imports. This procedure is incomplete when it is applied only to volume imports (in ECUs) from which a value-indicator is calculated; the difference between the import value-indicator (MVI) and the export value-indicator (XVI) is called the EURO-indicator (DIV). This dividend indicator remains a rough measure but follows the logic of the 'shift-share' technique.

Shift-share analysis enjoyed an initial success in regional economics because it bypasses the paucity of regional data and shows an implicit model structure (Isard, 1976). Applications in international trade suffer from the poor explanatory power of the technique. Some have endeavoured to compare model structures (Berendson, 1978), and a home-made software package on European trade won an award in the 'Jean Monnet' project of the EC

(Claessens, 1990b). Today the technique may benefit from the fact that European integration forges a unit in which the member states progressively behave as regions in a larger unit (nations). Therefore regional applications of shift-share analysis may gain momentum in this 'international' intra-European framework too.

The analysis follows Tables 6.3, 6.4 and 6.5, in which a few examples compare the agri-sector (vegetables, s. 2) with textiles (s. 11) and manufacturers (ss. 15 to 18).

Between 1976 and 1980 EC world imports rose by 14.77 per cent and intra-EC imports by 19.87 per cent. These average growth rates are called 'share-effects'. World imports of section 2 (agri-products of vegetable matter) dropped by 4.54 per cent or 19.31 below the 14.77 per cent average of EC world imports. In the shift-share jargon, this deviation is called the 'proportional product shift'. The intra-EC imports of these agri-products increased by 23.30 per cent, which produces a proportional product shift of 3.43 per cent relative to the intra-EC average of 19.87 per cent. Thus, the agri-sector fuels intra-EC trade and does not follow the average of EC world imports. A measure for this is simply the difference of the two proportional shifts (each relative to their average). Table 6.3 gives these calculations, including indices for the periods 1980–84 and 1984–87 (all only in volumes). The details of this for all trade MINEXE-sections are given in Table 6.4

The very positive 'Monnet index' for agri-products of vegetable matter strengthens the notion of a 'fortress Europe' for agriculture. Nevertheless, Table 6.4 shows that those very positive values drop. At the same time food trade (5.4) is initially very outward-oriented with a negative Monnet index and turns positive between 1984 and 1987. This example shows that basic agri-products (5.2) were dominating the internal EC market and are now progressively open to outside sourcing. At the opposite extreme, final products (food, 5.4) initially show a dominant external sourcing and tend to internal trade. Typical examples also are the negative value for chemical products (5.6) and the changing fortunes in vehicles trade (5.17). The arrows in the last columns indicate whether the Monnet index (m) synchronizes with

Table 6.3a Example of the 'Monnet index' 1976–80

1976–80:	'share'	– col. 2	= prop.shift	1980–84	1984–87
World-import	14.77	–4.54	–19.31	– 6.09	–10.54
intra-EG	19.87	23.30	3.43	15.59	8.29
Monnet index = intra – world			22.74	21.68	18.83

Source: numbers from section 2 in Table 6.4.

Internalization of EC trade 87

Table 6.3b: Product proportional shifts with 'Monnet index'

share:1976–80	(14.77)	1980–84	(4.07)	1984–87	(20.84)	intra-
share-intra:	19.87	intra:	13.24	intra:	22.23	effect
1. 18.88	4.11	11.88	7.81	15.02	–5.81	↓ ↑ a
1. 25.26	5.39	14.88	1.65	16.76	–5.47	▼ ▼ r
Monnet index	**1.28**		**–6.16**		**0.34**	▼ ▲ m
2. –4.54	–19.31	–2.01	–6.09	10.30	–10.54	↑ ↑ a
2. 23.30	3.43	28.83	15.59	30.52	8.29	▲ ▼ r
Monnet index	**22.74**		**21.68**		**18.83**	▼ ▼ m
3. 21.44	6.67	13.63	9.56	10.81	–10.03	↑ ↓ a
3. 29.52	9.66	30.19	16.95	14.00	–8.23	▲ ▼ r
Monnet index	**2.99**		**7.39**		**1.80**	▲ ▼ m
4. 21.18	6.41	11.90	7.83	14.12	–6.72	↑ ↑ a
4. 15.06	–4.81	16.51	3.27	18.90	–3.32	▲ ▼ r
Monnet index	**–11.22**		**–4.56**		**3.40**	▲ ▲ m
6. 30.73	15.96	22.93	18.86	26.89	6.05	↓ ↓ a
6. 31.00	11.13	24.21	10.97	19.72	–2.51	↓ ↓ r
Monnet index	**–4.83**		**–7.89**		**–8.56**	▼ ▼ m
7. 24.85	10.08	22.33	18.26	25.84	5.00	↓ ↑ a
7. 21.63	1.76	21.51	8.27	28.12	5.89	▲ ▼ r
Monnet index	**–8.32**		**–9.99**		**0.89**	▼ ▲ m
9. 11.79	–2.98	–9.43	–13.50	8.32	–12.52	↑ ↑ a
9. 11.82	–8.05	12.54	–0.73	32.31	10.08	▲ ▲ r
Monnet index	**–5.07**		**12.77**		**22.60**	▲ ▲ m
10. 18.25	3.48	15.89	11.81	15.55	–5.29	↑ ↑ a
10. 30.23	10.36	31.36	18.12	32.11	9.88	▲ ▼ r
Monnet index	**6.88**		**6.31**		**15.17**	? ▲ m
11. 2.72	–12.05	8.08	4.00	14.00	–6.84	↑ ↑ a
11. 6.31	–13.56	15.46	2.23	16.31	–5.92	▲ ▼ r
Monnet index	**–1.51**		**–1.77**		**0.92**	? ▲ m
13. 22.92	8.16	1.91	–2.16	13.71	–7.13	↓ ↑ a
13. 19.05	–0.82	1.97	–11.27	23.08	0.85	▼ ▲ r
Monnet index	**8.98**		**–9.11**		**7.98**	▼ ▲ m
14. 35.16	20.39	–18.89	–22.96	38.97	18.13	↓ ↑ a
14. 25.20	5.33	–25.45	–38.69	43.68	21.45	▼ ▲ r
Monnet index	**–15.06**		**–15.73**		**–3.32**	? ▲ m
15. 10.14	–4.63	–5.12	–9.19	13.24	–7.60	↓ ↑ a
15. 11.72	–8.15	–2.28	–15.52	9.94	–12.29	▼ ▲ r
Monnet index	**–3.52**		**–6.33**		**–4.69**	▼ ▲ m
16. 27.75	12.98	–2.77	–6.84	21.20	0.36	↓ ↑ a
16. 23.93	4.06	–5.63	–18.87	23.19	0.96	▼ ▲ r
Monnet index	**–8.92**		**–12.03**		**0.60**	▼ ▲ m
17. 29.45	14.68	–15.78	–19.85	35.77	14.94	↓ ↑ a
17. 4.24	–15.63	–5.20	–18.43	57.38	35.15	▼ ▲ r
Monnet index	**–30.31**		**–1.42**		**20.21**	▲ ▲ m
18. 63.84	49.07	–1.05	–5.12	28.94	8.10	↓ ↑ a
18. 24.29	4.42	20.65	7.41	26.81	4.58	▲ ▼ r
Monnet index	**–44.65**		**12.53**		**–3.52**	▲ ▼ m
20. 31.95	17.18	12.11	8.04	28.57	7.73	↓ ↑ a
20. 17.34	–2.53	5.50	–7.74	30.31	8.08	▼ ▲ r
Monnet index	**–19.71**		**–15.78**		**0.35**	▲ ▲ m

88 Economic integration between unequal partners

Table 6.4 Monnet index (1988–91) with import-value indicator

	volume: intra: Monnet:	14.35 15.51 1.16	value: intra; Monnet:	27.53 30.02 2.49	world intra MVI =	13.18 14.51 1.33	product CN sections
1.	12.18 12.35	−2.18 −3.16 −0.98	19.36 18.52	−8.17 −11.50 −3.33	world intra MVI =	−5.99 −9.32 −2.35	live animals animal products
2.	6.63 9.63	−7.73 −5.88 1.85	13.45 22.05	−14.08 −7.97 6.11	world intra MVI =	−6.35 −2.09 4.26	vegetable products
3.	21.60 21.92	7.25 6.41 −0.84	27.51 36.86	−0.02 6.84 6.86	world intra MVI =	−7.27 0.43 7.70	fats & oils
4.	13.87 19.56	−0.48 4.05 4.53	27.10 36.68	−0.43 6.66 7.09	world intra MVI =	0.05 2.61 2.56	prepared foodstuffs
6.	8.29 8.03	−6.06 −7.49 −1.43	23.25 23.65	−4.29 −6.38 −2.09	world intra MVI =	1.77 1.11 −0.66	chemical products
7.	29.22 25.66	14.87 10.15 −4.72	25.45 24.17	−2.08 −5.85 −3.77	world intra MVI =	−16.95 −16.00 −0.95	plastics & rubber
9.	5.00 20.13	−9.35 4.61 13.96	15.93 25.52	−11.60 −4.50 7.10	world intra MVI =	−2.25 −9.11 −6.86	wood, cork & articles
10.	18.21 23.95	3.85 8.43 4.58	18.20 23.38	−9.33 −6.65 2.68	world intra MWI =	−13.18 −15.08 −1.90	paper & pulp & articles
11.	15.23 15.54	0.87 0.02 0.85	31.89 28.24	4.35 −1.78 −6.13	world intra MWI =	3.48 −1.80 −5.28	textiles & articles
12.	34.72 23.32	20.37 7.80 −12.57	42.06 30.17	14.53 0.14 −14.39	world intra MWI =	−5.84 −7.66 −1.82	foot- & headwear
13.	21.49 16.52	7.13 1.01 −6.12	28.21 25.39	0.68 −4.63 −5.31	world intra MWI =	−6.45 −5.64 0.81	stone, cement ceramic, plaster
15.	17.90 17.98	3.55 2.46 −1.09	16.67 18.79	−10.86 −11.23 −0.37	world intra MVI =	14.41 13.69 −0.72	base metals & articles
16.	23.82 21.39	9.46 5.88 −3.58	32.08 33.45	4.55 3.43 −1.12	world intra MVI =	−4.91 −2.45 2.46	machinery & electrical equipment
17.	25.52 23.10	11.17 7.58 −3.59	52.65 50.46	25.12 20.43 −4.69	world intra MWI =	13.95 12.85 −1.10	vehicles & transport equipment
18.	26.54 31.19	12.19 15.68 −3.49	30.88 31.39	3.35 1.36 −1.99	world intra MWI =	8.84 14.32 5.48	optical, pre- cision & mus. instruments
20.	33.90 33.36	19.55 17.85 −1.70	40.63 36.84	13.10 6.82 −6.28	world intra MWI =	−6.45 −11.03 4.58	miscellaneous manufactured articles

Table 6.5a Export value indicator with EURO DIVIDEND INDICATOR

	volume: intra: Monnet:	11.48 13.86 2.38	value: intra:	22.88 27.29 4.41	world: intra: XVI:	11.40 13.43 2.03	import MVI: 1.33	EURO DIV.IN −0.7
1.	11.02 12.62	−0.46 −1.24 −0.78	16.07 17.05	−6.81 −10.24 −3.43	world: intra: XVI:	−6.35 −9.00 −2.65	−2.35	0.3
2.	14.18 15.22	2.70 1.36 −1.34	21.77 24.40	−1.11 −2.89 −1.78	world: intra: XVI:	−3.81 −4.25 −0.44	4.26	4.7
3.	12.47 15.29	0.99 1.43 0.44	23.77 32.51	0.89 5.22 4.33	world: intra: XVI:	−0.10 3.79 3.89	7.70	3.81
4.	14.18 13.49	2.70 −0.37 −3.07	32.43 35.40	9.55 8.12 −1.43	world: intra: XVI:	6.85 8.49 1.64	2.56	0.92
6.	6.71 6.47	−4.77 −7.39 −2.72	18.15 20.32	−4.74 −6.97	world: intra: XVI:	0.03 0.42 0.39	−0.66	−1.05
7.	15.50 20.17	4.02 6.31 2.29	16.20 21.23	−6.69 −6.06 0.63	world: intra: XVI:	−10.71 −12.37 −1.66	−0.85	−0.81
9.	22.48 14.46	11.00 0.60 −10.40	24.51 26.14	1.63 −1.15 2.78	world: intra: XVI:	9.37 −1.75 −11.12	−6.86	4.26
10.	22.80 19.90	11.32 5.94 −5.38	23.80 23.09	0.92 −4.20 −5.12	world: intra: XVI:	−10.40 −10.14 0.26	−1.90	−2.18
11.	10.18 11.16	−1.30 −2.71 −1.41	22.42 24.89	−0.46 −2.39 −1.93	world: intra: XVI:	0.84 0.32 −0.52	−5.28	−4.76
12.	21.50 19.70	10.02 5.84 −4.18	24.69 25.03	1.81 −2.26 −4.07	world: intra: XVI:	−8.21 −8.10 −0.11	−1.82	−1.71
13.	14.70 17.14	3.22<.br>3.28 −0.06	20.06 24.88	−2.82 −2.41 −0.41	world: intra: XVI:	6.04 5.69 −0.35	0.81	1.16
15.	10.55 16.21	−0.93 2.34 3.27	12.22 17.55	−10.66 −9.74 0.92	world: intra: XVI:	−9.73 −12.08 −2.35	−0.72	1.63
16.	16.32 19.44	4.85 5.57 0.72	26.85 29.41	3.96 2.12 −1.84	world: intra: XVI:	0.89 −3.45 −1.12	2.46	3.58
17.	14.51 23.28	3.03 9.41 −6.38	34.85 45.06	11.97 17.77 −5.80	world: intra: XVI:	8.94 8.36 −0.58	−1.10	−0.52
18.	16.42 33.48	4.94 19.62 14.68	22.51 29.76	−0.38 2.47 2.85	world: intra: XVI:	−5.32 −17.20 −11.88	5.48	17.36
20.	23.47 32.96	11.99 19.10 −7.11	24.41 34.83	1.53 7.54 6.01	world: intra: XVI:	−10.46 −11.56 −1.10	4.50	5.60

90   Economic integration between unequal partners

Table 6.5b   MVI-value indicator (5.2)

Monnet index:	m (value)	:	6.11
	m (volume)	:	1.85
MVI value indicator		:	4.26

see section 2 in Table 6.5a.

the proportional shift for intra-trade (r) and the absolute growth of intra-trade (a). For chemical products (5.6) all arrows go down.

Table 6.5 repeats the exercise for the later years (1988–91) with the new Combined Nomenclature (CN) and adds value trade (in ECU). The difference between the Monnet index for volume and for value is called the 'Import Value Indicator' (MVI).

A positive MVI means that intra-EC trade progressively becomes more value-oriented whereas world imports tend to low-value goods, such as semi-finished goods for inward processing.

A similar procedure can be followed for exports. Here the a priori signs should be the opposite (Table 6.6). The XVI (export value-indicator) should be negative, meaning that high-value products should tend to be exported outside the EC. The Euro Dividend Indicator is defined as : DIV = MVI–

Table 6.6   German proportional shifts and Euro Dividend

imports	value	–	tonnage	=	difference	
world	20.07		10.01		10.06	
intra	22.55		6.01		16.54	
----	----		----		----	
Monnet	2.48		–4.00		6.48	(MVI)
exports	tonnage	–	value		difference	
world	4.70		–4.29		–8.99	
intra	1.45		–9.21		–10.66	
----	----		----		----	
Monnet	–3.25		–4.92		–1.67	(XVI)

EURO DIVIDEND INDICATOR :   MV   –   XVI
                          8.15 = 6.48 – (–1.67)

XVI. When MVI > 0 and XVI < 0 both effects consolidate. Table 6.6 also repeats the MVI from Table 6.5 and shows the DIV in the last column.

The Euro Dividend indicates a growing value-added of intra-EC trade either by:

a. import substitution for high-value products (MVI > 0),
b. export penetration on extra-EC markets (XVI < 0),
c. a consolidation of both effects.

When any of the signs is 'wrong' the indicator presents a method of detecting the causes. The average, at least, causes problems since the average Euro Dividend is negative (–0.70). The decomposition means that the MVI (1.33) is not the source of problems but the XVI (2.03) has the 'wrong sign'. In other words, 'buy home' has been followed, but 'sell abroad' for high value products has not been sufficiently pushed.

3. Country growth and comparisons with the Euro Dividend

It is also tempting to compare the acceleration patterns by country, and to draw conclusions on the trade situation of the EC member states. The calculus uses 'proportional country shifts' in the same way that the 'proportional product shifts' established the concept of 'Monnet product index' in the previous section. The calculations are now carried out for the proportional shifts of German trade flows (Table 6.6).

The positive dividend for Germany follows from:

a. a positive Import Value Indicator (MVI = 6.48) expresses the fact that the German economy tends to obtain high-value imports relatively from the other EC members. The positive ratio is further sustained by a lower volume growth on the intra-EC market (negative Monnet index for tonnage of –4.00);
b. a negative eXport Value Indicator (XVI = –1.67) indicates that the high-value German exports go relatively outside the EC.

On average, Germany buys more high-value products from the internal market and sells the upgraded product outside the community. This calculation remains 'relative' to the average of the EC. Therefore there must be positive and negative deviations. Table 6.7 gives the numbers in an opposite situation which deals with the Spanish case.

The Spanish dividend is negative since, here, both the MVI and the XVI show the 'wrong' signs:

a. a negative iMport Value Indicator (MVI = –4.21) suggests that Spain tends to buy more expensive products from outside the community, more so in 1991 than in 1988;
b. a positive eXport Value Indicator (XVI = 1.53) suggests that Spain exports relatively expensive products from inside the community.

Table 6.7 The Spanish Euro Dividend indicator

imports	value	–	tonnage	=	difference	
world	24.11		16.81		7.30	
intra	28.66		25.57		3.09	
----	----		----		----	
Monnet	4.55		8.76		–4.21	(MVI)
exports	tonnage	–	value		difference	
world	18.88		–9.45		28.33	
intra	28.38		–1.48		29.86	
----	----		----		----	
Monnet	7.97		9.50		1.53	(XVI)

EURO DIVIDEND INDICATOR :   MV – XVI
                          –5.74 = –4.21 – (+1.53)

These calculations remain relative to the EC average. Therefore there must be positive and negative deviations. Table 6.8 gives an overview of the EUR-12 members. Among the larger countries only Germany and Italy show a positive dividend indicator. Remarkable also is the fact that most individual country calculations show negative results. This may indicate that a majority of member states have preferred to consolidate their position in the EC market after the 'deadline 92' message, rather than embarking on export opportunities outside the EC. In the recent literature (Haspeslagh and Jemison, 1992, p. 266) this would be called 'domain strengthening'.

A negative dividend indicator could also mean that a country tries to obtain inward processing for (re-exporting) to other EC member states. This processing may consist of 'cheap labour' assembly (e.g., Portugal) but it can also be restricted to mere trading and logistical services (Van der Hoop, 1992), viz. the distribution of imported goods (e.g., the Netherlands and the BLEU).

Table 6.8   Country statistics of Euro Dividend indicators

country	dividend
Greece	36.0
Germany	8.2
Ireland	5.3
Italy	3.3
United Kingdom	−2.6
France	−3.8
BLEU	−4.5
Spain	−5.7
Denmark	−6.3
Netherlands	−6.7
Portugal	−32.0

In spite of the fact that 'logistics' constitute a cluster of activities in Porter's value chains (Porter, 1991, p. 242), it may be feared that too many specialize in 'trading only' across the EC and too few embark in genuine value-added activities. This even results in a negative EC average dividend of −0.70 of which the composition is:

$$\begin{array}{r} (MVI: 1.33) \\ -(XVI: 2.03) \\ \hline = DIV: -0.70 \end{array}$$

This shows that for the EC as a whole inward sourcing is not the problem (since 1.33 is positive), but that there is a lack of sufficient outward selling (since XVI is positive also).

Even the cases with a positive dividend ought to be handled with care. In principle, the message of 'buy European' can be considered a positive factor indicating reliance on the home market. Central EC economies are indeed better (high-value) clients of the more peripheral members whereas the latter tend to act as gateways to the inland areas of the Community. This explains the German and Italian situation whereas the 'Atlantic-coast' countries, with their transit ports, obtain negative dividend indicators.

4. Trade balances

The previous analysis concentrated on the compound issue of European trade, its intra-share, and outward sourcing. The dividend indicator only presents a compound measure of import and export flows in relation to the

94 Economic integration between unequal partners

intra-EC trade. It does not illustrate the balance of trade. Trade balances, though, are very limited when they are restricted to product trade. Therefore, these balances are only presented as an annex to the previous analysis, to which they provide a welcome complement.

A preliminary way to identify balances is to look at the national share in intra-European imports and exports and to compare the percentage-point balances. This is done in Table 6.9. For the sake of clarity, the Table reports the old EC (EUR-9) in the old NIMEXE-nomenclature, and switches to new CN (Combined Nomenclature) for the 1988–91 period. Both 1988 and 1991 report the EC with and without the 'new Mediterranean' members (Greece, Spain and Portugal). The break between 1987 and 1988 is kept open in order to reduce potential trend irregularities (due to switching nomenclatures) to a strict minimum.

The 'winners' are clear. The major national surplus is registered in Germany and to a lesser extent in the Benelux countries. These countries show also more 'gain' from intra-EC trade after 1988 (i.e., including the new members). The BLEU features occasional deficits in 1980 and 1987. Ireland registers deficits in the 1970s but recovers later. All others show negative intra-EC balances throughout. Especially, the 'newcomers' (GR, E & P) show deteriorating import balances between 1988 and 1991.

Finally, it is possible to assess the balances also with the help of the shift-share technique. For this purpose we simply apply 'growth' within the same year from imports to exports. The 'share effect' should be zero for the intra-EC balance, but in practice it evens out potential errors and inaccuracies. A positive proportional shift then gives the net effect. This is, for example, positive for Germany (8.85 per cent), the Netherlands (17.25 per cent), the BLEU (6.23 per cent), Ireland (33.38 per cent), and Denmark (4.51 per cent), all of this excluding mineral products. The product-balance is negative for France (−5.22 per cent), Italy (−1.01 per cent), the UK (−8.80 per cent), and the new Mediterranean partners Greece (−56.82 per cent), Spain (−18.96 per cent) and Portugal (−32.32 per cent).

It is then possible to link the product balance with the dividend concept in a suggestive graph (Exhibit 6.10).

This graph suggests a constructive articulation of the positive balances where the dividend is instrumental in separating the 'processors' from the 'traders'. The negative balances invite further investigation of the causes. The Greek situation is extreme, since the country has an extremely developed service industry which is not included in the analysis. Nevertheless the growing product-deficit with the Community remains a source of concern. At the opposite extreme, the UK, by nature a trader, is cutting back the intra-EC deficit to normal proportions. As in the case of Greece, the British service sector is not included in the analysis, nor in the extra-EC trade.

Table 6.9   National % shares in intra-EC value trade

D	F	I	NL	BL	UK	IRL	DK	GR	E	P
24.5	19.9	12.0	13.7	14.2	10.6	1.7	3.3	1976		IMPORT
28.7	17.6	11.1	14.3	14.5	9.5	1.6	2.6	1976		EXPORT
4.2	−2.3	−0.9	0.6	0.3	−1.1	−0.1	−0.7	EXPORT	−	IMPORT
23.8	19.7	13.6	12.1	12.6	13.4	2.4	2.5	1980		IMPORT
29.7	17.0	12.5	13.2	12.1	10.4	2.5	2.5	1980		EXPORT
5.9	−2.7	−1.1	1.1	−0.5	−3.0	−0.1	−.−	EXPORT	−	IMPORT
23.8	19.0	13.4	11.4	11.4	15.9	2.2	2.8	1984		IMPORT
30.7	17.3	13.1	12.4	11.5	10.4	2.4	2.4	1984		EXPORT
6.9	−1.7	−0.2	1.0	0.1	−5.5	0.2	−0.4	EXPORT	−	IMPORT
23.0	20.2	14.1	11.4	11.2	15.4	1.8	2.8	1987		IMPORT
30.7	17.3	13.1	12.4	11.5	10.4	2.4	2.4	1987		EXPORT
8.6	−3.6	−0.8	1.4	−0.2	−6.0	1.5	−0.1	EXPORT	−	IMPORT
22.1	20.9	13.9	11.0	11.3	16.4	1.9	2.5	1988		IMPORT
29.8	18.2	12.8	12.1	11.6	10.9	2.4	2.2	1988		EXPORT
7.7	−2.7	−1.1	1.1	0.3	−5.5	0.5	−0.3	EXPORT	−	IMPORT
20.3	19.2	12.8	10.1	10.4	15.0	1.7	2.3	1.3	5.2	1.9
28.0	17.1	12.0	11.4	10.9	10.2	2.3	2.1	0.6	4.2	1.3
7.7	−2.1	−0.8	1.3	0.5	−4.8	0.6	−0.2	−0.7	−1.0	−0.6
26.5	20.7	13.8	10.3	11.1	13.5	1.8	2.3	1991		IMPORT
28.0	19.1	13.2	11.8	11.8	11.8	2.4	2.4	1991		EXPORT
1.5	−1.6	−0.6	1.5	0.3	−1.8	0.6	0.1	EXPORT	−	IMPORT
23.9	18.6	12.4	9.3	10.0	12.1	1.7	2.1	1.6	6.4	2.2
26.0	17.7	12.2	10.9	10.6	11.0	2.2	2.2	0.6	5.1	1.5
2.1	−0.9	−0.2	1.6	0.6	−1.1	0.5	0.1	−1.0	−1.3	−0.7
D	F	I	NL	BL	UK	IRL	DK	GR	E	P

Notes: all years reported for the EUR-9 configuration 1988 and 1991 also report the full EC (EUR-12).

Source: calculations on EUROSTAT COMEXT.

5. Evaluation

The issue of intra-EC trade offers greater possibilities for analysis than a mere comparison of internal and external balances. The current period offers an interface between previous separation and pending unification and provides a statistical basis for observation up to 1993. At that time the system is

Exhibit 6.10 Trade dividend graph

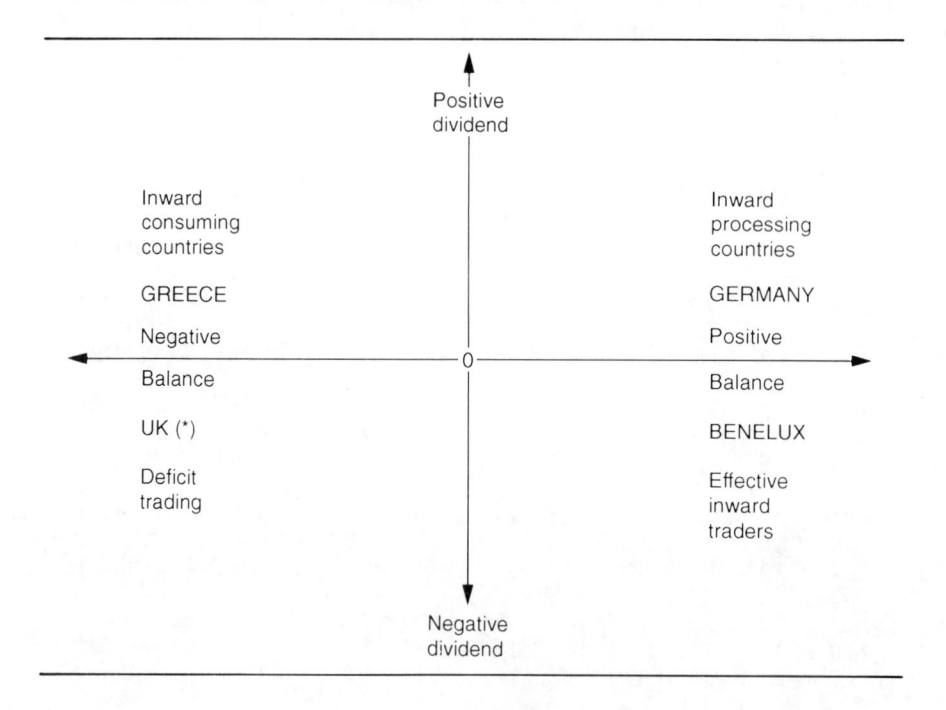

```
                        ↑
                    Positive
                    dividend

   Inward                              Inward
   consuming                           processing
   countries                           countries

   GREECE                              GERMANY

   Negative                            Positive
←──Balance────────────0─────────────── Balance ──→

   UK (*)                              BENELUX

   Deficit                             Effective
   trading                             inward
                                       traders

                        ↓
                    Negative
                    dividend
```

bound to suffer from another trend irregularity. It is worthwhile for the time being to await what happens and to suggest ways for the continuation of this work with the new data system which will record intra-EC trade from 1993 onwards. For this purpose the shift-share technique is flexible and suggests further directions for constructive and innovative research.

Bibliography

Beenhakker, A. and F. Damanpour (1992), 'Globalization of Foreign Trade Zones; The Case of the United States', *The International Trade Journal*, **VII**, (2), Winter, 181–203.

Berendsen, B.S.M. (1978), *Regional Trade and Development*, Leiden: Nijhoff.

Claessens, E. (1982), *European Transport During the Crisis Years, a Shift-share Statistical Investigation*, Liber amicorum prof. L. Baudez, Antwerp, 245–60.

Claessens, E. (1984), *Export Marketing Study for the Republic of Indonesia*, Embassy of Indonesia, Brussels.

Claessens, E. (1989), *Trade Analysis for an Export Marketing Study of Thai Exports to the European Community*, part 1: The Macro Study & part 2: The Market-share Study, Bangkok: BOI.

Claessens, E. (1990a), *Die Bundesrepublik Deutschland, ein erfolgreicher Nachbar*, working paper, Antwerpen: UFSIA, departement bedrijfseconomie, 90–129.

Claessens, E. (1990b), *M.O.N.N.E.T. (Methodology for Orienting Across Nations and Nomenclatures, the European External Trade Flows*, European Communities, DGX/C6, modules 90/30566 and 92/0030 and chair programme 'Jean Monnet' 91/0061.

Claessens, E. and P. Innegraeve (1983), *Positioning Auditing and Product Portfolio Planning in Foreign Trade*, VvE congres, Brussels, VUB.

Claessens, E., M. Kamel and A.K. Shanker (1984), 'Traffic and Trade Projections on the Eastbound Suez Shipping Route', *Maritime Policy and Management*, 1.

Dudley, James, W. (1990), *1992, Strategies for the Single Market*, London: Kogan.

EC (1990, 1991 and 1992), *Panorama of EC Industries, ed. 1990–91, 1991–2 & 1992–93*, Luxembourg, various chapters.

Green, Robert C. and Arthur W. Allaway (1985), 'Identification of Export Opportunities. A shift-share approach', *Journal of Marketing*, **49**, Winter, 83–8.

Haspeslagh, Ph. and D. Jemison (1992), 'Industry Restructuring, Acquisitions and the Value Creation Process' in K. Kool, Neven and Walter, *European Industrial Restructuring*, Macmillan.

Hitiris, T. (1988), *European Community Economics*, 2nd edition, New York: Harvester.

Isard, W. (1976), *Methods of Regional Analysis*, Cambridge, Mass.: MIT, 259–308.

Kahn, H. and A.J. Wiener (1967), 'The next thirty-three years; a framework for speculation', *Daedalus*, Boston: American Academy for Arts and Sciences, **96**(3), 705–32.

Lindberg, L.N. and S.A. Scheingold (1970), *Europe's would-be policy*, Prentice Hall, 314.

Mill, John Stuart (1861), *Considerations on Representative Government*.

Moini, A.H. (1991), 'EC 1992: Perception and Strategic Planning of Small- and Medium-sized Exporting Manufacturers', *The International Trade Journal*, 193–209.

Porter, M. (1991), *Competition Among Nations*, The Free Press.

Porter, M. (1993), 'Competition Among Nations and the New Europe' in *Quo Vadis Europe*, International Harvard Conference, Frankfurt, Harvard Club Rhein-Main.

Van der Hoop, J.H., (1992) 'The Single European Market: Optimizing Logistics Operations in Post-1992 Europe' in *Logistics, the Strategic Issues*, Chapman, 260–67.

Vernon, R. and L.T. Wells (1981), *Economic Environment of International Business*, 3rd edition, Prentice Hall.

World Bank (1991), *World Development Report*, 183 & 205.

7 Economic integration and unequal development: the experience of Greece[1]

Theodore Georgakopoulos

1. Introduction

Greece has been a member of the European Community since 1981. The performance of the economy after membership has however been very poor, despite the huge financial assistance the country has received from the European budget. The average growth rate of GDP for the 1980s was only 1.5 per cent, which is about 65 per cent of the EC average, compared to 4.7% for the 1970s, a rate more than 50 per cent above the EC average. Industrial production grew at an average rate of only 1 per cent (about 60 per cent of the EC average), compared to 6.9 per cent in the 1970s (about 2.5 times the EC average). Inflation ran at an average rate of 18.1 per cent (three times the EC average). The unemployment rate increased substantially, and from 2.2 per cent on average in the 1970s (about half the EC average) reached 7 per cent in the 1980s (about 80 per cent of the EC average). Finally, the trade balance deteriorated severely. Leaving out fuels, the overall trade deficit increased from less than 6 per cent of GDP in 1980 to over 17 per cent in 1990, whereas that with the Community increased from less than 5 per cent to about 13 per cent.

The above developments give rise to two important questions to which I will try to give an answer: firstly, are these developments, at least partly, the result of Common Market membership or are they due to other factors independent of entry? Secondly, to the extent that the negative results are due to accession, do they provide some evidence which could be generalized to other situations of economic integration among unequal partners or are they simply germane to the special conditions of Greece and the EC? To answer these questions, I will consider the major implications of entry for the Greek economy during the first decade of entry. In particular, I will discuss: (i) income transfers between Greece and the other EC countries, (ii) trade and welfare effects, (iii) effects on agriculture, manufacturing and the public sector, and (iv) the macroeconomic implications of entry. A summary of conclusions is given at the end.

2. Inter-country income transfers

Membership in the European Community implies two sorts of income transfers: (i) budgetary transfers, and (ii) direct transfers through trade. The former

Table 7.1 Greece's budgetary receipts and payments 1981–1993

Year	Gross receipts m.Drs	Gross payments m.Drs	Net receipts m.Drs	Growth rate	% of GDP	% of trade balance	% of government expenditure
1981	18 268	9 152	9 116	—	0.5	2.4	1.3
1982	59 168	18 652	40 516	344.4	1.8	10.1	4.6
1983	98 398	25 024	73 374	81.1	2.7	15.4	6.6
1984	112 333	28 612	83 721	14.1	2.5	13.3	5.9
1985	162 682	40 434	122 248	46.0	3.0	15.2	6.5
1986	273 666	91 896	181 770	48.7	3.7	20.6	7.8
1987	318 965	74 621	244 344	34.4	4.5	25.7	8.5
1988	348 680	88 795	259 885	6.4	4.0	24.0	7.7
1989	461 797	108 286	353 511	36.0	4.5	23.9	8.4
1990	595 686	120 907	474 779	34.3	5.1	24.3	9.2
1991	788 341	181 543	606 799	27.8	5.5	27.0	10.2
1992*	1 055 750	202 700	853 050	40.6	6.6	—	12.9
1993**	1 292 500	275 880	1 016 620	19.2	6.9	—	12.4

Notes:
* estimates
** forecasts

Source: Ministry of Finance, *Annual Budget Reports* for various years.

result from the operation of the European budget, since a country's receipts do not usually match its contributions. The latter follow from the higher prices that consumers of a member country pay to producers of other member countries as a result of discriminatory protective devices, especially of tariffs and variable levies.

Greece is a heavy beneficiary from the European budget. As Table 7.1 shows, Greece's net budgetary receipts are very substantial and have steadily increased over the years, so that from 0.5 per cent of GDP in 1981, they reached 6.5 per cent in 1992 and are expected to increase even further in future years. Today, these receipts cover more than one-quarter of the country's trade deficit and correspond to more than 10 per cent of the total expenditures of the general government.

The structure of Greece's receipts from the EC is, however, not equally satisfactory, since a large part comes from the guarantee section of FEOGA in the form of income support for farmers[2] and is used by them for consumption purposes,[3] so that the contribution to investment and growth is smaller than its size would suggest. It is only during the last few years that the contribution of the so-called structural funds,[4] which are supposed to improve the structure of the economy, has increased, but even a large part of these resources constitute consumption funds.[5]

Contrary to budgetary transfers, the direct transfers through trade leave a substantial negative balance for Greece. Negative transfers are caused by both tariffs and variable levies. In the case of tariffs the negative balance is due to two main factors: (i) Greece's total exports to the EC are only 40 per cent of its total imports (and in the case of manufactures only 30 per cent; (ii) Greece's imports from the EC are, on average, more luxurious products and they bear higher tariffs when imported from third countries than its exports to the EC. As a result, Greek consumers pay to EC producers higher prices for a larger volume of consumption than do EC consumers to Greek producers. In the case of variable levies, the balance is negative because Greece produces and exports mainly Mediterranean-type agricultural products, which are supported via variable levies and result in negative transfers. Previous studies (e.g. Georgakopoulos and Paschos, 1983, Georgakopoulos, 1986) indicate that, in 1981, the negative balance of the direct transfers more than outweighed the positive balance of the budgetary transfers; in 1982 it was about 50 per cent, whereas in 1984 it fell to one-third. Although no estimates are available for later years, it is probable that the relative size of the negative direct transfers remains at about the same level.[6]

3. Trade and welfare effects

Although Greece became an associate member of the EC as early as 1961, and tariffs on imports of manufactures had already been substantially reduced, and those on its exports to the EC totally abolished, the Greek economy was, at the time of entry, still heavily protected on the import side and widely subsidized on the export side. Protection was assured by direct controls, financial impediments (in the form of interest-free deposits to the Bank of Greece, settlement of import invoices only in cash, restrictions on the finance of imports etc.) and, above all, the tax system.[7] On the other hand, export subsidization took the form of direct money subsidies granted to exporters.[8]

The abolition of protection on the import side must have had a considerable impact on imports into Greece. The introduction of the Common Agricultural Policy has also had substantial effects on imports both because of the increase in imported food prices from the EC, and its direct impact on food imports, and the harm to competitiveness that possibly resulted from the cost–push inflation caused by these food price increases. No substantial favourable effects were expected on the export side because Greece's exports of manufactured products were already entering the Community free of tariffs from 1968.[9] On the contrary, Greek exports must have been severely hit after the abolition of the large subsidies granted before accession. Greek trade balances must therefore have substantially worsened as a result of entry.

Table 7.2 presents some well known indices which support this view. As the table shows, imports from the EC, as a percentage of GDP, doubled in the post-accession period whereas the percentage of imports from third countries increased only slightly. These developments caused a sharp increase in the share of Greek imports from the EC by 13 percentage points in the post-accession decade. The Balassa *ex post* income elasticity of imports from the EC increased from 1.3 in the 1970s to 6.5 in the 1980s, while the elasticity of imports from third countries increased from 1.5 to 3.4. Accession has therefore resulted in large overall trade creation. A similar conclusion is reached when the shares in apparent consumption are considered. Imports from both sources increased substantially at the expense of domestic production, with the domestic share having fallen by ten percentage points.

Coming to exports, we also observe a shift to the EC, but the overall level of exports as a percentage of GDP remained relatively constant. The share of Greek exports to total EC imports increased from 0.33 to 0.39, while their share in EC apparent consumption increased from 0.090 to 0.094.

The above *ex post* developments, of course, incorporate the impact of other factors as well, especially changes in the competitiveness of Greek products. However, as Constantopoulos (1992) has shown, for the whole decade on average the relative prices of traded goods in Greece remained unchanged, since the differential in the Greek inflation rate was counterbalanced by exchange rate changes.[10]

Table 7.2 Some indices of the trade and welfare effects of Greece's entry

		IMPORTS			EXPORTS		
Alternative indices		1970	1980 (71–80)*	1990 (81–90)*	1970	1980 (71–80)*	1990 (81–90)*
I.	PERCENTAGES OF GDP[1]						
	EC	9.7	10.3	20.6	3.9	5.7	8.0
	Third Countries	6.9	7.7	8.7	3.5	6.5	4.2
	Total	16.6	17.9	29.3	7.4	12.2	12.2
II.	SHARES[1]						
	EC	58.4	57.1	70.4	52.5	46.8	65.6
	Third Countries	41.6	42.9	29.6	47.5	53.2	34.4
III.	EX POST INCOME ELASTICITIES (BALASSA)[2]						
	EC		1.29	6.50	—	2.39	4.88
	Third Countries		1.49	3.39	—	2.95	–0.69
	Total		1.37	5.33	—	2.17	2.13
IV.	SHARES IN APPARENT CONSUMPTION (TRUMAN)[2]						
	EC share	6.8	7.6	17.7	—	—	—
	Third Countries' share	4.8	5.7	8.0	—	—	—
	Domestic share	88.0	92.2	82.1	—	—	—
V.	SHARE OF GREEK EXPORTS TO EC IMPORTS[3]				—	0.33	0.39
VI.	SHARE OF GREEK EXPORTS TO EC APPARENT CONSUMPTION[3]				—	0.071	0.094

Notes:
* For the Balassa *ex post* income elasticities and the shares of Greek exports to EC imports and apparent consumption.
(1) current prices (2) constant prices (3) averages for the period 1971–80 and 1981–90, respectively

Source: National Statistical Service of Greece, *Foreign Trade Statistics*.

4. The impact on agriculture

Entry into the EC affected the agricultural sector considerably, since it increased the level and changed the structure of support of the sector. Total subsidies to agriculture, before entry, amounted to just over 10 per cent of agricultural GDP, whereas immediately after entry they were increased to 25 per cent and, in 1990, they reached 30 per cent. The average rate of tariffs on agricultural products was 15 per cent before entry; it fell to about 4.3 per cent in 1981, immediately after the introduction of the CAP, and it was gradually aligned to the common customs tariff within the five-year transition period. On the other hand, imports of cereals and livestock products from third countries were heavily burdened by special levies, which, on average, amounted to about 35 per cent in 1981 and were gradually increased to 50 per cent in 1985.

The above changes have had a tremendous impact on the prices of some major imported agricultural products, and especially of livestock products.[11] On the other hand, the prices of Greek exportable agricultural products did not increase very much since they are not heavily protected in the European market (Georgakopoulos and Paschos, 1983). These price changes had substantial effects on the level and orientation of imports of agricultural products and harmed the Greek balance of trade in agricultural products. Indeed, as the first four columns of Table 7.3 show, the share of the EC in Greek imports of

Table 7.3 The impact of accession on trade in agricultural and manufactured products

		AGRICULTURAL PRODUCTS				MANUFACTURES		
Alternative indices		1970 (71–80)*	1980 (80–81)*	1981 (81–90)*	1990	1970 (71–80)*	1980 (81–90)*	1990
A.	IMPORTS							
	I. SHARES[1]							
	EC	26.7	40.9	72.1	78.6	70.6	66.1	69.2
	Third countries	73.3	59.1	27.9	21.4	29.4	33.9	30.8
	II. ELASTICITIES[2]							
	EC	1.88	442.67	146.65	8.83		1.10	6.44
	Third countries	0.05	−295.39	−67.97	0.28		1.74	4.56
	Total	1.05	2.94	37.38	4.17		1.39	5.78
B.	EXPORTS							
	I. SHARES[1] Third							
	EC	54.9	40.9	46.5	70.4	56.2	49.7	64.1
	Third countries	45.1	59.1	53.5	29.6	43.8	50.3	35.9
	II. ELASTICITIES[2]							
	EC	0.78	−40.00	26.49	5.88	—	3.46	3.94
	Third countries	3.20	−225.00	−44.59	−3.58	—	5.05	0.50
	Total	2.02	−157.22	−16.49	1.19	—	4.24	1.94
C.	EXPORTS/IMPORTS[1]							
	EC	2.66	1.49	0.76	0.73	20.0	41.4	29.6
	Third countries	0.79	1.49	2.25	1.12	37.3	81.7	37.3
	Total	1.29	1.49	1.17	0.83	25.1	55.1	31.9

Notes:
* For the Balassa elasticities.
(1) current prices (2) constant prices

Source: National Statistical Service of Greece, *Foreign Trade Statistics*.

agricultural products increased from 41 per cent in 1980 to 72 per cent in 1981, and further to about 80 per cent in 1990. Substantial changes in the destination of Greek exports of agricultural products also took place, with the share of the EC increasing from 41 per cent in 1980 to 47 per cent in 1981 and gradually to 70 per cent in 1990. The Balassa *ex post* income elasticities show tremendous trade diversion, especially in the first year of accession, but trade creation is even larger, so that the final outcome is trade creation. However, the balance of trade in agricultural products deteriorated severely with the ratio of exports over imports having fallen from 1.5 in 1980 to only 0.8 in 1990, the deterioration being mainly due to developments in Greece's trade with the Community, where the ratio fell from 1.5 to 0.7 over the same period.

Coming to the domestic market, we have had an increase in the price received by producers of agricultural products, but prices of inputs also went up materially. The increase in the price of final products overcompensated farmers for the increase in input prices so that the net price to producers went up as a result of entry. On average, the increase in the net price received by producers is estimated at about 8 per cent. This improvement is mainly due to the increases in the prices of livestock products which, on average, amounted to about 15 per cent, whereas the net price increase of crops to producers is estimated at about 1 per cent. These price changes have changed the structure of production, with the production of certain heavily supported products (e.g. hard wheat, maize, cotton, sunflower etc.) having increased very much, whereas the production of others has increased less or even fallen in the 1980s (Bank of Greece, 1991).

The above price and volume increases together with the increase in subsidies going to farmers, have increased farmers' incomes. The average income per employed person in agriculture, as a percentage of the average income in all other sectors, has increased from less than 52 per cent in 1980 to over 62 per cent in 1989 and part of this improvement must be due to entry. Previous studies (Georgakopoulos, 1988) show that the improvement in farmers' incomes because of entry must have been of the order of 8–10 per cent.

5. The impact on manufacturing

The impact of full membership on manufacturing was dubious before entry. It was argued that Greek manufacturing could benefit from the large market within which firms would be able to place their products without any restriction; but doubts were expressed as to whether the Greek industry would be able to compete with the more efficient European firms, as well as with firms from other developing countries which would obtain access to the Greek market. The last three columns of Table 7.3 give *ex post* developments in the trade of manufactured products.[12] As this table shows, the overall export over import ratio fell from 55 per cent in 1980 to 32 per cent in 1990, and the ratio of exports over imports with the EC fell from 41 per cent to 30 per cent, whereas the corresponding ratio for third countries fell from 82 per cent to 37 per cent. These developments may again incorporate the impact of other factors, but a careful consideration of the developments in trade reveals that entry is an important factor. During the first half of the 1980s when the discriminatory tariff changes took place and quantitative restrictions were abolished, the Balassa *ex post* income elasticities of imports from the EC increased from 1.1 to 9.4 per cent, whereas the elasticity of imports from third countries fell from about 2 to 1. On the other hand, imports from both sources increased substantially over the second half of the 1980s when the regulatory levy was gradually abolished.[13]

Coming now to exports of manufactures, Table 7.3 reveals that the impact of entry has not been substantial. Total exports have not increased very much, but exports to the EC have increased more than exports to third countries.

6. The impact on the public sector

The public sector underwent considerable alterations in the 1980s. Its size increased substantially, its structure changed, but its balance worsened materially.[14] These developments were mainly policy choices but entry into the European Community has had some impact. Concerning the size of the public sector, entry may account for part of the increase, for three main reasons: (i) Community funds are now spent by public authorities over and above what would be spent in the context of pre-existing national policies; (ii) Greece contributes to the structural funds, and this increases the size of the public sector to the extent that expenditures by the structural funds do not substitute for expenditures via national policies; (iii) entry has, as we shall see below, affected economic activity in the country negatively, and it may therefore have resulted in an automatic increased in the relative size of the public sector, if, as Buchanan (1977) points out, this sector has a momentum of its own, independent of developments in the economy.

Coming to the balance of the public sector, entry has had effects in both directions. Part of the expenditures that were financed by domestic sources is now financed by Community funds and this must have tended to reduce deficits. On the other hand, entry has increased deficits for three main reasons: (i) the loss of revenues from tariffs, which yielded about 6 per cent of total tax revenues; (ii) the loss of revenues from the gradual abolition of the regulatory levy, which, in 1984, brought in about 10 per cent of the total tax revenues; and (iii) the loss of revenues from the reduction in economic activity caused by entry.

7. Macroeconomic aspects

Accession to the European Community has affected the macroeconomic performance of the Greek economy. Both the level of economic activity and the inflation rate have perhaps been affected. The impact on domestic activity may have come from both the demand and the supply side and a complete analysis of the issue is impossible in the present context. The most important impact has probably come from the demand side as a result of the sharp increase in the marginal propensity to import which has reduced the multiplier and consequently the level and rate of growth of economic activity.

Accession has probably also accelerated the inflation rate. Again, the impact on inflation may have been the result of more than one factor, but two major inflationary sources should be mentioned here: (i) the large increase in food prices which resulted from the introduction of the CAP and has perhaps initiated some cost-push type of inflation, and (ii) the depreciation of the national currency, which was necessary to accommodate the huge trade deficits caused by entry.

More important however, accession to the Community has affected the mechanisms of macroeconomic stability and has reduced the power of exchange rate changes to correct trade imbalances. With the prices of agricultural products being fixed in ECU, any devaluation of the currency results in price increases of agricultural products to the extent that the green drachma is devalued. If the green drachma is not devalued to the same extent, the use of monetary compensatory amounts does not allow for any improvement in the competitiveness of agricultural products; currency devaluation therefore affects only trade in manufactures, whereas it leaves the agricultural trade balance intact.

8. Conclusions and overall evaluation

What conclusions can one draw from the above analysis and what answers can be given to the two questions set out at the beginning? It appears that the answer to the first question as to whether entry is an important causal factor of the hardships through which the Greek economy has been suffering must be in the affirmative. For, although the country has received truly substantial amounts of resources from the European budget, these are mostly consumption resources which do not play an equal role in the country's growth. Besides, a large part of these resources (about one-third today) are returned to other member countries in the form of higher prices paid by Greek consumers to EC producers over and above what EC consumers pay to Greek producers.

Also, Greece's full membership in the European Community has severely harmed its pseudo-competitiveness which was artificially created via extremely severe protective measures on the import side and extensive subsidization of exports, and has caused considerable trade imbalances with all their negative consequences for the economy. Besides, entry has redistributed income in favour of the agricultural sector, which may have been welcome on social grounds but is perhaps also growth retarding, whereas it substantially hit the growth of industry. Finally, entry probably contributed to the increase in size and worsening of the balance of the public sector and caused considerable problems in relation to the macroeconomic performance of the economy. The only beneficiaries appear to have been consumers, and especially farmers, who have benefited from both the budgetary transfers and trade creation.[15]

Concerning the second question regarding the general lessons one can learn from the Greek experience: it appears that a large part, if not all, the negative consequences of entry are indeed the result of special conditions applying to the Greek case. First, despite the long period of association, during which Greece was supposed to have gradually reduced protection and allowed smooth adaptation of the economy to the severe competition that full entry would entail, Greek authorities simply replaced protection by direct controls, financial stringencies and the tax system, for protection by tariffs. Secondly, wide subsidization of Greek exports was taking place before accession, something clearly odd for a country preparing for full entry into such a strongly competitive environment. Thirdly, Greece had already reaped most of the benefits that accession to a common market would entail because her exports of manufactures had been entering the Community free of tariffs since the late 1960s.

Notes

1. Research facilities provided by the Centre for Economic Research of the Athens University of Economics and Business are gratefully acknowledged.
2. Income support to farmers amounted to about 75 per cent of Greece's total receipts in the four years 1982–85, it fell to around 60 per cent in the following four years, while today it amounts to 55 per cent.
3. Private investment in the agricultural sector, at constant prices, fell from 4.1 billion Drs in 1980 to 3.2 billion Drs in 1990, whereas in the intervening years it was even smaller.
4. These include the guidance section of FEOGA, the Social Fund, the Regional Fund and the Integrated Mediterranean Programmes.
5. In 1991, for example, only 13 per cent of Greece's total gross receipts appear in the investment account of the Central Government, 9 per cent in its current account, 19 per cent appear in the accounts of third parties, and 59 per cent in the special guarantee account for farmers.
6. The recent reform of the CAP however will result in a reduction in these direct transfers from Greece to other Community countries.
7. The tax system differentiated the burden between imported and domestic products by both notional increases in the price of imports and differentiated nominal rates. This protection was incorporated into a special tariff, called the *regulatory levy*, in 1984 and was gradually reduced until totally abolished in 1989. The average rate levied on dutiable imports in 1984 was 11.1 per cent, which is about 60 per cent of the average protection accorded to domestic production by tariffs in 1961.

108 Economic integration between unequal partners

8. These subsidies varied considerably among the various products. At the beginning, they were supposed to counter-balance the tax burden levied on exports (Georgakopoulos, 1977), but their size increased and their scope widened in the late 1970s so that they came to be an important export promotion means. At the time of accession, the average rate for all exports was 20 per cent (Maroulis, 1991). They were gradually abolished between 1987 and 1992.
9. The only favourable effects on the export side were expected to result from the subsidization of Greek exports of agricultural products in the context of the CAP, but these were not very large.
10. The average rate of inflation in Greece over the period 1981–89 was 17.2 per cent, whereas the average increase in foreign prices was 4.2 per cent and the average depreciation rate of the Greek drachma was 13.3 per cent.
11. Between 1980 and 1981, the price of imported meat from the Community went up by 95 per cent, the price of milk by 50 per cent, the price of butter by 135 per cent and the price of cheese by 90 per cent.
12. For a detailed *ex post* study of the impact on manufacturing, over the first six years of accession, see T. Giannitsis (1988).
13. It must be noticed here that the extent of devaluation of the national currency during the second half of the 1980s was not sufficient to compensate domestic producers for the differential in the inflation rates (Constantopoulos, 1992). Part of the negative impact on trade during this subperiod may therefore be due to changes in competitiveness of the Greek products rather than to integration.
14. Total government expenditures as a percentage of GDP increased from less than 35 per cent in 1980 to 55 per cent in 1990, deficits increased from 4 per cent to over 20 per cent and the public debt increased from 30 per cent to over 100 per cent.
15. There is, of course, nothing wrong with this. A country's static benefits from an economic union are usually measured in terms of consumers' welfare and, from this point of view, Greece benefited substantially. But this is something different from the hardship the economy goes through after entry, which is what we are discussing here.

Bibliography

Balassa, B. (1967), 'Trade creation and trade diversion in the European Common Market', *Economic Journal*, 77.
Bank of Greece (1991), *The Governor's Report for the Year 1991*, Athens.
Buchanan, J. (1977), 'Why does government grow?' in Borcherding, T.E. (ed.), *Budgets and Bureaucrats: The Sources of Government Growth*, Durham: Duke University Press.
Constantopoulos, M. (1992), 'Exchange rate policy dilemmas in the presence of macroeconomic imbalance' in T. Skouras (ed.), *Issues in Contemporary Economics*, Athens, Greece: Proceedings of the 9th World Congress of the International Economic Association, 5.
Georgakopoulos, T. (1977), *Indirect Taxes and Greek Industry*, Athens: Institute of Economic and Industrial Research (in Greek).
Georgakopoulos, T. (1986), 'Greece in the EC: Inter-country income transfers', *Journal of Common Market Studies*, 25.
Georgakopoulos, T. (1988), 'The impact of accession on agricultural incomes in Greece', *European Review of Agricultural Economics*, 15.
Georgakopoulos, T. (1990), 'The impact of accession on food prices, inflation and food consumption in Greece', *European Review of Agricultural Economics*, 17.
Georgakopoulos, T. (1991), 'Trade effects of Common Market membership: Greece', *Economia Internationale*, 23.
Georgakopoulos, T. and P. Paschos (1983), 'The costs and benefits of the CAP', *European Review of Agricultural Economics*, 10.
Giannitsis, T. (1988), *Accession to the European Community and the Impact on Manufacturing and External Trade*, Athens: Foundation for Mediterranean Studies (in Greek).
Hitiris, T. (1972), *Trade Effects of Economic Association with the Common Market: The Case of Greece*, New York: Praeger.

Maroulis, D. (1991), *The Greek Balance of Payments: The Impact of Accession and the Unification of the Internal Market of the EC*, Report No. 5, Athens: Centre for Planning & Economic Research (in Greek).

Tsoukalis, L. (1979), *Greece and the European Community*, West Mead: Saxon House.

Truman, E.M. (1969), 'The European Economic Community: Trade creation and trade diversion', *Yale Economic Essays*, **IX**.

Zolotas, X. (1976), *Greece in the European Community*, Paper and Lectures, No. 33, Athens: Bank of Greece.

Zolotas, X. (1976), *The Positive Contribution of Greece to the European Community*, Paper and Lectures, No. 40, Athens: Bank of Greece.

8 The Common Agricultural Policy in the process of European integration and convergence
George P. Zanias

1. Introduction

Initially established as a customs union, the European Community (EC) has since changed considerably. At this stage, the EC is moving towards Economic and Monetary Union (EMU) and the ultimate goal of political integration is now more mature than ever.

For a long time, however, EC's only supra-national policy has been the Common Agricultural Policy (CAP). As such, and because it absorbs about two-thirds of the Community budget, the CAP purported to play a significant role in the process of European integration as well as in bringing the Europeans closer. Three aspects of this role of the CAP are briefly assessed in this chapter. First, its role as a political institution is examined. Second, some statistical evidence is reviewed regarding the way the CAP has influenced social cohesion and particularly convergence in agricultural incomes. Third, reference is made to the extent to which the CAP has led to the unification of spatial agricultural markets. These three issues are preceded by an introduction to the reasons that led to the establishment of the CAP, and to its main effects on European agriculture. At the end, the concluding remarks trace the major threads of the chapter and link them with the reform of the CAP and the completion of the single market.

2. Origin and outcomes

At the time the EC was formed, the original six member states had a variety of agricultural support policies which had implications for trade. Since abandoning intervention into agriculture was impossible, and the abolition of internal barriers would imply undesired changes in product prices, the existing policies had to be either coordinated or supra-nationalized. The latter proved easier and the CAP was born relying on price policy and variable import protection as the means of support. Price levels were initially set at the upper spectrum of existing national prices.

Mainly as a result of the CAP, which linked support to output, agricultural production increased very rapidly, exceeding the growth of domestic demand by about 1.4 per cent per annum (from the mid-1970s to late 1980s). In this way the degree of self-sufficiency rose rapidly too, leading to the creation of significant surpluses which need strong subsidization to be exported, since the EC agricultural prices are considerably higher than world prices. On the other hand, revenues under the CAP (mainly from agricultural import levies) remained stagnant.

These developments put considerable pressure on the budget (Table 8.1) and have been the major force behind the recently adopted reform of the

Table 8.1 Expenditure and revenue under the CAP

Year	FEOGA expenditure (million ECU)	% of total budget	Revenue (under the CAP) (million ECU)
1973	4 004.0	77.4	551.0
1974	3 356.7	67.3	330.0
1975	4 706.8	69.6	590.0
1976	5 803.3	69.3	1 173.2
1977	7 126.1	74.1	2 137.7
1978	8 996.3	76.3	2 278.9
1979	10 844.1	72.7	2 143.5
1980	11 918.0	69.4	2 002.3
1981	11 556.6	64.7	1 747.5
1982	13 055.6	63.1	2 227.8
1983	16 539.6	66.7	2 295.1
1984	19 022.7	69.9	2 436.3
1985	20 463.8	72.8	2 179.1
1986	22 910.9	65.7	2 287.0
1987	23 875.1	67.3	3 097.8
1988	28 829.8	70.1	2 895.3
1989	27 296.6	66.7	2 664.3
1990	27 402.1	64.0	2 084.0
1991	34 804.7	62.6	2 549.0
1992	39 006.6	62.3	2 589.1

Note: 1973–1980 EC-9; 1981–1985 EC-10; 1986–1992 EC-12.

Source: Commission of the European Communities: *The agricultural situation in the Community*, various years.

CAP. Developments in the Uruguay Round of GATT negotiations have been of secondary importance. The CAP reform attempts to break the link between output and support which had as a result a tremendous increase in production, the regressive distribution of support, high prices for consumers, and important implications for the environment. The new policy measures are expected to give greater play to market forces and bring closer EC and world agricultural prices.

3. The CAP and political integration

Since the establishment of the CAP, it has been hoped that this supra-national policy would promote European integration and lead to the establishment of other supra-national policies. In other words, it was hoped that the CAP would have spill-over effects leading to economic and ultimately to political integration (Koester, 1984). Since under the CAP the member states have given up their autonomy to a far greater extent than under other policies, while decisions on agricultural policies are expected to promote Community welfare at the expense of national interests, the functioning of the CAP can also act as a barometer of the willingness of member countries to promote the European ideal even when national interests are at stake.

Has the CAP lived up to these expectations? It is true that the CAP has been responsible for significant transfers of resources among the member states (Table 8.2). The reason is that the member states bear the marginal cost of increasing support prices according to the VAT valuation base rather than according to their contribution to these costs. Thus, countries like Greece and Ireland are gainers and countries like Germany and the United Kingdom are net losers from budgetary transfers. In addition to these, transfers also occur at the consumer level (because of the significantly higher prices) whereby net agricultural exporters gain and net importers lose.

The existence of such resource transfers can at first sight be considered as a success for the CAP. It would seem that member states do act in the European rather than the national interest. The European barometer would seem to run high. Things, however, are not quite so simple.

Probably the greatest defeat of the Common Agricultural Policy of the Common Market was the introduction of 'green' conversion rates and the Monetary Compensatory Amounts (MCAs). The former made possible the partial re-nationalization of the CAP, since common prices set in ECU are converted into local currencies using these artificial rates which, in practice, are determined by the member states according to their domestic priorities. The MCAs operate as taxes and subsidies on intra-Community trade and constitute significant trade barriers against the ideal of a common market. These internal border barriers came into existence very early and still remain

Table 8.2 Net budgetary transfers in the European Community (average 1986–90)

Member State	Total payments minus FEOGA receipts	Total payments minus Total receipts
	million ECU	
Belgium	–696	–567
Denmark	382	470
Germany	–4 313	–3 682
Greece	1 238	1 819
Spain	–968	–633
France	–933	–62
Ireland	916	1 362
Italy	–891	435
Luxembourg	–52	–47
The Netherlands	597	1 026
Portugal	–93	529
United Kingdom	–3 307	–1 998

Source: Commission of the European Communities: *Report of the Court of Auditors*, various years.

in force, although lately they have been a pale shadow of their former selves, and for most member states they are equal to zero.

The major decisions on the CAP are taken during the annual price review. Because of diverging national interests, such a seemingly easy task usually involves lengthy negotiations with failure often avoided only at the last minute. Many disputes have had to be resolved by meetings of the Heads of Government.

This happens despite the fact that the Commission's proposals, on which farm ministers decide, usually constitute an option of least political resistance rather than optimal EC welfare. Radical proposals have had very limited success (for example, the Mansholt Plan in 1968). During the first one and a half decades of CAP operation decisions were relatively easier to reach because of the externalization of costs to third countries (variable levies), consumers (higher prices), and taxpayers – all three parties not present in the negotiations. This was easier at that time because the degree of self-sufficiency was lower than today and the gap between domestic and world prices was not, in certain cases, as large. Furthermore, the Community was much smaller. Farm ministers have had their share in this externalization of CAP cost because they tend to support the interests of farmers, who are much better informed about the agricultural policy of the EC than consumers, and also represent a relatively cohesive block of voters. Domestic political sensitivities have led to considerable price increases at the EC level.

Externalization of costs has become increasingly difficult during the 1980s because of EC surplus production and lack of financial funds. Between 1980 and 1986 CAP expenditure doubled and in 1984 the Community actually ran out of money for the first time. The budgetary pressure led to two unpopular policy measures. In 1984 milk production quotas were imposed and in 1988 the so-called 'stabilizers' were introduced. These unpopular measures constitute rather heroic decisions. Still, however, these measures proved insufficient and after years of negotiations and under the threat of possible bankruptcy a more radical reform was decided on in May 1992 which, to a certain extent, upsets the balance of interests achieved so far. Although it took a long time and a lot of effort for these reforms to be decided one has to admit that the budgetary crisis caused by agricultural spending is now coming under control.

Thus, one may argue that member states tend to support policies in their national interest but that when a crisis develops decisions are taken which may not be in the interest of some member states. Has the CAP been successful then in its 'political' role? Although opinions differ, on balance it seems that the operation of the CAP has contributed to a better understanding among Europeans and has 'trained' them to decide together for Europe. The CAP, however, can be criticized for absorbing most of the Community's funds, thus making more difficult the emergence of other common policies the establishment of which it was supposed to promote. The counter argument in this case is that the member states have shown a reluctance to set up other common policies with the same degree of integration, requiring similar financial solidarity as the CAP.

4. The CAP, social policy and income convergence

The CAP was established to pursue a variety of objectives which are stated in the Treaty of Rome and specifically: to increase agricultural productivity, to increase the individual earnings of persons engaged in agriculture, to stabilize markets, to assure the availability of supplies, and to ensure that supplies reach consumers at reasonable prices (article 39). In some cases targets were reached rather quickly (increased productivity, regular supplies) while in other cases (reasonable prices to consumers) things went quite out of hand.

Of all the above objectives the CAP concentrated on supporting farm incomes. Especially during the past decade, there has been hardly any justification for the CAP on the grounds of economic efficiency. The CAP 'provides' (through budgetary and consumer transfers) a significant proportion of farming income; farm prices, especially of cereals, have risen well in excess of world prices, while the structural measures which purported to create a more viable agriculture were, until very recently, allocated only about five per cent of the agricultural fund. Clearly, to a great extent, the CAP owes its continuing existence to its social aspects, and the preservation of rural communities by keeping marginal producers in the sector, though these aspects also are pursued in an inefficient way.

What has been the record of the CAP as a social policy, and to what extent has it contributed to promoting social cohesion and (income) convergence in the Community? The available evidence suggests that the benefits of the CAP have been distributed regressively giving smaller benefits to lower income farmers while penalising low-income consumers. With the exception of Ireland (the agriculture of which is based on the heavily subsidized dairy industry), to the extent that a member state has lower income farmers and consumers, relative to the other EC countries, it will have received smaller benefits.

The consumers are in any case penalized by the CAP because they face, compared to world levels, higher prices. Since, however, lower income consumers spend proportionately more on food, their relative contribution to financing the CAP is greater. This does not necessarily lead to the conclusion that lower income countries pay proportionately more as consumers to the financing of the CAP. This depends also on the composition of consumer expenditure as well as on the farm trade balance of the particular countries.

Brown (1989) has calculated the distribution of CAP benefits (price policy only) by member state and various farm types and sizes, using basic data from the 1984/85 and 1985/86 FADN (Farm Accountancy Data Network) surveys. Tables 8.3 and 8.4 reproduce some of these results. According to Table 8.3, CAP benefits vary considerably across countries and across farm types. There is size category, and the farms in the highest income bracket receive a benefit 8.47 times that in the lowest income bracket.

Such a regressive distribution of benefits goes against any notion of a social policy or a policy which purports to keep people in rural areas. Some comfort from these results is given by the fact that the percentage of small farmers having a dual activity (and hence supplementary income outside agriculture) is considerably higher than that of large farmers. Even in this case, however, the distribution of benefits remains very skewed. The main reason for this distribution is the fact that support is linked to output. On the other hand, larger farms benefit from economies of scale and are more capital intensive, with both these factors contributing to larger incomes/benefits. This skewed distribution constitutes one of the reasons for the partial change in the support philosophy achieved in the latest reform.

Table 8.3 Magnitude of CAP benefits (1984/85 and 1985/86)

	CAP gains as a % of the farm value of production	CAP gains as a % of net farm value added
Cereals	28	77
General cropping	28	66
Horticultural	15	37
Vineyards	29	54
Fruits/olives	27	44
Dairying	30	91
Drystock	28	74
Pigs/poultry	8	34
Mixed	22	76

	Range of benefits over farm types by country	
BLEU	14–31	31–75
Denmark	3–23	10–92
France	27–35	54–101
Germany	5–32	25–143
Greece	17–26	33–46
Ireland	34–35	74–107
Italy	14–37	34–64
Netherlands	8–37	21–107
United Kingdom	23–34	78–109
EC–10	8–30	34–91

Source: Brown (1989, p. 32).

The skewed distribution of CAP benefits and the persisting inequality in farm sizes contributed to the persistence of the inequality in farm incomes also. Thus, following at most two-and-a-half decades of CAP application the earnings from agricultural activities vary considerably across member states, as is shown in Table 8.5, using both ECU and PPS (purchasing power standards). The four so-called 'cohesion' countries of 'Delors II', namely Greece, Ireland, Spain, Portugal, together with Italy, have incomes (real net value added at factor cost) per AWU lower than the EC-12 average, both in terms of ECU and PPS. For two of these countries, Greece and Italy, this is in line with the findings in Table 8.3 (lower part) according to which these two

Table 8.4 Distribution of CAP benefits (ECU) by income class and farm size (1984/85–1985/86)

	ECU per Annual Work Unit (AWU)				
Farm net value added/ AWU	≤ 4 000	4 000– 7 999	8 000– 11 999	12 000– 23 999	> 24 000
CAP benefit/ AWU	2 329	4 016	7 029	11 155	19 730

ESU[1]	2–4	4–6	6–8	8–11	12–16	16–40	40–100	> 100
CAP benefit/ AWU	1 466	1 970	2 315	3 253	4 422	8 210	13 821	14 703

Note:
1. European Size Units, equal to 1100 ECU of Standard Gross Margin (a measure of gross farm value added at constant – 1982, in this case) prices.

Source: Brown (1989). Extracts from tables in pp. 69 and 74.

countries receive the lowest CAP gains as a percentage of net farm value added. Of these, the Mediterranean member states are also associated with the smallest farm sizes in the EC. The remaining seven member states exhibit a considerable inequality in farm incomes. The index (with EC-12=100) varies from 120.6 (99.9 in PPS terms) for Germany to 276.8 (255.0 in PPS terms) for the Netherlands. The variation of agricultural incomes across member states with comparable non-agricultural incomes shows that there is variation in their parity ratios also. With regard to the 'Delors II' member states, in terms of the ratio between agricultural and non-agricultural incomes, they are in a situation similar to that of the other member states.

Thus, the common ECU prices under the CAP have not led to a convergence in farm incomes in the EC. With the exception of Ireland, farm incomes per person tend to decrease as we move from north to south. The higher incomes belong to the 'northern' group (Belgium, Denmark, the Netherlands, United Kingdom), the lower to the 'southern' group (Greece, Italy, Spain, Portugal), while the 'central' European group (Germany, France, Luxembourg) is associated with middle incomes per person.

The focus of the CAP on a price policy which links support to output has been the main reason for the situation analysed in this section. The EC has

118   Economic integration between unequal partners

Table 8.5   Net farm value added at factor cost per AWU in the EC

	B	DK	D	GR	E	F
'1981' ECU	240.8	204.9	117.0	82.4	59.9	148.5
'1990' ECU	230.5	214.0	114.9	87.9	85.2	137.9
'1981' PPS	213.9	157.7	100.7	88.8	69.7	130.0
'1990' PPS	224.2	162.0	101.5	95.9	90.7	130.7

Table 8.5   (contd)

	IRL	I	L	NL	P	UK	EC-12
'1981' ECU	72.5	93.8	132.0	263.0	18.3	190.6	100.0
'1990' ECU	84.4	87.0	137.3	274.6	18.2	137.6	100.0
'1981' PPS	68.1	107.8	119.9	223.9	31.4	168.6	100.0
'1990' PPS	83.8	83.9	132.8	264.1	27.8	141.2	100.0

Note:
'1990' = (1989+1990+1991)/3
'1981'+(1980+1981+1982)/3
PPS=Purchasing Power Standard.

Source: Eurostat, *Agricultural Income, 1991*.

failed to follow the principles laid down in the Stresa Conference in 1958 'ensuring that structural and price policies go hand in hand'. The recently adopted policy reforms go some way towards acknowledging these principles.

5.   The CAP and spatial market integration

The establishment of a truly integrated common market was a major objective of the EC. Progress, however, on this front was relatively slow and impetus was recently given with the '1992' ideal which aimed at the elimination of, mainly, physical, technical and fiscal barriers to intra-Community trade.

In the case of agriculture, it is often assumed that, because common policy measures are applied to the agricultural markets of the EC, a single barrier free integrated market already exists. Such an assumption, however, may be misleading, at least in certain cases. It should not be surprising that more than a third of the Commission's proposed regulations or amendments which must be passed in order to achieve the removal of trade obstructions to obtain a truly integrated market, affect directly the agriculture and food sector.

The most obvious barrier to intra-Community trade, in the case of agriculture, has been the existence of the MCAs, which operate as export subsidies/taxes, and have been in existence for more than two decades. Although at this stage for most member states the MCAs have been set equal to zero, in the past they were responsible for export subsidy/taxes exceeding, in some cases, 30 percentage points.

A very important category of barriers to trade in agriculture are the non-tariff barriers and they refer mainly to sanitary and phytosanitary restrictions. About 130 legislative items required for the completion of the internal market are related to these restrictions. These regulations and amendments are based on the 'mutual recognition' principle whereby products acceptable for sale in one member state must be accepted in another.

Although they do not operate as impediments to trade, the quantitative restrictions (quotas) introduced by the EC in an attempt to curb production and surpluses in the sugar and dairy sectors impair the realization of the full effects of integration. The reason is that these quotas, which are currently national in nature, tie production to certain regions and obstruct the operation of the comparative advantage. A possible solution to this problem would be to make the quotas transferable among EC member states. At this stage, however, there is no plan to abolish quotas nor to convert them into transferable ones.

It is clear that the agricultural trade among the member states is certainly not obstruction free and hence it is questionable whether the agricultural markets in the Community have become integrated. In the absence of such impediments efficient commodity arbitrage would ensure that, for the homogeneous agricultural products, the regions of the Community would belong to the same market in which a single price prevails [the 'law of one price' (LOP)].

But, are the forementioned barriers to trade sufficient to inhibit the validity of the LOP? Evidence on this issue is given in Zanias (forthcoming) where co-integration analysis is used to test whether the EC agricultural product markets are integrated. The testing procedure is applied to four products (soft wheat, milk, pigmeat, potatoes) which have different characteristics and policy regimes. The results show that in the majority of cases the LOP is valid, especially when the influence of MCAs is deducted, indicating once more the disruptive effect of the MCAs on trade. In a significant number of cases, however, the LOP was not found to be valid which is probably due to the impediments to efficient arbitrage and/or imperfect competition.

Spatial integration prospects, however, are better now. The '1992' ideal entailed the elimination of a large number of trade barriers while the MCAs will, in practice, be eliminated since the green rates are expected to be set, for the currencies included in the Exchange Rate Mechanism, equal to the central currency values. Furthermore, the adoption of a common currency later this decade will involve the dismantlement of the MCA mechanism also and a reduction in the effects of risk aversion in intra-Community trade.

6. Concluding remarks

Being the first and, for a long time, the only supra-national policy of the Community, the CAP was bound to play an important role in the process of European integration. Despite the difficulties encountered in reaching decisions at the Community level against some national interests, and the partial re-nationalization of this common policy through the 'green' conversion rates, the CAP managed to survive and promote, to a certain extent, the European ideal. However, despite its stated objectives, the CAP concentrated on supporting farm incomes and eventually became an important 'partner' for the EC farmers. In this way, the CAP ended up as a policy pursuing social rather than economic objectives. In this respect, it failed since it tends to penalize small farmers and low-income consumers. Furthermore, the large farm income differences among the member states have not shown any signs of convergence. Serious doubts can also be raised about the effectiveness of the CAP in promoting a single integrated market in agricultural products. On the other hand, the CAP promoted successfully the objectives of higher productivity and securing food supplies.

For these reasons as well as because of other domestic and external implications of the CAP, during recent years its critics have outnumbered its supporters. As a result the most radical reform of the CAP was recently achieved. One of the reasons leading to this reform was the skewed distribution of the CAP benefits. The reformed policy measures should go some way towards remedying this situation although the expected results on this issue should be rather moderate at this stage. It is rather difficult to predict the future but once the change of emphasis from supporting output to supporting people in rural areas has been gradually established, the CAP will be in a position to promote more effectively its social targets and eventually promote rural development. With the completion of the single market and the eventual abolition of the MCAs better integrated agricultural markets will also be established. It seems that in the future we will be able to talk about a CAP which will promote integration, social cohesion, and convergence more effectively than in the past, and play an important role in an enlarged Community including eastern and central European countries which have large agricultural sectors.

References

Brown, C. (1989), *Distribution of CAP Price Support*, Report No. 45, Institute of Agricultural Economics, Copenhagen, 45.

Commission of the European Communities, *The Agricultural Situation in the Community*, various years, Luxembourg.

Commission of the European Communities, *Bulletin of the European Communities*, various issues, Luxembourg.

Commission of the European Communities, *Report of the Court of Auditors*, various years, Brussels.

Commission of the European Communities Eurostat (1992), *Agricultural Income, 1991*, Luxembourg.

Koester, U. (1984), 'The Role of the CAP in the Process of European Integration', *European Review of Agricultural Economics*, **11**(2).

Zanias, G.P., 'Testing Integration in the European Community Agricultural Product Markets', *Journal of Agricultural Economics*, forthcoming.

9 Regional imbalances and national or federal social protection

Jozef Pacolet and Erik Gos

The discussion on Economic and Monetary Union in the Community has, up to now, largely focused on the monetary aspects of that Union. This chapter summarizes some of the most important findings of a study for DG XXII on the relationship between EMU, social protection and regional cohesion.[1] This report is one example of the greater interest of the EC in this relation between the social aspects and EMU, among other things how it is related to the issue of fiscal federalism.[2]

The European community attributes great importance to regional cohesion, and has confirmed this by its decision in Maastricht. A distinction can be made between economic and social cohesion. Economic cohesion concerns autonomous growth and the primary income generating capacity of a region. The EC focuses on this through regional policy aimed at improving infrastructure and productive investment. This is, however, a long-term strategy. We widened the definition of cohesion to include income redistribution (mostly by social insurance) and the distribution of social services (so-called tertiary income). Working conditions can be added to give an even wider definition of social protection (although it may be attributed to primary income conditions).

The EMU focuses on macroeconomic convergence: nominal convergence of inflation, interest rates, exchange rate stability, budget deficits, indebtedness, and real convergence of economic growth, unemployment. The strategy chosen for monetary integration implies a very short-term approach. Some people are afraid that regional cohesion will be weakened in a rapid transition to convergence and the realization of the internal market, with negative impacts on social cohesion as a result.

1. Methodology

The *fil rouge* of this chapter is linked with earned and redistributed income per capita. This is closely related with work and the cost of production in the economy. Social insurance and benefits in kind are financed by the fiscal and parafiscal burden. This has a direct impact on the competitive situation of regions and countries and the mobility of workers.

Factors causing regional discrepancies can be beyond the control of the region and can be of cyclical (external shocks), structural (industries in decline), historical or demographic origin.

We have defined macroeconomic shocks, structural disadvantage and demographic disadvantage as follows:

- macroeconomic shocks: deterioration of terms of trade, leading to lower GDP/employed and higher unemployment. There is a need for macroeconomic stabilization and consensus that this should be organized at the European level. Such an operation may be established through a European stabilization fund with the aim of compensating unemployment expenditures;
- structural disadvantage: this issue is again measured by high unemployment or low GDP/employed. In this case the structural funds may function as a European compensation mechanism;
- demographic disadvantage: this issue is concerned with the relationship between the population of active age and total population (see Figure 9.1).

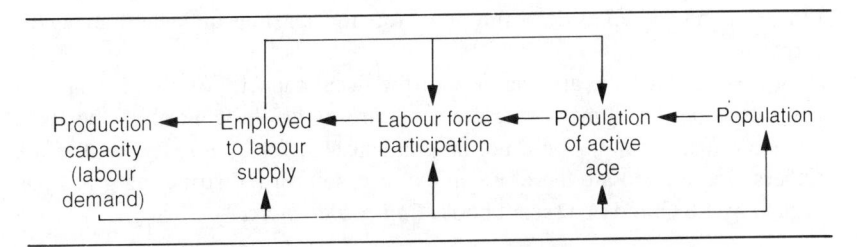

```
                ┌──────────────┬──────────────┐
                │              ▼              ▼
Production ◄── Employed ◄── Labour force ◄── Population ◄── Population
 capacity      to labour    participation      of active                ▲
 (labour        supply           ▲                age                   │
 demand)          ▲              │                 ▲                    │
    └─────────────┘              │                 │                    │
```

Figure 9.1 *'Behavioural' characteristics of the labour market*

This demographic factor leads to lower productive capacity, but also to higher social expenditures. Demographic elements determine, to a large extent, the 'needs' for a certain level of social protection (amounts for pensions, health care and care of the elderly care, education and policy towards (youth) unemployment).

Some of those elements are already accepted for EC-intervention purposes (see Figure 9.2) but others are not. The latter are related to social security and public services, and involve elements of interpersonal redistribution. Mainly for reasons of subsidiarity, the EC is not interfering in these areas.

The imperatives of nominal convergence endanger some of these systems even more, especially through the imposition of norms for indebtedness.

Empirical evidence on regional cohesion concerns mostly the economic aspects. Data on social protection are limited. This chapter starts from exist-

	Regional differences	Policies
Short term:	• Different sensitivity to external (business cycle) shocks due industry mix	→ Macroeconomic stabilization (now the objective of coordination)
Long term:	• industry mix (life cycle of industries) • demographic factors causing unemployment 　　　　　　　　　　causing other needs • basic infrastructure (private and public)	→ Present EC structural policies → Present EC structural policies → Little EC responsibility → Present EC structural policies

Figure 9.2   Reasons for regional divergence and EC policies

ing information to simulate the relation between regional distribution of mostly nationally financed social expenditures and regional cohesion. These simulations on social expenditures in the regions are related to the way social protection is organized. Social protection is influenced by the financing capacity of an economy, by political decisions on how large the share of GNP attributed to social protection is, and to need factors (for instance population older than 65 and 75 as determining factors for pensions and health expenditures).

In Box 9.1 we give an overview of the fiscal capacity of a region and its associated needs. Some of the elements are under the control of the local decision-makers, and should not be compensated for by a federal authority. Others are not, and are therefore an extra reason for redistributing grants, as argued by Le Grand in a recent book, *Equity and choice*.

2. Calculation of regional social protection

For each country we have data on social expenditures for four large categories, namely health, pensions, unemployment and education, the financing of those expenditures and the number of beneficiaries per category. This gives us for each country the amount of ECUs spent per sick person, per pensioner, per person unemployed and per student. Since regional information is only available for unemployment, we will estimate these expenditures assuming that in each region the national amount of ECU per beneficiary is given to each person in each category. This gives us a total per region of expenditures on health, pensions, unemployment and education, determined by the demographic structure of the region.

2.1   Absolute norm

The results of this simulation are presented in 'case 1: equal expenditures per beneficiary' in each country. This scenario reflects a 'needs' criterion.

Box 9.1   Decomposition of regional fiscal capacity and needs

In *Equity and Choice* J. Le Grand illustrates how redistributing grants are motivated from central government to local government. He looked for reasons of equity, that is those elements which are beyond the control of the policy-makers or the beneficiary. Although several elements are not further developed in this analysis, we give an (adapted) overview of his reasoning. His analysis is based essentially on the decomposition of the needs. We add to it the decomposition of the regional fiscal capacity per capita. Finally, even the production (per active person) could be decomposed (as is done in certain shift-share analysis) into national, regional and sectoral effects. The items market with * are more or less taken into consideration in our analysis. The **elements in bold** are elements that could be determined as beyond the control of the region, which means that they are reasons for compensating redistribution to achieve greater equity.

*Needs per capita (in annual sum per capita; social protection per capita, quantity)
- services necessary for eligible persons (for instance hospital beds per 1 000 elderly inhabitants)
  number of eligible persons (for instance elderly) as a share of total population*
- production function for those services (for instance required number of nurses)
- cost of those production factors (for instance annual wage of nurses)

*Fiscal capacity per capita
- **income per capita (for instance regional GDP)***
- effort or tax rate (for instance per cent of fiscal and social security contributions for health care)*
- desired saving *(unlikely) or accepted deficit (more plausible) rate; the deficit rate will be monitored by the EC*

*Determinants of income per capita
- **share of population of active age in total population; (depends on decisions on schooling age and pension age)***
- **participation ratio (share of population of active age, looking for a job: this is a cultural factor)***
- **share of employed in active population (determined by unemployment and distribution of available work)***
- **income per active person (is a productivity indicator)***

*Determinants of income per active person
- productivity per industry (production function, labour intensity)
- industry mix, including the share of public services
- cyclical situation of industry
- life cycle of industries
- competitive advantage of a country and a region at a certain moment in time

The results show that the expenditures, even if equally distributed according to beneficiaries, lead to very large differences in expenditures due to demographic reasons. Furthermore, this effect can be more pronounced depending on welfare levels. The Belgian example makes this clear: social expenditures vary from 21.6 per cent of GDP in Brussels to 44 per cent in Hainaut. This situation is partially influenced by demography, but, at the same time, it is also affected by the original GDP in that region. If the social receipts as a percentage of GDP are the same for all regions in the same country, namely the national percentage, then each region faces a different burden of social expenditures and deficits. If each region has to provide the same nominal amount of social expenditures per beneficiary then the poorer regions and those struck by demographically difficult situations would either have a high tax burden or a high deficit. National financing of these expenditures can prevent regional deficits; in other words, to prevent regional indebtedness and a consequential debt burden expenditures should be financed at national level.

There are some studies available in Belgium which illustrate that for some regions (the Walloon) the regionalized social expenditures and the yearly deficit lead to an important accumulation of debts which without measures to balance the expenditures and income, would lead to a debt GDP ratio of 361 per cent.[3]

If no indebtedness were allowed, and regions were compelled to finance their social expenditures by higher taxes, this would increase the competitive disadvantage of the poorer regions. Regions with a high 'demographic-social' burden would encounter the greatest economic difficulties.

2.2 Calculation of the regional social protection: relative norm

We see that the richer a country is, the more of its GDP is reserved for social protection. This is in line with the so called Wagner's Law and implies that there will be a large difference in social protection per capita. Now, if each country were to apply its national GDP share of social expenditure in each region, social protection per capita would differ significantly among regions (especially between those in a 'different demographic position'). This is simulated in Case 2. This scenario reflects an ability to finance (income) criterion. Within countries, the range of social expenditure per capita could be quite large (a difference of 100 per cent between the lowest and the highest figure), which if it held in reality would create unacceptable differences within one country. This is, however, the implication of a greater regional responsibility for social protection.

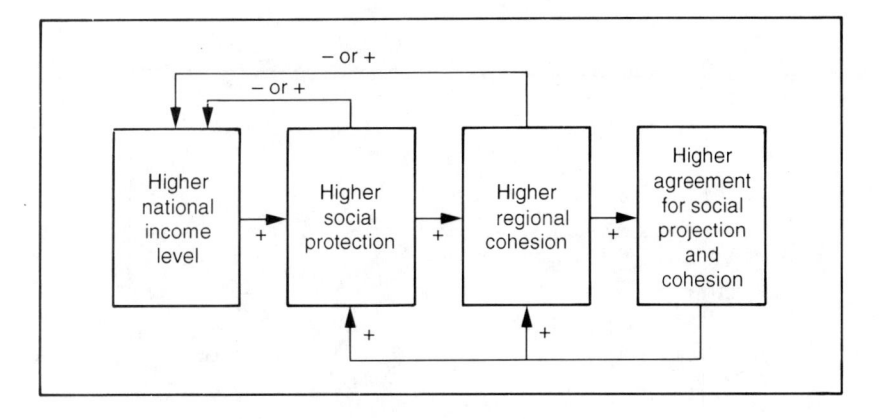

Figure 9.3 Relation between national income, social protection and regional cohesion

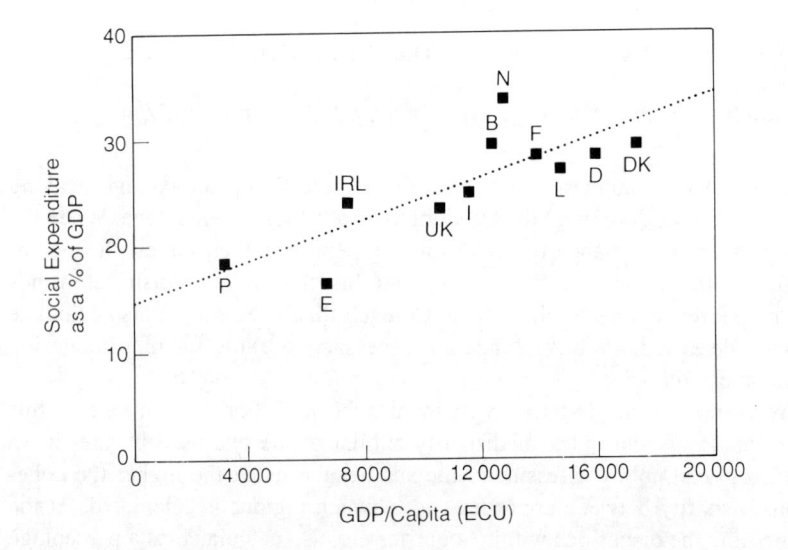

Source: Eurostat Regional Databank. OECD Health Databank. Own calculations.

Figure 9.4 Trade off between GDP and social expenditure, 1987

2.3 Introduction of a minimum for the poorest countries

At the moment there are no proposals for each EC country to apply the same percentages of social expenditures, which is one interpretation of harmonization of social protection. However, we will simulate the case where poorer

Figure 9.5 Trade off between GDP and GDP dispersion, 1987

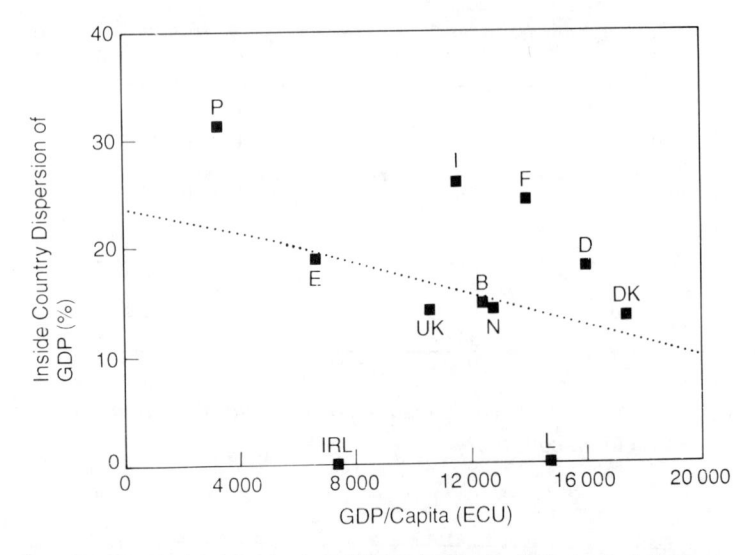

Source: Eurostat Regional Databank, OECD Health Databank. Own calculations.

countries would increase their percentage to the European average, leaving the others (core countries) the freedom to have a higher percentage. When the periphery has to finance this additional expenditure themselves, their competitive situation will get worse. To avoid this, the EC can redistribute funds to the poorer regions to allow them to reach this level. So we also calculate what federal redistributive funds are necessary to allow for more cohesion along these lines.

What now is the impact on regional cohesion? For the purpose of this analysis we use an index of disparity similar to the one used by the EC in their regional policy assessment: the smaller the index the higher the cohesion. Disparity between countries and between regions is calculated. At the same time the disparities within countries are also calculated as a percentage of the country average. When we plot the index of disparity against the welfare level of the countries and the percentage of social expenditures (index of inequality) we observe that richer countries are becoming more equal, contrary to the generally accepted view that there is a trade off between equity and efficiency. The difference between 'conventional wisdom' and empirical data is clearly illustrated.

Richer countries have a higher level of social protection, so that redistribution, regional equity and total welfare go hand in hand. Here again empirical

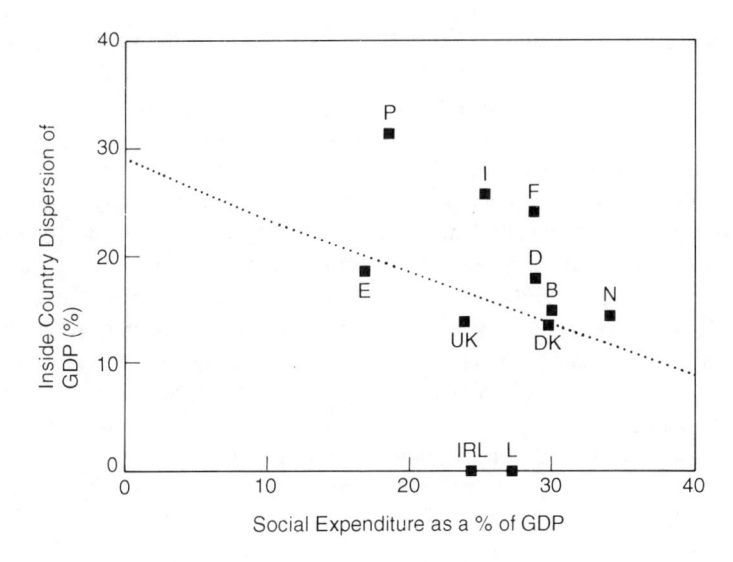

Source: Eurostat Regional Databank, OECD Health Databank. Own calculations.

Figure 9.6 Trade off between social expenditure and GDP dispersion, 1987

data are in contradiction with 'conventional wisdom' that too much public expenditure could damage economic growth. Social protection and regional cohesion are positively related and not opposed to high levels of income.

There exists a possibility often stated in Germany that regional redistribution is a political choice, partially argued economically. The title of the contribution of Sleijpen makes reference to this phenomenon. It may be the case that systems of social protection, including redistribution possibilities ('Ausgleich'), are acceptable only when income is already high and distribution equal. As Atkinson stated, with respect to the development of social protection over time: 'as the economy becomes richer, the constraints cease to bite, and the target level of benefits becomes attainable...'. This means that the principles governing benefit up-rating may change (which implies that even a higher share of GNP for social expenditures may be acceptable). Finally, 'increased real earnings may also be expected to ease these constraints and to permit those on benefit to share in rising national prosperity'. This quotation confirms that countries have to become richer to be able to grow more equally.

2.4 Regional disparity in scenario a and b

Table 9.1 gives the results of the different scenarios of the organization of social protection. We first give the actual dispersion in GDP per capita between countries and regions. Column 3 gives the result for a scenario in which each group of beneficiaries receives the same amount of social expenditure per beneficiary in ECU in all regions in the same country, namely the national amount per beneficiary. The total amount per subgroup (sick, pensioners, unemployed, students) is determined by the population structure. The system is based on needs, but also takes into account differences between countries in GDP/capita and share of social protection. The expenditure per capita due to the differences in prosperity in each country (amplified by the differences in percentage) are higher at the European level. This is not a perfect system of social protection in the sense that each country does not have the same percentage of social expenditure. The dispersion over countries is also significantly larger (index 39 instead of 28), while the already uneven dispersion over regions is also greater (39 instead of 35). When all beneficiaries in each country have the same expenditure, the index illustrates the diversity of the demographic structure.

Table 9.1 Results of the various simulations

	Dispersion of primary income per capita	Dispersion of social expenditures per capita		Dispersion of social expenditures	
		Each region same national amount	With a 75% minimum at EC level	National % in each region	With a 75% minimum at EC level
Dispersion of countries	28.12 %	39.38 %	30.38 %	39.51 %	30.65 %
Dispersion of regions	35.04 %	39.78 %	30.88 %	45.07 %	36.70 %

Scenario b supposes that each region spends the same national percentage of income on social benefits. This implies that the inequality between the regions in each country is the same as in the original distribution. Comparing scenario b to scenario a for each country clearly illustrates that scenario b leads to less regional equality. Instead it confirms the primary income distribution. When each country applies the same percentage in each region, the disparity between the regions is larger at EC level.

The existence of more equally organized systems of social protection (scenario a) in each country not only leads to higher equality between those regions in a country but also to higher equality between the countries in Europe. This solidarity is organized at national level and is incorporated in the public finances of each country. The harmonization of public expenditures and debt in the monetary union has to take this into account.

Since these financial flows are caused by essential economic and demographic factors, this calls for a third kind of intervention at federal level. If countries have to guarantee the same social expenditure per beneficiary in each region (cf. the discussion of L. Osberg for Canada),[4] they have to tax more in richer regions to subsidize poorer regions. This improves the social cohesion within the country and by definition within the EC. If they do not tax more on average, then they have to borrow. So, not allowing certain countries to borrow for redistribution purposes decreases the likelihood of greater social cohesion. Where the EC does not allow this to happen (as through the application of strict convergence criteria), they (the EC) should organize it themselves either by redistributing funds or by redistributing borrowing capacity.

In both scenarios we introduced a minimum at 75 per cent of the expenditure per capita of the EC average for those regions which are below this level.

The results are also given in the table. Scenario a assumes an equal amount spent per capita in each region of a country, combined with a minimum in the poor countries which are below 75 per cent of EC average expenditure. In scenario b we simulate a very decentralized and differentiated system of social protection, combined with a kind of minimum social protection.

The consequence of the latter scenario is that the disparity is (almost) the same when compensating the poorest regions at 75 per cent (36.7) as the regional social cohesion that is obtained allowing national solidarity (scenario a, index 39.78), but the EC has to use 2 per cent of EC GDP. The best results are obtained when regions get a federal minimum (requiring a budget of 1.7 per cent of GDP) mediated through national expenditures, making sure they are applied within each country in the same way. The national and regional disparity index diminishes from 39.78 to 30.88, a decrease of one quarter. European regional social cohesion is, therefore, best served by national social protection equally applied in the regions within each country, with a certain percentage financed from federal funds.

Our analysis also suggests that there need not necessarily be a levelling of differences between the northern and southern countries. However, the positive impact of some minimum threshold on distribution is also confirmed. The funds necessary for such redistribution are reasonable compared with mature federal states, but large compared to the present EC budget. Finally, for a country like Belgium, the message is that for internal social cohesion and equity, nationally funded systems of social protection are also preferable.

132   Economic integration between unequal partners

3.   Conclusions

What are the general conclusions? Social protection implies redistribution between persons and regions in the form of benefits (secondary income) and services (in-kind aid or 'tertiary income'). The level of this protection per capita or per beneficiary is determined by the share of GDP spent on social protection, and the demographic structure. The share of GDP (or the level of deficit financing) devoted to social protection is a political decision. The redistributive effect of social protection is further conditioned by the organization of social protection. In this study we have illustrated empirically the converging or diverging propensity of two different organizational forms of social protection. A first scenario illustrates a flat social protection per capita, fixed for each region within a country at national level. A second scenario illustrates a flat percentage of social expenditures of GDP for each region, fixed again at the national level. We then include for both systems a minimum social protection in the poorest regions (fixed at 75 per cent of the average social expenditure per capita at EC level).

The following observations can be made.

1. Regional disparities in GDP are already reduced by systems of national social protection and redistribution.
2. The EC should be aware that national constraints on the redistributional capacity of some member states endanger regional social cohesion at European level.
3. A system of national solidarity is better for European social cohesion than no such system, even when it is extended by a system of minimum social protection at 75 per cent of the EC average. Funded at EC level such a system would need ± 1.7 per cent of Community GDP.
4. Regional responsibility for the financing of social expenditures can lead to greater and sometimes unacceptable differences in social expenditure per capita.
5. Structural inequalities can change in the long run across regions. However there are 'historical' exogenous shocks (demography, industries reaching the end of their life cycle) that are very difficult for regions to absorb on their own, unless debt financing is available. Because of existing as well as potential debt burdens, there are real limits to intervention, especially at more decentralized levels. Debt financing at the national level at least allows some distribution of the burden and realizes some financing gains.
6. The existing difference in social protection among EC countries (on a per capita basis as well as share of GDP) implies the need for some progressiveness in fiscal burden. This would favour regional distribution in

primary income but may also lead to even more regional convergence if it is partly used in support of a minimum social protection scheme.

In the EMU discussion most attention is given to economic convergence. Some argue that the only instrument that is necessary is federal control of monetary aggregates.

We advocate a more interventionist approach, that is a fiscal corollary (a Euro-Fisc) to the proposed European monetary federation in order to offset the negative effects of integration and any asymmetrical shocks that may hit the Community. This implies a stabilization policy equal to the policies in mature federations.

A second field of EC policy on which a growing consensus exists is the policy of Structural Funds. However, they are, by definition and choice, a long-term strategy. They have to be considered as a policy to increase the autonomous growth potential of a region, certainly when this threatens to be eroded by the creation of the internal market.

Existing measures of redistribution such as the Structural Funds, while necessary, are not sufficient to reduce inequalities among regions. Too much emphasis has, so far, been placed on overcoming infrastructure and training inadequacies within regions. More flexibility should be associated with the use of Structural Funds. In addition, all aspects of cohesion should be looked at, particularly those policies which seek to promote interpersonal equality. The latter is sometimes forgotten in the push for greater regional harmonization.

Making reference to mature federal countries, and even generalizing to 'most countries with political subdivisions';[5] important redistribution streams from central or federal to regional and local level can be observed. The criteria are probably based on equity considerations, for those factors beyond the control of the regional authority. The EC has a long way to go before it matches existing federations with respect to implementing formal systems of redistribution. The problem is that social divergence is acute and cannot be solved by waiting until the second strategy (promoting autonomous growth) is realized. The problems can even get worse when the imperatives of the EMU limit some of the existing systems of redistribution at national or regional level. The empirical part of this report illustrates essentially the effects of those national redistributive systems. The financing burden to realize optimal levels of redistribution can be high, and is sometimes only possible through debt financing. It is precisely at this point that the EMU norms do interfere. Where the EC limits the national (and regional) level of indebtedness, it must compensate for this by debt financing at EC level, or through providing an equivalent system of solidarity to compensate for structural shocks of a demographic nature. Existing differences in social protection between the EC countries (per capita as well as by share of GDP) can only be accepted when they result from differences in preferences and where they imply some progressiveness in fiscal burden. Progressive tax systems improve the distribution of income and contribute to a spontaneous comparative advantage for low income groups, jobs, sectors, regions and countries.

There is no optimum blueprint for the journey between common market and full economic and monetary union. One approach to the problem is to use the principles of public finance to determine the most appropriate level of government intervention in the areas of economic and social policy. Accepting this approach rules out any slavish adherence to subsidiarity as an overriding principle in deciding on the allocation of public finance functions. A federal role in the area of interpersonal social protection is an important element of this allocation of functions. Despite the present trend, we are of the view that it is especially needed in the short run as the corollary of a short-run realization of the EMU.

The larger federal role with respect to interpersonal and interregional redistribution is more a priority in the short run, since in the long-run macroeconomic and regional convergence will potentially be realized. In the transition period, the greater federal distribution (and/or the leaving intact of national systems) is/are necessary to make the EMU politically acceptable.

Notes

1. Gos, E., E. O'Shea and J. Pacolet (1992), *EMU, Social Protection, Social Charter and Regional Social Cohesion*, Leuven, HIVA, p. 145.
2. Some references:
    - Papers prepared for DGII (1991) on several fiscal aspects of the EMU;
    - Papers prepared for DGXXII in the context of the TEPSA Study on Methods for achieving greater economic and social cohesion in the European Community (1991);
    - Conference of HIVA, Brussels, May 1992, on Social Protection and Economic and Monetary Union. Papers to be published in autumn 1992;
    - Conference of the CEPS, Brussels (June 1992), on Economic and Social Cohesion;
    - Workshop on European Integration in a Nordic Perspective, Stockholm, June 1992.
3. De Grauwe, P. (1991), *Denkoefeningen over de regionalisering van de Belgische overheidsschuld*, Leuven: Centrum voor Economische Studiën.
4. Osberg, L. (1993), 'Equity and efficiency in a decentralized federation, the role of a social charter' in J. Pacolet (ed.), *Social Protection and the European Economic and Monetary Union*, Aldershot: Avebury.
5. Le Grand, J. (1991), *Equity and Choice*, HarperCollins Academic.

10 Health expenditure and market integration in the European Community

Theo Hitiris

Introduction

The Treaty on European Union (TEU, the Maastricht Treaty) professes that '...the activities of the Community include... a contribution to the attainment of a high level of health protection' (TEU, 1992, Article 3). The European Community has also proclaimed that it will pursue Economic Union by upward *convergence* of economic performance for *cohesion* among the member states by effective policy action subject to the principle of *subsidiarity*. Health care has both economic and social dimensions which are subject to harmonization and, ultimately, integration in the European Community. It is, therefore, timely to take stock of current comparative conditions in the EC countries and to consider whether a common market in health services is a realistic proposition in the short run.

In this chapter we examine the current conditions and determinants of health expenditure in the member states of the European Community and discuss some of the implications of extending the common market to the sector of health. Section 1 briefly describes the existing health care systems in the member states of the European Community. In Section 2 we define the determinants of health expenditure and estimate a health expenditure function. We also consider the problems of developing a common market for European health care in the light of the results of our estimations. Finally, Section 3 presents some general conclusions.

1. Health care in the EC member states

In a wider sense, public health is the objective of several European Community policies, such as environmental policy, consumer policy and social policy. European 'socio-economic environmental research' and collaborative R & D into biotechnology also have implications for health. The Treaty of European Union specifies that the Community will contribute to ensuring a high level of health protection by encouraging cooperation between the Member States, if necessary, by lending support to actions taken nationally (TEU, Article 3). The principle of intervening in case of externalities between the member states and only by the rules of subsidiarity would suggest that Community action will be directed mostly towards 'preventive policies' against the spread of major health scourges, including drug dependency and environmental pollution. In this respect, the Commission and the European Parliament have recently had notable success in pushing preventive strategies onto the EC's agenda (Bomberg and Peterson, 1993).

In this paper we deal with health care in its narrow sense, the provision and cost of medical care and health care services at the level of the EC member states. Health care in the EC member states is the concern of the countries themselves. Although health care coverage is wide in every EC country, the systems they employ differ in organization, financing and delivery. In 1992, nearly 96 per cent of the population of the European Community member states were covered against medical costs by either of two systems (i) National Health Service (NHS), characterized by universal coverage, universal financing, and public provision in state-run institutions; and (ii) Social Sickness Funds (SSF), characterized by insurance (usually compulsory) financed by contributions paid by employers and employees. The United Kingdom (since 1948) and Denmark (since 1973) employ the first system. All other northern Member States practice the SSF system. Greece, Italy, Portugal and Spain changed from SSF to NHS, but late in the 1980s; therefore their systems are still closely linked to the former SSF. All countries finance health care by compulsory earnings-related contributions, social contributions and public funds raised by taxation. The exception is Denmark which finances health care entirely by taxation.

The EEC Treaty (1957) touched on some problems about health in its Social Policy section. In Articles 117 and 118, the member states 'agreed upon the need to promote improved working conditions and an improved standard of living of workers'. Therefore, the Community's task was to encourage cooperation for achieving this objective, but not direct harmonization or unification of health care. The Treaty on European Union has gone further in this direction by setting 'the raising of the standard of living and quality of life' and attainment of a high level of health protection (TEU, Article 3) as a Community target. Yet, there is nothing about aiming at a common market in health care. However, with integration advancing in the markets for commodities, services and factors of production, certain allocative disadvantages arising from different national regulations of health care markets could become more prominent. It is also possible that, with health care supplies differing in quantity and quality among the EC countries, inter-state patient flows could rise.

All these do not imply, however, that the Community has set or should set health care equalization among the member states as a target. The Treaty implies that, while health care will continue to be provided nationally by the member states, the EC will promote research into the causes and transmission of diseases while the member states would, in liaison with the Commis-

Table 10.1 Health care expenditure in EC member states, 1988

	GDP per capita		Health Expenditure	
Country	Market prices[1]	Per cent of GDP[2]	Per capita[1]	Per cent of GDP[1]
Belgium(B)	12 875	7.35	1 160	9.01
Denmark(DK)	13 641	8.04	1 380	10.12
Spain(E)	9 139	7.10	832	9.10
France(F)	13 883	8.62	1 454	10.47
Germany(D)	14 595	8.50	1 520	10.41
Greece(GR)	6 045	6.25	536	8.85
Italy(I)	12 833	7.82	1 260	9.82
Ireland(IRL)	7 766	8.42	834	10.74
Luxembourg(L)	15 166	9.04	1 736	11.44
Netherlands(NL)	12 383	8.45	1 346	10.87
Portugal(P)	6 690	6.52	542	8.10
U.Kingdom(UK)	12 853	6.57	1 085	8.44
EC	12 642	7.89	1 215	9.61

Notes:
1. In ECU, purchasing power parity (PPP).
2. In ECU, exchange rates.

Sources: *Health Policy*, Special Issue: Health Care in the EC Member States, Vol. 20, Nos. 1, 2 Feb. 1992; and *Basic Statistics of the Community*, Eurostat, 29th edition, 1992, Office for Official Publications of the European Communities, Luxembourg.

sion which may sometimes take the initiative, coordinate policies and programmes. The Council will adopt incentive measures, but any harmonization of the laws and regulations of the member states is excluded. In other words, no common health policy is planned, and no standardization of national health service systems or financing. Therefore, although coordination should become closer, the Community has no mandate to impose convergence of the different national systems of health care.

There is no doubt, however, that national health care systems are different among the member states. Table 10.1 presents comparative statistics of health care expenditure in the EC countries for 1988, confirming a wide variation between countries. For example, in purchasing power parity (PPP) values, among the EC countries Greece has the lowest health expenditure per head, 536 ECU (628 $US) and Luxembourg the highest, 1,736 ECU (2,033 $US), more than three times higher than that of Greece. Greece and Luxembourg are also the countries with the lowest and highest ratios of health expenditure to GDP, 6.25 and 9.04 respectively. Greece has also the lowest GDP per head, 6,045 ECU, while Luxembourg has the highest among the EC countries, 15 166 ECU, more than twice as large as that of Greece. The data also show that the four countries with the lowest income per capita are also the countries with the lowest health care expenditure per capita (GR, P. IRL, E). Whether GDP is a determinant of health expenditure, which these figures might suggest, is examined in the next section.

2. Determinants of health expenditure

The empirical literature on per capita health expenditure, E, has specified three main sources of determinants[1]: (i) per capita income, Y, often with an elasticity about 1; (ii) demographic factors, usually the age-structure of population, as revealed by the ratio of old and/or young in total population, P, which is expected to have a positive effect on expenditure; and (iii) the share of public expenditure in total health spending, H, which is assumed to be positively associated with the dependent variable. Some writers have also included a few other factors, such as the presence of a national centralized health system, N, the rate of inflation, I, or the relative price of health services, Z. Therefore, the general form of the health expenditure function is

$$E = f[Y, P, H, N, I, Z] \qquad (10.1)$$

Health expenditure functions like (10.1) have usually been estimated from small samples of cross-section observations which are available only for developed economies (Hitiris and Posnett, 1992). Moreover, for convenience of interpretation and estimation of elasticities, the functional form of equation (10.1) is usually assumed to be log-linear. For our purposes, we propose to estimate a form of equation (10.1) which, although ad hoc, is consistent with the existing empirical literature, but from a large sample of data from EC countries.

For the estimation, we rewrite equation (10.1) in regression form as

$$E = a + b_1 Y + b_2 P4 + b_3 P65 + b_4 H + b_5 D + u \qquad (10.2)$$

where E is per capita health expenditure both private and public, Y is the per capita GDP, $P4$ and $P65$ are the ratios of the less than 4 and more than 65 age groups in total population, H is the share of public expenditure in total health spending, D is a dummy variable to account for qualitative individual country characteristics and u is an error term.

The data set consists of observations for the 28 years 1960–87 from ten EC member states: Belgium (B), Denmark (DK), France (F), Germany (D), Greece (GR), Italy (I), Ireland (IRL), the Netherlands (NL), Spain (E) and the United Kingdom (UK). Data for Portugal and Luxembourg are not available. The statistics on health expenditure and GDP for each country are recorded at current prices in national currency units.[2] For the estimation, we converted these data to comparable figures by deflating the national currency values by the GDP purchasing power parity (PPP) index. Since the number of available observations for each country is inadequate for an unbiased time-series estimation of equation (10.2), we pooled the data of all the countries to form a sample of 280 observations (10-countries × 28-observations). This makes it possible to estimate the regression model from a larger sample using both cross-section and time-series information.

Two methods of estimation were used. Method A assumes that the cross-sectional units (that is the EC member states) are independent and the disturbance terms are cross-sectionally heteroskedastic and time-wise autoregressive. Method B assumes that the cross-sectional units are interdependent and the disturbance terms are correlated and time-wise autoregressive. The economies of the EC countries are interdependent in many other sectors but not much so in their health sectors. In practice, however, both methods of estimation have provided comparable results.

Despite the general preference for the log-linear rather than the linear functional form, we have found no significant difference between them. For selecting regressors, we have used the Amemiya Prediction Criterion (APC) and the Akaike Information Criterion (Maddala, 1988). On the basis of economic and statistical criteria, we have found only two of the main explanatory variables statistically significant: income per head, Y, and the proportion of aged, $P65$. Lagging each and all of the variables by one year led to similar results. Two of the shift-dummy variables were also found to be significant, those for the United Kingdom and Denmark, both with negative coefficients. The relatively low per capita health expenditure for the United Kingdom is often attributed to scale economies associated with its national health service systems (Leu, 1986). Therefore, Denmark's case could also be charged to similar causes and to under-reporting of certain types of cost, such as those for municipal nursing homes (Poullier, 1989).

The results of the estimations are shown in Table 10.2. Equations 10.1.1 and 10.1.2 were estimated by Method A, equations 10.2.1 and 10.2.2 by Method B. In equations 10.1.1 and 10.2.1 the Y variable is contemporaneous with the dependent variable, while in equations 10.1.2 and 10.2.2 it is lagged one year. All equations show a high goodness-of-fit statistic[3] and the estimated coefficients have the correct sign and are statistically significant; that is, they are reasonable by both economic and statistical criteria. The esti-

Table 10.2 Health expenditure in EC countries

Equation		10.1.1	10.1.2	10.2.1	10.2.2
independent variables					
constant	c	−4.895	−5.208	−4.620	−4.704
		(0.311)	(0.362)	(0.251)	(0.299)
income	Y	1.068	1.045	1.053	1.049
		(0.015)	(0.016)	(0.012)	(0.013)
aged	$P65$	0.803	0.965	0.702	0.758
		(0.125)	(0.143)	(0.098)	(0.118)
dummy UK	D_{UK}	−0.308	−0.315	−0.311	−0.304
		(0.043)	(0.052)	(0.027)	(0.034)
dummy DK	D_{DK}	−0.171	−0.138	−0.199	−0.184
		(0.072)	(0.075)	(0.038)	(0.040)
	R^2	0.968	0.966	0.976	0.972
	σ	0.911	0.909	0.908	0.900
	SSE	228.020	219.040	226.610	214.590
	APC	0.842	0.842	0.839	0.825
	AIC	−0.170	−0.172	−0.176	−0.193

Notes: The dependent variable is E = health expenditure per head. All variables are expressed in natural logs. Standard errors are in parentheses below the estimated coefficients. R^2 is the Buse R-square, σ is the standard error of the estimate, SSE is the sum of squared errors, APC is the Amemiya prediction criterion and AIC is the Akaike information criterion.

mates confirm that it makes no significant difference if the Y variable is lagged or not. Similar considerations apply to the other dependent variable, $P65$, and therefore the estimates with lagged $P65$ are omitted. The estimated income elasticity is consistently close to 1 and statistically significant, as found in previous research (Hitiris and Posnett, 1992). Per capita income is indeed the most important determinant of per capita national expenditure on health. This explains, therefore, the general observation that high-income countries spend more on health care than low-income countries.

The results of the empirical analysis have implications for the issue of health care in the EC for both convergence by market forces and coordination at the level of the Community. Convergence by the pure market approach would not be effective nor will it lead to Community socially-desirable results since it would be based on ability to pay and income is unequally distributed between states and income-groups within states. Solidarity and cohesion among the members states by upward convergence of state systems of health care would require an upward convergence of national income, which is the principal determinant of health care expenditure. This is a long-term objective of the EC but it cannot be reached before a long period of consolidated growth at the level of the Community with accelerated development of the least developed member states, suitably aided by the Cohesion Fund. Therefore, in the short term coordination for a common approach to common problems of health care is the only task which the Community can undertake with recourse to adequate funding.

3. Conclusions

The European Community has completed the Single Market in commodities, services and factors of production in an attempt to increase the quality of life and welfare in the member states. Internal market integration does not, however, include a single market in health care, which presumably is a contributor to quality of life. National health care differs between the member states in the quality and quantity demanded and supplied, which reflect different systems and different funding. The most important determinant of the provision of health care is, however, the level of economic development as displayed by GDP per head which decrees what a country can afford for health care. Therefore, only convergence in economic performance and growth would lead to convergence of health care standards. Health care convergence will occur when 'a harmonious and balanced development of economic activities ... the raising of the standard of living and life, and economic and social cohesion and solidarity among the Member States' (TEU, Article 2) are realized. Meanwhile, the main task of the Community is to assist the efforts of the member states to coordinate national health care policies and, when necessary, to take common action to prevent the spread of Community-wide health problems.

Notes
1. For reference see Hitiris and Posnett (1992).
2. The expenditure and GDP data come from OECD (1990) and the population data from United Nations, various issues.
3. In the estimation procedure the data are transformed to correct for heteroskedasticity and autocorrelation and, therefore, the usual goodness-of-fit statistics are inappropriate. We used instead the Buse R^2 which measures the proportion of the generalized sum of squares which is attributable to the influence of the explanatory variables (Buse, 1973).

References

Bomberg, E. and J. Peterson (1993), 'Prevention from Above? The Role of the European Community' in M. Miles (ed.), *British Politics, Health and Prevention*, Avebury Press.

Buse, A. (1973), 'Goodness of Fit in Generalized Least Squares Estimation', *The American Statistician*, **27**, (3), 106–8.

Council of the European Communities (1992), *Treaty on European Union*, Luxembourg: Office for Official Publications of the European Communities.

Hitiris, T. and J. Posnett (1992), 'The Determinants and Effects of Health Expenditure in Developed Countries', *Journal of Health Economics*, **11**, 173–81.

Leu, R. (1986), 'The Public–Private Mix and International Health Care Costs' in A.J. Culyer and B. Jönsson (eds), *Public and Private Health Services*, Oxford: Blackwell.

Maddala, G.S. (1988), *Introduction to Econometrics*, New York: Macmillan.

OECD (1990), *Health Care Systems in Transition*, Paris: OECD.

Poullier, J.P. (1989), 'Health Data File: Overview and Methodology', *Health Care Financing Review*, Annual Supplement, 111–94.

United Nations (various issues), *Demographic Yearbook*, annual, New York: UN.

11 An approach to economic integration of a small country
George K. Zestos

Introduction

After World War II the Greek economy began an era of phenomenal economic growth. During this period Greece gradually opened its economy to the rest of the world through trade liberalization. In November 1962 Greece became an associate member of the European community (EC). As an associate member Greece agreed to eliminate tariffs against the other EC countries according to a dual schedule of 12 and 22 years on two main groups of products. EC countries were to remove their tariff protection more quickly. Greece also aligned its trade policies with the EC *vis-à-vis* the rest of the world, by adopting the common EC external tariff, which was generally lower than the previous Greek tariffs. In 1981 Greece became the tenth member of the EC.

The opening of the Greek economy is demonstrated in Tables 11.A.1 – 11.A.3 in the Appendix. Table 11.A.1 presents real Greek exports (X), imports (M), trade balance ($X-M$), and Gross Domestic Product (GDP) for 1960–88, all expressed in 1985 drachmas. With very few exceptions, these variables increased over the entire period. The last variable in Table 11.A.1 is the sum of real exports and imports divided by real Gross Domestic Product. This variable is included to measure the degree of the trade openness of the Greek economy and it has also been gradually rising continuously since 1960.

Tables 11.A.2 and 11.A.3 show the geographic distribution of trade shares of Greek exports and imports. These tables show that Greece became a closer trading partner to the EC, for both its exports and its imports, after it became a member of the EC.

To study the effects of economic integration on the Greek economy, the method of factor growth accounting is adopted. The total economy of Greece is compared with the total economy of France and Germany. A time series data set was constructed for this purpose which consists of 27 observations on output (Y), capital (K), and labour (L).[1]

The aim of this study is to examine whether real economic convergence between Greece and the EC is taking place. Real economic convergence refers to the long-run process of reducing the disparities in the standards of

144 *Economic integration between unequal partners*

living between member states. This is an objective of the EC as explicitly stated in Article 2 of the Treaty of Rome which established the EC in 1957. The goal of real economic convergence was stressed again in the 1990-91 Annual Economic Report of the Commission of the European Communities.[2] Real convergence can be measured by the reduction in the disparity of the per capita GDP of the member countries.[3]

Factor growth accounting (FGA)

The method of Factor Growth Accounting (FGA) is utilized to study how the Greek economy has evolved during the twenty-seven years of this study. The main inquiry is how economic integration of Greece with the EC has affected the Greek economy. Was there a convergence or divergence in rates of growth of output, and labour and capital productivities, in the three countries? The rates of growth of output, and labour productivity, are decomposed into their contributing components, in order to aid the understanding of the sources of growth of the three economies. The aim is to show how the Greek economy compares with the other two, and to indicate the driving forces behind the rates of economic growth. France and Germany were chosen since both countries are original members of the EC. The factors contributing to growth of output are the inputs of production, while the remainder, after all inputs are accounted for, is attributed to neutral technical change. The idea of factor growth accounting has its origins in an important contribution by R. Solow (1957). A general production function can be written as:

$$Y = A(t)f(K,L), \qquad (11.1)$$

where capital (K), and labour (L), are the only inputs, and $A(t)$ represents total factor productivity (TFP). As equation (1) shows, TFP is independent of the level and qualities of the inputs. Because of this specification $A(t)$ is also called disembodied technical change. TFP can be thought of as a general improvement in production arising from innovations.[4]

Using a Solow-type production function that is homogenous of degree one[5] the growth of output and the growth of the Total Factor Input (TFI) are given by equations (11.2) and (11.3) below:

$$Y_g = TFI_g + TFP_g, \qquad (11.2)$$

$$TFL_g = S_L I_g + (I - S_L)K_g, \qquad (11.3)$$

where: Y_g = growth rate of output, L_g = growth rate of labour, K_g = growth rate of capital, TFL_g = growth rate of the two inputs expressed as a weighted average, TFP_g = growth of the total factor productivity, S_L = labour share of income, S_K = capital share of income.[6]

Equation (11.3) states that growth of the total factor input TFL_g is a weighted average of the two inputs used in the production. The weights of the two inputs are their share in the output (income). Since the production function is characterized by constant returns to scale, it is also true that $S_K + S_L = 1$.

To proceed with the FGA study, estimates on the shares of capital and labour are necessary; the former are not easily available. For this study, estimates for S_K were borrowed from three different sources.[7] The sample period in this study was divided into three subperiods to take into consideration the 1973–74 oil crisis and the year of the accession of Greece to the EC (1981). Equations (11.2) and (11.3) are utilized in Table 11.1 to study the sources of the growth of output Y_g in the three countries.

Table 11.1 summarizes the rates of growth of the outputs, inputs, and the *TFP* of the three countries. Greece surpassed the other two countries in the growth of all the variables presented in Table 11.1, with the exception of labour. The first subperiod, 1961–73, is the most impressive era of growth for Greece. Germany and France also experienced substantial rates of growth in output, capital, and *TFP*, but to a lesser degree. From 1974 to 1980 the oil crisis negatively affected all three economies; however, Greece's economy did not falter as much as the other two. Output growth declined to 4.2, while labour and capital growth rates were 0.44 and 5.0 respectively. The level of total factor productivity also remained relatively high at 2.92. During the third subperiod, 1981–87, the Greek economy revealed major weaknesses in all variables except for its capital stock, which grew at a rate of 2.89 per cent. All the other variables showed small rates of growth. Particularly, output and *TFP* grew at rates lower than the corresponding French and German ones. This constitutes a break in the convergence process of the previous two subperiods.

In the last four columns of Table 11.1, the contribution of the inputs and TFP_g to the growth of output are presented. The pattern for the three countries is very similar; TFP_g declined in all three countries, with time, while the contribution of capital rose. Labour was never an important source contributing to growth in any of the three EC countries.

Table 11.2 presents the growth of the two inputs, capital and labour as well as the growth of the capital-to-labour ratio. The growth of *K/L* has declined steadily from subperiod to subperiod. The growth of the factor substitution variable $S_K(K/L)_g$ displays a similar pattern. It can be determined from Table 11.2 that the growth of capital, the capital-to-labour ratio and factor substitution have declined in these countries. However factor substitution declined more in Greece than in the other two countries.

146 Economic integration between unequal partners

Table 11.1 Sources of growth of output for three EC countries' Gross Domestic Product, GDP

Greece
Capital Share = 0.20

	Average Annual Rates				Contribution to Growth of Output			
Variable	1961–73	1974–80	1981–87	1961–87	1961–73	1974–80	1981–87	1961–87
Total Output	7.35	4.2	1.17	4.5	100	100	100	100
Labour	−0.93	0.44	0.24	−0.45	−10.1	8.3	16.6	−8.1
Capital Stock	8.5	5.0	2.89	6.17	23.35	23.5	50.2	27.6
Total Factor Productivity	6.38	2.92	0.38	3.59	86.8	68.2	33.2	80.5

Germany
Capital Share = 0.348

	Average Annual Rates				Contribution to Growth of Output			
Variable	1960–73	1974–80	1981–87	1960–87	1974–80	1981–87	1981–87	1960–87
Total Output	4.5	2.38	1.65	3.2	100	100	100	100
Labour Input	0.05	−0.15	−0.10	−0.12	0.7	−4.2	−4.0	−2.4
Capital Stock	4.48	3.02	2.21	4.41	34.5	44.3	46.7	47.8
Total Factor Productivity	2.93	1.43	0.94	1.75	64.8	59.9	57.3	54.6

France
Capital Share = 0.308

	Average Annual Rates				Contribution to Growth of Output			
Variable	1960–73	1974–80	1981–87	1960–87	1960–73	1974–80	1981–87	1960–87
Total Output	5.53	2.24	1.78	3.74	100	100	100	100
Labour Input	0.84	0.22	−0.17	0.43	10.6	6.2	−6.6	7.9
Capital Stock	6.04	4.27	4.31	5.14	33.6	53.8	74.3	42.3
Total Factor Productivity	3.09	0.98	1.96	1.86	55.8	40.0	32.3	49.8

Table 11.2 *Factor input growth and factor substitution percentage changes (annual rates)*

Capital Share	GDP		
	$S_g = 0.20$	$S_g = 0.308$	$S_g = 0.348$

Gross Domestic Product (GDP)

Period and Variable	Greece	France	Germany
1961–87			
L_g	−0.45	0.43	−0.12
K_g	6.17	5.14	4.41
$(K/L)_g$	6.65	4.69	4.53
$S_K(K/L)_g$	1.33	1.44	1.46
1961–73			
L_g	−0.93	0.84	0.05
K_g	8.5	6.04	4.48
$(K/L)_g$	9.6	5.15	4.43
$S_K(K/L)_g$	1.92	1.59	1.59
1974–80			
L_g	0.44	0.22	0.15
K_g	5.00	4.27	3.02
$(K/L)_g$	4.57	4.05	3.18
$S_K(K/L)_g$	0.91	1.25	0.95
1981–87			
L_g	0.24	−0.17	−0.10
K_g	2.89	4.31	2.21
$(K/L)_g$	2.64	4.48	2.31
$S_K(K/L)_g$	0.53	1.38	0.70

In Table 11.3 the growth is decomposed into its contributing components, the TFI_g and the TFP_g. According to equation (11.2), $Y_g = TFP_g + TFI_g$. One point to be made here is that for all periods, except 1981–1987, Greece experienced the highest rates of growth in Output Y, Labour Productivity Y/L, and Total Factor Productivity *TFP*. Conversely, for the last subperiod Greece was lagging in all three variables. France and Germany while not performing

148 Economic integration between unequal partners

Table 11.3 Productivity, output and input growth average percentage change (annual rates)

	GDP		
Capital Share	$S_K = 0.20$	$S_K = 0.308$	$S_K = 0.348$

	Gross Domestic Product (GDP)		
Period and Variable	Greece	France	Germany
1961–87 (Y_g)	4.5	3.70	3.20
TFI_g	0.9	1.90	1.50
TFG_g	3.6	1.80	1.70
$(Y/L)_g$	4.94	3.30	3.30
$(Y/K)_g$	−1.61	−1.33	−1.50
1961–73 (Y_g)	7.4	5.60	4.50
TFI_g	1.0	2.50	1.60
TFG_g	6.4	3.10	2.90
$(Y/L)_g$	8.36	4.65	4.47
$(Y/K)_g$	−1.14	−0.48	−0.042
1974–80	4.3	2.40	2.40
TFI_g	1.4	1.40	1.00
TFG_g	2.9	1.00	1.40
$(Y/L)_g$	3.82	2.22	2.54
$(Y/K)_g$	−0.72	−1.75	−0.63
1981–87	1.2	1.80	1.60
TFI_g	0.8	1.20	0.70
TFG_g	0.4	0.60	0.90
$(Y/L)_g$	0.91	1.96	1.75
$(Y/K)_g$	−1.69	−2.42	−0.55

as well as in the first twenty years, surpassed Greece during the last subperiod in all the variables presented in Table 11.3. This is evidence of divergence of the Greek economy from the other two. Also in Table 11.3, the growth of labour productivity $(T/L)_g$ and capital productivity $(Y/L)_g$ are presented. While the growth of labour productivity follows a pattern similar to that of the growth of output Y_g and the growth of TFP_g, the growth of capital productivity is very different. Capital productivity $(Y/K)_g$ is negative for every subperiod and for all three countries. This could be an indication that all three countries over-accumulated capital stock.

Figure 11.1 depicts the Greek rates of growth of output Y_g, labour productivity $(Y/L)_g$ and TFP_g. Two main points are made: first, all three variables move closely together; second, the impact of the two oil crises (1973) and (1979) on the Greek economy is evident. While it is no surprise that Y and Y/L move together, TFP_g also follows the business cycle since innovations are more likely to be initiated and implemented during expansionary periods.

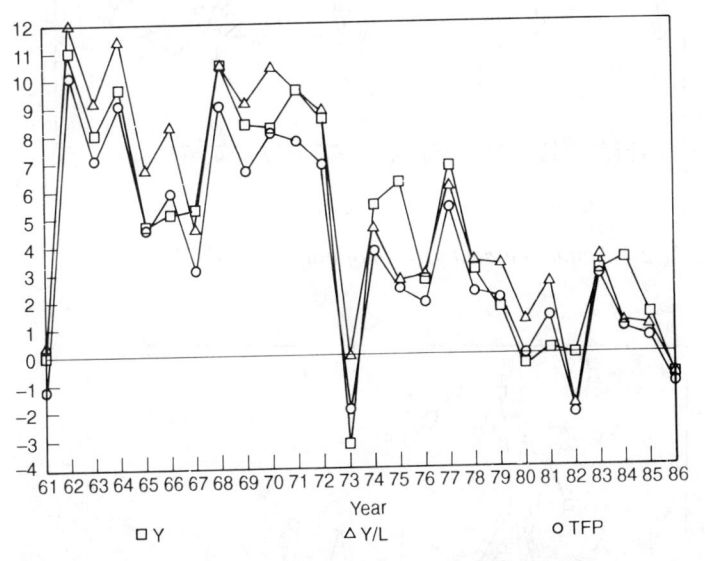

Figure 11.1   Annual percent growth of Y, Y/L and TFP, total GDP, Greece

Figure 11.2 shows the growth rates of output for these three countries. It can be seen that all three countries achieved high rates of growth in the first 20 years of the sample period but also high variability. During the 1980s the rates of growth dropped substantially (even became negative). The main reason that the economic variables of the three countries move together is that all three are open economies, members of the EC and subject to common external shocks.

Patterns of the growth of output are closely followed by the labour productivity and the TFP_g which are shown in Figures 11.3 and 11.4.

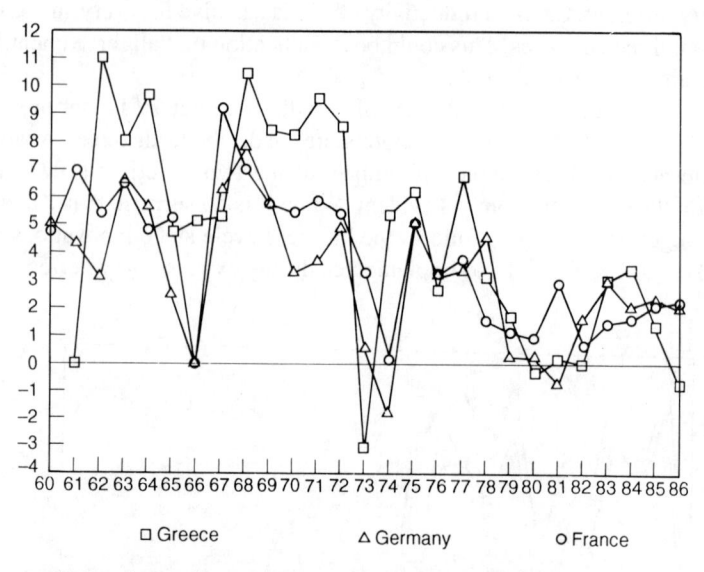

150   *Economic integration between unequal partners*

Figure 11.2   Annual percent growth of output, total GDP

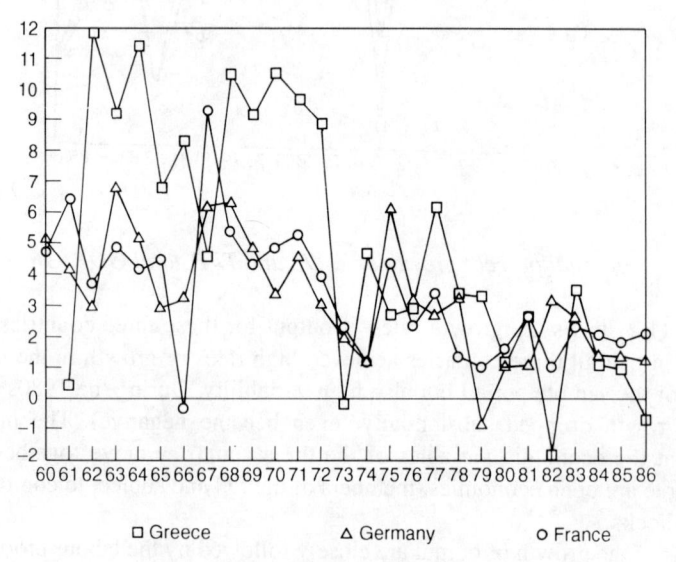

Figure 11.3   Annual growth of labour productivity, total GDP

Economic integration of a small country 151

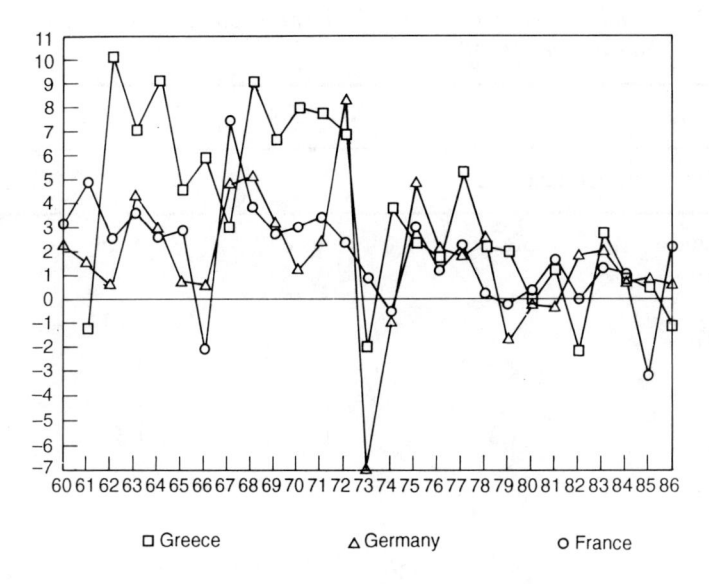

Figure 11.4 Annual percent change in TFP, total GDP

Sources of growth of labour productivity in three EC countries
To study the sources of growth in labour productivity we rewrite equation (11.2) as:

$$TFP_g = Y_g - S_L L_g - (1 - S_L) K_g \qquad (11.4)$$

It can be seen from (11.4) that TFP_g is the residual in the growth of output after the contributions of the two inputs have been accounted for. Equation (11.4) can also be written as:

$$(Y/L)_g = TFP_g + S_K (K/L)_g^8 \qquad (11.5)$$

Equation (11.5) states that the growth of the labour productivity depends on the growth of two components, the TFP_g and the growth of the factor substitution $S_K (K/L)_g$. Note that the last term, the factor substitution, is the growth of the (K/L) ratio multiplied by the share of capital. When TFP_g increases, labour productivity $(Y/L)_g$ increases. Similarly, increases in the capital-to-labour ratio result in an increase in labour productivity.

In Table 11.4, the growth of labour productivity is broken down into the growth of *TFP* plus the growth of factor substitution. The factor substitution declines in all three countries. The interpretation of this result is that while an increasing capital-to-labour ratio affects the labour productivity favourably,

Table 11.4 Labour productivity, total factor productivity and factor substitution, GDP

Capital Share	$S_K = 0.20$	$S_K = 0.308$	$S_K = 0.348$
Gross Domestic Product (GDP)			
Period and Variable	Greece	France	Germany
1961–87			
$(Y/L)_g$	4.9	3.3	3.3
TFP_g	3.6	1.9	1.7
$S_K(K/L)_g$	1.3	1.4	1.6
1961–73			
$(Y/L)_g$	8.3	4.7	4.5
TFP_g	6.4	3.1	2.9
$S_K(K/L)_g$	1.9	1.6	1.5
1974–80			
$(Y/L)_g$	3.8	2.2	2.5
TFP_g	2.9	1.0	1.4
$S_K(K/L)_g$	0.9	1.2	1.1
1981–87			
$(Y/L)_g$	0.9	2.0	1.7
TFP_g	0.4	0.6	0.9
$S_K(K/L)_g$	0.5	1.4	0.8

this effect weakens with time. A reason for this is that capital accumulation makes factor substitutability in production more difficult. Once physical capital is added, firms cannot respond readily to changes in factor prices.

Conclusion
Relying on factor growth accounting it was found that Greece had a different developing path from the other two countries. Greece had a fast and vigorous start which was reversed in the 1980s, when every economic variable except the capital stock ceased growing. Germany and France experienced a similar slowdown, but not to the same extent as Greece. Considering the fact that Greece is a developing country, while the other two are advanced industrial-

ized economies, the experience of the 1980s indicates a break in the integration process.

Furthermore, it was found that the TFP_g declined in all countries; more in Greece than in France and Germany. It cannot be known with certainty what caused TFP to decline more in Greece than in the other countries. A possible explanation could be the fact that Germany and France spent more than Greece in research and development (R & D). The two countries rank third and fourth in spending on R & D, led only by the USA and Japan.

Another major problem faced by the three countries is that all three experienced 'over-accumulation' of capital. The latter resulted in negative rates of growth in the marginal product of capital in all three countries. As a result of the excessive capital deepening, factor substitution has declined in all three countries, but more in Greece than the other two countries.[9] Reduction of factor substitution had a direct impact on labour productivity. The problem is of great dimension since many studies found that production technologies are putty-clay.[10] This means that factors of production are substitutable only during the time of new addition to capital. Consequently, firms cannot take advantage of changes in relative factor prices in decisions regarding their entire capital stock.

Appendix

Table 11.A.1   Greece: exports imports and trade openness

Year	Exports X	Imports M	Net Exports X–M	GDO Gross Domestic Product	Trade Openness (X+M)/GDP %
1960	107 074	221 737	–114 663	1 308 609	25.1
1961	122 626	249 909	–127 283	1 454 513	25.6
1962	134 846	275 185	–140 339	1 476 818	27.8
1963	143 823	317 525	–173 702	1 626 510	28.4
1964	146 196	365 948	–219 752	1 760 832	29.1
1965	164 713	443 451	–278 738	1 926 221	31.6
1966	221 414	441 345	–219 931	2 043 706	32.4
1967	232 616	472 856	–240 240	2 155 723	32.7
1968	230 292	521 756	–291 464	2 299 391	32.7
1969	263 868	602 562	–338 694	2 527 022	34.3
1970	296 484	639 702	–343 218	2 728 041	34.3
1971	331 651	688 591	–356 940	2 922 260	34.9
1972	407 552	794 742	–387 190	3 181 751	37.8
1973	502 732	1 050 979	–548 247	3 414 739	45.5
1974	503 335	879 747	–376 412	3 290 502	42.0
1975	556 862	935 173	–378 311	3 489 594	42.8
1976	648 087	992 669	–344 582	3 711 521	44.2
1977	659 576	1 071 812	–412 236	3 838 771	45.1
1978	767 717	1 148 454	–380 737	4 095 871	46.8
1979	818 772	1 230 760	–411 988	4 247 023	48.3
1980	875 601	1 132 623	–257 022	4 321 449	46.5
1981	823 686	1 173 927	–350 241	4 323 831	46.2
1982	764 454	1 256 431	–491 977	4 340 897	46.6
1983	825 426	1 338 936	–513 510	4 358 329	49.7
1984	965 225	1 341 727	–376 502	4 478 295	51.5
1985	977 623	1 513 529	–535 906	4 617 747	53.9
1986	1 114 930	1 571 106	–456 176	4 653 331	57.7
1987	1 293 090	1 831 403	–538 313	4 650 839	67.2
1988	1 390 870	1 950 223	–559 353	4 834 554	69.1

Notes: In millions of 1985 drachmas.

Source: OECD National Accounts 1960–1988.

Table 11.A.2   Greece: geographic distribution of trade, 1980–1987 (in percent of total)

Greek exports to:	1980	1981	1982	1983	1984	1985	1986	1987
Industrial Countries	57.4	56.4	59.8	63.1	68.3	68.2	76.4	80.3
Germany	18.5	18.4	19.0	20.0	19.7	20.1	23.7	24.3
Italy	9.7	7.1	8.8	13.6	13.7	11.3	13.5	16.2
France	7.3	6.7	7.0	7.4	8.4	7.9	9.5	8.6
United Kingdom	4.1	4.9	4.8	4.9	6.2	7.0	6.8	8.2
USA	5.6	8.8	8.7	6.2	8.4	8.1	7.1	6.8
LDCs Non-Oil Producing	19.1	19.1	18.1	15.6	14.9	15.8	11.8	11.4
Oil-Exporting Countries	15.3	18.7	15.8	15.6	11.9	9.6	7.4	4.5
Communist Countries	7.7	5.8	6.2	5.4	4.6	6.1	3.8	
EEC	48.0	43.4	46.3	52.5	54.1	53.1	62.5	66.9

Source: International Monetary Fund, *Direction of Trade*, 1987 and 1989 yearbooks.

Table 11.A.3   Greece: geographic distribution of trade, 1980–1987 (in percent of total)

Greek imports from:	1980	1981	1982	1983	1984	1985	1986	1987
Industrial Countries	63.8	66.8	65.3	65.8	65.3	63.3	72.8	73.9
Germany	13.9	19.6	17.0	17.4	16.9	17.0	22.2	22.0
Italy	8.5	9.7	9.2	8.9	9.8	9.4	12.1	12.5
France	6.2	6.5	7.0	6.9	7.0	6.5	8.1	7.7
United Kingdom	4.6	4.9	3.6	4.1	4.0	3.8	4.0	4.8
USA	4.6	5.1	4.2	3.6	3.0	3.2	3.2	2.7
LDCs Non-Oil Producing	20.4	16.7	8.8	8.1	8.1	7.8	14.0	12.8
Oil-Exporting Countries	10.7	10.4	21.0	21.2	18.8	22.1	12.7	9.1
Communist Countries	4.6	5.7	4.5	4.6	7.4	6.5	4.6	
EEC	39.9	50.1	46.0	48.7	47.8	46.8	56.7	60.7

Source: International Monetary Fund, *Direction of Trade*, 1987 and 1989 yearbooks.

Notes

1. Data on the output and labour are published in the *National Accounts* of the OECD while capital data are published in several issues of the *Flows and Stocks of Fixed Capital* of OECD. Data on Greek labour were provided by the Central Bank of Greece. Twenty-eight observations constitute the data set for France and Germany. Output and net capital stock of the three countries are measured inconstant 1970 prices in the respective national currencies. Labour is measured in thousands of workers per year.
2. *European Economy*, December 1990.
3. More popular in the literature of economic integration and the news media is the term nominal convergence which refers to convergence in the rates of inflation, interest rates, government debt, and deficits as a percentage of GDP. Nominal convergence is believed to guarantee the success of the European Monetary Union (EMU). The economic variables mentioned were the main focus in the Maastricht Agreement in December 1991.

4. Once data on output and inputs are available, *TFP* can also be estimated using regressions analysis. In regression it is usually called neutral technical change. An advantage of the FGA over regression analysis is that this method does not suffer from the familiar econometric problems.
5. Production functions which depict increasing returns to scale might be very desirable for empirical work within the FGA framework. However, use of such production functions has not been successful. Constant returns to scale production functions for the three economies are also supported by regression analysis using the same data set, in Zestos (1990).
6. The above notation and model specification is used by Todd ((1984) and (1988)).
7. The first source is Steven Englander and Axel Mittelstadt (1988), who studied twenty-two OECD countries and cover almost the same sample period as the present work (1960–1986). Englander and Mittelstadt divide their sample into three subperiods, 1960–73, 1974–79, and 1980–86. However, in this study, the subperiods are 1960–73, 1974–80 and 1981–87. These are exactly the same periods that were used also in Zestos (1990). The other two sources of estimates for S_K are from Kintis (1985) and Todd (1984).
8. Equation (11.4) can be written as

$$TFP_g = Y_g - S_L L_g - K_g + S_L K_g$$
$$TFP_g = Y_g - K_g - S_L (L_g - K_g)$$

and now replace S_L with $1 - S_K$:

$$TFP_g = Y_g - K_g - (1 - S_K)(L_g - K_g)$$

and by multiplying out:

$$TFP_g = Y_g - K_g - L_g + K_g + S_K L_g - S_K K_g$$
$$TFP_g = Y_g - L_g - S_K (K_g - L_g) \text{ or } Y_g - L_g = TFP_g + S_K (K_g - L_g)$$

and in a more compact notation is written as:

$$(Y/L)_g = TFP_g + S_g (K/L)_g.$$

9. Reduction in factor substitution can be supported by many studies which calculate the elasticity of factor substitution based on estimation of production functions. Based on a transcendental production function Zestos (1990) found continuous decline of the elasticity of substitution between capital and labour in different sectors of the three economies.
10. See Fabinne Ilzkovitz (1987).

Bibliography

Davidson, L.S. and M. Fratianni, 'Economic Growth in the 1970s and Beyond', *Economic Notes*, **14**(3), 17–37.

Englander, S. and Mittelstadt (1988), 'Total Factor Productivity: Macroeconomic Aspects of the Slowdown', *OECD Economic Studies*, 12.

Ilzkovitz, F. (1987), 'Capital/Labour Substitution and Its Impact on Employment', *Economic Papers*, Commission of the European Communities, 57.

Kintis, A.A. (1985), 'Patterns and Sources of Growth in Greek Manufacturing', *Greek Economic Review*, **7**(2), 144–60.

OECD, *National Accounts*, several volumes.

OECD, *Flows and Stocks of Fixed Capital: Paris*, several issues.

Solow, R.M. (1957), 'Technical Change and the Aggregate Production Function', *Review of Economics and Statistics*, **39**, 312–20.

Todd, D. (1984) 'Factor Productivity Growth in Four EEC Countries', *Economic Papers*, Commission of the European Communities, Oct., 34.

Todd, D. (1988), 'Total Productivity Growth and the Productivity Slowdown in the West German Industrial Sector, 1970–81' *Weltwirtschaftliches Archiv*, Mar., 108–26.

Zestos, G. (1990), 'The Effects of Economic Integration on a Small Economy: The Case of Greece and the EEC', Unpublished doctoral dissertation, Indiana University, Bloomington, IN.

PART III

THE POLITICAL ECONOMY OF ECONOMIC INTEGRATION

12 Trade among partners who differ in their economic development
Ingrid H. Rima

There are few areas of economics in which the disparity between economic theory and economic practice is wider than it appears to be with respect to international trade. Political and popular attitudes and practices relating to trade deviate substantially from mainstream theory, which is unequivocally in support of free trade. Since the days of David Ricardo, economic principle has maintained that nations trade to exploit differences in the comparative costs with which they and others can produce goods and services.

Mainstream economists typically overlook that Ricardo's rule about comparative cost differences as constituting the basis for trade was offered as a prescription for raising profit rates by substituting lower cost imports, chiefly food, for domestic production (Rima, 1993). Ricardo's argument related to England as the most developed economy of the 19th century whose trade was with the basically agrarian economies elsewhere in Europe. It is the argument of this chapter that if the special context of Ricardo's theory were more widely appreciated, contemporary writers about trade issues would be less pressured to rationalize free trade almost irrespective of the differences among economies in the stages of their economic development.

The policy implications of differences among nations with respect to their stage of development is manifested in numerous (and contradictory) ways. Specifically, nations are now behaving in ways that are contrary to the General Agreement on Tariffs and Trade (GATT) to which 96 nations agreed after World War II. The 'new protectionism' in the form of a host of tariff and non-tariff barriers to trade now affects on the order of 50 per cent of world trade. Without exception leading industrial countries are imposing restrictions of one sort of another on the importation of automobiles, consumer electronics, steel, and textiles as well as on agricultural products. Most countries also subsidize their aircraft, computer and high-tech industries.

There are, to be sure, countervailing efforts to negotiate limits to protectionism through bilateral trade arrangements. These are now blossoming into major trading blocs, specifically those of the European Community (EC) and the North American Free Trade Agreement (NAFTA). The likelihood is that a Pacific Rim agreement which includes Japan, Australia and other Asian countries will eventually convert the world into three distinct trading blocs. While it is a strong possibility the latter is, of course, still an arrangement of the future and NAFTA was only recently negotiated (August 1992). Thus it is only from the EC experience that some tentative observations can be made about the gains from freer trade to which economies at different stages of economic development are likely to have access. The EC includes several economies, Greece and Spain among them, which have not been short-term beneficiaries of economic gains as a consequence of accession. When their experience is evaluated in the long view of history there appears to be an analogy to the early 20th century experience of England which reflected the latter country's loss of her earlier comparative advantage *vis-à-vis* the United States, Canada and other Commonwealth countries. The effect on the terms of trade culminated in compromises to England's free trade policy including, ultimately, resort to currency devaluation, which proved an extreme measure of dubious value. This comparative historical analysis suggests that the gains from free trade among partners whose stage of economic development is substantially disparate may be marginal to the least developed among them to a degree that may compromise the success with which their trade barriers can be removed.

This chapter proceeds first by examining the special context within which Ricardo offered the principle of comparative advantage as the basis for trade between England which was 'the most manufacturing country' of the 19th century and her less developed, largely agrarian trading partners. Their subsequent development by the first quarter of the 20th century enabled them to surpass England in basic heavy industrial exports. The US and some Commonwealth countries were also producing agricultural raw material and foodstuffs by means of large scale cost-reducing production units akin to those of British manufacturing industries. The outcome was a worsening in England's terms of trade which decreased the income per unit of employment to a degree that provoked 'beggar they neighbour' remedies in the hope of improving her balance of payments.

The second section of this chapter suggests that the history of England's shifting competitive position *vis-à-vis* her trading partners provides a historical case study about the relevance of differences among trading partners in their stage of economic development and the reasons why these differences are more likely to compromise than to facilitate the move towards the textbook ideal of free trade. While the European Community is a strong institutional vehicle for accomplishing the removal of all tariff and non-tariff barriers by January 1993, less developed partners like Greece and Spain appear to have benefited only marginally from accession.

The final part of this chapter takes the position that, from a global perspective, the critical need is for international economic cooperation to restore growth rates in the developed economies. Only then can the problem of reducing strains between the more developed and the less developed economies, the natural proclivity to beggar one's neighbour, be addressed.

Classical theory: comparative cost as the basis for trade

The classical theory of international trade was formulated primarily with a view to addressing the questions of national policy that arose in the context of the issue of restoring the Corn Laws. The Smithian case for free trade derives from his recognition that there is an advantage to a country in importing those commodities which either cannot be produced at home at all or can be produced only at a cost absolutely greater than that at which they could be acquired in exchange for native products. This view is the source of the classical free trade doctrine that was abridged by the Corn Laws.

Ricardo wanted to abolish the Corn Laws to lower the cost of grain as the chief staple of wage earner consumption in order to raise the rate of profit. Though 'comparative advantage' is what has been transmitted as Ricardo's chief contribution, the main point of his stance on the Corn Laws was that England's absolute disadvantage in corn production coupled with her absolute advantage in manufacturing is the rationale for abolishing the Corn Laws in favour of free trade. Ricardo (1817; 1886, p. 211) argued as follows:

> In rich countries, on the contrary, where food is dear, capital will naturally flow, when trade is free, into those occupations wherein the least quantity of labour is required to be maintained at home: such as the carrying trade, the distant foreign trade, and trades where expensive machinery is required; to trades where profits are in proportion to the capital, and not in proportion to the quantity of labour employed.

Ricardo's stance against reviving the Corn Law can be interpreted as a proposal to facilitate the emergence of industrial capitalism by enhancing the process of accumulation and productive investment by means of policies favourable to capitalist profits (Rima, 1993). Expressed in terms of the contemporary macro model, Ricardo envisioned closing the savings–investment gap by imports of cheap food. This would keep the profit rate higher than it would be if the supply of corn were chiefly produced at home. By checking the rise in wage costs it would provide more funding for capital expansion and economic growth financed, at least in part, by England's trading partners. The special context of Ricardo's argument and its critical connection to the profit rate is thus missed by most contemporary discussion. Later neoclassical expositions of the comparative advantage principle focus almost entirely on the gains from trade that can be achieved by *all* trading partners. This focus has overshadowed that aspect of the classical theory and trade policy that envisioned the gains to England, given her small amount of land, from concentrating her labour and capital on industries enjoying increasing returns in order to buy the products of 'increasing cost' industries abroad. Thomas Malthus was particularly appreciative of this point and how it relates to a country's stage of economic development, for he emphasized that the gains from trade do not simply derive from the possibility of obtaining cheaper commodities (1820, p. 462).

The terms of trade under free trade
Tariffs were generally lowered over a large part of Europe in the third quarter of the 19th century and England adopted free trade in agricultural products. The most rapidly growing sector of world trade was that among the industrialized countries.

Britain's increasing industrial development during the 19th century went hand in hand with a rapid expansion of trade as well as in international investment and finance. Trade among industrialized countries was the most rapidly growing component of world trade. By the beginning of the 20th century Britain's trade rivals, Germany and the USA, were beginning to surpass her in exports of basic heavy industries dependent on iron and steel and also goods produced by new industries dependent on applied scientific skills, among them chemicals, electrical supplies and machines. Her agricultural prosperity was also substantially at an end by the 1870s, which led her to abandon her earlier efforts to excel in the production of grain. Other Commonwealth countries and Argentina soon exported not only food stuffs but also agricultural raw materials into England. These highly developed rural economies were producing with large-scale cost-reducing production units which were structured essentially like British manufacturing industries. This kind of import reliance was essentially different from that of the 18th and 19th centuries, when England was the indisputable workshop of the world. Thus by 1923 J.M. Keynes (1931; 1972, p. 482) evaluated the change in Britain's foreign terms of trade since 1900 as reflecting a deterioration to a degree that 'we are no longer able to sell a growing volume of manufactured goods (or a volume increasing in proportion to population) at a better real price in terms of food'. Along with Sir William Beveridge, Keynes recognized that the worsening in the terms of trade (that is, relative to the price of exports) represented a decrease in income per unit of employment for the country as a whole. In the short run, at least, a worsening in the terms of trade for a major trading country is likely to produce a neo-mercantilistic reaction in the form of beggar-thy-neighbour remedies via exchange depreciation, wage reductions, export subsidies and/or restrictions of imports by means of tariffs and quotas. The object of these expedients, each of which has important effects on the distribution of employment and income between industries in the home country, is to improve the balance of trade. This increases employment and income in the export industries, but it also raises the home price of export goods that rival imports. Although such policies have the effect of reducing average real wages, they are nevertheless viewed as beneficial when circumstances dictate that the game of beggar-thy-neighbour is the appropriate policy. Even Pigou, though he was otherwise orthodox in his thinking about trade, recognized that in the short run, a tariff could increase employment (1947, p. 224).

A worsening in the terms of trade (i.e., relative to the price of exports), represents a decrease in income per unit of employment for the country as a whole. In the short run at least such a worsening in the terms of trade for a major trading country will produce a neo-mercantilistic reaction in the form of beggar-thy-neighbour remedies either via exchange depreciation, wage reductions, export subsidies and/or restriction of imports by means of tariffs and quotas. Their objective is to improve the balance of trade. Such a policy, as Keynes recognized in *The General Theory*, is perfectly rational under conditions of chronic demand deficiency. Thus, the interwar period taught by painful experience the lesson that the presence of a foreign sector confers a degree of latitude for increasing domestic absorption that is not available to a closed economy, but that its pursuit is likely to be confrontational *vis-à-vis* its trading partners.

This confrontation was clearly at the heart of the US Smoot–Hawley Tariff of 1930 which ushered in an era of American protectionism that extended until the General Agreement on Tariffs and Trade (GATT) which was established after World War II. GATT established four main principles: (1) that member countries should work to reduce trade barriers, in particular, those that operate through quotas; (2) that barriers to trade be applied on a non-discriminatory basis to all the participating countries; (3) that the rescinding of trade concessions is forbidden unless there is compensation to trade partners; and (4) that trade disputes be addressed by negotiations and consultation.

Seven 'rounds' of trade negotiations were sponsored under GATT jurisdiction between 1947 and 1979 which produced cuts in tariffs which were of the order of 40 per cent in the 1940s to less than 5 per cent in the 1980s (Salvatore, 1993). These reductions produced an increase in the merchandise trade of industrial countries of the order of 8 per cent per year during the 1950s and 1960s.

These steps toward free trade notwithstanding, the gains from multilateral trade have been short-lived. The present era of modern capitalism is characterized by industrial economics in pursuit of two main neo-mercantilist goals; to maintain near full employment and stimulate GNP growth. Both for the newly emerging ex-colonial industrial economies and the older, now mature industrial economies, neo-mercantilism is an essentially new phase in the historical development of modern capitalism. The objective of using trade to increase the nation's absorption rate has now become a globalized objective.

It has been argued that the basic reason for the high Japanese savings rate and her high growth rate is that her people 'desire to accumulate wealth in order for their children to live as well as Americans do' (Hayashi, 1986, p. 199). Had Japan followed the conventional wisdom, she would have adopted free trade and would have specialized in industries of the labour intensive variety. Instead, the Ministry of International Trade and Industry established industries predicated on intense employment of capital and modern technology. This policy choice, which also severely limited Japanese imports, is absolutely irrational within the context of traditional theory. But over the longer period, the industries which MITI promoted are ones in which labour productivity rises fast. The outcome of these policies is analogous to the increasing return industries which England chose to support when she abolished the Corn Laws to pursue free trade in primary commodities. For 19th century England the substitution of cheap imports of food raised the profit rate which, in turn, facilitated industrialization and provided access to world markets. In the case of contemporary Japan, her policy makers concluded that the lateness of her industrialization would only be compatible with protected domestic markets which encouraged a high savings rate. These policies encouraged her rapid growth and became the basis for her world export market. The international economic order has thus come full circle in terms of policy. This point of fact supports the inference that the *raison d'être* of international trade has historically been to effect a real resource transfer from one's trading partners.

The countervailing influence of the EC
The seemingly natural tendencies which nations have toward mercantilistic restrictions on imports can only be counteracted by their joint actions to work towards the removal of restrictions. The objective of the European Community (EC) to completely remove all barriers to the internal flow of goods among its 12 member nations by the end of 1992 has already shown itself to be a powerful countervailing influence to the propensity of individual nations to redirect trade, whether by means of tariffs or quantitative restrictions. It is manifestly clear that a nation will normally lower its trade barriers only if its trading partners make comparable concessions. This is a fact of economic life, whether the reductions at issue involve very large numbers of nations such as the ninety-nine involved in the Multilateral Trade Negotiation (the so-called Tokyo Round) or the substantially smaller number comprising the EC or NAFTA.

Qualitative restrictions, tariffs and/or subsidies to encourage exports and limit imports represent economic distortions that alter the allocation of resources from their competitive ideal. Price theory implies that the price established in a competitive market is optimal in the sense of being both fair to consumers and remunerative for sellers. When competition is constrained, as it becomes in the face of mercantilistic trade practices, the optimal method for restoring the desired set of prices is to encourage the restoration of competition. The critical problem inherent in accomplishing this objective, even within the framework of collective action, is that the markets of the competitive ideal have largely been superseded by oligopolistic fix-price markets which clearly favour the economic agents of the potentially powerful countries *vis-à-vis* those of the LDCs and the more recently developed economies of the EC, notably Greece and Spain. Oligopolistic power concentrated in the major industrialized economies of the world has become the chief vehicle for raising profit rates by facilitating the transfer of real and financial resources during the second half of the 20th century. It has, in essence, thus served the same objective for these countries as did free trade for England in the latter part of the 19th century.

The success with which the industrial economies have been able to accomplish a positive sum trade game has, to be sure, been mediated by the success of OPEC producers (and a few other mineral exporters) in creating and exploiting a sellers' market in oil. They have been further compromised by the emergence of newly industrialized economies, in particular Japan, and more recently South Korea and Taiwan, who have carved out powerful positions as exporters of steel, automobiles and electronic products. These structural changes have, in effect, generated a new generation of oligopolists (which are typically the product of policies such as those of Japan's MITI) whose goal is to alter the cost structure of specific industries with a view to enabling them to establish positions in foreign markets, if necessary by dumping. The effectiveness with which these 'new oligopolists' have been able to operate is evidenced by the fact that balance of payments surpluses have been generated chiefly by the OPEC countries and Japan (and occasionally by Germany).

Oligopolists, most of whom are industrial producers, are price makers while primary producers (with the notable exception of the OPEC oil cartel) are 'price takers'. Their different responses in terms of price cuts versus output cuts in the face of reductions in demand is at the heart of the downward trend in the terms of trade for less developed members of the EC, much as it is for third world countries. This suggests that the stabilization of commodity prices is critical to the management of trade among partners whose economies are at different stages of development. This is certainly the case with respect to Greece and Spain, neither of which has reaped substantial benefits from accession. In the Greek case Community officials have judged her performance as less than satisfactory, given the degree of support received from the Community. Greece has been a full member of the EC for ten years, but the economy has not thrived despite the assistance that has been received.

'Foot dragging' and 'boon doggling' inevitably accompany such fundamental changes in the economic life of a nation as full union in the European Community. Yet, it is quite possible that those who judge Greece's performance as inadequate have underestimated the costs of adjustment. The problem stems in at least some measure from the fact that Greece's Mediterranean type of agricultural production confronts a different kind of support from either the 'northern' agricultural products (in particular, livestock and grains) or the manufactured products she imports. Since accession Greek consumers have paid EC producers larger increases in unit prices in comparison with the payments to Greek producers by EC consumers. While the negative balance to Greece from transfers attributable to trade is outweighed by the positive balance resulting from budgetary transfers from the European budget, the increase in Greece's income from trade with the Community falls short of aggregate direct gains from export trade to Greece (Georgakoupoulos, 1994). In this sense accession has thus far been a negative sum game for Greece.

The Spanish experience with accession is similarly less than positive. Accession has led to a sharp decrease in her trade balance which has deteriorated for every major Spanish export industry (Walcott, 1993). The Spanish case is rather different from that of Greece. Specifically, the most important Spanish export industries are also those of the EC9 countries. Four industries dominate: transport equipment, basic iron and steel, machinery and industrial chemicals. Exports and imports of all of these products increased as a result of new private business initiatives by Spanish firms. Spain's historical ties with North European business firms, especially those in Germany and the Netherlands, also appear to have moderated her adjustment costs *vis-à-vis* those of Greece. There are, therefore, inequalities in trade even among those who are themselves unequal. Thus the shift of resources from north to south may well be less painful for Spain than for Greece. The cases of Turkey and Portugal, also unequal partners in trade, are no doubt as individual as those of Greece and Spain.

Concluding remarks
The effectiveness and speed with which the north–south shift of resources will be able to proceed will be closely linked to the domestic prosperity of the more economically developed countries. The critical need in a world characterized by trading partners who are at substantially disparate stages of economic growth (and therefore in per capita GDP) is to systematically encourage the flow of capital and technology from the more developed to the less developed economies. This will ultimately also be to the advantage of the developed economies for they will increasingly find markets for their goods in markets which they help to flourish. The great impediment to the necessary resource transfer towards the less developed economies is the

problem of unemployment and declining rates of growth in the developed countries. These problems impact on their political stability which, in turn, has engendered the neo-mercantilist policies that impede the flow of resources among nations.

The absence of an international hegemon, such as Great Britain was before World War I and the US became after World War II has deprived the world of the leadership essential for international cooperation. International cooperation for addressing the crisis of unemployment and severely lagging growth is now virtually non-existent. In its absence, the problems inherent in a world comprised of unequal trading partners appear increasingly to be addressed by a return to various policies of beggaring one's neighbour as a way of increasing or, at least, preserving domestic standards of living.

Bibliography

Bhagwati, Jagdish (1989), *Protectionism*, Cambridge, MA: MIT Press.
Georgakopoulos, T. (1994), 'Economic Integration and Unequal Development: The Experience of Greece', in this volume.
Hayashi, Fumio (1986), 'Why is Japan's Savings Rate so Apparently High?' in S. Fischer (ed.), *NBER Macroeconomic Annual*, Cambridge, MA: MIT Press, 147–210.
Keynes, J.M. (1929), 'The German Transfer Problem', *Economic Journal*, 39, March, 1–7. 'A Rejoinder', ibid., June, 179–82. 'A Reply', September, 404–8.
Keynes, J.M. (1931; 1972), *Essays in Persuasion*, Collected Writings, Vol IX, London: Macmillan.
Keynes, J.M. (1946), 'The Balance of Payments of the United States', *Economic Journal*, 56, June, 404–8.
Malthus, Thomas (1820), *Principles of Political Economy*, Reprints of Economic Classics, New York: Augustus Kelley, 1964.
Pigou, A.C. (1947), *A Study in Public Finance*, third edition, London: Macmillan.
Ricardo, David (1817), *Collected Works, Volume on Principles of Political Economy and Taxation*, edited by J.R. McCulloch, London: John Murray, 1886.
Rima, Ingrid H. (1993), 'Neomercantilism: What does it tell us about the political economy of international trade?' in *The Political Economy of Global Restructuring*, Volume II, Chapter 2, Aldershot, Hants, England: Edward Elgar.
Robinson, Joan (1967), 'Beggar My Neighbour Remedies', *Essays in the Theory of Employment*, 2nd ed., Oxford: Basil Blackwell.
Salvatore, Dominick (1993), 'Trade Protectionism with Voluntary Export Restraints' in *The Political Economy of Global Restructuring*, Volume II, Chapter 4, Ingrid Rima (ed.), Aldershot, Hants, England: Edward Elgar.
Walcott, Susan (1993), 'The Impact of Accession with the European Community on Spanish Industry' in *The Political Economy of Global Restructuring*, Volume II, Chapter 8, Aldershot, Hants, England: Edward Elgar.

13 Triple 'A' trade: asymmetry, access and adjustment, the inflexible limits of trade blocs

Daniel Drache

Introduction

Regional trading blocs come in all shapes and sizes. At one extreme is the European Community that gives Brussels sweeping powers over its 12 participating members (Hufbauer, 1990). When completed, it will result in a vast single economic space for the free circulation of goods, services, capital and people – a single currency, a central bank and a common defence policy. At the other end of the spectrum is NAFTA. It is a far simpler but equally radical variant of the free trade ideal. It creates an immense North American market between Mexico, Canada and the US by integrating the three economies, grants new rights to business to invest and divest with minimum restriction in resources, finances and manufacturing, and imposes a multitude of restraints on the Canadian and Mexican governments in the hope of creating a level playing field (Grinspun and Cameron, 1993). What is special about this trade bloc is that it does not have any provision to establish a supranational authority to coordinate joint decision-making between the parties. Everything is to be market-driven. The only special institutional arrangement is provision for a court of last resort to settle trade disputes.

Despite these very real differences in design, practice and intent NAFTA and the EC have at least one thing in common.[1] These bold schemes have convinced public policy-makers that trade liberalization strategies are their 'first best' policy option to counter the worst economic crisis since the depression. With Western economies looking at zero growth rates and double digit unemployment for the foreseeable future, governments everywhere are looking to trade blocs to kickstart their troubled economies.

For élites, regional trade blocs appear as an unlimited investment frontier capable of delivering new productivity growth and new jobs.[2] What is driving this agenda? Why are states rushing to open their economies regardless of the costs and consequences (Drache and Gertler, 1991)?

A trade regime defined

The formation of trading blocs provides a unique opportunity to examine the power of the global economy to restructure national economies. A trade regime is more than a means to build an integrated market of gigantic proportions based on economies of scale and market niches for the fortunate few. At a minimum, it has to be thought of as a unique kind of economic system anchored in the international economy but having its own set of institutional forms. This includes a growth model of production to set the broad terms of the compromise between capital and labour, a compromise that affects both work organization and the lifestyle of wage earners (Boyer, 1991). It also functions as a powerful regulatory device to redefine the rules of the game for fiscal, monetary and industrial state policy as well as to establish the ground rules and conceptual framework for competition policy.

From this perspective the heart and soul of a free trade regime are the linked issues of *access* – how to enhance it, *asymmetry* – how to neutralize it, and *adjustment* – how to plan and pay for job loss and economic restructuring. Providing answers to these strategic concerns enables trade blocs to keep the wheels of integration turning. If a free trade bloc has not provided for a strong set of non-market regulatory institutions to counter market imperfection and failure, free trade arrangements cannot make good their promise to deliver long-term growth or to provide a higher standard of well-being for the majority. Indeed, in these circumstances trade regimes such as the NAFTA and the EC are more likely to become victims of the current structural global crisis rather than be any kind of viable alternative.

The argument that will be made is that NAFTA and the EC represent two of the boldest attempts by governments, to date, to use the new competitive pressures to accelerate social, economic and political change. However, far from stabilizing these new trading arrangements, this strategy renders trade blocs unstable and, in the long term, unsustainable in their present form. The place to begin to get a handle on this complex story is by examining the transformation of the Cold War ideal of free trade into a global concept of free trade for all (Bhagwati, 1989).

Cold war free trade
Free trade zones are not a recent invention (Tovias, 1991). In the immediate postwar world the free trade ideal was believed to be the most effective way to organize trade on a non-political basis by putting its organization beyond the reach of non-economic considerations (Friedman and Lebard, 1991). Thus, 'the power of nations to impose relative advantage by political or military means was banned' (Friedman and Lebard, 1991, p. 195) The national fortunes of countries would have to depend in the future on macroeconomic factors such as savings, cost of raw materials, investment flows and a virtuous cycle of growth that linked increased productivity to rising patterns of consumption. Countries were required to specialize in the production of goods in which they had a competitive cost advantage. This vision of the

international order allowed countries to compete for access to markets and resources on a more secure basis than ever before.

For industrial nations, export-led growth was seen to be compatible with Keynesian precepts of the dynamic benefits derived from long production runs, Fordist mass production techniques and stable consumer markets. Gains from scale economies promised a higher standard of welfare and, most importantly, high levels of demand and continual economic growth (Boyer, 1989). For the better part of two decades, trade was deemed employment-friendly. Adjustment was left to the market and, with industrial economies growing at better than six per cent annually, workers losing their employment in the low-productivity sectors did not have much trouble finding better paying jobs in the competitive side of the economy (Lawrence and Litan, 1986).

This system of liberalized trade not only provided an economic framework for governments, it also had a powerful political dimension. The creation of strong market economies took place in an alliance led by the US and under the authority of GATT. This international organization set the rules of the trade game and it addressed the question of access in a rather straightforward manner. Countries were required to open their economies gradually to competitive pressures. The chosen instrument was the most-favoured-nation concept, a legal obligation requiring countries to dismantle their tariff walls.

Almost all countries could accept this institutional imperative because the GATT permitted them to protect their economies or key sectors when they were threatened for limited periods in difficult economic circumstances (see GATT article XVIII). Faced with exceptional conditions, GATT members could invoke safeguard measures or rely on other forms of contingent protection to address large-scale adjustment problems. These escape measures were not difficult to justify and were quickly accepted as the cost of trade liberalization (Nelson, 1989).

Almost immediately, GATT recognized that modern European governments could never rely exclusively on trade to shape their competitive edge. Countries saw that a liberal trade system needed to be supplemented by industrial strategies. Germany took the lead in using co-determination as a prototypical industrial arrangement in its iron and steel industry (Wallace, 1990). Such a strategy specifically required German authorities to be interventionist in protecting jobs and the environment. Other countries also used the state to build strong industries. France, Italy, Denmark, Belgium and the Netherlands all relied on state enterprises to supplement and bolster their so-called 'revealed' comparative advantage (Albert, 1991). Thus GATT reconciled itself with the Keynesian reality that markets were too important to be left to the short-term needs of the private sector. But, even more was needed.

Mechanisms had to be created to settle trade disputes (Ruggie, 1983). Thus, a dispute settlement mechanism was established. The principle was that countries or industries would be forced to settle their differences by arm's length international panels. Trade jurisprudence emphasized negotiations between the parties to settle countervail and anti-dumping conflicts. Importantly, the costs were born by governments, not the private parties. Overall, the system bore results. Internationally, GATT acquired a reputation for fairness in settling trade disputes (Bhagwati, 1989). Though never without its critics who complained that the agreement did not do enough to promote a more vigorous form of 'pure' free trade, a minimum level of transparency was established to oversee the international trade in goods and commodities. Contentious areas such as agriculture, services, textiles and intra-firm trade were kept outside GATT. The spoiler was the US, who chose not to be bound by the general rules of the trading club with respect to agriculture, clothing and voluntary export controls. Washington designed its own parallel system of trade remedy laws to further its domestic interests internationally.

This picture of the international trade order is deliberately incomplete. It describes the legal features of the system, not its political and power base. The foundation of the postwar free trade system was, first and foremost, an American invention for, during this time, the US had unchallenged hegemonic power as leader of the Free World bloc. Trade liberalization was one of the pillars of the Cold War system underwritten by the American-sponsored Bretton Woods Agreement. Those inside the system stood to benefit directly. As members of the alliance they were in a privileged position to receive technology and investment flows from US multinationals. These were the critical components of the liberal trade model that ensured its success. Enhanced investment prospects, not export markets, made the wheels of trade liberalization turn.

Between 1950 and 1975, foreign investment and technology transfers played a critical role in maintaining high growth rates for the industrialized core members of the trading club. Those outside the American alliance paid a high price; the third world found the industrialized markets closed to their products. If they expected to join the club, they had to accept the rules of the liberalized international system as written by the advanced industrialized world. These rules put them at a huge disadvantage because their cheaply manufactured exports in the clothing, textile and other similarly competitive industries were largely not wanted in first world markets. The price was right but the costs of adjustment prohibitive. Open markets meant labour-shedding and no government wished to be seen to be creating unemployment in the core industrial sectors of the economy.

Global free trade for all
Liberalized trade in the 1990s is a very different scheme of things from its Cold War predecessor. Internationalism has been redefined beyond recogni-

tion. Internal free trade zones in North America, Europe and elsewhere are the first step towards fragmenting markets by regionalizing them.[3] The ability to regionalize markets does not depend on taking politics out of trade but actually involves the reverse. The principal mechanism for achieving such regionalization is by invoking 'rules of origin'. This is a legally-sanctioned way of achieving a powering form of embedded protectionism against non-members while still conforming to GATT rules. The way this kind of international norm works is quite straightforward. Rules of origin are customs practices that enable trading blocs to protect their markets against outsiders. If trade blocs did not keep out imports they would not offer any advantages to the participants. Therefore, rules are designed to ensure that production is regionally-based and locally-sourced. Products defined by customs officials as being manufactured within the trade bloc (i.e., North America) are given preferential treatment while goods, products and producers coming from outside the region are disadvantaged.

All of this requires politicizing trade to an unprecedented degree. The introduction of free trade zones in the 1990s has put the organization of international exchange squarely within the reach of non-economic considerations. The leading nation in each bloc will be able to rely on its political and military power to coerce other nations to sell their commodities at lower prices or to force them to buy goods produced by the dominant partner at higher prices. The principle of segmented markets means, in effect, that economic well-being will rest with the dominant trading partner which can divert resources to its own markets. Such a 'partner' is in a strong position to close off its regional markets to competitors.[4] With these unequal dynamics, what tangible benefits can the small and medium countries of trading blocs realistically expect from a free trade zone? Can trade blocs serve the diverse and contradictory developmental needs of countries like Spain, Portugal, Greece, Mexico and even Canada, that have few national champions, high levels of foreign ownership, large regional disparities and too little governmental machinery to coordinate domestic development?

With a new set of rules governing the organization of trading blocs in this post-national world, measures such as liberalization, harmonization and integration are automatically redefined. With the rules of the game so favourable to the dominant party in any trade bloc, the distribution of benefits is skewed. Preferential trading arrangements pose a range of difficulties for participants. The most important is that small- and medium-sized countries will be forced to adjust their wage and cost structures as well as other employment-related policies to that of the dominant member. Why does this happen? Triple 'A' trade supplies a powerful insight into trade dynamics.

a. The magnitude of adjustment

Even though free trade zones create mega-markets with new opportunities for some businesses, the magnitude of adjustment has proven much more difficult than ever anticipated. The EC has created a market of over 300 million people but is now struggling to come to terms with how it is going to restructure its ten steel industries, six automotive sectors, a dozen textile clusters and the dozens of shipbuilding firms which currently operate in various regions of the Community. To address this problem, Brussels has introduced various regional industrial and competitive policies, but none of these has proven adequate to the task for which it was designed (Hufbauer, 1990; Sbragia, 1992). The Community does not have the authority nor the resources to build strong European industries or to tackle double digit unemployment. Because of this, the real costs of integration frequently outweigh the potential benefits derived from larger markets. This is why countries continue to rely on state aids and other national policies.

b. The complexity of asymmetry

Even though trade blocs promote cooperation between governments in ways never before contemplated, such agreements do not diminish the asymmetry between member states. In fact, the complex rules, regulations and directives of the Single European Act, the Maastricht Treaty and the NAFTA create a juridical framework which permanently imbeds this inequality in the structure of each agreement. Because these texts are rules-driven rather than results-oriented, they favour the interests of the dominant and the powerful over any substantive concept of the collective.

This is illustrated, by the way, in the way each trade bloc is dominated by a single nation. The European Community is a Deutschmark bloc governed by Germany's central bank. North America is a dollar-bloc controlled by the US Federal Reserve. This dominance is reflected not only in the trade flows between the parties but also at an even more fundamental level.

In the case of NAFTA, with a combined GNP of around 6 trillion US dollars and a population of more than 357 million, there is little question that the US will dominate it. The US accounts for more than 85 per cent of the regional output and nearly 70 of its total population (Hufbauer and Schott, 1992). Not surprisingly, these large and irreconcilable market imbalances translate into recalcitrant trade difficulties.

Canada's trade with the US has become increasingly unbalanced as it has become more integrated into the US economy. This is the principal finding of Michael Porter's study especially commissioned for Canada's most powerful business lobby, the BCNI. Canada's exports became more specialized in the primary sector throughout the 1980s at the expense of boosting its manufacturing exports (Drache and Gertler, 1991). In essence, Canadians sell resources in largely unprocessed form and import sophisticated end-products, equipment, machinery and computers in return. Canada's deficit in high-tech equipment and machinery has soared since the signing of the Canada–US FTA. In terms of employment, the US is the winner in this two-way trade because resource extraction is capital-intensive but not labour-intensive. This puts Canada in the disadvantaged position of having to buy back manufactured goods made from its own resources. In terms of adjustment, Canada's job-loss total is four times the US figure.

The picture for Mexico is different in respect to detail but is very similar with respect to the basic issues (Congress of the United States, 1992). Mexico's trade with the US is equally unbalanced. In 1991 it had a $22 billion trade deficit with the US. Mexico imports US consumer and capital goods and exports finished products and sub-assembly parts to the US. Just how advantageous this is to the US economy can be seen by the fact that manufactured exports to Mexico increased by 40 per cent in 1991 alone while Mexico's exports to the US increased by only 8 per cent. Even in the auto industry, the country's economic miracle of the 1990s, Mexico had a $1.5 deficit in auto and auto parts with the US. The only bright spot in its export picture is the country's publicly-owned energy sector which generated a huge surplus. Energy exports and not manufactured exports continue to drive Mexico's debt-ridden economy.[5]

c. *The artificiality of enhanced access*
The goal of every trade agreement is to augment market access and strengthen the employment prospects for its members (Harris, 1989). Studies such as Emerson's and Huhne's prestigious *The ECU Report* (1991) and Hufbauer and Schott's highly optimistic predictions in support of North American Free Trade (1992) promise that the relentless drive to increase exports is, on balance, job-friendly and that the increased internationalization of the economy will lead to a higher standard of living and a brighter economic future for all. Thus far, the drive to be more competitive has been accompanied by intensified job-slimming. Hardly a day passes without an IBM, a Siemens, a General Motors, a Renault, a Volkswagen, a Pratt and Whitney or a Stelco announcing another massive reduction of their work-force. In these circumstances, the real costs of technological change outweigh most, if not all, of the tangible benefits of employment-creation that are supposed to result from increased access to bigger markets.

Many of these dramatic announcements come from the most competitive and export-oriented side of the industrial sector. Economic theory predicts that labour-shedding is supposed to occur when marginal firms in a given industry close down operations, workers lose their jobs and then seek employment in the sunrise, better-managed sectors. What is causing serious misgivings in the 1990s is that these static losses are occurring in the leading edge sectors, that the biggest firms are repeaters and that the layoffs are permanent rather than temporary. Statistics Canada has reported that many of the plant closures are directly due to increased competitive pressures. It is estimated that over 800,000 jobs have disappeared from factory closures in Canada since the FTA was signed in 1989. While not every plant closure is a FTA victim, what has changed is that the number of branch plants which have closed and moved their operations back to the US has increased substantially. These kinds of static losses far exceed any other single category. It is estimated that the FTA has cost Canada almost one in five jobs in its manufacturing sector. Compared to the US, Canada has lost four times as many jobs.

There are long-term consequences that result when a firm or industry closes down its operations in a region. Consumers have to foot the bill when whole regions and sectors are marginalized as a result of a country joining a so-called dynamic trade bloc. The region loses its social vitality as well as its economic viability.

The recent closure of the north-shore fisheries in Newfoundland is one of the most dramatic cases in recent times of this phenomenon. The fisheries shutdown affects 30,000 fishermen but more than 120,000 people, in total, if their dependants are included. The shutdown is due to overfishing by the European Community offshore fleets and the absence of any effective conservation measures on Ottawa's part. If the fisheries are not re-established in two years time when the ban ends, this temporary situation becomes a dynamic loss.

Another equally disturbing example of a static loss becoming a dynamic one is in the declining British coal industry. In early 1993, the British government announced its decision to close 51 of the 80 remaining pits, thus instituting a direct employment loss of over 30,000 jobs and an indirect loss of over 120,000 according to mine equipment makers.[6] Similar shutdowns are being discussed for the German coal industry which receives more subsidies than any other single coal industry in the European community. Dynamic losses are also observable in the case of Greece. Despite all the subsidies it has received, the Greek economy remains structurally weak and is less productive than before it joined the EC.

For the EC as a whole, regional inequality has increased as European integration has advanced. Critics argue that the growth in inequality is linked to measures resulting from extending the common market. After a decade in which structural funds are the largest component of the EC's budget – not including the CAP – figures published in 1991 reveal that 40 per cent of the Community's citizens have a per capita income that is more than 40 per cent below the average (CEC, 1991).

Corporate efficiency or social welfare

The failure to close the 'inequality gap' of triple A trade is at the heart of the problem. Trade blocs are driving a permanent wedge between the corporate drive for efficiency and the commitment of governments to maintain high levels of social welfare. So far the pendulum seems to be swinging towards the efficiency end of the scale. Traditional trade theory with its optimistic assumptions about the automatic, flow-through and continual benefits from trade creation sheds little light on any of the above issues.[7] With tariffs at an all-time global low, trade has become a means to another end – two ends, to be precise.

First, the most important 'innovative' part of a trade regime is that it gives new rights to business to invest and divest with fewer restrictions than ever before. Trade regimes demand the end of all restrictions on foreign investment; they require the free movement of capital and the patriation of profile and dividends. They entail the extension of national treatment to foreign capital which will render the entire banking sector more mobile than ever and less responsive to regulatory norms than previously. In NAFTA and the Single European Act, thousands of pages are devoted to changes in investment practices, the liberalization of the banking sector, the deregulation of capital markets as well as other measures designed to make capital a supranational force. The demand to denationalize financial markets in order to accelerate this process has been the most important strategic goal for every trade bloc in the world (de Carmoy, 1990; Spero, 1988; Ohmae, 1990).

None of the foregoing is unexpected or surprising. The fact is that commodity trade which sustained the free trade ideal of the 1960s is no longer the driving force of the world economy in the 1990s. Trade used to be defined as the international exchange of national products (Strange, 1985). It was measured by the volume of exports and imports exchanged between countries. Today's bilateral trade deals are very different creations from the conventional image presented by neo-liberal trade enthusiasts. The 'World Investment Report' for 1992 singles out the importance of foreign direct investment as the most important global force. Trade blocs render such investment even more influential. '[It] has now become the primary means by which a growing number of countries are integrated into the international economy.'[8]

The UN reports that there are now more than 35 000 transnational corporations in existence with more than 150 000 affiliates. The TNCs manage these investment flows worldwide and three-quarters of these take place between developed countries of the Triad, the yen bloc along with its Deutschmark and dollar counterparts. Ten developing countries receive *two-thirds* of all the investment funds from first world countries. The TNCs have become the engines of growth controlling over $200 billion outflows in 1989. The growth of foreign direct investment has been phenomenal in the 1980s, increasing at an annual rate in nominal terms of 34 per cent as countries have opened their economies. Measures such as privatization, trade liberalization and deregulation measures have increasingly made the TNCs, in the words of this important new study, 'the driving force of international transactions'. The unprecedented growth of foreign direct investment has given them exceptional power over their host countries and this has forced governments to tailor their industrial policies to support the investment needs of these global players.[9]

Second, free trade zones want to make full-employment a thing of the past. This requires wholesale changes to labour's entitlements and the Keynesian-Beveridge postwar accord that enabled organized labour throughout the industrial world to make rapid economic gains for the better part of a quarter of a century (Drache and Glasbeek, 1991; Boyer, 1989). While each national approach developed its own trajectory, the essential story was remarkably similar in broad outline in all industrial countries. The state developed an imposing level of involvement in the economy. This permitted labour to be recognized as a partner in the postwar growth coalition. Collective bargaining rights were upgraded and extended; collective bargaining was regularized for core industrial workers, often including the public sector in Western European countries, and the net result supported a flow-on effect by bidding up the price of labour for the unorganized sectors.

The effect of these measures was both immediate and far-reaching. Real wages rose along with productivity gains. The consequence on the standard of living was equally dramatic. Consumer norms were transformed and the Western working class enjoyed an unparalled increase in its standard of living. Along with this reform, the social wage was deepened; social welfare nets were extended and broadened. In the area of industrial strategy, states could and did regulate corporations. Governments through tax and fiscal policy had a primary role in shaping capital markets with interventionist policies. Interest rates and money supply played a crucial role in protecting national economies from global shocks and were an integral part of any industrial policy worth its name (Armstrong, 1991; Esping-Andersen, 1990).

Global free trade vs. the goal of full employment

Now, global free trade has a very different agenda. Wages that were taken out of competition through collective bargaining are to be set in response to market forces (Emerson, 1988). The justification is that wage rigidity is held responsible for slowing technological progress. The theory of the new economics is that when output is thought to be lower than could be achieved by the market mechanism, static inefficiency obtains in labour markets. The leading assumption found in many OECD reports and studies is that unions and workers are deemed to be inflexible in pay negotiations if they ignore the drive to be competitive. The larger issue is not wage flexibility, which could be negotiated between the parties, but private sector power. This is the subtext found in many of the OECD's studies of wage rigidities. The message that is being sent to governments is that management's bargaining position is weakened by existing institutional guarantees which take the wages of the core group of workers out of competition.[10] What the OECD studies propose are new institutional forms to change individual and collective behaviour.

The neo-liberal alternative as developed by Michael Emerson, one of the leading architects of the new Europe, is to replace the state's commitment to full employment with one of high employment. High-employment capitalism requires individuals to stay in the workforce longer, have fewer entitlements, less job security and to pay a larger share of whatever entitlements they receive. In this paradigm shift, new production relations require new social relations and, above all, new institutional arrangements. For these social engineers, the free-trade zone becomes the chosen instrument to force a wholesale change in society and, in particular, redefine the terms and conditions of the capital–labour compromise. This is possible because trade now directly affects the wage structure of all workers in a way which was never before possible.

Wages in an open economy

Factory workers have long understood that they can lose their jobs if their employer chooses to compete with foreign rivals. Traditionally, organized labour has been cautious about the benefits of economic integration. Unions have seen that global trade wars bid down the price of labour because companies are forced to produce more for less. This compels corporations to ask for concessions and demand wage cuts. For unions, this problem is manageable so long as a country's exports and imports are only a small part of its gross domestic product. Once they are a major element and the economy is wide open, the effect is seismic.

Trade dependence is the ratio of exports to total economic product. For most countries in the 1960s it constituted a relatively small part of a country's overall GDP. This left a large part of the domestic economy shielded from international instability. But, this is no longer the case. Trade liberalization has integrated the nation-state into the global economy as never before. As shown in Table 13.1, by 1990 exports equalled 39.7 per cent of Germany's GDP; 25.2 per cent of France's; 47.3 per cent of Portugal's; and 29 per cent of Canada's. The one country which did not fit this profile of growing trade dependence was the US.

But this is no longer so. In the past 20 years the US has caught up. The above figures fail to capture the full extent to which the US manufacturing sector is now subject to international competition. The more revealing measurement is the combined weight of exports and imports of goods as a share of

Table 13.1 Trade dependence of core industrial economies

	[Exports as a percent. of GDP]			
Country	1960	1972	1985	1990
Canada	17.2	22.0	28.4	29.2
United States	5.2	5.8	7.1	10.5
Japan	10.7	10.6	14.6	18.1
West Germany	19.0	20.9	32.4	39.7
France	14.5	16.7	23.9	25.2
Italy	13.0	17.7	22.8	23.8
United Kingdom	20.9	21.8	29.1	29.4
Spain	10.2	14.6	20.1	19.6
Portugal	17.3	27.2	37.3	47.3

Source: OECD National Accounts, vol.1: Main Aggregates 1960–88, Paris 1990.

total US manufacturing output. Using this figure, imports and exports rose from 58 per cent in 1979 of total US manufacturing output to 82 per cent a decade later. Meanwhile average wages and benefits fell 6 per cent after inflation while plant productivity rose 42 per cent (Business Week, 1992). When this happened, imports began to displace workers in industries such as textiles, auto parts and electronics.

In Canada, with its much more open economy, the effects have been considerably greater. In 1990 total industrial production amounted to 77.7 billion dollars. Imports and exports as a share of total Canadian manufacturing output amounted to 287 billion dollars. The drive to be competitive has triggered a brutal round of layoffs and factory closings. Since 1989 unemployment has risen by more than 120 per cent in Ontario, Canada's most heavily industrialized province, that is, from just under 4 per cent of the workforce to more than 10 per cent. If discouraged workers are included in this figure, it is not difficult to conclude that Ontario faces an unprecedented employment crisis. In the NAFTA setting, global free trade is now a job-*killer* (Sharpe, 1993).

On the wages front, the evidence of the way an open economy has fuelled income inequality is equally apparent. Dick Leaner, an economist at UCLA, has calculated that between 1972 and 1985 liberalized trade cost non-professionals $46 billion in lost wages. For professionals, liberalized trade boosted their income by $33 billion. This widening income inequality will likely grow as many of the American industries compete on wages (Business Week, 1992).

Inequality and competitiveness

The US is not the only country where the wage structure is being revised downwards. The welfare state always acted to keep threatening wage pressures in check. As full employment was reached in the 1960s, workers demanded renegotiation of the postwar contract. Low unemployment gave organized labour a powerful instrument. Governments responded with a variety of measures including deflationary policies – Italy, France and Denmark in 1963, West Germany in 1965 and Great Britain and Sweden in 1966. Nordic countries responded with incomes policies of different kinds. Later in the 1970s Britain, France and Italy experimented with institutional reforms to accommodate labour's newly found power. Sweden went furthest in using an active labour market policy to include unions in key decision-making and promised to upgrade social benefits in return for short periods of wage restraint (Esping-Andersen, 1990, pp. 170–73). The net effect of these different regulatory instruments was to bolster the role and importance of the welfare state. It helped keep wage pressures in line with productivity growth and also ensured that such pressures did not feed inflationary price movements.

In the 1990s, institutional accommodation is meant to end social-wage bargains based on long term productivity accords, and to replace them with market-based bargaining for the foreseeable future. Not surprisingly, static income inequality, once kept under control through the tax system, public expenditures and regularized collective bargaining has been transformed into a dynamic form of wage and income inequality in almost every industrial country (Albert, 1991).

In Western Europe, for instance, wages have either remained stagnant for the better part of a decade or have been cut, while personal taxes have increased (Boyer, 1991). What this trend points to and, indeed, highlights is the shift in macroeconomic conditions that enables trade-generated competitive pressures to become a wage-setting mechanism for the entire manufacturing sector. Trade competitiveness along with the introduction of labour-saving technologies makes a potent combination, particularly for countries with decentralized bargaining systems where unions are weak or where the governments in power have no plans to restructure their weak industries other than to open their economies to liberalized trade.

Conclusion

Just two years ago, there was no stopping the momentum behind completion of the single market in Europe or the realization of NAFTA. Now, however, the tide is beginning to turn and second thoughts are in order. So too in Europe. Rising unemployment throughout Western Europe is forcing many Euro-enthusiasts to reconsider the current plan for a single market. This shows that regional trade alliances are reaching their inflexible limits and new strategic initiatives are badly needed to create a stable and results-driven international order.

From this perspective, NAFTA is the least stable of any current trade bloc project on offer. For the economic élites of the three countries involved, the free-trade zone becomes a source of empowerment over the existing nation-state structures. This vision of global markets and the dynamics of this trade bloc must be regarded sceptically because they are so fundamentally different from the economic theory which entices countries to pool their resources to form larger markets. Without a redistribution mechanism, NAFTA is incapable of delivering what it promises: more jobs, cheaper goods and a higher level of well-being.

Notes
1. Market integration has a complex history on both sides of the Atlantic. No one can or should ignore these differences. The point of this paper is to suggest that there has been a dramatic amount of convergence at both the political and macro-economic levels in the mid-1980s. See Drache (1993) for a detailed examination of the forces that have brought this about.
2. Regional and interregional trade amounted to $575.3 billion in 1972 and by 1990 total trade from regional blocs had soared to $3 484 billion worldwide (de la Torre and Kelly, 1992). Free trade zones have risen to such prominence by the end of the 1980s that 41.4 per cent of world trade fell within existing regional trading arrangements. This figure is expected to grow another 5 per cent when new arrangements are concluded between Eastern Europe and the EC as well as between the US and Mexico.
3. This is in part the thesis developed by George Friedman and Meredith Lebard, *The Coming War With Japan*, New York: St. Martin's Press, 1991. As the text clearly shows, I am indebted to them.
4. Friedman and Lebard add that 'this was the essence of the old European imperial system. The question is whether this system will emerge again', p. 197. In many respects, the NAFTA and SEA conform to the basis thrust of their argument. The proliferation of bi-lateral arrangements raises many questions about whether they are the most efficient way to organize trade on a global basis. A recent paper published by the IMF warns that this 'undue emphasis on regionalism undercuts the multilateral trade system' (de la Torre and Kelly, 1992).
5. In the case of the EC, asymmetry also looms as a large and intractable issue. Until German reunification, Germany ran persistent trade surpluses with almost all of its partners. For a discussion of this and other aspects of European integration, see Sbragia (1992).
6. See *Financial Times*, Oct. 17/18, 1992, p. 26.
7. Conventional trade theory underestimates just how complex markets are and shows little understanding of why this mechanism does not respond easily to external shocks. But the real difficulty is of a more fundamental kind, as the rest of the paper makes clear.
8. *IMF Survey*, July 20, 1992. See the actual study, 'World Investment Report' (1992). It is significantly subtitled 'Transnational Corporations as Engines of Growth'.
9. The UN agency warns countries of the need to change their perspective if they are to grasp the totality of this new development in the world economy and to devise policies that are appropriate to it.
10. From a neo-liberal standpoint viewpoint, labour power was also held responsible for the growth of the public sector. The expansion of health, education and welfare services increased the burden of taxation and public spending was singled out to be the principal reason for the slowdown in private sector investment and the fall in productivity growth.

Bibliography

Albert, Michel (1991), *Capitalisme contre capitalisme*, Paris: Seuil.
Armstrong, Philip, Andrew Glwyn and John Harrison (1991), *Capitalism Since 1945*, London: Blackwell.
Best, Michael (1990), *The New Competition Institutions of Industrial Restructuring*, Cambridge, Mass.: Harvard U.P.
Bhagwati, Jagdish (1989), *Protectionism*, Boston: MIT.
Boyer, Robert (1989), 'New Directions in Management Practices and Work Organisation: General Principles and National Trajectories', *Technical Change as a Social Process*, Paris: OECD.
Boyer, Robert (1991), *The Transformations of Modern Capitalism in the Light of the 'Regulation' Approach and Other Political Economy Theories*, Comparative Governance of Economic Sectors Conference, Bellagio, May 29th to June 2nd, revised November 1991, CEPREMAP paper no. 9134.
Business Week (1992), 'The Global Economy: Who Gets Hurt?' August 10.
CEC (1991), *The Regions in the 1990s*, Directorate-General for Regional Policy, Brussels.
Commission of the European Communities (1990), *Employment in Europe 1990*, Directorate-General for Employment, Industrial Relations and Social Affairs, Brussels.
Congress of the United States (1992), *US–Mexico Trade: Pulling Together or Pulling Apart?*, Office of Technology Assessment, Washington.
Cox, Robert (1991), 'The Global Political Economy and Social Choice', in D. Drache and M. Gertler (eds), *The New Era of Global Competition*, Montreal: McGill–Queen's U.P.
Daubler, Wolfgang (1991), *Market and Social Justice in the EC – the Other Side of the Internal Market*, Gutersloh: Bertelsmann Foundation.
de Carmoy, Hervé (1990), *Global Banking Strategy, Financial Markets and Industrial Decay*, Cambridge, Mass.: Basil Blackwell.
de la Torre, Augusto and Margaret R. Kelly (1992), *Regional Trade Arrangements*, International Monetary Fund, Washington, Paper 93.
Drache, Daniel (1993), 'Trade Blocs and Free Trade in the Post-Modern Era: Are NAFTA and the EEC Converging?' York University, January.
Drache, Daniel and Meric Gertler (eds) (1991), *The New Era of Global Competition*, Montreal: McGill–Queen's U.P.
Drache, Daniel and Harry Glasbeek (1991), *The Changing Workplace: Reshaping Canada's Industrial Relations System*, Toronto: Lorimer.
Emerson, Michael (1988), *What Model for Europe?*, Cambridge: MIT Press.
Emerson, Michael and Christopher Huhne (1991), *The ECU Report The Single Currency – and What It Means to You*, London: Pan Books.
Esping-Andersen, Gösta (1990), *The Three Worlds of Welfare Capitalism*, Princeton: Princeton U.P.
Friedman, George and Meredith Lebard (1991), *The Coming War With Japan*, New York: St. Martin's Press.
Grinspun, Ricardo and Maxwell Cameron (eds) (1993), *The Political Economy of North American Free Trade*, Montreal: McGill–Queen's U.P.
Harris, Rick (1989), 'Market Access in International Trade' in Robert M. Stein, *Trade and Investment Relations Among the United States, Canada and Japan*, Chicago: University of Chicago Press.
Hufbauer, Gary (ed.) (1990), *Europe 1992: An American Perspective*, Washington, DC.: The Brookings Institution.
Hufbauer, Gary Glyde and Jeffrey J. Schott (1992), *North American Free Trade Issues and Recommendations*, Washington, DC: Institute for International Economics.
Jackson, Andrew (1993), 'A Social Democratic Economic Agenda for the 1990s: A View from the NDP', *Canadian Business Economics*, **1**(2), Winter.
Jacquemin, Alexis and André Sapir (1988), *European Integration or World Integration?*, 124:1.
Lawrence, Robert A. and Charles L. Schultze (eds) (1990), *An American Trade Strategy: Options For the 1990s*, Washington, DC: The Brookings Institution.

Lawrence, Robert Z. and Robert E. Litan (1986), *Saving Free Trade: A Pragmatic Approach*, Washington, DC: The Brookings Institution.
Nelson, Douglas (1989), 'Domestic Political Preconditions of US Trade Policy: Liberal Structure and Protectionist Dynamics', *Journal of Public Policy* **9**(1), January/March.
Ohmae, Kenichi (1990), *The Borderless World. Power and Strategy in the Interlinked Economy*, New York: Harper Business.
Petrella, Riccardo (1989), 'Globalization of Technological Innovation', *Technology Analysis & Strategic Management*, **1**(4).
Porter, Michael (1991), *Canada At the Crossroads*, Ottawa: Business Council of National Issues and Minister of Supply and Services.
Ruggie, John Gerard (1983), 'International Regimes, transactions, and change: embedded liberalism in the postwar economic order', *International Regimes*, Ithaca: Cornell University Press.
Sbragia, Alberta M. (ed.) (1992), *Euro-Politics Institutions and Policymaking in the "New" European Community*, Washington: The Brookings Institution.
Sharpe, Andrew (1993), 'The Rise in Unemployment in Ontario' paper presented at the Conference on Unemployment: What is to Be Done?, Laurentian University, Sudbury, Ontario, March 26–27.
Spero, Joan (1988–89), 'Guiding Global Finance', *Foreign Policy*, **73**, Winter.
Strange, Susan (1985), 'Protectionism and World Politics', *International Organization*, **93**(2), Spring.
Strange, Susan (1988), *States and Markets*, New York: Blackwell.
Tovias, Alfred (1991), 'A Survey of the Theory of Economic Integration', *Journal of European Integration*, **15**(1).
United Nations (1992), *World Investment Report 1992: Transnational Corporations as Engines of Growth*, New York: United Nations.
Wallace, William (1990), *The Transformation of Western Europe*, London: The Royal Institute of International Affairs, Pinter Publishers.

14 Economic integration: 'gobble-ization' or partnership? The case of Southern Europe
O.F. Hamouda

It is undeniable that in the 1980s and 1990s the world economy has been undergoing an accelerated structural change which is affecting more than ever government sovereignty and the political balance of power in a nation's economic decisions. In order to sustain and accommodate prosperity and technological progress, nations or regions are pressed to integrate economically: to join economic unions, to accept a much greater degree of openness, and to bring down the traditional economic barriers. In the course of economic integration, transformations occur in trade restrictions, tariff barriers, fiscal harmonization, and in the standardization of the means of payment and the means used to transport goods and resources. Western Europe is presently witnessing many of these transformations. It is the pace of its economic transformations and the focus of its regulations or deregulations which are proving to interest economists. Today, economists are attempting to theorize about this currently emerging form of market organization, just as when, during the birth of the socialist countries, much was written about the different welfare theories of the market and planned economies.

In today's world, an economic community in Western Europe, already in the process of being formed, is inevitable. For that reason discussion ought even now to have moved beyond the question of whether an economically trailing or unhappy country should step outside or stay within the community to the analysis of how the new trans-border institution forces smaller or/and trailing nations or regions to cope with a new economic and political restructuring. Since, quite chauvinistically, every member country attempts first to strengthen its own relative position within a union regardless of regional imbalances or relative economic development, how thus can a country as member best take advantage of an economic structure which is most likely not to disappear but to strengthen itself and in which social welfare depends on political bargaining? To assist in answering the question the case of Southern Europe within the EC will serve as an illustration.

The literature on the making of the EC is now abundant. Studies such as Gibson and Tsakatos (1992), Larre and Torres (1991), Bliss and Braga de Macedo (1990), El-Agraa (1990), Molle (1990), Nevin (1990) and others all contain good indications of the future for the Community and member countries, while also revealing different aspects of the difficulties of an economic integration in the making. What seems, however, little discussed in the same literature is the implications of the integration in terms of a theory of social welfare.

It is argued in this chapter that while economic unions undeniably offer economic reward, there are no economic criteria in terms of social welfare that can determine a single suitable distribution of the ensuing gain among member states of the union. For one, the economic evaluation of the so-called 'catch-up' is problematic, and it is not surprising that its discussion is often shifted from economics to politics. Economic union and political union are entangled, and yet, while economic integration forges ahead, political disagreements tend to drag on endlessly. The present study is an exercise which draws from Arrow's discussion of social choice and suggests its implications for welfare economics. Since there is no criterion for resolving the impasse of social choice on purely economic grounds, it is suggested in this study that various scenarios for 'resolution' must be contemplated, each one describing a vision of economic union in which the economic and political strategies of both strong and trailing countries are discussed. Before presenting the scenarios, a brief explanation as to the reasons for a nation wanting to expand its market area and form an economic union or common market are given.

1. The reality of economic integration and political union

The dynamics of market economies are characterized both by domestic and foreign competition to control a viable share of the market and by progress, which each imply a continuous search to improve the efficiency of the production process and the quality of products. These dynamics both cause and are driven by technological changes which constantly affect the labour market, the standard of living, and a country's relative prosperity. One of a nation's domestic economic objectives is constantly to create jobs to compensate for job losses resulting from obsolescence and more labour efficient processes. In a democratic society a high level of unemployment is a potential source of social instability. Thus, there are built into the democratic political system domestic social pressures to restrain employment from dropping. In changing modes of production, the number of new, more efficient, processes must increase more than the number of old processes in order to absorb displaced labour and to accommodate the arrival of the new, young labourers, in which instance production may increase beyond desired demand and the country may find itself either with accumulating surpluses (as is the case in the agricultural and manufacturing sectors) or with the need to limit its size and employment to market circumstances.

Economic unions are often seen as the answer, to allow domestic markets to expand and prosperity to be maintained. They are usually initiated, encouraged and led by the relatively more developed nations. Economic unions are also formed as a response to external pressures, such as the emergence of other competitive, stronger and larger economies. In reaction, a group of countries forms its own free trade bloc, as not to match the external competition would jeopardize both domestic employment and prosperity. Faced with international competition, a country's size and degree of development are strong factors for union: the smaller the country and the less it is developed, the higher its incentive to join. Economic unions are from the start not necessarily composed of countries of equal strength, size, or of similar motivations for joining; they will differ in financial structure, productivity, production activity and so forth.

The births of the EC and NAFTA and the emergence of a Pacific Rim alliance are all examples of unions resulting from both internal and external economic pressures. Once the process of economic integration reaches a global scale, economic blocs will have to strengthen their positions even more. It is to this end that the EC is in the process of defining itself.

In such a dynamic configuration of an economic union in gestation, made up of countries of different economic strengths and different financial structures, many questions arise. First of all, in this context what do 'economic globalization', 'economic integration', 'political union' and 'social welfare' mean? Can economic union be achieved without political union? How can the welfare of individual member states be taken into consideration?

The last quarter of the twentieth century can be characterized by the domination of financial capital over physical capital and the proliferation of financial intermediaries which make the circulation of that capital more fluid than ever. Economic globalization in this context is an acceleration of capital integration beyond national borders. It is the result of ongoing economic forces whereby, first, capital flows where return is highest and, second, resources are combined to capture the largest share of the market. To sustain consolidation in an ever competitive world, firms not only attempt to conquer international markets but to make sure that their presence is felt physically beyond their domestic borders through branch plants or more importantly through mergers. As international economic integration is forming, the old national political institutions are slowly yielding their power to economic force, while new trans-border institutions are being created.

Identifiable with the end of the century is also a transformation in market organization. The market has been defined according to a specific geographic area where a firm operates. Sovereign countries have tended to protect markets confined within their national borders by tariffs, quotas or simply by a ban on foreign competition. Economic unions which allow the expansion of a national market area are causing a change in the concept of market into trading bloc. The ensuing economic integration (whether in the form of customs union, common market, or free trade) is the elimination of barriers to trade and the commitment by a group of nations to facilitating the formation and flow of capital, resources and goods.

None of these economic changes is achieved without altering the existing political setting. An economic union cannot be realized without some form of political union. At the very least, economic union will require a loose political union in which inter-national political intervention eliminates trade barriers and ensures that trade between member countries in the union functions freely. In its strongest or most integrated form, political union becomes a federation in which at least economic and social policies are harmonized through common political institutions. In the case of full political union within an economic union, no economic advantage internal to the union exists for any of its strong members and collective advantage exists for all *vis-à-vis* economic market outside the union.

Although the general structure of *economic integration* might look simple, the dynamics of its various components are terribly complex. Since, however, the potential advantages from it are easy to envisage, emphasis and discussion in the EC is being placed on this form of union. Meanwhile, *political union*, the only source of long range stability for the economic union in Europe, while in principle much simpler to configure (albeit, given the principles of democracy and the ever-present divergences of opinion, often unwieldy to bring to unanimity or consensus), is following slowly behind.

It is the choice in the degree of political union, from loose to strong to full, apparently offered to an economic union which is the source of some difficulty. In the case of the EC, while many economic advances are noticeable, politically there remains much friction and disagreement. For example, it is specified in the Maastricht Treaty of February 1992 that the economic social objectives of the Community are:

> the promotion of employment, improved living and working conditions, proper social protection, dialogue between management and labour, the development of human resources with a view to lasting high employment and the combating of exclusion. (Protocol on social policy: Article 1)

Despite its lofty declarations, the Treaty leaves the implementation of its economic policies vague, witness alone the conflicts in the following statement in the Protocol on social policy, Article 1:

> To this end the Community and member states shall implement measures which take into account the diverse forms of national practices, in particular in the field of contractual relations, and the need to maintain the competitiveness of the Community economy.

and the overriding Maastricht principle of subsidiarity, that action shall be taken:

> if and only in so far as the objectives for the proposed action cannot be sufficiently achieved by the Member States and can therefore, by reason of the scale or effects of the proposed action, be better achieved by the Community (Article 3b).

Since the interpretation of each proposal is highly subjective, it is not quite clear whether the EC ends are to be achieved by market forces or by economic policies, by the Community as a whole or by the members individually.

Two broad possibilities present themselves. One, if the union is very loose politically and market forces are left to determine the outcome, then it does not really matter whether it is the Community or the member states which enforces the free economic practices. The declared social objectives, similar to those usually advocated by conservative political parties, will be the fruits of market efficiency. Since the market presents the 'best' alternative, there is no need for policy intervention and 'national practices' will be superfluous. Political proclamations will prove to be rhetorical or highly symbolic.

Second, if a strong political union is formed, then the declared social objectives will be implemented by economic policies, along the lines of those of a traditional welfare state. Here, it makes a great deal of difference whether the policies are 'better' conceived and enforced collectively by the Community as a whole or diversely by individual states. The distribution of policy responsibility will depend at least on the interpretation of the Protocol on social policy and of the principle of subsidiarity. In the case of divergence of interest, an impasse may arise at the initial level of interpretation of the political proclamations, let alone at the point of policy conception.

Of course, the actual debate within the EC tends to vacillate between tempered versions of these two extreme forms of union. It is thus not surprising to see strong division among supporters of the idea of economic union on how to carry out the process of building the union. Approaches to the process of integration continue to vary from that of immediate liberalization to those of gradualism, and from the policies of Keynes to those of the rigorous monetarists. Also represented are those who maintain that the Community must strengthen itself through an increase in institutions and those who are antagonistic to any more bureaucracy. These discussions are simply a preamble for emerging debates concerning the objectives, role, and power of the European Bank and who will control it, as well as those concerning centralized fiscal policies.

Within this setting, it is the issue of economic welfare in the EC which is of interest. To sum up, in a world where economic progress and technological change are both desirable and irreversible and where the assumption of the overall gain from trade is accepted, custom unions are inevitable, and capital integration is difficult to resist. Doubtless, economic unions do have their economic rewards, usually undisputed if measured according to Paretian criteria. They are, however, undeniably, not always achieved smoothly, without either individual friction and hardship caused by readjustment or the competitive struggle to secure relative regional advantage. Indeed, by joining forces and resources, countries can benefit from economies of scale and size; however, the outcome in terms of the social welfare effect of redistribution in the new economic situation is less certain.

2. Individual preferences, social preferences and social welfare

From modern economic welfare theory, it is well known that in any group where decisions are taken on the basis of different individual preferences, the resulting outcome will not reflect everyone's choice. There is no one economic mechanism that, purely economically, ensures that within any group each one gets a fair share. Not only is the mechanism chosen selected from one of a number of possibilities, but also the recognition and weighting of individual preferences to determine social preferences is based on value judgement. It is the lack of a singular value-free social result from an economic change which shifts the difficult decisions about social welfare from the economic to the political sphere. It is thus not surprising to see the myriad political ramifications emanating from the economic union of the EC.

In his *Social Choice and Individual Values*, Arrow (1963) identifies two forms of preference, individual and social. The discussion here makes use of Arrow by modifying slightly his categories of preferences. In the case of an economic union, one has to distinguish between three types of preferences: individual preference (expressing the choice of the individual as loner), collective preference (expressing the individual's choice influenced by the sense of belonging to a group) and social preference (expressing the preference of the group). The collective preference is most particularly influenced by a group's conditioned level of economic development. This influence on collective preference is particularly striking when member states of a union have diverse cultural habits and customs.

Arrow paints a very bleak theoretical picture for taking individual preferences satisfactorily into consideration at the social level and states clearly:

> If we exclude the possibility of interpersonal comparisons of utility, the only methods of passing from individual tastes to social preferences which will be satisfactory and which will be defined for a wide range of sets of individual orderings are either imposed or dictatorial. (Arrow, p. 59)

Arrow defines a 'satisfactory method of passing from individual tastes (or preferences) to social ones' as a method which takes into consideration everyone's individual preferences such that their ordering is reflected in the social welfare outcome. The attempt here is to see what the implications of the assertion of his possibility (or impossibility) theorem is for the social welfare of individuals and countries in economic unions. This is rather an important issue, for it can easily be argued that it is impossible, when formulating state social decisions, to take all collective preferences into consideration when those preferences are conflicting. For the good of the state, some preferences are left out. When, however, the same argument is applied to a group of nations (as stated above in the EC's principle of subsidiarity), it is difficult to argue that, for the good of the union, in some cases a nation's social preference can be completely left out. To understand the extent of preference conflicts within modern economic unions, one might examine a smaller organization. Recognition of the difficulties raised by the assumption that a union which is formed to take advantage of size can be managed analogously to a smaller social entity is not new. It seems that, as long ago as the ancient Greek philosopher Aristotle, there was awareness of the problems which might arise with changes in the scale of social organization. For Aristotle, smooth economic relations demand minimal conflict in individual and collective preferences. Along the lines of Arrow's possibility theorem, Aristotle thus restricted unencumbered economic relations to the family; in his model, the household of father, mother and children is a well-defined entity in which preferences are conditioned to fit together or are at least harmoniously expressed and accommodated. If the family members differ among themselves, in a setting in which the rules and distribution of responsibility are clear, it is the preference of the head of the household which will prevail.

In noting that 'economics is prior in origin to politics' (*Oeconomica*, 1343a, pp. 14–15), Aristotle expressed the complexity of economic relations for any social organization larger than the extended family. To deal with economic issues at the level of the 'polis' or state, politics is a necessity. Inter-personal relations, economic and social, within the state are unclear, due to the relative indeterminacy of each individual's role within the social group, and are complex, due to scale. Collective preferences cannot be taken for granted from any of the guidelines used within the family: social position, gender, age, etc. Individual preferences cannot be addressed directly by one person who determines social preference. At the level of the state, scale and social ambiguity drive economics into politics. At the level of the mega-polis, the foundation for economics is even more ambiguous. From a pragmatic point of view, since in an economic union there is no single way to optimize social welfare which will be satisfactory to everyone, how is a solution to come about? It seems that a procedure will emerge in the form of one of

'Gobble-ization' or partnership? 193

several possible scenarios which take into account in different manners the diversity of preferences and in each of which only some, not all, preferences will be satisfied. To consider possible scenarios for an economic union such as the EC, take the following theoretical configuration as the model.

Let the union consist of two types of member states: Fatlands of greater relative economic prosperity and Thinlands of lesser relative economic prosperity. While no one Fatland has absolute political dominance in the union, one, Domiland, may have relative economic dominance. All member countries of the union are democracies which became part of an economic community on a voluntary basis and which recognized their respective economic developments as unequal at the union's starting point. Each member state's economy has its own distinct marginal rate of return on capital, rates of technological progress and labour productivity, and consequently its own specific levels of income. The union is one in which all member individuals freely express their preferences; they pursue their own individual interests while at the same time acknowledging that they belong to a union sub-group, a member state, according to which they express their collective preference.

Consider six possible scenarios of economic union relations (Table 14.1). In each a different group would emerge as the decisive one, i.e., the group whose social preference determines the social preference of the union. The decisive group is identified, as are the circumstances which determine that role for the group. An analysis follows to determine which scenario, from the Thinlands' perspective, would yield the best outcome for them. Extreme hypothetical cases for the emergence of a single preference from a decisive group are the following two:

Scenario 1: The decisive group is comprised of one individual from the union. In the entire union, no two individual preferences are alike; the social preference reflects no more than one individual's individual or collective preference. For only one individual are the social and collective and/or individual preferences one and the same. That one individual's preference overrides the preferences of all other members in the community. That person can be either a dictator within a weak political union and impose by force his or her preferences (Scenario 1a) or a leader within a strong political union in which any one member might be chosen to lead (Scenario 1b). While in each case all are obliged to adhere to the social order of the decisive individual, in the case of Scenario 1b there exists a form of consolation: the possibility for each that he or she would be the next chosen leader.

Scenario 2: The entire community of union members (i.e., the countries and the individuals composing them) is the decisive group. Whether out of ideological commitment (Scenario 2a) or religious conviction (Scenario 2b),

Table 14.1 Decisive group

	LOOSE ECONOMIC UNION		STRONG ECONOMIC UNION	
	1 individual	1 Domiland	Many Fatlands	All individuals
LOOSE POLITICAL UNION no compensation	1a Dictatorship	3 Domiland: Domination Thinlands: Free trade	5 Fatlands: Rationalization Thinlands: Customs union	2a Ideological commitment (Utopia)
STRONG POLITICAL UNION compensation	1b Leadership	4 Domiland: Joint venture Thinlands: Free ride	6 Fatlands: Socialization of investment Thinlands: Redistributive policies	2b Religious conviction Redistributive charity

individual preferences dominate | social preferences override individual preferences | collective preferences dominate

Individual preference: expressing the choice of the individual as loner,
Collective preference: expressing the individual's choice influenced by the sense of belonging to a group and
Social preference: expressing the preference of the group.

The collective preference is most particularly influenced by a group's conditioned level of economic development. This influence on collective preference is particularly striking when member states of a union have diverse cultural habits and customs.

all individuals have the same individual and collective preferences, the unanimity of collective preference renders the social preference like that of the collective, and thus social preference reflects both individual and collective preference(s) without misrepresentation. Having accepted their different economic levels within the union as an initial given, the member states proceed within a strong economic union according to Paretian criteria. This is the only scenario that satisfies all five conditions of Arrow's possibility theorem (free triple, responsiveness, independence, citizen sovereignty and nondictatorship; Arrow, pp. 22–31; Quirk and Saposnik, pp. 105–16) and thus in which individual (and collective) preferences are satisfactorily translated into social ones.

Four intermediary and more plausible cases for the emergence of a single preference from a decisive group in an economic union are:

Scenario 3: The most dominant Fatland, Domiland, is the decisive group. For each individual within the union his or her collective preference reflects the sense of belonging first and foremost to a country, rather than to an encompassing union, and thus each country within the union retains a national identity. The social preference of one country, Domiland, is imposed on all other union member countries. This is a case of a minimal or loose economic union and minimal political integration or loose political union among member states. There is overt economic domination of all member states by one country with an unabashed eye to its reaping economic and thus social advantage for itself without considering the preferences of others. All other countries, including the Thinlands, find themselves in a free trade relationship with Domiland in which they can gain, provided they are shrewd and take an active role in areas where they have a comparative advantage.

Scenario 4: Domiland is the decisive group. As in Scenario 3, union member countries retain their national identity through the collective preferences of their citizens, while the social preference of Domiland determines that of the social preference of the union. In this scenario, however, along with the imposition of preference, Domiland, in a stronger political bond, offers economic compensation to one or more member states in order further to bring about its vision of the union. Domiland sees itself as involved in an economic joint venture with the Thinlands which, since they benefit from the infusion of economic compensation, for their part view their relationship to Domiland as an economic free ride. If they take the initiative, this association offers them the opportunity to orient in their favour the thrust of the joint venture.

Scenario 5: Among the group of member countries, there is no one predetermined national decisive group. Since collective preference is expressed by individuals with reference to a nation, member countries preserve the features of their national identity, except for any pre-union restrictions on market forces. Market forces are thus totally free to be subject to and to determine social preferences. Although no national group is pre-determined to be decisive, nonetheless, the market forces of one country will formulate the decisive social preference, and this will undoubtedly be that of one of the Fatlands. This is the effect of a union bound to full economic integration, (i.e., the free mobility of goods and resources) with minimal political interference, in which all members have different economic starting points. Both the Fatlands and Thinlands find themselves within a customs union. The Fatlands will use the situation to rationalize their investment. The Thinlands, for their part, provided their products are lower in cost than those of any other member country, can benefit from their competitive position, if they know how to take advantage of the market opportunity.

Scenario 6: One decisive group emerges within the fused political environment of the union. Along with full economic union, the community has also integrated itself into a strong political union or federation. While nations and regions, former Fatlands and Thinlands, may well preserve a traditional culture, their earlier identities are no longer identifiable through political convention which now reflects collective preferences expressed according to the sense of individuals' belonging predominantly to the union. Both market and political forces are free of being defined by pre-union sub-groups; management of them is effected in newly distinct divisions within the federated union. The group whose social preferences become those of the community acquires its decisive role through special interest dominance in the context of economic policies coordinated and harmonized union-wide. In this scenario, due to the political commitment to socializing investment throughout the union, disadvantaged regions (probably among the former Thinlands), with the possibility of a political voice, will aspire to benefit from redistributive policies.

When one is tempted to ask which of these scenarios most closely resembles that of the EC, it is perhaps most surprising to discover that there is no one answer.

3. Visions of political union in the EC

In reflecting on the six scenarios, both Scenarios 1 and 2 merit only fleeting comment as to why they are not really in the running as scenarios for the EC. Scenario 2 is a virtual impossibility. There is nothing binding to sustain the unanimity of collective preferences even if they stem from a shared ideological commitment; long-term unity of preferences is thus totally utopian. If the union-wide unanimity derives from religious conviction, the bond might be reinforced through the 'compensation' of redistributive charity. As Arrow (1963, pp. 1–2) has pointed out, however, regardless of 'compensation', sustaining agreement in the interpretation of religious doctrine is extremely difficult. How often will even three individuals opt unanimously for one preference, let alone a country and group of countries!

Scenario 1 requires a few more words to dismiss. Aside from the fact that it bars any combining of forces among individuals, an unlikely eventuality, the spectre it presents of an extremely strong leader or dictator in Europe is foreboding and reminiscent enough to surmise that it would be the vision of the EC for only a very small group of individuals, and certainly not of one whole European country. After the elimination of Scenarios 1 and 2, surprise at the current discord over a vision of the EC might further be tempered by the recognition that indeed as long as state distinctions still stand, each EC country would like to be itself, or at least to be a part of, the decisive group. It is that drive to have one's own national social preference determine the social preference of the union which fuels the contemplation of different scenarios as visions for the form of economic union of the EC.

Of the six scenarios, not all are considered to be equally satisfactory to each of the different countries of the EC. Scenario preference seems to depend highly on the relative economic and political power of the different countries within the EC. Fine distinctions in the economic and political relative positions of countries in the union have an apparently greater effect in determining scenario preference among the EC Fatlands than among the Thinlands. The scenario preferences of Fatlands differ more widely among themselves than do those of Thinlands, and a Fatland's particular vision, be it that of Germany, France, or England, for example, has thus far been more adamantly pronounced and defended than the chosen visions for the EC of the group of Thinlands, Greece, Spain and Portugal.

Depending on the Fatland, Scenario 3, 5 or 6 is a possible choice. Germany, to start, has appeared to have favoured either Scenario 3 or 5, depending on the security of its own economic situation. At times when it has anticipated remaining strong both within world markets and relative to the other EC countries, its confidence of risking little under the full rein of market forces seems to have led it to push for Scenario 5. At other times when its relative strength seems to falter as it has under the strain of reunification, Germany appears to press to retain its dominance, along the lines of Scenario 3's minimal collective economic and political responsibility, which would permit it to raise interest rates unilaterally as it did very recently.

As a Fatland, England's internal political forces as well as internal and external economic conditions appear to have led it to see Scenario 5 as the best for its state interests. Its interpretation of subsidiarity, with great emphasis on the ability of the member states to handle independently most of the political/social issues confronting Europe, bears witness to its intent on a loose political union and rationalization of its economy.

France, as especially the more socialized of the EC Fatlands, entered the union with a state economy so very determined by national political forces that its vision of the EC seems also to have become one of full political and economic integration. At the same time, since full political integration entails relaxing not only state geographical frontiers but also the reinforcement of national identity by political territorial definition, France and other member states are uneasy about the effect of political integration on the very programmes which are so much a result of their state politics. Acceptance of Scenario 6 seems thus, for each of the countries which might advocate it, to mean adoption of the very concept of political and economic integration which currently reigns in each of their countries. In general, Scenario 6 represents the socialization of investment for the Fatlands, and beneficial redistributive policies for the Thinlands. Specifically, Scenario 6 is as individual as the particular countries which envisage its effectiveness. By those who adopt it, that one scenario is being divided into as many sub-scenarios as there are EC member countries.

What scenarios then are the choices of the EC Thinlands, Greece, Spain and Portugal? Will any and every scenario lead to 'gobble-ization'? Like each of the Fatlands, each of the Thinlands, whether Greece, Spain or Portugal, would like to be, at least, part of the decisive group. They are each, however, quite aware of the fact that this role could not be obtained based on the strength of their economies. In other words, they recognize that a conception of the EC in which one of them would play the part of Domiland is excluded from the start. The present economic situation of the Thinlands is revealing. The relative position of Fatlands and Thinlands in terms of the GDP per head has remained much the same over the period 1970 to 1990 with Germany leading the way. What is more striking is that this relationship has remained the same for each Thinland even after it joined the EC (Greece, 1981, Spain and Portugal, 1986). Admittedly the economies of Spain and Portugal appear to have experienced a slight acceleration in the growth of their GDP since they joined, but this is definitely not the case for Greece.

Does this mean, however, that a scenario with a Domiland would be rejected? Not necessarily, for one or more of the Thinlands might find either its social preference echoed or even taken into consideration. The social preferences of Domiland and Thinland might coincide, and thus Scenario 3 would be an acceptable, though precarious, vision of the EC for a Thinland. Scenario 4 would be a somewhat less uncertain option, for, since it is seen by Domiland as a joint venture between the two countries, it includes both political recognition of, and economic action in the form of compensation based on, the social preferences of Thinland. The measure of the consideration of Thinland's preferences and of Thinland's satisfaction within Scenario 4 would be the degree of compensation or free ride offered to the Thinland by Domiland.

The European Thinlands might also consider Scenarios 5 and 6 as possible visions for the EC. Since Scenario 5 would force them to adjust to complete market freedom without political encumbrances, with any one of the Fatlands holding forth, their role within the economic union might be effectively no different from that under Scenario 3. Anyone of the Fatlands, economically stronger at the outset of the union, would, as Domiland, be able to dominate the Thinlands in turn.

Scenario 6 might be seen to hold the most promise for the EC Thinlands. Much of their chance to be a part of the decisive group rests upon their preferences being recognized. In the absence of a particular economic advantage a Domiland might reap from listening to a Thinland, as in Scenario 4, the only way the Thinlands are likely to be heard within an economic union is if that union also integrates itself politically. There is, of course, no mention within Scenario 6 about the distribution of political power and therefore, no guarantee that the Thinlands would acquire any power to speak of in such a new federation. Nonetheless, as in countries today where some of the social preferences are those originally expressed by very small political parties, such as the preferences of the Greens at their beginnings, their preferences can frequently be allied in some way so as to render their voice powerful within a decisive group. Hence, Scenario 6 might be seen ultimately to speak best to the interests of Thinlands within the EC.

Conclusion
Given that there is no way of satisfying everyone's individual or collective preference, social preference will always reflect the preference of a subgroup. At any time, in any economic union of heterogeneous nations it is therefore unlikely that the union's preference will reflect that of all member nations. In an economic union, economic strength is the most crucial factor in determining social preference. Thinland member nations will thus always find themselves at a disadvantage, if not in the discussion process of political decisions, then undoubtedly in the shaping of economic trends.

The various scenarios discussed in this Chapter present fundamental differences in terms of both economic organization inside the union and its relation vis-à-vis the rest of the world. From the perspective of the economic welfare of the Thinlands, it is, however, not sufficient to push for the one which offers the strongest political representation, say, either Scenario 5 or 6, or to side with those advocating the most promising economic advantages, as in, say, Scenario 3 or 4. No matter which scenario a Thinland supports the long-term beneficial outcome will depend on whether or not the Thinland can take advantage of the economic structure of the union to become a Fatland. If an economic union remains a community of independent nations, then different Thinlands may find it advantageous to choose to support different scenarios. Their choice will depend on their size, their economic structure and strength, and their current economic relations with other member states.

If on the other hand, a scenario of strong political union, such as Scenario 6, is pursued to the limit and the union becomes a federation in which the national level of existing governments is removed or drastically weakened, collective and subsequently social preferences expressed on a basis of national differences might disappear. The issue of preference differences in the decision process would still remain, however, as it does within any political union, such as a single nation. Arrow's dilemma would reappear in a manner closer to its initial form. In the case of the federation scenario, the Thinlands will simply be gobbled up by the union, and the decisive group will ultimately reflect the collective preference of a trans-European interest group. Division within the union will no longer be along national lines and between Fatlands and Thinlands, but rather between the strata of Fatgroups and Thingroups.

Bibliography

Abramovitz, M. (1986), 'Catching up, Forging ahead, and falling behind', *Journal of Economic History*, **XLVI** (2), June.
Aristotle (1921), *Oeconomica*, tr. E.S. Forster, *The Works of Aristotle*, gen. ed. W.D. Ross, Oxford: Clarendon Press.
Arrow, K.J. (1963), *Social Choice and Individual Values*, Second Edition, New Haven: Yale University Press.
Bergson, A. (1938), 'A Reformulation of Certain Aspects of Welfare Economics', *Quarterly Journal of Economics*, **LII**, February, 310–34.
Bliss, C. and J. Braga de Macedo (1990), *Unity with Diversity in the European Economy: The Community's Southern Frontier*, Cambridge: Cambridge University Press.
El-Agraa, A.M. (ed.) (1990), *Economics of the European Community*, Third Edition, London: P. Allan.
Gibson, D.H. and E. Tsakotos (eds) (1992), *Economic Integration, Financial Liberalization: Prospect for Southern Europe*, London: Macmillan.
Larre, B. and R. Torres (1991), 'Is Convergence a Spontaneous Process? The Experience of Spain, Portugal and Greece', *OECD Economic Studies*, No. 16, Spring.
Molle, W. (1990), *The Economics of European Integration (Theory, Practice, Policy)*, Aldershot: Dartmouth.
Nevin, E. (1990), *The Economics of Europe*, London: Macmillan.
Quirk, J. and R. Saposnik (1968), *Introduction to General Equilibrium Theory and Welfare Economics*, New York: McGraw-Hill.

15 Peripherality and divergence in the EC: the need for industrial policy

Philip Arestis and Eleni Paliginis

1. Introduction

The theoretical view on divergence within the area of Political Economy, as it relates to capital accumulation and economic development in the European Community (EC), is the subject-matter of this chapter. The divergence view is closely related to what have come to be known as Fordism and Peripheral Fordism (see also Arestis and Paliginis, 1993).

This Chapter argues that the present economic structures within the EC are such that divergence rather than convergence should be expected. We argue the case by first looking at the theoretical developments underpinning the possibility of divergence before we look at the evidence. A final section concludes and summarizes the argument.

2. Fordism and Peripheral Fordism

The Fordist thesis refers to the industrial structures developed in the core European countries in the postwar period. It is characterized by large multi-plant enterprises taking advantage of economies of scale provided by big markets. This concentration was relevant both in terms of industrial production and employment and was thought to be remarkable because of its size and consistency in many countries, especially in the EC (Keeble et al., 1983). A historical compromise manifested itself in the relationship between capital and labour. Productivity gains produced steady improvements in workers' real incomes, institutionalized as an 'inflation plus' norm for wage deals. The Keynesian welfare state at the same time expanded the social wage along with the private wage. The institutions of collective bargaining, the relation between banks and industry and the role of the state are central issues in Fordism. This 'inflexible' Fordist regime leads to divergence. Dynamic economies of scale, the importance of productivity growth and the specialization ensured by the creation of new markets, clearly implied 'cumulative causation'. A clearer distinction between core and periphery countries within Europe developed at this time.

The late 1960s crisis of the Fordist regime of accumulation is viewed as the result of *intensive* accumulation which led to the collapse of *productivity* and ultimately *profitability*. Thus Fordism required modification by way of transition from one regime of accumulation and mode of regulation (that is institutional support) to another. Mass production, mass consumption and a monopolistic form of regulation (Keynesian policies and collective bargaining), all these three elements combined produced Fordism. The crisis of Fordism is, then, followed by a *transition* period which is characterized by both new structural tendencies and continuities with the previous regime of accumulation. Mass production and mass consumption are still very much in evidence but in a modified form: there is, now, the internationalization of Fordism spread by the activities of transnational banks and multinationals, along with the persistence of monopolistic types of regulation in the form of financial and industrial 'cities of capital'. New types of information and communication technologies emerge along with vertical disintegration in production.

The crisis in Fordism caused by the collapse of profitability is seen as responsible for an emerging new pattern of capitalist development. Multinationals, in particular, in their attempt to recover profitability, sought refuge in the New Industrialised Countries, the Peripheral Countries, where low-wage and high-productivity possibilities existed. This development is precisely what Lipietz (1987) has labelled 'Peripheral Fordism'. It is Fordism in as much as it involves intensive accumulation and mass consumption, especially of consumer durables. And it is peripheral in that the centres of 'skilled manufacturing' and engineering are not located in these countries. Exports of cheap manufacturing goods to the centre are the other dimension of the local markets. So, an obvious difference between Peripheral Fordism and Fordism itself is that, unlike the latter, the former cannot regulate demand or indeed adjust it to local Fordist branches, given that it is world demand that is involved in this case. So that, while in the traditional Fordism the link of consumption to productivity was met by monopolistic regulation of wage relations, in Peripheral Fordism this came about through increases in the income of the middle classes. Industrialization is achieved through imports from the centre which are paid for by exporting cheap manufacturing goods to the centre. But ultimately Peripheral Fordism should only be contemplated 'when growth in the home market for manufactured goods plays a real part in the national regime of accumulation' (Lipietz, 1987, p. 80). The finance of Peripheral Fordism has taken the form of borrowing on the international capital and money markets. Such financing in the pre-Peripheral Fordist period had been channelled through direct investment. Following the emergence of Peripheral Fordism, however, financing through direct investment became inadequate and international bank finance began to replenish the shortfall. This development gave rise to what has been known as the *international credit economy*, with some key 'capital cities' around the world, such as London, Frankfurt, New York, etc.

The section that follows attempts to relate these theoretical developments to the 'stylized facts' of European peripheral development.

3. Stylised facts and EC peripherality

Greece, Ireland, Portugal and Spain are considered the peripheral countries of the EC. Their 'peripherality' is determined by a lower than average per capita GDP, a large and inefficient agricultural sector and a late developing industrial sector, partly controlled by multinational capital. Convergence between members, in terms of per capita GDP, is what the EC Commission was set to achieve. Per capita GDP, in 1992, as forecast by the EC Commission is expected to be, in Greece 52.1 per cent of the EC average, in Ireland 68.9 per cent, in Portugal 56.3 per cent and in Spain 79.9 per cent.

One important determinant of the degree of development of the European economies is given by the sectoral distribution of labour. In all the peripheral EC countries the agricultural sector is large and inefficient. Adverse historical events prohibited these countries from developing their industrial sector and kept them as agrarian ones. In Greece, employment in agriculture represents 26.6 per cent of employment, in Portugal 18.9 per cent, in Ireland 18.9 per cent, and in Spain 13 per cent, while the EC average is 7 per cent. The high level of employment in this sector is not the result of a natural endowment, but the result of lack of opportunities in alternative ones. This is shown by the disproportionate contribution of this sector to GDP.

The existing indigenous industrial structure, although not homogeneous in all the peripheral countries, is either characterized by a labour intensive industrial sector, concentrating in sectors of low demand such as food, textiles, clothing and paper (Greece, Portugal), or by the domination of foreign multinationals. The former is characterized by a large number of small size companies, experiencing low levels of productivity. In Greece, 40 per cent of the employment is generated in units of less than ten individuals and the average size of the firm in 1986 was 4 to 5 employees (Katseli, 1990). Similarly, in Spain, in the same period, 80 per cent of companies in the manufacturing sector were employing less than 10 workers and only 0.2 per cent more than 500 (Vinals et al., 1990). A few capital intensive industries, such as oil refineries and cement, were relatively large both in terms of output and employment. These were of an import-substitution nature, often dominated by multinationals and protected from outside competition by high tariff walls. The incorporation of these countries in the EC removed the primary incentives and weakened these industries.

Turning our attention to investment, we observe that in 1992 the levels of investment in Portugal and Spain were 26 per cent and 24.1 per cent of GDP respectively against a 19.6 per cent average for the core EC countries. This represented a positive step towards convergence between core and periphery countries. However, this period coincided with a decrease of the price of oil and was particularly stimulated by the expansion experienced by core countries. Higher levels than the present ones were experienced by both countries in the 1960s, 1970s and, indeed, early 1980s. In both Ireland and Greece investment was lower during the 1980s than in the core countries and lower than in previous periods.

The increase in investment in the mid-1980s had, as an effect, an increase in industrial production in the peripheral countries, bringing it above the EC average, thus creating optimistic claims about a fundamental shift in economic structures. This increase in industrial production was primarily the result of MNEs and not of domestic activities. The entry of Portugal and Spain into the EC stimulated the inflow of multinational capital. Although this is a welcome increase, there are pitfalls attached, as the transfer of production from domestic to MNE capital weakens the role of domestic capital, reduces the ability of the government to regulate the economy and further intensifies instability, given the foot-loose nature of these companies.

As a result of the structural problems of the peripheral countries, unemployment and underemployment are serious problems and are expected only to worsen. In Spain and Ireland unemployment is consistently higher than the EC average. Although there was some fall in the unemployment rate in Spain in 1992, a 15.5 per cent level is still unacceptably high. In Ireland the rate for 1990 was 15.6 per cent, expected to rise to 18.1 per cent in 1992. The lower rates registered in Greece and Portugal can be explained by the lack of welfare benefits which hinders registration of unemployment. Further, underemployment or parasitic employment in both the agricultural and the state sector is widespread in both countries. Lack of possibilities for work in the industrial sector inflates the numbers of self-employed individuals and the effort of the state not to allow unemployment to rise beyond an acceptable level creates a large and bureaucratic state sector.

As a result of the structural problems of these economies and the opening of markets, there are serious effects on the balance of payments. There is an increased dependence on the core countries for imports, both of capital and consumer goods. In the case of Greece the gap between imports and exports more than doubled during EC membership, while for Portugal and Spain the gap between 1986 and 1990 increased almost five times. Capital movements smoothened this event, but a large proportion of these were portfolio and real estate investment (Spain and Greece), while the repatriation of profits by far outstripped the inflow of capital (Ireland). Thus, membership of the EC has so far had both a trade creation and trade diversion effect. Trade within the EC increased and it was diverted away from traditional markets to the new EC partners. Trade creation, in the manufacturing sector, benefited the core countries and led, in many cases, to the destruction of already weak indigenous manufacturing sectors in the peripheral ones.

4. European peripherality and EC policies

Convergence is the ultimate aim of the EC, as was explicitly claimed in Maastricht. Regional policies and later the Structural Funds aimed to decrease discrepancies between states and regions. In this section we examine the existing EC policies and consider whether they set the prerequisites for the economic development of the periphery.

Experience from both the old and the newly industrialized countries, as well as the European periphery, shows that the manufacturing sector has consistently been the main contributor to economic growth. The economic development of the periphery necessitates:

(a) The decline and restructuring of the agricultural sector.
(b) The development of the manufacturing sector.
(c) The education/training of the labour force with special emphasis on young people and women and the retraining of part of the existing working force.

In a new integrated approach to regional policy the Structural Funds, which include the European Regional Development Fund (ERDF), the European Social Fund (ESF) and the Guidance section of the European Agricultural Guarantee and Guidance Fund (EAGGF), were expected to play a central role. They were reformed in 1988 and their funding was to be doubled by 1993. To increase their efficiency, the Funds concentrated in the most needy regions in accordance with five objectives set by the Community for dealing with aspects of restructuring, both of the peripheral regions and of the regions of the developed countries suffering from de-industrialization.

An important hurdle to the successful use of EC convergence policies is the existence of the Common Agricultural Policy (CAP). Its size and regressive nature act against any real changes. Approximately 60 per cent of the EC budget is spent guaranteeing farmer's incomes. This represents hand-outs to farmers and does not necessarily involve any restructuring of the agricultural sector. Although the main recipients of the Guarantee Fund are the rich farmers of France and the Netherlands, peripheral countries such as Ireland and Greece have also benefited substantially. In 1990, contributions from the Guarantee part of the EAGGF represented 74 per cent of total EC contributions in Ireland, 64 per cent in Greece, and 57 per cent in Spain, though they totalled only 30 per cent in the case of Portugal. The rest was mainly contributions through the Structural Funds. The bulk of EC contributions are not directed towards a long-term restructuring of the peripheral economies and, further, the existence of large payments in the form of guaranteed prices creates a disincentive for real changes.

In contrast to the CAP, more positive attitudes towards the development of regions are adopted by the EC through the ERDF, the ESF and the Guidance section of EAGGF. However, the quantitative constraints on these Funds and the lack of more direct intervention in the development of the manufacturing sector prohibit any serious restructuring of these economies. The contribution of the EC to the development of the secondary and tertiary sectors appears in the Community Support Framework, CSF, which represents programmes co-financed by the EC through the Structural Funds (SF) and the national governments. The emphasis in all of them is the development of the infrastructure. Provisions such as road construction, and sewage are necessary, but not sufficient, prerequisites for the development of these countries. These provisions are compatible with the neo-liberal attitudes of the 1980s. They provide a basis, leaving the rest to the private sector. The lack of infrastructure was neither the only, nor the main, reason holding back investment.

In recognition and compensation for the negative effects arising from Maastricht and the Single European Market, a Cohesion Fund was created and directed to regions or states with a per capita GDP of less than 90 per cent of the EC average, the main effect of which will again have to be on infrastructure. As the main effect from the Single Market will be on the manufacturing sector of the peripheral economies (as the latter are weak and unable to compete) compensation for these negative effects with funds which primarily affect the infrastructure do not represent a true recompense and do not lead to convergence.

It has been suggested that the development of the manufacturing sector is to be considered the main and only way for the development of the peripheral EC countries. The attraction of multinational capital was considered as an alternative to the development of domestic capital. They were expected to have significant effects on the levels of employment and output and on the balance of payments. Inflow of foreign direct investment (FDI) in these countries increased substantially, but at different rates, in the 1980s, reflecting the peculiarities and different advantages offered by the peripheral countries. In Spain and Portugal a substantial increase in FDI coincided with full membership in the EC. Relatively cheap labour, particularly in Portugal, proximity to the markets, stable domestic policies and an improvement in the rate of return in capital, led to the inflow of FDI. Ireland, having the advantage of a well-educated workforce and with English as the spoken language, had always been particularly attractive to both non-EC and EC MNEs. Nonetheless the capital intensive nature of FDI in Ireland led to high levels of unemployment, while high levels of profit repatriation and serious dependence on the MNEs created an unstable outcome. The most disadvantaged country is Greece. Its geographical isolation and continuous economic and political problems and social unrest had a negative effect on the MNEs. The inflow of MNEs in the 1970s was largely of an import substitution nature and the removal of tariff barriers, together with an increase in wages in the early 1980s, raised the real unit cost of labour and led to a decline in FDI.

MNEs could be a source for the development of the manufacturing sector in a country, as experience from South East Asia shows. Nonetheless, this development is fraught with problems. It poses problems of macroeconomic control over the economy, such as the efficacy of fiscal and monetary policy, the level of employment, conditions of service, the movement of profits, etc. The foot-loose nature of these companies, and the constant need to compete with Eastern Europe and the rest of the developing world through low wages, creates an undesirable basis for development. However, multinationals could assist the development of the peripheral regions of EC if their activities are centrally controlled and they are a part of an overall plan of development. The expectation for development in the EC should be based on active industrial policies and within this context the MNEs could play a complementary role.

The importance of developing 'niches' for small to medium enterprises (SMEs) may be considered as an alternative or complementary instrument for growth, along the lines of post-Fordist theories. The development of the 'third Italy' is an example of such possibilities. Although it is true that 'third Italy' developed along these lines, the existence of close linkages with a developed industrial North and the availability of both skilled and unskilled labour were some of the special conditions which allowed this development. SMEs have a role to play in a developmental process. Their size and flexibility may be better suited to local uniqueness, but because of their inability to generate large economies of scale, they cannot become an alternative to large enterprises. Their role is mainly complementary.

The 'nicheing' of the market requires a labour force possessing education and technical skills. High current levels of unemployment are considered to be the result of low levels of education. Nonetheless, with the exception of Portugal, years spent on education and the number of students in higher education are not substantially different from the core countries. In 1987/88, in Germany, 13 per cent of the population were full-time students in higher education, 9 per cent in Greece, 10 per cent in Spain, 6 per cent in Ireland, 5 per cent in Portugal, 6 per cent in Britain and 9.7 per cent in France. Nonetheless these aggregate statistics do not examine the quality and the marketability of these skills. The extension of education and the improvement of educational standards are a necessary, but not sufficient, requirement for escaping the vicious circle of Peripheral Fordism. Education and training could bring desirable effects only if they are a part of balanced development.

Lack of opportunities for people to use their talent within their own communities will involve the migration of young educated and skilled people from the peripheral countries, thus negating the desirable social effects that education and training could have on these regions.

5. Conclusions

EC contributions aim not only to overturn years of underdevelopment in the peripheral areas but also to cushion the effects that the Single Market and EMU are expected to bring. The withdrawal of protection, the opening of markets and the loss of domestic monetary policy could have detrimental effects on them. Yet, despite the concern for peripheral countries the prospects for development are rather poor.

The development of these regions depends on the development of the manufacturing sector as a result of all the effects mentioned earlier. This development has to be based primarily on the development of indigenous forces. Regulation failed in the 1970s because national states could not reinforce it within their own boundaries. The existence of large multinational capital, mainly from the USA and Japan, together with the existence of a plethora of different customs and habits, will make it very difficult, at least in the immediate future, for the EC to play the regulatory role that national states were playing in the 1950s and 1960s. Yet this control is a precondition for satisfactory regulatory policies either on a national or 'super national' level.

These countries have not experienced the Fordist type of development at a national level. The belief that structures such as SMEs could produce the springboard for their development is optimistic. Development will have to be based on the advancement of the manufacturing sector, taking into consideration local uniqueness. Taylorism would not need to be a constituent of any form of production of this type. Modern technology could bring some improvement through the introduction of more flexible forms of production.

The limited programme for industrial development within the EC context and an excessive reliance on market forces do not create a basis for a sound development. Yet, until there is an improvement in the real economy of these countries we will not be able to see improvements in rates of inflation and the balance of payments. The demands for convergence by 1999, as set out in the Maastricht agreement, will not be met.

References

Arestis, P. and E. Paliginis (1993), 'Financial Peripherality and Divergence in the EC', *Journal of Economic Issues*, June.

European Economy (1991), 'Strengthening Growth and Improving Convergence', EC Commission, December.

Katseli, L. (1990), 'Economic Integration and the enlarged European Community', in C. Bliss and J. Braga de Macedo (eds), *Unity with Diversity in the European Economy: The Community's Southern Frontier*, Cambridge: Cambridge University Press.

Keeble, D., P. Owens and C. Thompson (1983), 'The Urban–Rural Manufacturing Shift in the European Community', *Urban Studies*, 20.

Lipietz, A. (1987), *Mirages and Miracles*, London: Verso.

Vinals, J. et al. (1990), 'Spain and the "EC cum 1992" shock' in C. Bliss and J. Braga de Macedo (eds), *Unity with Diversity in the European Economy: The Community's Southern Frontier*, Cambridge: Cambridge University Press.

16 The 'sensitive issues' of the EC-1992 programme and US business
Mike Pournarakis

The reaction of the US business world to the EC-92 programme of market unification came with a considerable time lag. Indeed it took three years, after the signing of the *White Paper* in 1985, for American firms to respond seriously to the Single Market programme. The Single European Act that followed in 1986 did not convince the world that the EC countries were actually going to abdicate important government powers to Community authorities. It would take too much of a dramatic change for the EC to shake off the inertia on integration that prevailed in the previous fifteen years. It was actually the Second Banking Directive in 1988 that triggered a reaction mechanism by the US transnationals which, all of a sudden, visualized the possibility of a 'Fortress' Europe with EC-wide protection and discrimination against American firms. In the original proposal of the Second Banking Directive the idea of 'mutual recognition' was carried too far concerning participation of non-EC countries in banking activity in the Community and called for a *'mirror image'* type of reciprocity which could result in discrimination against the United States. In response to the US firms' protest, the original proposal was substantially modified to require *national treatment* type of reciprocity. By April 1989, when the modified Second Banking Directive came out, United States businesses were convinced about the intentions of the EC to make compromises in order to cooperate with the United States.

The positive attitude towards EC-92 by US business and government authorities after mid-1989, is reflected in the handling of what could be termed 'sensitive' issues in US–EC relations. In what follows I will look into some of these issues in order to assess the expected incidence of the relevant directives of the EC-92 programme on US trade and investment activity in the European Community.

The issue of standards
Complying with product standards set by a country could be a serious problem faced by exporters. A key issue in the EC-92 programme is that of standards. More than half of the directives originally programmed in the 1985 *White Paper* pertain to standards. Standards harmonization by the European Community could potentially develop into a source of barriers to trade

and discrimination against non-EC countries. The adoption by the EC of standards not used internationally could result in export losses by these countries. It makes sense, therefore, that the US firms hedge against unexpected developments while at the same time they demand representation in the standardization activities of the European Community.

Obviously, harmonization of standards and adherence to it by the 12 EC countries is of key importance for intra-EC trade. The bad experience of the EC with the standards issue up to the mid-1980s led to the adoption of the so-called 'New Approach' according to which legally marketable products in one EC country automatically gain admission to markets of all other member countries. The 'New Approach' abstained from developing standards (rewriting them) through the Commission for individual products. This function is performed by the three non-Commission organizations: The European Committee for Standardization (CEN), the European Committee for Electrotechnical Standardization (CENELEC) and the European Telecommunications Standards Institute (ETSI). These organizations, on the basis of EC directives, which define broad requirements for categories of products, draft the standards to meet the requirements for each product. In this sense, the 'New Approach' is more flexible in that manufacturers are only required to legally meet the EC directives that pertain to *general* or *essential* requirements such as safety, health, and the environment. As for the conformity with specific standards for individual products the product is no longer bound by technical specifications included in EC directives as in the 'Old Approach'. Instead, producers have a choice of standards developed by the private sector which function as market codes rather than binding regulations.

West European countries are officially represented in the Standardization Committees with members of their government with voting privileges. How open is standard setting to the private sector outside the EC? Exporters consider the standards setting process a 'European affair'. Since United States firms have no input during the drafting period they are in no position to acquire promptly information on new standards. The lack of transparency and direct contact caused concerns among US firms about the EC's standards programme. Reactions by US businesses ranged from cautious optimism to fears that the EC used standards to effect a pro-Community and anti-United States policy.[1] The time lag involved in the access of information would make it difficult for US firms to make the required adjustments. Furthermore, the standards setting (private) organizations might adopt standards other than the ones used internationally. It is possible that, in the interest of standards harmonization, certain companies may promote EC-wide adoption of their own standards, securing in this way privileges for themselves and discrimination against US firms.

No doubt the 'New Approach' in standardization presents many advantages over the old one both for the EC member states and the rest of the world. Although complete harmonization may not occur in the near future, for the most part foreign firms will no longer be faced with different standards for each member state. In effect the standards on specific products of the 12 member countries are equivalent as long as the products imported into the EC satisfy the basic or general requirements which are adopted, by vote, in the EC. No longer will the United States exporters have to meet the requirements of each of the EC states. Unified standards in the Single Market present a definite advantage for the United States firms already operating in the EC. Harmonization of standards opens up substantial possibilities to economize in cost through upgrading scale production in a fashion similar to the one used in the United States. Especially large firms already in existence in the EC are expected to capitalize on the advantage of EC-wide product standards and realize substantial economies of scale.

US industry in response to the 'New Approach' as revised and presented in the final 'Green Paper' supports the overall objective. The reservations expressed[2] on matters of transparency and lack of input by non-EC countries were responded to by the EC. In cooperation with the American National Standards Institute (ANSI) and the International Standards Organization (ISO) the EC standards section organizations immediately make available information on developments and proposals on the standards issue. Furthermore, the ISO provides the liaison for proposals, requests and comments on standards activity in the EC.

Finally, on the issue of the need for standards-internationalization there is convergence both as a matter of principle and in terms of implementation. The US Department of Congress admits that 'there is a clear commitment to international standardization' on both sides.[3] Currently cooperation of EC and US standards bodies 'focuses on setting priority areas for developing international standards, speeding the standards development process, establishing implementation and monitoring procedures for these standards and setting up an information system easily accessible to manufacturers from the EC and the United States'.

Testing and certification
The issue of standards is closely related to that of 'Testing and Certification'. The latter refers to the procedures to ensure the conformity of products to the agreed standards. As in the case of standards, the 'New Approach' aims at unifying different national product certification requirements. In the past, separate approvals from national and local regulatory authorities led to duplication of tests and documentation causing unnecessary delays and costly undertakings. The Single Market programme, through a set of directives, advances the replacement of national product certification procedures with a simplified single set of conformity assessment requirements. This procedure

is viewed as an extension of the *harmonization* of standards and is applicable for directive-regulated products concerning safety, environment and consumer protection.

From a non-EC country point of view, the above conformity requirement must be met in order for foreign products to be placed on the EC market. These common rules must be observed by all national authorities in the EC. More important, for non-EC countries national governments in the community have to accept certification in other member countries. This *mutual recognition* requirement is of key importance and underlines the 'Global Approach' character of testing and certification in that it makes the EC market more transparent and accessible since non-community products have access to the same certification system that applies for community products.

The EC-wide product testing and certification programme spells out in a number of directives detailed requirements for conformity assessment and lists government appointed assessors (notified bodies) for certifying conformity of products to specific requirements. A 'CE' mark ('Communauté Européenne') affixed to the tested product is required to signify that all legal requirements are met. To acquire the CE mark, manufacturers can certify product conformity via various means depending on the product. Options range from manufacturer's self declaration of conformity to quality assurance audit by agencies authorized by EC member states with approval of the EC commission.

Consistent with the standards programme, testing and certification procedures advance the general principle of less regulation and more freedom of choice for community and non-community business. In this sense and assuming that implementation will do justice to the philosophies underlying the Single Market concept, the 'New Approach' to testing and certification should lead to 'trade creation' results for the Community internally and externally. In the case of the United States the benefits expected to accrue are very substantial since close to two-thirds of US exports to the EC belong to sectors that require harmonization of standards and EC-wide testing and certification.

As time drew closer to EC-1992 the US business community seemed more positively disposed and more optimistic over potential uses related to testing and certification that could entail costs for US exports. Most of the concerns centred around the question whether testing of US products could take place by entities located in the United States. In the early stages US firms expressed concern over the fact that the 'New Approach' would upset existing bilateral arrangements between US laboratories and EC states which did not require additional tests in Europe. Also, the principle of mutual recognition could not be extended to cover US exports to the Community and declarations of conformity from US companies could not be accepted on an equal basis with those of European producers.

Most of these fears were dispelled following a meeting of US and EC authorities in Washington DC in June 1991 where progress was made on the issue of mutual recognition agreements. Subject to certain EC conditions, US agencies will qualify to certify adherence to EC standards by American exporters. The qualifications of certification and testing centres will be assured by the National Institute of Standards and Technology (NIST).

Rules of origin, local content and public procurement
Local content requirements and rules of origin are high on the list of potential sources of discrimination against non-EC producers. The local content requirement spelled out by EC directives forces foreign firms in the Community to use domestic inputs so that a large amount of the value added of the firm must come from materials and services made domestically. The process for determining the origin of different products is notoriously complicated and there is no reference to internationally accepted rules to determine the patrimony of products and inputs. Such rules actually do not exist. Outside some general guidelines provided by the GATT there are no uniform procedures to determine rules of origin.

Foreign firms in general and US industry in particular fear that in view of the loose legal provisions on the issue, the EC could arbitrarily manipulate rules of origin in the name of anti-dumping policies in order to affect foreign interests and protect certain industries in the EC.[4] In a sense, United States concerns are well founded and they stem from the policies followed by the EC on certain electronic products, especially semi-conductors. EC regulations since 1989 on integrated circuits and assembly processions reflect the intentions of the Community to enhance its self-sufficiency and competitiveness in electronics production. In particular the intent is to boost semi-conductor manufacturing with silicon chips made in the EC. This, of course, presents the foreign-based companies with difficulties. Foreign assembly firms in the semi-conductor industry do not secure EC origin if they do not use EC-made silicon chips. In general, stringent local content requirements with strict rules of origin of the type used in semi-conductors and television discriminate against products made outside the Community as well as those assembled in the EC. The so called 'screwdriver rule' was instituted recently and allows anti-dumping practices by the EC in the case of certain imported products assembled and sold in the EC at prices lower than their per unit cost. In order to escape anti-dumping duties these products must be made with parts and materials which originate in the exporting country to an extent of no more than 60 per cent.

Public procurement in a broad sense (including purchases by public enterprises) represents close to 15 per cent of Gross Domestic Product of the EC member states. Long-standing barriers at the member state level and failure to open public sector purchasing to EC-wide competition has proved very costly to the Community budget. In an effort to encourage more open public procurements and secure transparency, competition and non-discrimination, the EC adopted what became known as the 'Excluded Sectors' Directive on September 1990 to be effective on January 1, 1993. The award of large works and supplies contracts is subject to regulations and requirements that promote intra-EC competition in the so-called excluded sectors (water, energy, transport, communications). However, the directive allows exclusion of contract proposals in the excluded sectors that are not at least 50 per cent of EC origin. In case of equivalent tenders preference should be given to the tenders of EC origin. 'Tenders are to be considered equivalent if the price difference does not exceed 3 per cent.' This means that in order for non-EC bids to be considered they must offset the 3 per cent price preference in favour of the EC contracts.

Obviously there is a clear-cut case of potential discrimination against foreign-based producers. American producers point to the arbitrariness that may arise in the process of evaluating bids from non-EC producers. Furthermore, as long as the 50 per cent requirement is not met and unlike the 'Buy American' practice in the United States, EC authorities are allowed to reject any foreign bid. Therefore foreign firms are forced to increase their EC content to more than 50 per cent in order to be considered by the examining agencies.

The financial sector and the notion of 'Fortress Europe'

There are close to 30 directives dealing with the financial sector of the EC. In addition to banking and the capital market, insurance and securities are covered. Emphasis is placed on the free movement of capital among EC members. Also, in the context of pursuing the goal of monetary unification, financial firms can operate in any one of the member states if they get authorization to provide financial services and security activities in one country. This *single license* objective enables the financial firms to operate throughout the EC under a set of regulations spelled out in the Second Banking Directive.

The Second Banking Directive, by requiring a minimum level of EC-wide regulation, aims at creating the necessary harmonization (or equivalence) of the 'essentials' in the interest of pursuing integration of the financial sector. This concept of 'mutual recognition' among EC countries was carried too far by the Second Banking Directive concerning the participation of non-EC countries in banking activity in the Community. Indeed, the original proposal of the Second Banking Directive called for reciprocity by the outside world to the effect that non-EC financial markets were expected to accommodate the EC banking firms through laws and regulations equivalent to those of the

Community. This actually amounts to a 'mirror image' type of reciprocity and gave rise to negative reactions and protest by the non-EC countries. It was at that time that reference to 'Fortress Europe' was made by American officials of the Reagan Administration. Europe's response was prompt and the directive was modified substantially, and in its final form the Second Directive required *national treatment* type of reciprocity according to which foreign and domestic financial firms are accorded identical treatment by a country.

Trade and investment gains

On the question of how the chosen regulatory format of the Single Market will affect the United States economy, the interest is centred on the areas of trade and investment. In both areas a unified and more open market of 345 million consumers could potentially bring about substantial gains for the US economy. The EC remains the largest trading partner of the United States and accounts for about one-fourth of its total trade. In the last four years there has been a dramatic improvement in the US trade balance with the EC. Furthermore, the prospects for continuation of favourable trade balances in the future are good considering the potential of EC growth due to the unification of its market.[5]

Inevitably, the interest of the United States is even keener for the future of US direct investment in the EC. European Community–based American affiliates account for a very large percentage, 80–85 per cent, of the availability of US goods in the Community. Unlike other industrial economies the United States relies on investment-based exports to the EC. In the case of Japan the reverse is true; Japanese affiliates in the EC supply only 20 per cent of their country's sales while the remaining 80 per cent comes from exports.

This striking contrast of an investment-based and a trade-based economic relationship of the US and Japan with the EC is expected to give rise to different investment policies by the two countries. In the case of Japan, export-substituting investment strategies take priority. To defend their market share against possible regional protection, exporting firms may switch to investment within the region to produce locally the products formerly exported. A more offensive investment strategy may be the result of an attempt by foreign firms to position themselves at an early stage in the integrated area in order to capture the growth of the unified market.

In the case of the United States, with an already significant presence of capital stock in the EC, priority is expected for adjustments of direct investment to the new regional environment. Following market unification and elimination of borders in regional trade, region-based affiliates are expected to engage in large-scale realignment of investment activity. Cross-border investment with mergers and acquisitions is expected to characterize corporate restructuring and investment in new ventures.

As shown in Table 16.1 between 1988 and 1989 US firms restructuring increased in terms of number of deals both in an absolute and relative sense (the relative dimension measures US mergers and acquisitions in the EC as a percentage of total deals by US firms). Valuewise, however, there is a decrease in the emphasis on Community-asset transactions through cross-border merger and acquisitions. This suggests that at this stage there is a shift of emphasis to cross-border restructuring among small firms. To the extent that these deals constitute first time foreign investment this finding implies mobilization of American business activity in the community at the small and medium size level which involves what we called earlier aggressive, trade-replacing investment policies.

Table 16.1 Cross-border mergers and acquisitions in the Economic Community 1988–1989

	Number of cases		Value (mill. of $)	
	1988	1989	1988	1989
United States	121	192	6435	8700
EC as percentage of total	26	46	69	48
Japan	11	30	2280	3009
EC as percentage of total	14	23	21	31
All Countries	753	1190	31417	32769

Source: United Nations, *Regional Economic Integration and Transnational Corporations in the 1990s*, Series A, No. 15, July 1990.

Finally, we should add here the widely held view that in the case of the United States, its EC-based affiliates enjoy a definite advantage at this point in that they are better positioned in the Single Market than their Japanese and even their European counterparts. It is widely recognized[6] that the United States affiliates have long established positions in the EC. The EC-based affiliates of the United States, close to half a trillion dollars in assets, are in a position to capitalize on their experience and take advantage of the opportunities presented by the EC-92 programme to shift their scope of competition from the national to the EC-wide level. It is evident therefore, that restructuring with cross-border asset transactions is the top priority for the United States transnationals.

Closing remarks

Obviously, the EC-92 programme does not reflect, in some areas at least, the universalist philosophy of the GATT. Also, its implementation was not synchronized with the Uruguay Round. It proceeded at a faster pace and, in so doing, it created *faits accomplis* on several issues on trade and Trade Related Investment Measures (TRIMS).[7] Obviously, this leaves the GATT talks with less flexibility to the point that the Uruguay Round is destined to last longer while its chances of success become smaller.

In a sense, this is the result of the abrupt change in the EC from 'Eurosklerosis' to 'Euroenthusiasm' for the Single Market in the mid-1980s. The timing of the EC-92 programme suggests that Europe had suddenly awakened to the fact that it was lagging behind in the technological race of the members of 'Triad'. The other two members, USA and Japan, had already dominated certain high technology areas like the semi-conductors and telecommunications. The formation of the Single European Market with a pro-European regulation structure was, therefore, seen as an immediate need even at the expense of causing difficulties to the Uruguay talks.

Under the circumstances the EC directives were bound to reflect the philosophy 'Europe for Europeans' concerning the share of gains from the formation of the Single Market. Europe was not going to miss the chance to reap massive benefits from a truly integrated market with a single regulation structure.

In reviewing the developments on the so-called 'sensitive issues' we see that the slogan 'Europe for the Europeans' may overstate the issue of conflicting interests between the two economic blocs, the EC and the US. So far we witness a set of directives which aim at the pursuit of self-interest in the context of the GATT principles of trade liberalization.

The progress made in harmonizing standards and testing and certification procedures opens the way for future Mutual Recognition Agreements (MRA) between the US and EC. These agreements will enable product certification in the United States that will be accepted by the EC. Up to very recently US exporters were concerned that, for certain products, they would have to go though certification procedures both in the US and in EC. Talks are under way already to explore the possibility for MRAs in several sectors.

The case of MRAs as well as the amendment of the Second Banking Directive are examples of intentions of the EC to make compromises in the spirit of cooperation with the US in the process of implementing unification of the European markets. Convergence is expected to prevail in the areas of public procurement, the energy market and transportation.

Finally, it would seem that the United States is in a position to capitalize on the benefits to accrue from the unification of the European markets. US business, as the best positioned in the EC, should enjoy an advantage over other non-EC countries. The local content requirement presents no problem for the US firms based in EC since they are self-sufficient in terms of productive capacity and do not have to rely on imports from the United States. It is estimated that their imports from the US as per cent of the sales of EC-based American manufacturing affiliates is only 5 per cent.[8] This is a striking contrast to the situation faced by Japanese firms which rely very heavily on imports from home to supply their affiliates.

Notes
1. This was the interpretation of the EC's 'Green Paper', released on October 8, 1990, printed in the *Official Journal of the European Community*, January 28, 1991.
2. See National Association of Manufacturers (1990), *Statement on European Commission Green Paper on the Development of European Standardization*, December 20.
3. US Department of Commerce (1991), *Europe Now. A Report*, Sept.
4. US International Trade Commission (1991), *The Effects of Economic Integration within the European Community and the United States*, Washington, DC, July 1991.
5. For example P. Ceccini (1988), *The European Challenge 1992*. A more optimistic view is found in R. Balusn, 'The Growth Effects of 1992', *Economic Policy*, November 1989.
6. For example see T. Divinney and W. Hightower (1991), *European Markets after 1992*, Lexington Books.
7. For a discussion of this point see R. Sehwok (1991), *US–EC Relations in the Post-Cold War Era*, Oxford: West View Press.
8. R. Lipsey, 'American Firms Face Europe 1992', Working Paper No. 3293, National Bureau of Economic Research.

PART IV

MONETARY AND FINANCIAL ASPECTS OF THE INTEGRATION PROCESS

17 Financial integration in the EC: conceptual approach and implications
Sotirios Kollias[1]

1. Introduction
The 1985–86 period was a turning point in the history of the European Community. Conscious that integration was slow, its twelve member states found the political will to speed up the process, in particular to complete the internal market by the end of 1992, and thus increase the internal and external competitiveness of the EC economy.

An important part of the 1992 project is the creation of an integrated European financial area, the main components being the full liberalization of capital movements and the free supply of financial services across borders.

Financial integration has, however, implications that go beyond the efficiency aspects. It will affect significantly monetary and budget financing policies in the member states and may present a challenge to the exchange rate stability which (until recently) had been ensured through the successful functioning of the European Monetary System (EMS).

The present chapter highlights the nature of financial integration, the programme formulated by the EC Commission and the legislative work in progress. It also discusses the broad implications of such integration and the problem of distortions due to disparities in capital income taxation across the EC.

2. The financial dimension of the Single Market
The European Community project to complete the internal market has a financial dimension. It includes the free circulation of capital and the free cross-border supply of financial services. The two freedoms together form the basis for the creation of the common market in banking, securities and insurance. Supplemented by other parameters, such as fiscal convergence and exchange rate stability, they can lead to integration of national financial markets, to the approximation of national financial systems and ultimately to the creation of a *European Financial Area*, not as the simple sum of twelve national systems but as a space with internal cohesion and external identity.

As with the integration of the economic sectors, financial integration is expected to bring important efficiency gains through more competition and exploitation of economies of scale, thus implying a wider choice, at lower prices, of financial products for consumers, and increased international competitiveness. From this point of view, it is an integral part of the 1992 project.

However, owing to the multiple role (payments system, protection of savings, allocation of financial resources, monetary policy implementation) that the financial sector plays in an economy, financial integration has implications that go beyond the efficiency aspects: first, it will change radically the conduct of monetary policy and the management of public debt; and second, it presents, during the adjustment period, a challenge to exchange rate stability. For these reasons, although a part of the 1992 project, financial integration tends to be a programme in itself, which the EC Commission has elaborated conceptually, and it is currently being enacted in the form of Council directives at such a pace that it has reinforced the overall drive towards the 1992 objective.

3. The potential for financial development

The European Community seems indeed to have a large financial potential. It saves a substantial part of its income and exports more than the United States and Japan, both in absolute and relative terms (Table 17.1). However, the use of EC currencies in international operations is not commensurate with its economic and trade importance. In 1989, 59 per cent of international reserves were held in US dollars and only 26 per cent in EC currencies (Table 17.2). Similar discrepancies are seen in the denomination of international bonds and bank loans, although the use of EC currencies has increased in recent years. Moreover, a substantial part of EC exports and imports is invoiced in non-EC currencies.

The potential is also evident if we compare stock market capitalization as a percentage of GDP. With the exception of Luxembourg and the United Kingdom, stock markets in Europe play a relatively small role in the financing of the economy as compared with Japan and the US (Table 17.3). This implies a lot of room for developing capital markets in the EC and reducing the

Table 17.1   Exports of goods and services, 1991 (by major areas)

	% of GDP	% share in world exports
EC	28	40
intra	17	25
extra	11	15
USA	10	12
Japan	11	9

Source: Eurostat, OECD.

Table 17.2 Use of currencies in international financial transactions (% share of outstanding volumes)

	Bonds and bank loans		International reserves	
	1989	1991	1989	1991
EC currencies	26	30	27	31
USD	50	44	59	56
Yen	13	13	8	11
Other	11	13	6	2

Source: BIS.

Table 17.3 Stockmarket capitalization, 1991

	% of GDP	% of World index
Luxembourg	114	0.11
London	91	10.35
Amsterdam	44	1.47
Brussels	33	0.69
Dublin	32	0.12
Copenhagen	27	0.41
Paris	25	3.17
Madrid	24	1.12
German Exchange	22	3.47
Athens	19	0.13
Lisbon	13	0.09
Milan	12	1.35
EC-12	34	22.50
US	66	37.80
Japan	85	30.80

Source: Federation of Stock Exchanges in the EC.

financing costs of enterprises. Particularly low is the relative importance of stock markets in France, Germany and Italy.

Many other indicators at the national or sectoral level could be given to show that there is potential to improve the allocation of financial resources and the payments system. The removal of barriers to capital movements and to financial services, by throwing national markets into competition, can lead to exploitation of this potential.

4. The conceptual framework of financial integration

The requirements for financial integration are shown in Table 17.4. Full *liberalization of capital movements* is the cornerstone. Exchange controls deprive residents of access to foreign 'financial products' which may be better suited to their needs and possibly cheaper. Moreover, they insulate domestic financial institutions from competition and therefore imply higher financing costs and reduced quality of services.

Table 17.4   Programme of financial integration

I. *Basic Requirements*
   freedom of capital movements
   freedom of establishment of institutions
   free cross-border supply of services in the
   – banking
   – securities markets
   – insurance
   harmonization of prudential rules

II. *Other parameters*
   relations with third countries
   stability of exchange rates
   fiscal aspects
   – approximation in company taxation
   – approximation in interest income taxation
   – elimination of tax discriminations
   social aspects: measures to combat money laundering
   pension funds: freedom to invest abroad
   payments system: cross-border efficiency

Full liberalization of capital movements is a necessary condition for the *free supply of financial services* directly from the home base of the institutions. Combined with *freedom of establishment*, it implies increased competition and expanded activity, and hence reduced costs and economies of scale.

Freedom of bankers, investment firms and insurers to establish in another member state and/or to export services are essential elements but not sufficient to bring about effective competition and integration without *harmonization* of prudential and regulatory systems which vary enormously from one member state to another. Without such harmonization, the suppliers would have to face twelve different regulatory and supervisory systems which have been built up historically. Because of the specific role the financial sector plays in the economy, it has been necessary to impose a variety of rules in order to protect consumers and ensure the stability of the financial system from miscalculation of risks and mismanagement.

Harmonizing twelve different and complex regulatory frameworks is a difficult task. Table 17.5 shows the approach of the EC Commission to this crucial issue. The principles of 'single licence', 'mutual recognition' and 'home country supervision' play a crucial role in dealing with the problem. They ensure consumer protection, solvency of institutions and 'level playing field' conditions in a flexible market environment which is created by the implementation of basic freedoms outlined above.

Table 17.5   Harmonization of prudential rules

Objectives	Protection of investors and depositors
	Solvency of financial institutions
	Equal conditions of competition (level playing field)
Principles	Single licence permitting a financial institution to set up a branch in the other States without new authorization and new capital endowment
	Harmonization of basic definitions and rules, in particular those concerning capital adequacy and the covering of risks
	Mutual recognition of rules and standards not harmonized at Community level
	Home country control, i.e. supervision of branches abroad by the country where their head office is located

Besides the above basic requirements, *other conditions* must be fulfilled for the creation of an integrated financial area. For instance, exchange rate stability is essential if the integration process is to be irreversible, while differences in the taxation of interest income, if not narrowed, will distort the allocation of capital and jeopardize the expected gains. Similarly, it is necessary to improve the payment systems across countries so that the freedom of transferring funds abroad is not choked off by large costs and undue delays. On the other hand, measures must be taken to prevent the use of the financial systems for money-laundering.

By the end of 1992, almost all measures needed to create the common market in financial services had been enacted in the form of directives. The legislative task has been facilitated by the Single European Act which instituted the adoption of directives in this field, as in many others, by qualified majority (56/74 votes). The main directives and the date they come into force are shown in Table 17.6.

Table 17.6   Financial integration: main EC directives

	Effective
Capital movements	
1. Complete liberalization	1.7.1990
Credit institutions	
2. Second banking	1.1.1993
3. Solvency ratios	1.1.1991
4. Own funds	1.1.1991
5. Annual accounts	1.1.1993
6. Consolidated supervision	1.1.1993
7. Money laundering	1.1.1993
8. Large exposures	1.1.1994
Securities market	
9. Investment services	1.1.1994
10. Capital adequacy	1.1.1994
11. Prospectus	17.4.1991
12. Insider dealing	1.6.1992
13. Major holdings	1.1.1991
Insurance	
14. Second life	20.11.1992
15. Second non-life	30.6.1990
16. Third non-life	1.7.1994
17. Third life	1.7.1994
Pension funds	
18. Freedom of investment	proposal

5. Implications
The free circulation of capital, combined with the free supply of financial services and the single European market in general, has far-reaching implications for the operators of government policy. It is not possible here to do more than highlight some of these implications.

5.1 General
The process of financial integration will force member states to restructure their *financial systems* in order to make them more efficient and competitive. The existing developed financial centres (UK and Luxembourg) will try to maintain their lead. Other centres, like Paris, Frankfurt and Amsterdam, are making efforts to exploit the new opportunities and emerge as leaders. The process of securitization which has been going on during the last ten years will continue as a result of the structural changes. Non-bank financial intermediaries, such as unit trusts, pension funds, leasing companies, etc., will assume increased importance in countries where banking has traditionally dominated the intermediation process. Moreover, money and capital markets will be developed both for reasons of competition and the effective conduct of monetary policy.

5.2 Economic agents
Households will be free to diversify the portfolio of their financial assets: invest in foreign securities, open deposit accounts and buy bank and insurance services anywhere in the Community. Moreover, the structure of their domestic asset holdings may change as a result of the development of the securities markets and increased competition between the financial sub-sectors.

For *enterprises* financial integration will mean:

(I) A wide choice of instruments (domestic and foreign) in which to place their liquid assets and therefore more rational cash and portfolio management.
(II) Access to international loans and credits for smaller amounts than is now the case and at better terms.
(III) A wider choice of banking and insurance services at reduced prices.
(IV) Elimination of restrictions concerning their international commercial operations: freedom to invoice and settle in any currency and no obligation to repatriate export proceeds or to settle import payments within a limited period.
(V) Under conditions of exchange rate stability, reduced costs for covering exchange risks. If there is a unique currency then there will be the elimination of exchange risk costs and a reduction of transaction costs.

5.3 Financial intermediaries

Banks, insurance companies and *other financial* institutions will have the opportunity to extend their activities in all member states and in new products, like consumer and mortgage loans and various types of insurance. But they will be exposed to increased competition which may lead to reduced prices of financial services and intermediation margins. Banks, in particular, face lower profit margins in the future as investors turn directly to the capital markets to raise capital or allow rival institutions to manage their funds. In view of the single market and the tendency for the generalization of the universal banking model in Europe, banks and the other financial institutions will look for strategies which will open new horizons of activity, such as mergers, acquisitions and intersectoral alliance agreements. For instance, the highly developed pension funds of the UK may seek to expand their activity in Germany by using the dense banking network of the latter.

5.4 Monetary policy

The integration of national financial markets, in particular the free circulation of capital, will propogate monetary shocks more quickly and directly from one country to another. Substitutability between domestic and external financing will tend to become 'perfect'. The options that national central banks will have for influencing interest rates and monetary aggregates in their own countries will be limited.

Direct credit controls will not operate since households and enterprises can turn to external sources of credits. Moreover, *reserve requirements* on bank deposits will lose much of their relevance as, in an integrated financial area and a single market, member states will tend to reduce or eliminate them so as to enhance the competitiveness of their banks and financial centres. This, in turn, should lower the cost of credit to enterprises. This tendency will be reinforced by other factors, such as the challenge to banks from non-bank competitors on both the asset and liability sides, or growing disintermediation as a result of the direct recourse of high-quality debtors to the capital market, for instance, by issuing commercial paper. Thus, monetary regulation will have to be based principally on *indirect management techniques* through the manipulation of short-term interest rates and open-market operations.

5.5 Financing of government budgets

The need for effective monetary policy and competitive financial markets will lead to the elimination of compulsory or privileged methods of financing the public deficit. Four such methods can be distinguished :

(I) Fiscal incentives which encourage investments in government securities. Most member states apply various forms of such incentives. In

some cases, the advantages are offered to the whole range of domestic securities, thus discriminating against the purchase of foreign securities. This practice must be eliminated since it is incompatible with the free circulation of capital in the Community.
(II) Compulsory investment by banks in government securities, often at interest rates below those prevailing in the free market. At present some member states apply such investment ratios but the trend is towards their elimination.
(III) Compulsory investment by institutional investors (insurance companies and pension funds) in domestic government securities. Although traditionally imposed on prudential grounds, such rules will be removed or relaxed as a result of the directives on insurance services and pension funds which will abolish the localization of their assets. In an integrated financial area the currently applied rules seem to go beyond the objective of prudential regulation.
(IV) Direct and automatic access of the Treasury to Central Bank credit or advances at a rate below the market rate. This method of financing tends to disappear as countries make efforts to create the conditions of sound monetary policy.

Overall, the public sector will be forced to face the same market conditions for the financing of its deficit as the private sector. This implies a more rational management of the public debt and, therefore, a tendency to contain the deficit through more rational budgetary policies.

6. Exchange rate stability

In view of the high degree of openness of the EC economies and the increasing over time intra-EC flows of goods, services and capital, exchange-rate stability is vital not only for avoiding competitive devaluations but also for contributing to price stability which is necessary for investment planning, optimal allocation of resources, sustainable growth and employment. Therefore, since the collapse of the Bretton Woods system, a constant EC goal has been the creation of a zone of monetary stability.

Since 1979 this goal has been pursued via the European Monetary System (EMS), in particular via the Exchange Rate Mechanism (ERM) which limits the fluctuation of exchange rates. Monetary policy of countries participating in the ERM is therefore geared to maintaining exchange rates within the permitted bands of fluctuation.

Before 1992–1993 ERM discipline had gradually brought convergence of inflation and interest rates across Europe towards those of Germany, the country with the strongest currency and monetary policy assigned credibly to price stability. The monetary policy of the other ERM participants closely followed that of Germany, mainly via similar movements in short-term interest rates, with virtually no room for independent manoeuvring, either for domestic policy objectives or *vis-à-vis* third currencies. This ensured price stability, confidence in their currencies and a reduction in long-term interest rates which determine the financial cost of investment.

The obligation to fully liberalize capital movements initially raised concerns about the stability of the exchange rates and the working of the ERM. It was argued that at the same time there cannot be full capital mobility, fixed exchange rates and independent monetary policy. Until September 1992 these concerns were thought to be exaggerated for a number of reasons: a static view of the argument, the fact that many ERM participants were already 'liberal', the gradual removal of exchange controls in the 'restrictive' countries, transitional arrangements for those with a less developed financial system, and monetary policies already geared to that of Germany. However, the monetary crisis of September 1992, which led to devaluations and the exit of the UK pound and the Italian lira from the ERM showed the inherent incompatibility of free capital mobility and rigid exchange rates in the absence of closer monetary integration and convergence of economic policies.

Exchange rate stability through the reduction of exchange risk is an important factor for effective financial integration in the EC. In particular, the single currency will eliminate such risks and will in turn facilitate the movement of capital and trade in financial services. It can be argued that the various hedging techniques permit cover against exchange rate movements and that therefore there is no need for exchange rate stability. The answer is that they are costly. Moreover, the institutional investors, which account for about 70 per cent of capital market activity, will be subject to currency matching rules for their liabilities and thus severely limited in their ability to invest abroad.

7. The fiscal dimension

Another aspect of financial integration is the fiscal dimension. It is admitted that the allocation of resources in the Community cannot be optimal if it is not governed by economic criteria. Nor can the financial intermediation process be cost-effective if capital movements take place not because of differentials in the rates of return but because of differences in taxes.

Unfortunately, the taxation of savings varies enormously within the Community. Some member states operate a withholding tax which ranges from zero in Luxembourg and Germany to 30 per cent in Italy and Ireland (Table 17.7). Two states, Denmark and the Netherlands, operate a direct reporting system by banks to the fiscal authorities. Moreover, most of them do not tax savings of non-residents. This implies that each State is a 'tax haven' for the other.

Table 17.7 Taxation on interest from deposits (% coefficients)

	Residents	Non-residents
B	10 (*)	0
DK	reporting system	0
D	25	0
GR	15 (*)	0
E	25	25
F	25 (*)	0
IRL	30	0
I	30 (*)	0
L	0	0
NL	reporting system	0
P	20	20
UK	25	0

Notes: (*) final tax.

A proposal for a 15 per cent minimum withholding tax has not been adopted, as opinions differ between the EC countries and adoption of directives in the fiscal field requires unanimity. Concerns about the flight of capital to other parts of the world with zero taxation have played an important role. Without some kind of harmonization, however, competition among the national tax systems will bring rates downwards to economically meaningful levels. In fact, some countries with high rates have already adjusted downwards, while Greece and Germany have gone in the opposite direction (from zero rates).

In company taxation, after twenty years of inaction, agreement has been reached on a package of three measures intended to facilitate cross-border cooperation between firms operating in the Community:

(I) A 'mergers' directive providing for the imposition of tax on capital gains arising from a merger, hive-offs, transfers of assets or an exchange of shares only when these have been actually realized, and not at the time of the operation in question.

(II) A 'parent company/subsidiary company' directive which aims to eliminate the double taxation of dividends distributed by a subsidiary established in one member state to its parent established in another member state.

(III) An 'arbitration procedure' convention intended to ensure, within a specific time-scale, the elimination of double taxation which may arise in the case of adjusting the profits of associated companies by national tax authorities. There still remains under discussion a proposal on the offsetting of losses made by a subsidiary in one member state against the profits of its parent company based in another. Another proposal provides for the abolition of withholding taxes on interest and royalties paid to a company by companies belonging to the same group and established in other member states.

Note

1. The views expressed in this Chapter are personal and may not correspond with those of the Commission of the European Communities.

18 Monetary union and economic integration: the less developed areas of the European Community

A.J. Kondonassis and A.G. Malliaris

1. Introduction

It is important to underscore that the Treaty of Rome which established the European Community (EC) did not list monetary integration as one of its primary goals. Actually, European monetary integration has been a vague objective of the EC, which has only received periodic attention, instead of a persistent priority, often as a result of financial crises of certain magnitudes.

The first move towards monetary cooperation occurred during the early period 1958–61 and was caused by the reality of persistent balance of payments surpluses in the original six members of the EC. During this period the EC established the Committee of Governors of the Central Banks to coordinate issues of exchange rate management and international monetary policy.

The increasing monetary instability of the late 1960s, created primarily by the inflationary pressures of the Vietnam war, generated financial dangers that appeared to threaten the existence of the European customs union. These concerns were expressed in the Barre Report which recommended the setting up of a machinery for monetary coordination. At the December 1969 Hague summit, the Barre Report motivated a detailed discussion on the issue of a coordinated European monetary policy. However, differences of opinion existed among the finance ministers and, as a compromise solution, it was suggested that a study group be formed to review these issues carefully. The chairmanship of this group was assigned to M. Pierre Werner, the then Prime Minister of Luxembourg.

It is the purpose of this chapter to present a framework for the evaluation of the European Monetary Union. The establishment of a financial common market with free capital movements requires a higher degree of monetary and fiscal cooperation than exists presently. The steps needed to improve such cooperation are examined and the guidelines established at Maastricht are reviewed. Section 2 offers a brief historical background while section 3 reviews some experiences with monetary integration in the EC. In section 4 a framework is presented for the evaluation of monetary integration between unequal partners. The last section offers our conclusions.

2. The history of European monetary integration

The Werner Report, published in 1970, has become a significant document on the topic of monetary integration. It recommended the development of the European Currency Unit (ECU), a centralized European credit policy, a unified capital market policy, a common policy on government budgeting finance and the gradual narrowing of exchange-rate fluctuations.

The monetary crises of the early 1970s that led to the rescinding of the gold convertibility of the dollar on 15 August 1971 and the floating of the guilder and mark created great pressures for finding an alternative solution to the abandoned Bretton Woods system of fixed exchange rates. The major economic powers, known as G-7, in their Smithsonian Accord agreed to allow their participating currencies to fluctuate within a 4.5 per cent band *vis-à-vis* the US dollar and EC currencies to vary as much as 9 per cent against each other. It was agreed that if a participating country's currency moved outside such a band this country's central bank was responsible for sufficient intervention to re-establish the acceptable range.

EC countries concerned about the difficulties that such a wide variation in their exchange rates implied for their Common Agricultural Policy proposed a more limited exchange-rate mechanism which was called the *snake*. Such a snake allowed a maximum total band of 2.25 per cent against the EC currencies. However, because some EC countries were unable to maintain such a narrow band, Denmark, France, Ireland, Italy and the UK left the arrangement at various times during 1973 and 1974. In October 1977, Roy Jenkins, President of the Commission, reactivated the EC's efforts at establishing a European monetary union. His efforts were supported by the French–German alliance and led to the birth of the European Monetary System (EMS) which became operational in March 1979. At the time all EC members joined in the EMS with the exception of Italy, whose currency, the lira, was allowed a wider margin of fluctuation and the UK, which did not become an active participant because of concerns about national sovereignty. Actually the EMS is basically a supersnake that imposes less strict exchange-rate conditions on the participating currencies because it is founded on the ECU. As such the EMS does not attempt to maintain direct parity with currencies outside the EC, specifically the US dollar or the Japanese yen. The details of the EMS and a brief evaluation of its performance will be presented in the next section. Here we wish to conclude the historical evolution towards a European monetary integration with two additional events: the Delors Plan and the Maastricht meeting.

At the Hanover summit of June 1988, the Council agreed that in adopting the Single European Act an implicit objective was monetary integration. The task for making such a goal explicit was assigned to a committee headed by Jacques Delors and the analysis, findings and recommendations of this committee are known as the Delors Report. This Report contains three major stages. Stage One was unanimously adopted by the EC members at the June 1989 Madrid summit.

The first stage of the Delors Report addressed the issue of the non-participating member states in the exchange rate mechanism of the EMS and the expansion of the role of the Committee of Central Bank Governors in coordinating monetary policy. The second stage would create a European System of Central Banks (ESCB) much in the spirit of the US Federal Reserve System. The Euro-Fed would be responsible for price stability, exchange-rate and reserve management, banking and monetary policies and general support of macroeconomic policies agreed upon at the EC level. Finally, the third stage of the Euro-Fed would be to transfer the control of monetary policies to the EC and to establish such a narrow band for the existing exchange rate fluctuations of the 12 currencies that effectively convergence would occur to one ECU.

Although the Delors Report outlined the process towards monetary integration, it was in the December 1991 Maastricht summit that the EC addressed a little more specifically the timetable of the various stages. In the detailed 90-page treaty on European monetary union produced at the Maastricht meeting, the EC heads of state reached an agreement which is aimed at fixed exchange rates and a single currency by 1 January 1999. More specifically, EC members must abolish all restrictions on the movement of capital and adopt, if necessary, multi-annual plans intended to ensure the lasting convergence necessary for monetary union.

Between January 1994 and January 1996, each member of the EC will start the process leading to the independence of its central bank. To facilitate this process a European Monetary Institute (EMI) will be established to strengthen the coordination of monetary policies between central banks, to monitor the functioning of the EMS and to facilitate the use of the ECU. At this summit, it was agreed that the ECU would eventually replace the D-Mark. This ECU will not be the current composite basket of EC currencies but rather a new currency representing irrevocably fixed values of existing national currencies. The EMI, as a precursor of the Euro-Fed will oversee and promote the development of the ECU.

According to the agreement, if a majority of member states meets the strict economic criteria necessary for European Monetary Union (EMU) (i.e., an inflation rate not more than 1.5 per cent higher than the three lowest rates among the members; a budget deficit not higher than 3 per cent of GDP; a long-term interest rate no more than 2 per cent higher than the EC's three lowest; no devaluations of a currency against any other currency within the exchange rate mechanism (ERM) of the EMS for at least two years) by the end of 1996 then stage three of the EMU will be implemented.

If the criteria established are not met as outlined above, the EC leaders will decide in 1998 which countries are ready for EMU and, without the requirement of a majority of the members, those countries meeting the criteria will proceed with a currency union on 1 January 1999.

3. Experiences with monetary integration: the EMS and the Maastricht Treaty

The aim of the EMS was to establish closer monetary cooperation leading to a zone of monetary stability in Europe. Stability applies to exchange rates between EC currencies and is part of a wider strategy that involves overcoming inflation and promoting economic growth. The achievement of both external and internal stability is considered essential for a long-term growth policy.

Deravi and Metghalchi (1988) examined the variability of exchange rates before and after the implementation of the EMS. They concluded that the EMS had successfully reduced the variability of the exchange rates of the EC countries. Their results coincided with an earlier study by Horst Ungerer et al. (1986).

Several studies investigate the important issue of convergence of monetary and fiscal policies. Artis (1987) has concluded that there was convergence for fiscal policy among EMS countries contrasted to a control group including such different experiences as the USA's expansion and the contraction in Japan and the UK. However, Artis (1987) found mixed results for monetary policy; there was some convergence but the dispersion of monetary growth rates remained very high.

Coffey (1991) argued that the goal of monetary stability had been served satisfactorily by the EMS. At the beginning of the operation of the system rates of inflation tended to rise but later tended to fall. Moreover, there has been an expansion in the commercial use of the ECU. Businessmen view the ECU as a model of stability and a risk spreader. It is now among the top 5 currencies used for international loans.

Our look at available pre 1992–93 data suggested that there were continuing problems of convergence that must be addressed. The rates of inflation were quite high in Greece and Portugal in 1991, 18 per cent and 11.5 per cent respectively, and substantial differences have existed in the public finances of the EC members. In 1991 net borrowing in Greece was more than 15 per cent of GDP and in Italy about 10 per cent of GDP. In 1991 the debt/GDP ratio was 128 per cent in Belgium, 86 per cent in Greece, 97.4 per cent in Ireland, 103.3 per cent in Italy and 63.8 per cent in Portugal. Greece also has had a serious continuing current account imbalance.

The above studies and data do not offer conclusive evidence that the EMS disciplined the monetary and fiscal policies of all its members. Although it is true that inflation rates and interest rates dropped in countries of the EMS, the same could be observed worldwide during the same period.

Finally, because of exchange rate crises in the ERM in 1992 and 1993, whatever results exist can only be viewed as tentative and certainly not all-inclusive.

An uncertain picture has also emerged concerning the Maastricht treaty. Between October 1991 when the Maastricht treaty was proposed and ratification in November 1993 several significant events had taken place. First, the Danes on 2 June 1992 narrowly rejected the Treaty while the Irish on 18 June 1992 approved it. In France, renewed populism induced the French President to announce a Maastricht referendum which turned out in support of the Treaty by a very small margin. Although such approvals have prevented dealing a death blow to the Treaty, Germany's insistence on tight monetary policies to fight inflation resulting from unification costs has brought major turmoil in European financial markets and a serious blow to the European Monetary System in general and to the British, Spanish, French and Italian currencies in particular. At this time, it seems reasonable to argue that the European financial turmoil and the political demands imposed by the Treaty will probably make its amendment or renegotiation an eventuality. As Kondonassis (1989) has remarked, 'Europe, notwithstanding its dynamism and the progress it has made towards integration, may have to be satisfied with a half loaf rather than a full one'.

4. The future of European Monetary Union

We will turn our attention now to the future of the European Monetary Union between unequal partners. The conceptual framework we employ to analyse and evaluate both the benefits and costs of the EMU consists of: (1) microeconomic efficiency; (2) macroeconomic stability; (3) equity and welfare issues between countries and regions.

First, concerning the EMU, in terms of microeconomic efficiency one can argue that the benefits outweigh the costs. Furthermore, there appear reasons to believe that less developed countries such as Greece, Spain, Portugal and Ireland may benefit proportionately more than the advanced countries. To substantiate these claims consider the two standard reasons: transaction costs and reduction in risk and uncertainty.

Transactions costs of exchanging bank-notes between major and minor currencies can be high. A single currency will eliminate such costs. Emerson and Huhne (1991) offer that the resulting saving can be about 0.4 per cent per annum of the EC's GDP. The larger members of the EC, whose currency is extensively used as a means of international payments may benefit by between 0.1 per cent and 0.2 per cent of GDP, while the less developed areas which constantly convert their currency to a stronger one may stand to gain around 1 per cent of their GDP.

Transaction costs are also more harmful to small and medium sized firms engaged in intra-EC trade than large multinational companies. Total transaction costs incurred by firms are estimated by Emerson and Huhne (1991) to be an average of 15 per cent of profits made on exports to other EC countries, and such costs may be twice as high for smaller firms.

The second aspect of microeconomic efficiency is financial risk. A potentially very important gain could arise from EMU, again with much greater benefit to countries such as Greece, Portugal, Spain, and Ireland, from the reduction of the overall uncertainty for investors. Such a reduction in uncertainty, due to a single currency and an independent and credible monetary policy by a Euro-Fed, could lower risk premiums and would greatly increase investment. Furthermore, such a reduction in uncertainty could also encourage future expectations for improved economic conditions and further stimulate new economic growth. Actually, opinion surveys suggest that EC industrialists expect significant benefits from a single currency.

On the question of macroeconomic costs and benefits one may first ask whether monetary union would have any adverse effects on the less developed areas of the union. There is little doubt that the elimination of a separate currency and of an autonomous exchange rate policy would deprive the lagging areas of a mechanism to handle shocks and to cushion the process of adjustment to such shocks. In this regard the single currency would involve a sacrifice for countries like Greece and Portugal. Yet, the bottom line is whether the poor region would accrue benefits which will more than offset the loss of independence associated with a separate currency. It can be argued that a favourable macroeconomic environment resulting from monetary union may offer an attractive option. Major advantages can be cited as regards better overall price stability, both in terms of low average inflation and low inflation volatility. Standard recent economic reasoning about rational expectations suggests that high inflation leads to a reduction in output and employment, in contrast to the earlier literature on the Phillips curve, which taught that reduction in the unemployment rate could be achieved through tolerance of a higher rate of inflation. The evidence of Greece, Spain and Portugal supports this point. Benefits from low inflation include a stable demand for money from productivity gains. However, to achieve such price stability the Euro-Fed would have to conduct an independent and credible monetary policy which would need to be supported by the budgetary policies of the EC members. Monetary union also means complete freedom of capital movements and irrevocable fixity of exchange rates. When Portugal and Greece will be able to lift exchange controls is not clear.

As indicated above, the challenge of the EMU is not strictly monetary. EMU requires the design of a European fiscal regime that allows sufficient autonomy, yet is tightly coordinated. High and growing public deficits by the less developed regions, such as Greece, would lead to pressures on Euro-Fed to either soften its fight against inflation or allow certain countries to default on their debt with enormous financial disasters for such a country's public finances. Also, large deficits and/or high debt to GDP ratios in some countries may undermine fixed exchange rates. If a given member uses a large portion of the available volume of savings within the EC, that may induce high interest rates, crowding out private investment with adverse effects on the union's exchange rate.

Let us look at another possibility with regard to Greece. Suppose that the EMU occurs without Greece's major overhaul of its public finances. The loss of Greece's monetary autonomy would reduce Greece's ability to finance its public debt and thus would make it necessary to offer both the flow and stock of its debt at higher interest rates. Such rates would have to be sufficiently high to compensate investors from the possible risk of default. However, for a country like Greece where public debt interest payments account for about 10 per cent of GDP, further increases in interest rates could be devastating. Hereby lies one of the most serious problems of EMU. A long transition period would be required for Greece to fix its public finances, with enormous costs to be borne by its social programmes in the form of major cuts in benefits.

Equity and welfare concerns have been expressed at every stage of EC's development since the signing of the Treaty of Rome. Yet, after more than thirty years, economic disparities continue to persist. While theoretical models of economic integration optimistically suggest convergence of economic growth between developed and less developed regions, economic experience demonstrates that the existence of structural disadvantages and inefficient institutions limit competition, growth and technological innovation in certain regions. Among the problematical factors of the lagging areas is the lack of certain types of infrastructure, including transport, communication and social facilities. Lower quality of labour because of poor performance of the educational systems also appears to be an important factor. There is no known answer at this point for stimulating fast economic growth in the lagging regions other than EC assistance through the Community Structural Funds. All three southern states, i.e., Greece, Portugal and Spain have made it a strong point that membership in the EMU must be accompanied by increased structural funds. Under a 1988 agreement these funds are scheduled to be 18 billion ECUs per year beginning in 1993. Total EC support (including agricultural) now accounts for 5.1 per cent, 5.9 per cent, and 2.3 per cent of the GDP of Greece, Ireland and Portugal respectively. The key question is whether these funds are sufficient to produce the needed economic and social cohesion in the EC? The poorer regions argue for further strengthening of the EC structural policies and in support of this it is pointed out that structural funds currently account for less than 0.25 per cent of the EC GDP. There is no question that economic and social development is a complex process and it takes time. Continued large regional imbalances would pose an economic as well as a political threat to economic and monetary union.

5. Conclusions

This paper traces the monetary dimension of 'Europe 1992'. A brief history of key monetary developments and a more detailed analysis of the EMS show that whatever progress has been achieved enormous challenges are ahead.

We have also proposed a framework for assessing potential benefits and costs for individual members of the EC under the assumption of an eventual EMU. It appears that the EMU is not a zero-sum game with total benefits experienced by some members equalling the total losses to be incurred by the rest. Rather it is a positive sum game with gains for all. Actually substantial gains are potentially available to less developed areas, provided major steps are taken during the transition period to help their economies converge with the rest. But if things, for whatever reasons, do not work out, the possibility of a two-speed Europe cannot be ruled out.

References

Artis, Michael J. (1987), 'The European Monetary System: An Evaluation', *Journal of Policy Making*, **9**, 175–98.

Coffey, Peter (ed.) (1991), *Main Economic Policy Areas of the EEC Toward 1992*, Third Revised Edition, Dordrecht, Netherlands: Kluwer Academic Publishers.

Deravi, M. Keivan and Massoud Metghalchi (1988), 'The European Monetary System: A Note', *Journal of Banking & Finance*, **12**, 505–12.

Emerson, Michael and Christopher Huhne (1991), *The ECU Report*, London: Pan Books, Ltd.

Kondonassis, A.J. (1989), 'The European Economic Community Thirty Years Later', *The Journal of Applied Business Research*, **6**(1), 1–7.

Ungerer, H. et al. (1986), *The European Monetary System : Recent Developments*, IMF Occasional Paper No. 48, December.

19 The macroeconomic and microeconomic consequences of alternative exchange rate regimes: implications for European Monetary Union

John Smithin and Bernard M. Wolf

Introduction

The Maastricht Treaty of 1991 calls for a European Union (EMU) with a single European currency. The treaty makes exchange rate stability a precondition for participating in the monetary union. To join the EMU, a country must not change its currency's par value relative to other members of the Exchange Rate Mechanism (ERM) for two years prior to accession. In reality, instead of no changes, September 1992 brought a major currency crisis in which Britain and Italy opted out of the ERM and in the process devalued their currencies. At the same time, Spain devalued the peseta. In November 1992, the crisis erupted again and Spain once more devalued its currency, this time accompanied by Portugal. The Irish punt joined the devaluations in January 1993, followed in May 1993 by further devaluations of the Spanish peseta and Portuguese escudo. In July/August 1993 another exchange rate crisis led to a dramatic widening of the permitted bands of fluctuation for the remaining ERM members. Do these devaluations merely achieve the adjustments in parities needed ultimately to drive the European Community (EC) toward a single currency? Or, do they represent a continuing need by EC countries to change their parities when the costs of fixed rates become too high? We think it is the latter.

Our assessment of the EMU proposals in light of both macroeconomic and microeconomic theory suggests that the potential costs in terms of employment and output of a single EC currency may be too high.[1] Hence, we argue that the EMU proposal should probably be abandoned for a majority of the EC nations. A European single market does not require a EMU, but rather only relatively stable real exchange rates and this can be achieved by other means. Padoa-Schioppa (1988) has referred to the impossibility of reconciling what he calls the 'inconsistent quarter' of free trade, full capital mobility, fixed exchange rates and national autonomy in the conduct of monetary policy. As the EC increasingly adopts the first two of these items, he argues, it is clearly the fourth that will have to go. Our view is that abdication of national control of monetary policy is far more costly than eliminating fixed exchange rates. As long as instruments for hedging foreign exchange risk are available, and as long as severe misalignments are ruled out by reasonably sensible macroeconomic policy, the existence of separate national currencies subject to exchange rate changes should not provide any serious impediment to trade.

Macroeconomics and the EMU

Our consideration of the macroeconomic implications of the single currency involves two major points. First, monetary policy is at least as important for real economic outcomes as it is for inflation. Hence, it should not be left to a EC central bank which might impose an inappropriate monetary policy, either for the Community as a whole or the individual regions. Secondly, under conditions which allow for changes in exchange rates, countries can maintain a relatively independent monetary policy. They cannot do so under a single currency or some other form of fixed exchange rates.

In terms of macroeconomics, the main grounds for opposition to the single currency are that it would eliminate freedom to use monetary policy and bar changes in exchange rates when these policy tools may be the least cost option for achieving desirable economic goals such as full employment and economic growth. As presently envisioned it also generates an EC monetary policy with an undesirable deflationary bias. Unlike the monetarist model, which centres exclusively on the impact of interest rates and money supply on inflation, we would place equal emphasis on the real effects of monetary policy. We argue that high real interest rates have negative effects on investment, capital accumulation and economic growth (Smithin, 1990). For example, Canada's experiences of the 1980s and early 1990s certainly show that it is always possible to 'cure' inflation by driving up real interest rates sufficiently to provoke a severe recession in real economic activity. What they also show, however, is that recovery of the real economy from such episodes can be painfully slow, especially in terms of national unemployment. Hence, we have suggested elsewhere (Smithin and Wolf, 1993) that a more stable and sensible monetary policy rule would be to stabilize real interest rates at low but still positive levels. We argue that this would be the best contribution monetary policy could make to provide an environment conducive to sustainable economic growth and high employment. On the inflation front, even though this rule would obviously not squeeze all inflation out of the system, it would at least avoid the severe inflationary episodes which ensue when real interest rates are allowed to become negative as in the 1970s. If all countries in a trading bloc followed such a rule, this would not be likely to lead to severe inflationary pressure and/or competitive devaluations. Competitive devaluations would not be a problem if the economies in the area are all expanding; they would not then need the competitive stimulus of a devaluation.

Empirical evidence (Frankel, 1992) suggests that in spite of the vastly increased capital mobility of the modern era, substantial real interest differentials between different jurisdictions do remain. This indicates that even with contemporary 'global capital markets' assets denominated in different currencies are not perfect substitutes. In these circumstances it continues to be feasible for at least the 'medium-sized' individual jurisdictions to pursue an independent monetary policy in the sense of a different real rate of interest from that prevailing elsewhere. However, to do so requires the right to make changes in the real exchange rate through nominal exchange rate changes. For example, a monetary policy generating lower real interest rates than prevailing elsewhere implies a real depreciation of the currency and an increase in the real net foreign credit position, but, as shown by Smithin (1994) and Paschakis and Smithin (1992), the process is not necessarily unstable. The lower real interest rate will stimulate investment, output and employment. The lower currency value will make the country's activities more competitive, thereby increasing exports and decreasing imports. The ideal situation within a trading bloc would be for all members to pursue sufficiently expansionary policies to safeguard sustainable growth and full employment. However, it also seems to be important for the individual jurisdiction to continue to possess the tools to be able to achieve this independently even if the other players are pursuing a different policy. Even under modern conditions, the abandonment of control over domestic monetary policy implied by the concept of monetary union represents a greater sacrifice than has usually been suggested. The losses from the elimination of monetary policy as a stabilization tool will, of course, be greatest for countries within the EMU for whom the centre's monetary policy is least appropriate.

Monetary policy in the EMU
This brings up the question of what monetary policies are likely to be followed by the EMU's central bank. In the existing ERM, the German Bundesbank has been the lynchpin, more or less determining monetary policy in the entire EC. It has generally followed a tight monetary policy emphasizing deflation. In fact, it is largely the tight money (high interest rate) policy pursued by the Bundesbank, to fight inflationary pressures stemming from the unification of Germany, which precipitated the September 1992 currency crisis. To take Britain as an example, under the ERM the British were compelled to maintain their exchange rate *vis-à-vis* the other members including Germany. Part of the reason for joining the ERM was supposedly to benefit from the low inflationary policies of the Bundesbank. By having to defend the exchange rate, which, however, most commentators felt represented an overvaluation even at the start (Williamson, 1993), anti-inflationary discipline would be imposed.[2] However, Britain got more than she bargained for.

When the Bundesbank increased interest rates, Britain was forced to follow although her own economy was in recession and clearly warranted lower interest rates. Britain in the ERM in 1990–92 was following the same type of high exchange rate deflationary policies as she did in 1925–31 when she reinstituted the gold standard at the pre-World War I parity. Fortunately, this time around the inappropriately fixed rate lasted only for two years. No doubt Keynes (1925), had he lived to see them, would have denounced the tight money policies of the 1990s as soundly as he did 70 years before. After leaving the ERM in the autumn of 1992, Britain reduced interest rates and saw the value of its currency fall substantially, with the result of a reviving economy relative to most of its competitors.[3] At the time of writing, the UK is the only major EC country with positive economic growth.

In the proposed EMU, the central bank is to be relatively independent of the member states' governments. Yet, it seems virtually certain that as Germany is the largest economy in the EC, views analogous to those of the German Bundesbank will be a powerful influence on EC monetary policy. Already in the announced convergence criteria for admission to the EMU there is a strong message that the focus will be exclusively on low inflation policies implying tight money and, when deemed necessary, high real rates of interest. The criteria set down in the Maastricht Treaty revolve around price-stability and non-excessive government deficits. For example, 'achieving a high degree of price stability' is interpreted to mean an average rate of inflation that does not exceed by more than 1.5 percentage points the average of the three lowest inflation performers over the past year. There is no mention of performance in terms of output or employment levels (Kenen, 1992).

Microeconomics and the EMU

We now turn to a consideration of the microeconomic implications of the EMU. Here the issue is how well the European Community fits the requirements of an optimal currency area, a notion originally formulated by Mundell (1961). The two chief criteria for such an area are relatively similar economic structures in the regions it comprises and a high degree of factor mobility (particularly labour mobility) between them.

Consider first the question of economic structure. If the economic structures of the different regions are dissimilar, the likelihood of asymmetric shocks is much greater.[4] Unpredictable shifts in region specific demand and/or supply conditions may well lead to situations in which the principal industries in one region are depressed while those in the other are booming. A common monetary policy which then focused exclusively on reducing inflationary pressures in the latter region would simply exacerbate the depression in the former. An obvious recent example of an asymmetric shock is, of course, the unification of Germany which, also, particularly in its monetary aspects (the 1-to-1 and 2-to-1 conversion rates for the two currencies), well illustrates the difficulties caused when the option of exchange rate policy is not available to ease the difficulties of restructuring.

A look at the European Community suggests substantial differences in economic structure among the member countries. Particularly striking are differences between countries in the north and those in the south. Hence, on the economic structure criteria the EC is a poor bet as an optimal currency area. Moreover, there is no reason to infer that regions suffering from demand shortfalls will be able to sustain rapid falls in wages and prices any more than in most industrial nations around the world. Therefore, the various regions within the EC may well benefit from some degree of exchange rate flexibility between them.

In response to economic shocks which affect one region differently than another, an absence of exchange rate flexibility must throw the burden onto some alternative adjustment mechanism. With reductions in interest rates and devaluation ruled out, either wages and prices in the depressed region would have to fall rapidly in order to increase employment and output, or alternatively a high degree of labour mobility out of the region could eliminate some of the unemployment. This is where the second criterion for an optimum currency area comes into play.

In terms of labour mobility, the EC also rates rather poorly in view of differences in culture and language. It should be noted that even in the existing 'currency unions' in countries spanning a large geographical area, such as the United States, labour mobility has never really been adequate to remove all regional disparities. Yet the US certainly has fewer language difficulties and traditionally a much greater degree of labour mobility than the EC. Currently, the New England region and California are suffering unusually high rates of unemployment. Historical experience suggests that these disparities will not be eliminated quickly. In Puerto Rico, where language and culture differ more radically from the continental US, and in spite of being a full member of the American currency and customs union with the opportunity for some labour mobility, per capita income is still less than half of that in Mississippi, the poorest US state (Eichengreen, 1990). Note also that disparities within existing federal structures such as the US and Canada continue to persist, in spite of the existence of a substantial tax transfer redistribution mechanism via fiscal federalism. These examples suggest that the EC could not rely on labour mobility to eliminate regional disparities and maintain high levels of income and employment.

In the absence of both symmetric economic structures and a much greater degree of labour mobility than currently exists, the EC is not a particularly good fit for the classic definition of an optimal currency area. Thus, from a microeconomic as well as a macroeconomic point of view, it is evident that situations could easily arise in which ameliorating monetary policy and exchange rate changes, if these continue to be available, might well come to seem the least cost method of handling structural change.

Policy options
Based on both macroeconomic and microeconomic considerations, it therefore seems that the EC is unlikely to fare well with a single currency. What then are the alternatives? As discussed earlier, we favour a regime in which all member countries in the area pursue a rule of stabilizing real interest rates at low but still positive rates. However, before expanding upon how this notion fits into the EC context, we consider a number of the other major policy options which have been suggested.

1. Return to something like the pre-September 1992 ERM. EC currencies not in the exchange rate mechanism could join or rejoin the ERM, retaining the previous band of plus or minus $2^1/_4$ per cent around the central rate for some countries and plus or minus 6 per cent for others who find it more difficult to stabilize their exchange rates. Changes in parities would be allowed, as in the earlier years of the system (up to 1987), in contrast to the situation which developed in the late 1980s and early 1990s when changes in parities apparently became politically unacceptable and hence exacerbated the domestic difficulties of many participants. Of course, reinstating the ERM in something close to its original form would not eliminate the deflationary bias stemming from the Bundesbank's influence. The ERM in this form also has the drawback that once a currency gets close to the limits of what has come to be perceived as an untenable band, driving it out of the band becomes a virtually costless one-way bet for speculators. The autumn 1992 crisis provides ample evidence.

    Eichengreen and Wyplosz (*The Economist*, June 5, 1993) advocate a temporary measure to reduce speculation on virtually costless one-way bets against ERM currencies. They suggest imposing deposit requirements on institutions that take open positions on foreign exchange. The cost would be passed on to speculators, discouraging one-way bets. While the measure does have the advantage of dampening speculation, speculation would not be eliminated since the measure could apply only to institutions within the EC. Reducing speculation would potentially allow for more orderly realignments, but it is unclear whether countries would take the initiative when realignments are required without being forced to. If they did not, the inevitable and necessary realignments which must arise from time to time would be delayed.

2. A 'soft' ERM. The influential periodical *The Economist* (May 8, 1993) which before the autumn 1992 currency crisis was a strong supporter of the EMU, has now switched to advocating a 'softer' ERM with more flexibility. It suggests that the exchange rate bands be widened; that bands should have 'soft buffers', which would allow members to let a currency move outside its band under certain circumstances; and that there be frequent, possibly automatic, realignments of the central rates, to take into account differences in rates of inflation. The latter would have the effect that the band would be around a central value of the currency's real exchange rate rather than its nominal exchange rate. This proposal is similar to that advocated earlier for the whole international monetary system by Williamson (1985) and Williamson and Miller (1987). The Williamson scheme calls for countries to calculate 'fundamental-equilibrium exchange rates' (FEERs), rates consistent (according to some underlying economic model) with a readily financeable current-account position.

The scheme proposed by Williamson and *The Economist* has the advantage of providing some real exchange rate stability for countries within the EC member nations without having to surrender all discretion over monetary policy. However, the difficulties with the proposal relate to the question of the determination of the FEERs and deciding when they should be changed. Speculators would still have a relatively costless one-way bet when a currency comes to the edge of a band (now defined in real terms), which the markets regard as unsustainable.[5] Given that the scheme does not call for maintaining nominal exchange rates, the problem of deflationary bias would not be as great, but in practice, countries may still be reluctant for political reasons to engage in nominal exchange rate changes and hence may still follow German monetary policy.

3. A 'two speed' Europe, with Germany forming a monetary union with countries opting for similar monetary policies and conforming to the criteria for an optimum currency area. The other members could stick to one or another form of the ERM, or make some other arrangement.

4. Eliminate the ERM and allow all currencies to float freely, with each member pursuing their own, possibly inconsistent, monetary and fiscal policies. Such an arrangement without any attempt at policy coordination could result in very unstable exchange rates which would cause difficulties for the completion of the Single European market. The unsatisfactory experience with floating exchange rates in the 1970s and 1980s explains why this option is not popular. Note, however, that the unstable exchange environment of these years was itself the product of unstable national monetary and fiscal policies as expressed in the unprecedented and extreme volatility of real rates of interest (Smithin and Wolf, 1993).

Our proposal that monetary policy should focus on stabilizing real interest rates in each jurisdiction, even in the context of a trading bloc like the EC, represents a fifth alternative to any of these four. It does not focus on exchange rate policy *per se*, but if there were general agreement on the objective and a commitment to policy coordination in achieving the interest rate targets, the result in practice would be a fair degree of real exchange stability consistent with the goal of stabilizing expectations and promoting trade. An advantage of our rule as compared to say the Williamson approach is that it focuses on the key factors in real exchange rate determination rather than arbitrarily picking an exchange rate target which may or may not be credible in terms of the economic fundamentals (Currie, 1993, p. 182). Above all, the rule would stimulate economic growth and high employment throughout the EC, which in turn are the prerequisites for harmonious trading relationships. Alternatively, if there cannot be agreement on monetary policy coordination at the EC level, it would at least remain open for an individual jurisdiction to retain an escape route from excessive deflationary pressure applied at the centre.

Conclusion

The present, albeit weakened, ERM carries with it opportunities for virtually costless speculation and the deflationary bias of the German Bundesbank. Although the adoption of the EMU in the EC would eliminate the costless speculation, as well as reduce transaction costs and hence arguably strengthen the single European market, the costs of inappropriate monetary policy (most likely deflationary) would be too high. Of the various alternative proposals, the ERM targeted nominal exchange rates and the 'soft' ERM (as proposed by Williamson and *The Economist*) targets real exchange rates. Our monetary policy targets real interest rates. The result of the latter would still be relatively stable real exchange rates, which would be desirable for the promotion of the single European market, but without the costs of deflationary bias and the abdication of national control over monetary policy.

Notes
1. We recognize the savings in transactions costs resulting from a single currency but believe these are outweighed by the various considerations discussed in this chapter.
2. Of course, a fixed exchange rate regime can promote inflationary pressure throughout the system depending upon the policies of the key player. See Smithin (1991) and Currie (1993).
3. By mid-June 1993 the pound had fallen relative to the German mark by 13 per cent. (It fell by even more against the US dollar, 22 per cent, and the Japanese yen, 32 per cent.)
4. Eichengreen (1992) points out one impact of the EC 1992 programme will in fact be increased regional specialization which paradoxically increases the likelihood of asymmetric shocks.
5. Williamson (1993) suggests that to avoid speculators benefiting from one-way bets there should be no attempts to defend a disequilibrium exchange rate and parity changes should always be made within the width of the band.

References

Currie, D. (1993), 'International Cooperation in Monetary Policy: Has it a Future?', *Economic Journal*, January, 178–87.
The Economist (1993), 'Can Europe Put EMU Together Again?', May 8, 17–18.
Eichengreen, B. (1990), 'One Money for Europe? Lessons from the US Currency Union', *Economic Policy*, No. 10, 117–87.
Eichengreen, B. and C. Wyplosz (1993), 'Mending Europe's Currency System', *The Economist*, June 5, 89.
Frankel, J.A. (1992), 'International Capital Mobility: A Review', *American Economic Review*, **82**(2), May, 197–202.
Kenen, P. (1992), *EMU After Maastricht*, Washington: Group of Thirty.
Keynes, J.M. (1925), *The Economic Consequences of Mr. Churchill*, London: Hogarth Press.
Mundell, R. (1961), 'A Theory of Optimal Currency Areas', *American Economic Review*, **51**, September, 657–65.
Padoa-Schioppa, T. (1988), 'The European Monetary System: A Long Term View', in F. Gravazzi, S. Micossi and M. Miller (eds), *The European Monetary System*, Cambridge: Cambridge University Press.
Paschakis, J. and J.N. Smithin (1992), 'Is Monetary Sovereignty an Option for the "Medium-sized" Open Economy?', Paper presented at the International Conference on Economic Integration Between Unequal Partners, Athens School of Economics and Business, Athens, Greece, August.
Smithin, J.N. (1990), *Macroeconomics After Thatcher and Reagan: The Conservative Policy Revolution in Retrospect*, Aldershot: Edward Elgar.
Smithin, J.N. (1991), 'European Monetary Arrangements and National Economic Sovereignty' in A. Amin and M. Dietrich (eds), *Towards a New Europe: Structural Change in the European Economy*, Aldershot: Edward Elgar.
Smithin, J.N. (1994), *Controversies in Monetary Economics: Ideas, Issues and Policies*, Aldershot: Edward Elgar.
Smithin, J.N. and B.M. Wolf (1993), 'What Would Be a "Keynesian" Approach to Currency and Exchange Rate Issues?', *Review of Political Economy*, 5(3), July, 365–83.
Williamson, J. (1985), *The Exchange Rate System*, Washington: Institute for International Economics, revised edition.
Williamson, J. (1993), 'Exchange Rate Management,' *Economic Journal*, January, 188–97.
Williamson, J. and M. Miller (1987), *Targets and Indicators: A Blueprint for the International Coordination of Economic Policy*, Washington: Institute for International Economics.

20 The Greek financial system: strategies for convergence

Themis D. Pantos and Christos C. Paraskevopoulos[1]

I. Introduction

One of the most important trends, since the early 1980s, has been the growing integration of financial markets around the world. As part of this trend, financial institutions have abandoned their previous confinement to domestic capital markets and have turned increasingly to the international arena.

On top of this, a number of worldwide events such as the North American Free Trade Agreement (NAFTA), the Asian Pacific Rim agreements, and most importantly the recent push toward full capital market integration in Western Europe – under the banner 'EC – 1992' have completely transformed the world's financial markets into 'global markets', characterized by innovative methods of conducting financial transactions. The 'globalization' of international financial markets, however, is the result of many factors, including the increased volume of international trade, technological improvements, the deregulation of cross-border transactions, and the push towards economic growth.

One of the key questions in growth economics is whether the poorer countries tend to grow faster than the richer countries and thereby converge, or catch up, in living standards. For countries open to world trade and financial flows, there would seem to be strong reasons to expect convergence. International evidence on convergence is mixed. Within Western Europe, there is evidence of a strong tendency towards convergence in the post-World War II period. The poorer countries, such as Greece, Italy, Portugal and Spain, tended to grow more rapidly than the wealthier core, which includes France, Germany, the Netherlands and the United Kingdom, and thereby closed part or all of the gap in per capita income. For a wider sample of developing and developed countries, however, the evidence shows that the tendency towards convergence between rich and poor countries is present, but is relatively weak.

Proponents of the Neo-Marxist school of economics have stressed a number of regressive effects of processes involving market integration between developed countries and less developed ones, and have expressed fears with regard to the prospect of economic divergence.

It has been argued, that the less developed financial systems will not be able to absorb these global changes and trends, and therefore will be vulnerable to competition from their stronger partners. In this context, Greece's financial system is at risk as it enters the critical decade of the 1990s.

The objective of this paper is twofold. First, to demonstrate that the Greek financial system is at risk not because it cannot be cost-effective or it cannot adapt to new competitive forces, but it is at risk because Greece's economic and regulatory climates both create serious impediments to constructive financial innovation.

Based on this view the paper goes on to frame principles of regulation, and to consider strategies for implementing them. The Greek authorities must start now to legislate and regulate by principle rather than to react *ad hoc* to specific crises real or perceived. If they don't, Greece's financial system will be a spent force in a fiercely competitive global environment, will not meet convergence criteria, and will never exploit potential advantages and benefits stemming from economic integration and globalization of the Single Market.

Second, to introduce financial innovation that offers better ways of handling risk and gives added versatility to borrowers, investors and institutions. Hence the basic function of financial innovation is to increase the efficiency of the functions of the financial system. The efficiency of a financial system is thus determined by the degree of competition in its different markets, where all impediments to entry are being removed.

The paper is organized as follows. Section II describes the six fundamental directives in a chronological order, as they related to 'Banking 92'. Section III examines the workings of the Greek financial system and the Athens Stock Exchange (ASE). Section IV highlights, introduces and proposes strategies that will enhance the effectiveness of the Greek financial sector, namely Re-regulation, Consolidation (Mergers and Acquisitions, Strategic Alliances), Financial Innovation, and Securitization. Finally, in section V, conclusions are reached and personal thoughts are expressed.

II. Banking in the European Community 'Project '92'

The creation of the Single Market Act was intended to include three areas of reform: the free movement of capital, the right to sell across frontiers without a local establishment, and the right of establishment in other member countries of the EC without authorization by host country regulators.

To unravel the likely impact of 1992's changes, one must consider the events in a chronological order, as they related to 'Banking 1992'. Banking 1992 is defined as encompassing the full range of services offered by financial institutions in Europe including securities, mutual funds and investment banking.

A number of enabling laws were required to implement the Single Market Act. The centrepiece of this plan consists of the following technical directives. (A technical directive is a binding policy that each member state is free to implement in its own way.)

- **Freedom of Establishment Directive**
  Adopted in 1973, this directive prohibited discrimination against a financial institution from one member state, which sought to establish itself in another member state territory.
- **First Banking Coordination Directive**
  Adopted in 1977, this directive stated that all member states should have an authorization system for credit institutions and outlined basic criteria for authorization including separate capitalization and reputable management. Risk/Asset ratio, Debt/Equity ratio, profitability ratio and liquidity ratio guidelines were stipulated.
- **Consolidated Supervision Directive**
  Adopted as early as 1983, this technical directive required that financial institutions should be supervised on a consolidated group basis as well as on a company basis.
- **Bank Accounts Directive**
  Adopted in 1986, this directive will apply to financial institutions' annual accounts after 1993 and will eliminate the use of hidden or undisclosed reserves. This binding policy also recommended but did not impose that a deposit protection scheme should be created and certain types of economic accounting and transaction exposures should be banned in order to avoid bank runs and different contagious effects associated with these particular events.
- **Second Banking Coordination Directive**
  Adopted in 1988, this directive stated that financial institutions authorized by their home member state will be allowed to conduct numerous banking activities in any other member state, provided its home state authorization applies to these activities. Thus, with an EC licence, a financial institution can offer its services in any EC country, provided of course that these services are offered at home. It granted, also, the right to host countries to impose any additional liquidity rules that seem necessary to protect the investors as well as any other rules aimed at preventing financial manipulation and insider trading activities.
- **Own Funds Directive**
  Adopted in 1988, this directive defined what kind of financial resources should be classified and treated as capital. Standard measures of holding core capital were introduced at a minimum of 4 per cent in accordance with the Basle Accord 1988 rulings. Core capital is defined as equity capital plus undisclosed reserves.

- **Solvency Ratios Directive**
  Adopted also in 1988, this directive classified on and off balance sheet items and commitments (options, swaps, and interest rate caps) into different risk categories. A Minimum Risk Asset ratio of 8 per cent was enforced and complemented the rulings of the Basle Accord 1988 agreement.
- **The Free Capital Movements Directive**
  Adopted in 1988, this directive called for the complete elimination of exchange and capital controls by the end of the year 1992.

The foregoing discussion suggests that the main objective of the EC banking directives is to ensure equal access by EC banks to all EC markets, through the EC banking licence. The key innovation is the introduction of the concept of 'mutual recognition' of individual country standards and regulations.

Financial institutions that meet minimum standards, such as capital requirements, should be able to operate throughout the Community subject to a single licence granted by the EC country in which they are established. Their right to operate would be determined by their domestic authorities (home country rule), though the way in which they advertised and marketed their products would still be subject to the rules that applied in the country whose consumers they were targeting (host country control). The treatment of foreign banks by the EC has not yet been decided. The original proposal of reciprocity, which would have been problematic for non-universal bank countries like Japan and the United States, has been replaced by the proposal of equal treatment: foreign banks are to be treated in exactly the same way as EC banks are treated in the country in question. If there is no difference between the way home country and EC banks are treated, as is the case in the United States, foreign banks will not be discriminated against.

III. The Greek financial system

This section describes the workings of the Greek financial system, highlighting the elements that might seem to enhance the effectiveness of the regulatory framework. Of particular significance in this regard are the low level of development of the capital market and the authorities' tight control over the banking system.

The Greek banking system operates in a highly regulated environment, imposed by the government through the Bank of Greece. This control is exercised directly through banking regulations, which have often been changed in the past to reflect the government's short-term goals of economic and monetary policy and indirectly through control over the major Greek commercial banks. Current regulations cover the following: reserve requirements;

permission for incentives to the banks for the granting of loans to certain types of enterprises; and foreign exchange control measures.

There are presently over 20 Greek banks and 18 'branches' of foreign banks operating in Greece. In addition, a number of foreign banks maintain representative offices. The Greek banks account for over 85 per cent of the total volume of loans and deposits and dominate the drachma oriented business. The foreign banks tend to concentrate on internationally oriented business, with shipping companies, multinational corporations, and large Greek industrial and public sector corporations.

Banking related activities like leasing have recently been introduced in Greece, whereas other activities like factoring are in their embryonic stage. The lack of a developed capital market has led industry to rely largely on bank loans for a high proportion of their funding. The commercial banks remain the prime source of loan finance for Greek industry and commerce.

The capital market
The capital market in Greece is not well developed. The securities market (Athens Stock Exchange) accounts for a very small fraction of external financing in the Greek economy. New issues of stocks and bonds constitute an insignificant source of funds for the private non-financial sector, which meets most of its financial requirements by borrowing from the banking system.

The low level of activity in the capital market can be attributed to the inadequacy of both the supply of and the demand for securities. Large industrial firms have little incentive to issue securities because they can usually meet all their financing needs by borrowing from commercial banks on favourable terms. Individual investors may be reluctant to hold corporate shares owing to the family character of most private companies and the uncertainty over their dividend policies. This uncertainty derives from the fact that the directors of the boards of such companies are usually members of the controlling family, allowing them to inflate their salaries at the expense of profits.

Larger institutional investors such as pension funds, mutual funds, and insurance companies are either prohibited by law from holding private securities or have insufficient resources to make any significant contribution to the level of activity in the stock exchange.

The banking system and credit policy
In Greece, the financial system consists of a government bank with the available financial securities, cheque accounts, time deposits, term life insurance, and government pensions. As we have mentioned earlier, the Greek financial system should change its primitive capital market to a secondary

market more sophisticated, offering to the individual a variety of pension and insurance products, deposits and direct claims issued by corporations.

The Bank of Greece, in addition to performing the usual function of a central bank, provides funds for the specialized credit institutions and occasionally engaged in direct lending to the private sector. Commercial banks obtain most of their funds by attracting deposits and extend loans to most economic sectors. The local banks also own or have interests in some major insurance companies and industrial and tourist enterprises, as well as in the investment banks, which engage in long-term financing and participate in the equity capital of industrial enterprises. Finally, the specialized credit institutions obtain most of their funds from the central bank, which also dictates how these funds are to be used. As a result, the assets of these institutions consist mainly of loans to agriculture, long-term loans to industry, housing loans to low-income groups and public employees, and loans to public utilities and public enterprises.

Unlike the specialized credit institutions, the commercial banks, which supply about 50 per cent of total bank credit, have considerable discretion over their operations. Monetary and credit policies are thus intended mainly to control commercial bank behaviour through a wide range of rules and regulations. This control is enhanced by the highly oligopolistic structure of the banking system and by state ownership of the two largest commercial banks. These two banks also hold controlling interests in the five smaller commercial banks, giving them effective control of around 70 per cent of commercial banking activity.

Restrictions on portfolio policies of commercial banks
Banks are required to deposit a fraction of their deposits in a non-interest bearing account with the central bank and to invest an additional fraction in treasury bills and government bonds. The authorities set ceilings on commercial bank deposit and loan rates in an effort to influence the demand for various types of deposits and loans. The monetary authorities set upper limits on the size of specific types of loans as well as on the overall supply of credit to certain sectors of the economy.

The regulation of the Greek financial system
In the 1970s and 1980s, control of the banking system had become a major preoccupation of every Greek government. This preoccupation had focused on two separate types of control: prudential control, designed to ensure that banks are prudently run, with the aim of protecting depositors and avoiding major upheavals in confidence and the movements of funds; and monetary control, design to use the banking mechanism as a positive tool in the conduct of macroeconomic policy generally or, at the very least, to prevent the

banking mechanism from pulling in the opposite direction from, and thwarting other measures of economic policy:

Two frequently mentioned goals in terms of security market regulation were:

1. The protection of the 'innocent' consumer from informational asymmetries, and
2. The creation of an efficient securities market (Athens Stock Exchange).

Moreover, other reasons for regulation stated from representatives of the Greek government were to achieve certain social goals, and to prevent excessive concentration of economic power.

A clear articulation of the above mentioned arguments will be a three pillar system, which can be justified on the grounds that it would:

- ensure that the attention and resources of the banks are concentrated on their banking activities, and not spread over too large an area.
- avoid concentration of powers and conflict of interest for bankers.
- avoid giving banks an unfair competitive edge.

Effectiveness of regulation and selective credit policies
The foregoing discussion suggests that the Greek authorities should be able to direct the flow of financing to the private sector with relative ease. Credit is channelled almost exclusively through the highly regulated and centralized banking system, which is mostly state-owned. As a result, the authorities have direct or indirect control over the terms, conditions, and quantities of credit allocated to the various sectors of the economy, and on the regulatory framework.

Nevertheless, there is evidence suggesting that, despite the apparent strict regulation of the Greek banking system, the effectiveness of selective credit controls has been limited by the ability of lenders and borrowers to behave in a way that frustrates the authorities goals. Although most of the banking system is state-owned, banks have often tried to evade credit regulations, acting as if they were profit-maximizing firms.

IV. Strategies for convergence

Regulation in the new era
Greece is a player in an increasingly integrated, worldwide financial system. This system has changed importantly over the last two decades and continues to change rapidly. The changes driven by underlying economics are altering the organization of financial activity, both internationally and domestically.

Individual countries' financial systems are now much more closely linked with the world financial system than before, and these closer financial links are also limiting the ability of national authorities to act independently. This means that Greek financial regulation must be accommodated to world developments in regulatory policy.

Hence we propose a 're-regulation' of the Greek financial system in order to keep up with this rapidly changing world environment and the new era. Even in a rapidly changing world, regulation can make effective contributions to financial system functioning. It can do so mainly by encouraging system efficiency, using regulations which provide for greater competition through greater freedom of entry, fuller disclosure of pertinent information, and by affording similar functions similar treatment. In addition to fostering these goals, supportive regulation also encourages rapid adaptation wherever change is profitable and should not resist market driven change. We elaborate on these six specific implementation strategies below:

1. **Financial System Efficiency**

    The efficiency of a financial system is determined by the degree of competition in its different markets, by ready client access, by the competence and integrity of financiers, and by widespread availability of pertinent information. Good regulation enhances these qualities. The kinds of regulation that enhance competition will sometimes make it more difficult for unsound firms to survive. It is a necessary property of a truly efficient financial system. The important goal for regulators is not to prevent firms from failing, if they are badly run, but to publicize such firms' difficulties early on so the corrective action can be taken by all parties concerned. Unsophisticated depositors are an exception. They should be protected with insurance, but only up to a stipulated maximum sum.

    By efficiency, economists usually have in mind three attributes:

    - Allocational Efficiency
    - Informational Efficiency and
    - Operational Efficiency

    i) Allocational Efficiency refers to a variety of financial securities available. Borrowers and lenders usually have different preferences for financial securities, based upon their own views of the economy, the particular risks that they face, and their own circumstances. Hence, a capital market is efficient if it allows individuals to choose the financial security that is most appropriate to their needs.

ii) Informational Efficiency refers to the accuracy of the prices determined in the financial system. If these prices are inaccurate, then individual borrowing and lending decisions will not be optimal and resources in the economy will be misallocated. The two most important aspects of this informational efficiency are fraud and the impact of new information.

If fraud is believed to be rampant in equity markets because prices are thought to be manipulated or because of insider trading on privileged information, then funds will not be invested in those securities. As a result, prices will be lower than they should be as lenders reduce to invest. Consequently, some firms will not be able to finance profitable investments.

Similarly, if legitimate good news about a company's prospects fails to increase its stock price, then again the firm may be unwilling to raise equity funds as 'depressed prices' and investments are deferred.

Athens Stock Exchange (ASE) and market efficiency
A market is said to be efficient in relation to a particular set of information if market traders cannot realize positive abnormal returns from devising and executing trading strategies based on that data set. Empirical tests of market efficiency in Greece have uniformly found that markets are not efficient in the 'weak form'. That is, abnormal returns can be made by trading on the basis of historical price movements. We believe that the ASE displays an uneven degree of informational market efficiency, high degree of illiquidity of most listed stocks, high degree of thin trading, and a high degree of share ownership concentration, and pervasive interconnectedness of corporate relationships. These Greek market peculiarities have been often ignored. We urge regulators to stop simply reacting to what's broken. We need thoughtful regulations based on sound principles and specific research. Fundamental changes in global equity markets and the environment they operate in are raising the pressure for reform of Greece's equity markets. These fundamental changes must be accommodated by the following tactical manoeuvres:

- The abolition of fixed commission rates;
- Increasing transaction volumes;
- Developing and expanding over-the-counter markets;
- Introducing derivative markets (options, swaps, etc.) which must interact with the cash markets;
- Movement towards international regulatory and security clearance systems.

iii) Operational or Transactional Efficiency simply means that the intermediaries in the capital market perform their functions at minimum cost, so that as much money as possible is transferred from lenders to final borrowers for use in real investments.

Operating an oligopoly or cartel to fix minimum commission rates is an obvious example of an operational inefficiency that restricts transactions and ultimately, the flow of capital to real investment.

2. **Freedom of entry**

Competitiveness can be encouraged by removing impediments to entry, whether to an industry such as the insurance business or to a particular market such as the market for consumer credit. This kind of regulation that enhances competition will sometimes make it more difficult for unsound firms (eg. Greek banks) to survive.

3. **Full disclosure**

One of the most constructive actions regulators can take is to ensure effectively timely information release. All financial firms, including market intermediaries such as securities brokers and dealers, should contribute to the public information base. They should report balance sheet and income statement data at the same time and as far as possible on the same basis. Financial firms' balance sheets and the quality of their assets should regularly be inspected by regulators whose assessments are then recorded in the public information base. Competition is enhanced by increasing the availability of information regarding both profitability and risk. In particular, publishing information about asset portfolios' quality will affect financial firms' ability to raise funds, either through deposits or through securities issues.

4. **Competition versus solvency**

Safety is better sought by using incentives rather than constraints. A combination of publicity, graduated penalties and flexible rewards could be used to encourage intermediaries to evolve gradually over the medium term, entering new lines of business flexibly but slowly enough to allow regulators to assess the new developments' effects on system safety.

5. **Fairness**

The same kinds of financial function must be afforded the same kind of regulatory treatment, both within a given jurisdiction and between jurisdictions. If different kinds of domestic institutions are not treated the same way, business usually gravitates towards the least restrictive, which does not always result in the most efficient form of system organization. If different jurisdictions employ widely varying standards, a competition in regulatory laxity can result, which in turn will produce poor business practices.

6. Conflict of interest
Prohibitions of conflict of interest are costly, ineffective and misallocate resources. The best way to deal with conflict of interest is to make financiers liable for damages caused by mismanaging conflict.

Market integration and industry consolidation
The prospect of an integrated EC marketplace has triggered a wave of consolidation in many financial industries. Industries are becoming more concentrated and will become more so, primarily via mergers and acquisitions and secondarily via strategic alliances. Consolidation will continue beyond the level required to attain scale economies, as major financial firms scramble to strengthen their positions prior to the 1992 deadline.

Mergers and acquisitions
Mergers have become a matter of interest and discussion in recent years. Greek financial firms must see a merger as a way to increase market share and as a result become a market/price leader or at least a significant player in their industry and, by extension, be in a position to deter the entry of other firms.

We turn our attention to the horizontal types of mergers (e.g. firms in the same line of business). A horizontal merger is a cheaper way of achieving production of financial services expansions.

Firms capture efficiency rents through economies of scale and synergies, such as increased productivity for R & D, financing advertising risk-taking ability and decreasing agency costs and inefficient management. The above argument is particularly valid in Greece, where the marketplace is small and cost could be reduced by a rationalization of product lines, a decrease of product differentiation and an increase in the length of runs per product at plant level. This reorganization would bring financial firms down to or at least closer to, minimum efficient scale and allow them to be more competitive on an international scale.

Mergers can create substantial benefits because of the minimization of the weighted average cost of capital and the existence of scale and scope economies. Hence, by merging, financial institutions take advantage of economies of scope. Product lines of traditionally heterogeneous financial institutions are rapidly fusing into a homogeneous blend. Mergers help institutions to reshape themselves to lower the cost of servicing customer demand for financial services, and to become leaders in the financial industry. Economies of scope exist when the total cost of producing the two goods jointly is less than the combined cost of producing the same amounts of each good separately.

Strategic alliances
These alliances usually involve some combination of: (1) licensing of technology in a joint venture; (2) a distribution agreement tied to a joint venture; and/or (3) swapping or sharing products between two or more companies. A strategic alliance must clearly be one that is of significance to, or has an element of the strategy of, the organizations involved. It is a coalition of two or more organizations to achieve strategically significant goals and objectives that are mutually beneficial. These goals and objectives can be pursued in either the economic or political arena, and can be either short or long term in orientation. Mutually beneficial does not imply equality of benefits, but does mean that both (or all) receive benefit from the alliance in some proportion to contributions made. Moreover, the stability of the alliance will be a direct consequence of these benefits, outweighing those of alternative arrangements.

V. Financial innovation
Financial innovation offers better ways of handling risk and gives added versatility to borrowers, investors and institutions. The pace at which financial innovation has proceeded through the 1980s has opened up additional opportunities for both producers and users of financial services. These opportunities can be translated into:

1. increasing portfolio diversification, through new products and the relaxation of investment guidelines;
2. expanding business opportunities for financial institutions, including the networking of different institutions.
3. pricing and enabling risk to be transferred between different parties according to their ability to absorb it;
4. improved risk management, both for those who seek protection and for those who wish to profit from risk-taking.

Research costs for financial innovation are small. Financial innovations are easily copied because no production patterns exist. Accordingly, financial innovations could be easily transferred from one market to others at a very minimal cost.

Financial innovation has led to the introduction of new products that might not be covered under existing capital adequacy and liquidity rules. These include derivative securities and off-balance sheet items such as Currency Swaps, Interest Rate Swaps, and Currency and Interest Rate Options. The introduction of these trading financial instruments will give a competitive edge to Greece's financial system because of its ability to design, produce and market goods and services the price and non-price characteristics of which form a more attractive package than those of competitors.

Briefly, we now define the various kinds of financial innovations which must be deployed in a strategic fashion in order to create buyer value and increase the liquidity, the breadth and the competitiveness of the Greek financial system.

1. **Options**

   An option contract conveys the right, but not the obligation, to purchase or sell a specified asset at a specified price on or before a specified date. The specified asset can be any one of many possible assets, including common stock, gold, foreign exchange, a stock market index, debt instruments and futures contracts. An option contract entails a specified amount of the asset. The specified price is determined at contract inception and is known as the option's exercise price or strike price. If the option buyer has the right to purchase the underlying asset, then the buyer holds a call option. Alternatively, if the option buyer has the right to sell the underlying asset, then he is said to own a put option.

   Option contracts can be either European or American. With a European option the buyer may exercise only at expiration. With an American option, however, he may exercise prior to the option's maturity.

   There are two sides to every option contract. On one side is the investor who has taken the long position (i.e. has bought the option). On the other side is the investor who has taken a short position (i.e. has sold or written the option). The writer of an option receives cash up front but has potential liabilities later. Four basic option positions are possible.

   1. A long position in a call option
   2. A long position in a put option
   3. A short position in a call option
   4. A short position in a put option

   Payoffs:
   It is often useful to characterize European option positions in terms of the payoff to the investor at maturity. The initial cost of the option is them not included in the calculation.

   If X is the strike price and Z is the final price of the underlying asset, the payoff from a long position in a European call option is: $\max[Z - X; 0]$. This reflects the fact that the option will be exercised if $Z > X$ (in the money option); and will not be exercised if $Z < X$ (out of the money option).

   The payoff to the holder of a short position in the European call option is: $-\max[Z - X; 0]$ or $\min[X - Z; 0]$.

The payoff to the holder of a long position in a European put option is: max [X − Z; 0]. This reflects the fact that the option will be exercised if X > Z (in the money option), and will not be exercised if X < Z (out of the money option).

The payoff to the holder of a short position in a European put option is: − max [X − Z; 0] or min [Z − X;0].

Ignoring transaction costs, option trading represents a zero sum game. In other words, any profits (losses) experienced by option buyers are offset by the losses (profits) experienced by option writers. Once transaction costs are included, however, total option trading must be a less-than-zero sum game. Still, options trading may result in utility gains through the transfer of risk between the market players. These players are option hedgers, speculators and arbitrageurs.

1. **Hedgers**: If an option buyer or writer employs the option to reduce risk, then he is said to be a hedger. Option hedging generally eliminates downside risk while allowing the hedger to capture any potential upside gain. Options can facilitate the transfer of price uncertainty (risk), thus enhancing the utility of risk-averse hedgers.
2. **Speculators:** If an option buyer or writer uses options primarily to profit, then he is a speculator. In principle, a speculator accepts the hedger's unwanted risk in order to generate profits. Since speculators are, by definition, less risk averse than hedgers − that is the cost of risk to the speculator is comparatively less − then the transfer of risk from hedgers to speculators can result in net utility gains. Such potential gains are what underlie the very existence of options.
3. **Arbitrageurs**: The third important group of market participants in derivative securities markets. Arbitrage involves locking in a riskless profit by simultaneously entering into transactions in two or more markets. An option player who engages in arbitrage should be regarded as a type of speculator who engages in trading to exploit profit opportunities that are rarely risk free.

2. **Swaps**

Swaps are private agreements between two 'counterparties' to exchange cash flows some time in the future according to a predetermined formula. They can be regarded as portfolios of forward contracts. A currency swap allows two firms to exchange currencies at recurrent intervals and is usually used in conjunction with debt issues. For instance, each of two firms may issue fixed-rate debt in a unique currency, then swap the proceeds of the issues and assume each other's obligation to pay principal and interest payments. This swap of currencies can allow each firm to make payments without exposure to exchange rate risk.

An interest rate swap occurs when a firm that has issued one form of debt agrees to swap interest payments with another firm that has issued a different form of debt denominated in the same currency. For instance, a firm that issued floating-rate dollar-denominated debt agrees to swap to make fixed-rate payments to another firm that issued dollar denominated fixed-rate debt. In return, the second firm makes floating-rate payments to the first. Such a swap may result in net savings and represent an efficient vehicle for transferring interest rate risk from one party to another.

Currency swaps evolved from back-to-back loans and parallel loans, which came into popularity in Britain in the 1970s as a means of circumventing foreign exchange controls implemented to prevent the outflow of British capital. The controls were usually in the form of taxes imposed on foreign transactions. Back-to-back loans were made between two national firms, each making the other a loan in its respective currency. Parallel loans were made by one multinational to another multinational's subsidiary. Here, each multinational made the loan in its respective currency, and each subsidiary was located in the other's country. The principal and periodic interest payments on these loans were structured to coincide, and since the loans were repaid with foreign revenues from ongoing operations, the tax on currency translations was avoided. Note that such loans achieved the basic structure of a currency swap which minimizes the multinationals' exposure to risk.

Interest Rate Swaps

Interest rate swaps evolved in the early 1980s as a special case of a currency swap in which all payments are made in the same currency. In the classical example of an interest rate swap, borrowers who are creditworthy, with a cost advantage in both the fixed-rate and floating-rate debt markets, but who exhibit a comparative advantage in the fixed-rate market, may borrow in that market and swap the fixed interest payments for floating payments with another, less creditworthy borrower who issues floating-rate debt. Interest payments, but not the principal, are swapped, and payments are conditional in that, if one party defaults, the other is absolved of its obligation. Since the principal is not swapped, we say that it is notional. The gains from this swap are allocated between the two parties and, typically, a financial intermediary who facilitates the swap.

In the classical example of an interest rate swap, the swap itself results from credit-market comparative advantage. 'Gains from trade' come into play similar to those gains arising from any specialization of trade arrangements.

3. **Interest rate caps**

   The most popular interest rate option is a cap. A cap provides the purchaser with a guarantee that the rate of interest on a floating rate loan will not rise above a certain level. This level is known as the cap rate. Whenever the relevant floating rate is above the cap rate, the writer of the cap pays the difference between the floating rate and the cap rate to the holder. A cap is effectively a portfolio of call options on an interest rate.

4. **Floors and collars**

   The opposite of a cap is a floor. Thus a floor is effectively a portfolio of put options on an interest rate. Floors pay off the amount by which the floating reference rate of interest is less than the floor rate. If a company has a floating rate loan and thinks low rates are unlikely, it might be prepared to give up the benefits from any low rates that might occur in the future. Thus it might consider writing a floor. One popular contract is a collar or a floor-ceiling agreement. This is where a company buys a cap and sells a floor. It has the effect of ensuring that a floating rate loan never costs more than the cap rate nor less than the floor rate. Often, the collar is structured so that its initial cost is zero. The value of the cap purchased by the company then equals the value of the floor sold. When the cap rate equals the floor rate in a zero cost collar, the collar has the effect of fixing the rate paid on the floating rate loan at this rate. The collar then serves the same purpose as an interest rate swap. Not surprisingly, the cap/floor proves to be the same as the corresponding swap rate in this case.

5. **Average rate caps**

   Average rate caps are an interesting variant on the standard product. They do not provide insurance against the rate on every reset date being above the cap rate. Instead, they guarantee that the average rate paid during the life of the cap will not be above the cap rate. Average rate caps are relatively rare, but they may become more widespread in the future. Arguably, from the point of view of the purchaser, average rate caps have some advantages over the plain vanilla caps described earlier. They are less expensive and, if a treasurer is concerned about the total cost of a floating rate loan during its life, they offer a more relevant insurance contract. From the point of view of the financial institution selling a cap, an average rate cap has the disadvantage that it is more difficult to value than a regular cap and the advantage that, once a good valuation procedure has been developed, it is generally easier to hedge. Floors and collars based on the average interest rate are also occasionally traded.

6. **Swaptions**

   A swaption is an option on an interest rate swap. It gives the holder the right, but not the obligation to enter into the interest rate swap in the future. An American swaption can be exercised anytime during its life. A European swaption can only be exercised at expiration. A quasi-American swaption can be exercised at a number of times during its life.

   An interest rate swap can be viewed as an agreement to exchange a fixed rate bond for a floating rate bond. A swaption can therefore be regarded as an option to exchange a fixed rate bond for a floating rate bond. The future value of a fixed rate bond is uncertain but we can be sure that the future value of a floating rate bond will be very close to par. A swaption therefore gives the holder the right to exchange a fixed rate bond for its par value. If a swaption gives the holder the right to pay fixed and receive floating, it is a put option on a fixed rate bond with a strike price equal to the par value. If a swaption gives the holder the right to pay floating and received fixed, it is a call option on the fixed rate bond with a strike price equal to the par value.

7. **Securitization**

   Securitization is the process of packaging loans into pools of securities and has become an important financial innovation in the face of the global economy. This process benefits financial institutions, investors and borrowers as well as the economy as a whole. Securitization allows financial institutions to free up capital for increasing lending, make better use of their capital base and enable them to specialize in areas where they have a comparative advantage in the management of risk. In short, securitization contributes to the overall efficiency of the financial system.

V. Conclusions

The functions of the financial system have not changed: borrowers still want to raise money by instruments that best manage their business, interest rate, and exchange rate risk; and lenders still want to invest funds to buy repackaged securities, like pensions and insurance products, as well as portfolios of direct securities, like equities and bonds. What has changed is the incidence of system risk, the sophistication of the system's participants, and the integration of the Greek system into the global financial system.

Financial innovation is the necessary and sufficient condition that will facilitate the Greek system to raise its standards and obtain the benefits from the process of globalization of the world's financial markets.

Re-regulation of the financial system will be the route to enhance competitiveness of the Greek financial sector, and, together with the introduction of the new financial instruments which open up new sources of funds, will help the Greek economy to converge towards the more developed European financial systems and obtain the benefits of economic integration.

Notes
1. The authors would like to thank Lawrence Booth, Paul Halpern, John Hull, and Alan White for their comments. The usual disclaimer applies.

Bibliography
Brealey, M. and Conor Quigley (1989), *Completing the Internal Market of the European Community*, London: Graham & Trotman.
Commission of the EC (1985), *The White Paper on Completing the Internal Market*, Brussels.
Dassesse, M. (1991), 'Banking in Europe – Restrictions and Freedoms', *International Banking Law*, **9**(8), January, 385–6.
Dixon, R. (1991), *Banking in Europe: The Single Market*, London: Routledge.
Erdilek, A. (1991), 'The Financial Integration of the European Community in Project 1992', *Case Western Reserve Journal of International Law*, **2**, 245.
Ewing, A. (1990), 'The Single Market of 1992: Implications for Banking and Investment Services on the EC', *Hastings International and Comparative Law Review*, **13**, Spring, 453.
Hankey, S. (1989), 'Pride, Prejudice and Reciprocity in the Single Market', *Journal of International Business Law*, **4**, 49.
Johnson, H. (1990), 'European Single Financial Area Takes Big Step Forward?' *International Banking Law*, **8**(10), March, 150.
Rugman, Alan M. and Alain Verbeke (1990), *Global Corporate Strategy and Trade Policy*, London: Routledge.
Rugman, A.M. and A. Verbeke (1990), 'Competitive Strategies for non-European Firms' in B. Burgenmeier and J.L. Mucchielli (eds), *Multinationals and Europe 1992*, London: Routledge, 22–35.
Toll, C.T., (1990), 'The European Community's Second Banking Directive: Can Antiquated United States Legislation Keep Pace?', *Vanderbilt Journal of Transnational Law*, **23**(3), 615–52.

PART V

LESSONS FROM THE UNIFICATION OF GERMANY

21 Unequal integration: the case of German re-unification

Horst Tomann

Introduction

Since *Ricardo* we have known that unequal partners may benefit from establishing trade relations. If production costs are lower in one country, it is nevertheless beneficial to exchange products with other countries according to the principle of comparative advantage in production. Economic integration via international specialization produces its beneficial effects without any reliance on factor mobility.

German re-unification is not a case in point. It is true that economists have complained of the substantial increase in the wage level in Eastern Germany since unification (see, for example Sinn, 1990; Akerlof et al., 1991). High real wages have been regarded as a main cause of the break-down in production and employment and a main reason why the economy's take-off has been delayed. Without the high wage level, it is argued, Eastern Germany would have had enough Ricardian goods to benefit from trade and integration. Unfortunately, however, this argument overlooks the fact that labour is mobile within Germany. The consequence was absolutely clear to Ricardo who expressed the view that there was no reason to expect different profits of capital employed in London and Yorkshire because 'capital and population' are mobile within a country (*Principles*, p. 134).

This paper first provides an overview of the sequence of events in the process of re-unification. This is to underline that the usual approach of economic reasoning does not apply. It continues by exploring and evaluating monetary integration, wage policy and privatization policy, respectively, which have been the main elements in the process of economic integration. It concludes with a short outlook.

The sequence of re-unification

The peculiar circumstances of German re-unification can be summarized as follows. The process started with an integrated labour market. When the wall was opened on 9 November 1989, it meant that the West German labour markets were opened up to East Germans. Large income differentials and a high demand for qualified labour in Western Germany induced emigration from East to West. This situation was highly unstable and pressurised the government to speed up the restructuring of the GDR economic system. As a main response to those tensions, a monetary reform exchanging the former currency for the DM took place in mid-1990. Hence even before German unity (3 October 1990) a monetary union was established supplying a hard and convertible currency. Thereby the signals were set for a fundamental structural change. The federal government provided for massive income transfers to build up a social security system in East Germany. In addition a Unity Fund was established to finance public investment in East Germany. On the other hand, although much political pressure had been applied, the East German states were not immediately integrated into the system of tax revenue redistribution (Finanzausgleich). This system is due for reform and will not be re-established before 1995 for the whole of Germany. At the same time, considerable administrative support was provided to establish an administration at state and local levels. The government privatization agency, the Treuhand, was taken over by West German staff. This indicates that a rapid process of social learning was initiated both in public administration and in the enterprise sector.

The German Monetary Union (GMU)
As far as monetary conditions of economic development are concerned, I propose to distinguish two different types of transition problems: (1) how to convert money assets and liabilities (the stock problem), (2) how to restore the competitiveness of the GDR economy (the flow problem). First as to the conversion of money assets, the money stocks accumulated in the past represented an obstacle to further development in that there were no real capital values of equivalent size (money overhang). However, it was clear that within a monetary union the money overhang would no longer be a GDR problem but would be transformed into a common German problem. There are two (conflicting) aspects of this problem. On the one hand, conversion of Mark to D-Mark at a favourable rate could create an inflationary potential. An additional money supply in excess of an amount determined by the increase of productive capacity would have violated the Bundesbank's quantity-of-money rule. The expansion of the money supply due to GMU was estimated to amount to 120 billion DM (10 per cent of M3), approximately the additional potential output (Deutsche Bundesbank, 1990). In fact the money supply increased at a higher rate (14 per cent). None the less, inflation was still moderate in the autumn (annual rate: 3 per cent) partly owing to the fact that supply in tradable goods markets is presumably rather elastic. Hence part of the additional demand was matched by an import increase that helped to reduce Germany's huge current account imbalances. In some narrow markets, for example, the market for second hand cars, prices increased sharply, however.

On the other hand, the conversion rate for money assets determined the extent of the capital transfer flowing from West Germany to East Germany. This transfer has usually been treated with respect to its distributional consequences but it has a developmental role as well. Money assets were in the hands of private households and small-scale enterprises. A favourable conversion rate for money assets would indeed have provided for equity finance to small business, thus stimulating economic growth. As for private households, incentives to save (a right to buy their dwellings or shares of 'people's ownership' in the productive sector) could have produced similar effects.

The government neither introduced such incentives nor a scheme of freezing private households' savings, tolerating a temporary boom in private consumption. The conversion ratios for money assets were differentiated according to social criteria only. Up to a limited amount per person a ratio of one to one was applied, above that amount the ratio was two to one.

Whereas the conversion of money assets actually increased the real wealth of private households and small-scale enterprises, the West German government did not intend a net capital transfer of equivalent size to the East German economy. Rather, the Deutsche Bundesbank proposed (and the governments by the State Treaty approved) that liabilities should be converted at the same ratio (two to one) that was in general applied to money assets. Hence a compensatory item amounting to not more than 26.4 billion DM was necessary to balance assets and liabilities after the conversion act. However, by limiting the banking sector's claims against government – and accordingly limiting the interest burden on the federal budget – the credit banks were left with overvalued assets. In particular the Deutsche Kreditbank (DKB), a credit bank founded as a daughter of the former GDR Staatsbank, inherited dubious credits to industry and the housing sector which amounted to 330 billion Marks (before conversion). It should have been clear that the DKB, which was to undertake profit-oriented banking activities, could not reach a sustainable position under these conditions. The basic shortcoming in the Bundesbank's proposal was to calculate the conversion of money stocks by simply adapting the socialist accounting system without questioning the rationale of its evaluations. In the socialist planning system, firms' debt burden had no economic meaning as investment risks were non-existent. The underlying reason for the firms' debts was taxation: firms were not allowed to accumulate profits and the 'value added' accrued to the government. In exchange for the fiscal drag, the government granted loans, thereby controlling the overall level and allocation of investment activities.

A market economy by contrast requires equity finance in order to provide for a firm's ability to bear investment risks. Hence by simply transforming the past pattern of liabilities at a two-to-one ratio into hard currency the government ended up with a systemic over-indebtedness of firms. It has been argued that a 'general' debt release would not be in order, since it would induce misallocation. It runs the other way around: the government imposed a general tax on firms to finance the burden of a generous conversion of money assets. This major transition problem has only recently been recognized. The Treuhandanstalt, the state's trustee agency responsible for privatization, will take on these liabilities. Hence, firms will be able to start new activities without the burden of past debts reflecting the peculiar financial relationships of the socialist system.

Wage policy
As regards the flow problem, the main determinant of the East Germany economy's competitiveness – after monetary union – was wage policy.

Initially, on the basis of (dubious) productivity calculations an evaluation of income flows at a ratio of one-to-one seemed to leave industry with a competitive cost level. However, markets for Eastern tradable products broke down completely as East Germans showed frantic demand for Western products; Eastern Europe was no longer willing to pay in hard currency for East German goods. Moreover, in expectation of the monetary union, substantial wage increases had been negotiated in several industries. That pushed up the overall wage level in East Germany by an estimated 20 per cent in 1990. As the wage rise was based on short-term contracts further substantial increases had to be expected.

In early 1991 a new wage settlement negotiated by IG Metall, followed by other trade unions and their employers' associations, clarified the situation. Essentially long-term contracts were agreed upon, fixing wages per hour to the West German level starting with an initial 0.6 ratio followed by annual increases offering a catching-up by 1994. These contracts provided reasonable perspectives for both sides. From the employee's standpoint a catching-up process of income was guaranteed. That provided favourable prospects as real income differentials were smaller owing to subsidies on non-tradables in East Germany, especially housing. On the other hand employers could count on substantial wage differentials for at least the next three years. In particular, fringe benefits and a shortening of the working week had been excluded from the contracts. Hence even if the contract holds total labour cost per hour will still be 20 per cent below West German costs by 1994.

These wage settlements have been questioned on the neoclassical assumption that lower wages would have avoided the sharp rise in unemployment which is actually under way. In particular this argument was raised in a study undertaken by Akerlof et al. (1991), and was underlined by a recent OECD (1991) study on Germany.

The Akerlof study argues on the basis of some 400 inquiries in East Germany that migration is driven by unemployment, not by wage differentials. It suggests, therefore, that wage increases are counterproductive as they cannot prevent migration. On the contrary, migration would be reinforced by such a wage policy.

The Akerlof study recommends a scheme of wage subsidization. There are two arguments against financing unemployment on the job. First, from the employers' point of view, low wages diminish the pressure for productivity increases and delay the catching-up with Western productivity standards. To avoid this kind of adverse incentive the Akerlof study recommends a scheme of decreasing subsidization. However, if the objective is to keep firms sustainable, the subsidy should be bound not to wage levels but to investment. Second, there are other adverse incentives in such a scheme even for the subsidized workers. The recent government policy of subsidizing unemployment on the job by paying wage differentials (of up to 100 per cent in the case of short-term labour) is evidence of that. Many first complained that workers had no incentive to accept retraining or re-education programmes because participation in such a programme would reduce their income.

The government stopped the programme of financing unemployment on the job in mid-1991. As a main provision against rising unemployment, a scheme of separating labour contracts from the employment relation was designed. Firms are allowed to lay off workers and end contracts if that is what is required for restructuring. On the other hand, contracts are offered by specific associations to the laid-off workers, providing them with remuneration and employment in communal programmes. These associations are temporary and should stimulate retraining of the labour force.

By the end of 1992 these associations employed 400,000 persons, that is, 7 per cent of the active labour force. The main argument against this kind of employment policy is that the communal programmes contest the markets for small-sized private firms. Hence, employment policy impedes the emergence of a spontaneous market order which is a fundamental element of transition to a market economy (McKinnon, 1992).

In 1992 East German labour market conditions worsened dramatically. That was an opportunity for the employers' associations to question the consensus on East German wage policy. In the metal industry employers gave notice regarding the 1991 three-year contract in order to avoid a 26 per cent wage increase which was scheduled to become effective on 1 April 1993. This brought the metal industry to the edge of the first big conflict in East German labour relations. Employers complain that a cost squeeze during a period of shrinking demand would drive many firms into bankruptcy. The trade union claims that contracts have to be honoured (there are no escape clauses in the contracts). Moreover, they point to the workers' situation who have suffered real income losses since subsidies on housing and public utilities have been substantially cut on 1 January 1993.

It seemed that employers had a good chance to get out of their obligation for substantial wage increases. They could take advantage of a dramatic fall in industrial employment. In December 1992, East German industry and mining still employed 828,000 persons, that is 37.9 per cent less than at the end of 1991. The resulting huge excess supply of labour strongly supports the employers' position to provide for compensation for inflation but to postpone real wage increases in East Germany. It does not seem, however, that East German industry would suffer a cost squeeze if the wage increases settled in 1991 were enacted. During 1992, the number of working hours in East German industry fell by 23 per cent, and industrial production fell by approximately 5 per cent. Hence productivity (per hour) increased by roughly a quarter. This may continue in the years to come since there is still unexploited productivity potential in industry. On the other hand there is a joint interest – with the trade unions' unspoken agreement – in high retained profits to provide for a sound financial basis for new investment which enacts productivity potential and creates new jobs.

The solution to this conflict lies in schemes offering workers' participation in expected profits. In the process of transition such schemes were, from the beginning, a neglected alternative to traditional wage policy (Sinn and Sinn, 1993). In March 1993 it was still an open question if profit sharing schemes providing for the firms' short-term financial viability and at the same time securing the workers' long-term claims could be negotiated.

Privatization
In Eastern Europe and the former Soviet Union, privatization is regarded as a catch-all instrument. Filatotchev (1991) enumerates the following objectives:

- Stabilizing the monetary system and absorbing the money overhang.
- Diminishing public budget deficits as firms' losses are no longer subsidized.
- Increasing public revenues by asset sales.
- Developing an entrepreneurial culture.
- Increasing efficiency of state owned firms.
- Stimulating competition and dissolving monopolistic structures in the economy.

Referring to the literature on principal–agent problems we would expect, above all, incentives for increased efficiency via privatization. In particular the following arguments are crucial for an economy in a state of transition:

- Privatization is a precondition for a capital market to be established.

- Privatization has the fundamental effect of restraining the influence of the political 'Nomenklatura' (the former ruling class) on the economy.
- Privatization of firms and the banking sector provides for hard budget constraints throughout the economy.

German experience

The government's trust agency 'Treuhandanstalt' (THA) was originally created to manage 'people's ownership' under the Modrow government. By mid-1990 the THA was redirected to implement the Federal Government's privatization programme.

Generally the THA's objectives have been to either privatize or close down firms. Therefore the agency's very existence was to be temporary. By the end of 1992 the first branches of this agency were closed down. The agency will definitely have finished its activities by the end of 1994. The agency might support a firm's restructuring and redevelopment strategy and actually was entitled to approve those strategies, that is to act like a supervisory board. This caused much bureaucratic delay to the process of privatization. By September 1991 about 80 per cent of the firms under control of THA had delivered their opening balance sheets (in DM) and enterprise concepts. The THA, however, was just starting approval of these concepts.

In addition the THA aimed at decomposing the huge, vertically integrated industrial complexes, 'Kombinate', which were typical of the socialist system. To indicate the magnitude of this task THA representatives typically counted the 6,000 companies which they still commanded by mid-1991 as being equivalent to about 40,000 firms in a market economy. Decomposition normally ends up with 'raisin picking', and the unsaleable remainder is left with the THA.

Finally, the THA was restrained from acting as a market agent by industrial policy objectives, especially regional employment objectives. This has been particularly the case whenever big firms were the major employers of a whole region. Furthermore, the THA was restricted in its pricing policy by fiscal constraints. In 1992, these constraints have been lifted by allowing debt releases for firms eligible for redevelopment. The debt release was carried out by simply providing the firms with compensating assets (to be drawn on the THA) which balanced the firms' debts, and then shortening the balance sheets. Furthermore, a debt-for-equity swap was offered to the firms in order to increase their risk capital endowment required by the creditors. The objective was that a restructured firm should start with a capital endowment equivalent to the industry average.

Consequently, the Federal Government – the owner of the THA – eventually acted as a lender of last resort, steering restructured firms into a viable starting position. That was done by a case-by-case procedure, however, and took time.

Means of privatization
The THA has been criticized for relying predominantly on customized sales and making no use of the capital market. Indeed, the THA has found itself in a seller's market, although a very tight one. At the present time, however, the firms controlled by the THA do not fulfil the legal requirements for admission to the stock exchange. Offering shares to the public has not yet been tried. As the firms consolidate their balance sheets, access to the stock market will become more and more an option for privatization. The THA is also thinking of using the assistance of investment banks, in particular to attract investors from abroad.

Meanwhile, the THA has shifted to a supportive strategy concerning management-buy-outs and management-buy-ins (MBOs/MBIs). The main problem with this instrument of privatization is a lack of risk capital and managerial experience. The THA assists MBOs by offering specific grants and credit guarantees. In mid-1992 there existed about 1,500 MBOs or MBIs, approximately 20 per cent of all privatizations.

Subsidization
To date, subsidization of THA companies was restricted to liquidity credits (although most firms claimed a roll-over of these credits) and wage subsidies for shortened hours of work. The wage subsidy scheme was phased out by mid-1991, mainly because this scheme exerted a disincentive for workers to quit and apply for re-education and retraining. In addition, the THA took over interest payments on old debts as a temporary measure.

More important than these temporary measures will be the debt release for firms eligible for redevelopment. The government issued a decree on debt release by September 1990. Its implementation, however, was started only by the end of 1991.

Subsidization will continue and will even have to be increased for companies which cannot be privatized but also cannot be closed down for reasons of regional employment. This long-term task will fall back to the politicians. When the THA has finished its activities, a public budget will be established, jointly financed by local governments, the states and the federal government, to support what have been labeled 'industrial core areas'. This solution at least provides for clarity on the cost of regional employment policy.

Concluding remarks
In contrast to Central and Eastern European countries, East Germany enjoys favourable conditions for economic development. Macroeconomic stability

is secured as the monetary union provides for price level stability, and the level of aggregate demand is supported by generous income transfers from West German public budgets. Hence, in implementing measures towards the required structural change, the government can be sure that adverse effects on the macroeconomic equilibrium are balanced.

On the other hand, two basic government decisions concerning property rights turned out seriously to hinder economic development. First, the re-unification treaty assigned property rights on real estate to ancient owners, not to the present ones. Hence the restitution blocked the disposition of property which must be regarded as an essential precondition for the functioning of the capital market. Secondly, the government missed the opportunity to combine the Monetary Union with a genuine monetary reform. That would have required the revaluation of firms' liabilities on realistic terms. These decisions were corrected later on, however, when the government took a more pragmatic stance, thereby confirming that the process of transition is virtually an open process.

Bibliography

Akerlof, G.A. et al. (1991), 'East Germany in from the cold: the economic aftermath of Currency Union', Paper presented at the Conference of the Brookings Panel on Economic Activity, Washington, DC.

Deutsche Bundesbank (1990), 'Die Währungsunion mit der Deutschen Demokratischen Republik', *Monatsberichte*, **42**(7), July.

Filatotchev, J.V. (1991), 'Prospects for privatisation in the USSR', Paper presented at the annual EARIE Conference, Ferrara.

McKinnon, R.I. (1992), 'Spontaneous Order on the Road Back from Socialism: An Asian Perspective', *American Economic Review*, Papers and Proceedings, May.

OECD (1991), *OECD Economic Surveys: Germany 1990/91*, Paris.

Ricardo, D. (1817), *On the Principles of Political Economy and Taxation*, edited by P. Sraffa, Cambridge: CAP, 1951.

Siebert, H. (1990), 'The economic integration of Germany – an update', *Kiel Discussion Papers*, 160a, September.

Sinn, G. and H.-W. Sinn (1993), *Kaltstart – Volkswirtschaftliche Aspekte der deutschen Vereinigung*, 3rd edition, Muenchen.

Sinn, H.-W. (1990), 'Macroeconomic aspects of German unification', *Münchner Wirtschaftswissenschaftliche Beiträge*, Discussion Papers, November.

22 Restructuring the East German economy
Jürgen Müller

1 Introduction

The economic reform in East Germany has been among the fastest in Eastern Europe. After the peaceful palace revolution of October 1989 and the first election of April 1990, a currency reform with West Germany was implemented on July 1, 1990. This also implied the adoption of the most important business laws and the abolition of all tariff barriers with West Germany and therefore the EC.

The major instrument for entrepreneurial development, namely a stable, legal macroeconomic environment was therefore quickly created. The trust institution Treuhandanstalt (THA) that had already been established before the currency reform was made the centrepiece of the privatization drive through a new set of guidelines in June 1990. After some start-up problems, specifically concerning the rights of previous owners and the issue of compensation vs. restitution, privatization was speeded up considerably. As a consequence, private enterprise activity could not only take place via entry of new firms, but also via privatization (including management buy-outs and management buy-ins) and reprivatization of those firms that were returned to their original owners.

These favourable conditions for private enterprise must be seen against the difficult macroeconomic climate as a consequence of the currency reform (a revaluation of the currency by between 200 and 400 per cent), the reduction of trade barriers, the exposure to highly efficient West German and EC industry and the subsequent reorientation of trade. Without sufficient process and product know-how on the part of East German firms, and given the rapidly rising wage level, the market became quickly swamped by West German and West European products. Furthermore, the major part of the traditional export market of East Germany, namely the Comecon region, was lost as a result of the currency revaluation and the change over to trade on the basis of hard currency. Another important difficulty of the East German companies is the lack of managerial and administrative talent. Such skills as marketing, procurement, finance, controlling, etc. were largely missing on the enterprise side.[1]

2 Industry structure in East Germany

Before the division of Germany in 1948, East Germany was one of the main centres of economic activity. Berlin dominated as a centre of transport and services. It was the headquarters of banking and finance and the home of major industries. Even small scale industry, especially textiles and light manufacturing was important there. The other important regions were Saxony, Saxony-Anhalt and Thuringia (if we ignore for the moment upper Silesia, which was handed over to Poland after 1945). There the chemical and machine tool industry dominated, but also many small and medium sized enterprises, such as publishing in Leipzig.

After the initial 'socialization' of the large manufacturers under the Soviet occupation (1945–50), 42 per cent of the workforce and 31 per cent of the GNP was still accounted for by small and medium sized private enterprises. At first this sector lost only slowly, but after the erection of the wall in 1961, dramatically, in importance. In 1972, 6,700 small semi-stage enterprises,[2] 2,900 private enterprises and 1,900 cooperatives were taken over by the state, eliminating the private sector almost completely. Most firms were organized in large administrative units (Kombinate, 126 altogether, plus 95 district enterprises), which led to a very unusual size distribution (the so-called socialist hole, since most small- and medium-sized enterprises were missing). Before the currency reform and unification, the tradition of small entrepreneurship in East Germany had therefore mostly disappeared, either by forced take-overs or by tax expropriation.[3] In 1989 the private sector produced only about 3 per cent of GNP, with the highest participation in trade and services and the retail trade.

The economic structure of East Germany, especially compared with West Germany, was heavily concentrated on traditional industries like mining, energy, manufacturing and construction. These sectors employed almost half of the labour force, an unusually high proportion for such an industrialized country. The manufacturing sector, similar to that of West Germany, is dominated by chemical, electrical engineering, machine tools and optics. The resource base of the economy, especially for the chemical and energy sector, was largely based on domestic lignite (with very high environmental costs) and imported energy from the USSR.

The industrial sector was organized into large combines with a high degree of vertical integration. For example, the automobile combine IFA employed 55,000 people, the computer and office equipment combine Robotron 69,000 people. Even the average enterprise size within these combines was quite large with 893 persons, compared to only about 190 employees in a typical West German company.

The East German economy – with a trade share of 30 per cent of its GNP – was less open than Western countries of a similar size (the Netherlands had a trade share of almost 50 per cent in 1988). Almost 40 per cent of its trade was with the Soviet Union, and almost 30 per cent with its other CEMA neighbours. Trade with West Germany and OECD countries was only 20 per cent.

If one compares the two countries one can see the much more autarkic character of the East German economy (the higher importance of non-durable consumer goods, light industry, textiles and foodstuffs). West German industry on the other hand is much more specialized in the production of capital and durable consumer goods, but also in chemicals.

The events after the fall of the Berlin wall led very quickly to a change of power. After the caretaker government of the Modrow regime, a grand coalition of Christian Democrats, Social Democrats and Free Democrats took over after the fist East German elections on April 18, 1990. Given the continued outward migration to West Germany (almost 3 000 people a day), and the imminent collapse of the East German economic system, the new government decided quickly to accept the economic and monetary union with West Germany that had been proposed by Chancellor Helmut Kohl in February. This led to the currency reform on July 1, 1990, and, under the jurisdiction of the Bundesbank, to the creation of a two-tier banking system. At the same time most of the economic laws of West Germany were adopted and all trade barriers with the EC eliminated.

With the currency reform, a completely new fiscal system was created, with the adoption of the West German system. But the elimination of the many subsidies took a long time, as did the attempts to implement tax collection. As a consequence, major budget transfers from West to East Germany had already taken place early in 1990 even before unification on October 3, 1990.

The government changed the status of all the state owned firms to limited stock companies and placed them in a trust agency, the Treuhandanstalt, in March 1990. Its status was changed in June 1990 from a holding company to a privatization organization, whose major aim was to reorganize and preprivatize owned firms. Joint ventures with foreign firms were permitted from January 25, 1990 and the setting up of private companies was greatly facilitated.

The centralized state system in East Germany was replaced by a federal one, in which five new federal states were created. The old planning ministries and all the central apparatus was almost completely abandoned, while at the same time the administrative structure of the new five states had to be created.

3 Initial reforms

The first effects of the reform were:

- macroeconomic adjustment problems as a consequence of the currency reform, and
- the effect of the integration of the East German economy into the EC trading system.

The currency reform resulted in a revaluation of 200 to 400 per cent. Given the lack of modern products and, in many cases, modern production processes and the continuous increase in wages, almost all tradable East German products were immediately priced out of the East German market. Their place was taken by West German or international products (for example in the area of consumer electronics). The move to a hard currency and the enormous revaluation also implied almost a complete loss of comparative advantage in East European markets, which had before made up almost 70 per cent of East German exports. The transfer rouble agreement in the second half of 1990 softened the adjustment somewhat. But the transfer of CEMA trade to convertible currencies and the economic problems of the USSR led to an almost complete collapse of that market from early 1991. As a consequence, industrial production dropped (nominally) to almost 30 per cent of its 1990 level, and the unemployment rate (including those workers on short time) reached over 20 per cent.[4] But large transfers from West Germany to the tune of over 150 billion DM in 1991 after 80 billion DM in 1990 and a number of new financial programmes helped, not only to maintain, but also to increase the standard of living in East Germany.

4 Private enterprise and the role of the THA

Private enterprise could be stimulated in four ways.

i) Growth:
   Expanding from the small base that already existed in the handicraft and trade sector.
ii) Entry:
   Via the creation of new firms.
iii) The restitution of small- and medium-sized firms that were expropriated (mainly from the 1972 Act).
iv) Restructuring:
   Those individuals with a sufficient capital base (very few) could buy firms that were privatized through the THA, or take part in management buy-outs and management buy-ins, or take over parts of enterprises that are liquidated by the THA.

It is clear that growth does not affect the number of entrepreneurial enterprises, but only their economic importance. Since restitution is part of restructuring, entry and restructuring are the crucial policy variables for the creation of private enterprise. As almost 97 per cent of economic activity was carried out by state-owned enterprises, the role of the THA is crucial for this development. It directly affects *restructuring* and, through access to assets of liquidated enterprises, *entry*.

It is therefore important to look at the task of the THA in more detail. It had to solve three important problems.

- To transfer the publicly owned enterprises into a legal form with limited liability (legal restructuring).
- To solve the problem of the treatment of former owners (restitutions vs. compensation).
- To privatize, once questions of property rights were settled.

The first task was carried out by the old THA under its March 1990 guidelines. Its companies were changed either to stock companies (Aktiengesellschaften) or to limited liability companies (GmbHs).

With the revised law of June 1990 the THA received revised objectives:

- To hold the shares of the enterprises and to control their performance.
- To reorganize the companies from their old structure (needed for the implementation of the planning process) into a sensible corporate structure that could be better managed, monitored, and eventually privatized (this included the spin-off of many of the vertically integrated activities that were not essential parts of the 'core' activities of the firms in a market environment).
- To privatize the profitable enterprises.
- To restructure the unprofitable enterprises into those which had to be closed down and those which afterwards, with restructuring, technology and management transfer and some financial help, could be saved ('Sanierung').

The conflict between these two last objectives, given the depressed economic state of East German enterprises and the extraordinarily high level of unemployment led to repeated disagreements about whether stabilization or privatization are to be the main task of the THA.

5 Initial progress

Initially privatization through the THA proceeded slowly, because of:

- the time needed to make the THA an efficient administrative organization

- the question of restitution.

The THA was created with the first THA law of March 1, 1990. The state-owned firms were to be transferred to the state holding company THA, and formed into limited companies (either AGs, KGs or GmbHs). Its initial aim (under the pressure of the 'round table') was to 'maintain' in a coordinated way the assets assembled by the state and to prevent asset stripping by opportunistic party officials.

This objective was changed with the second THA Law of June 17, 1990, now under the newly elected de Maiziere government. While headed by a West German (first Rainer Golke, later Detlev Rohwedder), its staff was mainly drawn from the old planning ministries and the management of the large combines. Only after the unification on October 2, when the legal responsibility moved to the Ministry of Finance, was a large build-up, with an influx of Western experts, possible. By February 1991, it had reached a size of 3,000, with many of its 1,000 Western experts being on short-term loan from the major West German firms and banks. Smaller sales were delegated to 15 regional directors. By then, most firms had been catalogued, and the THA could move from the role of a passive seller (essentially reacting to offers) to an active seller, in which many merchant banks and outside advisers also played a significant role.

But then, it was the uncertainty of disputed ownership which still held up many company sales. Most of the publicly owned enterprises had been expropriated either by the Russian administration (1945–1949) or the East German State (1949–1989) and could therefore not be sold until the question of the treatment of previous owners had been settled. Given the protection of property rights under the German constitution (Article 14), and its importance in the unification treaty, restitution to previous owners was to be the norm. Only property that was confiscated between 1945 and 1949 by the occupying Russian administration would not have to be restituted to previous owners, but somehow compensated. Given the large number of expropriations in East Germany between 1949 and 1989 and the treatment of the property of many of those who had left East Germany during that time, this administrative led to more than 1 million (sometimes competing) claims on East German property. But given the lack of administration and properly functioning offices for property records, this issue could not be quickly dealt with. This development more or less blocked the privatization activities of the THA until an amendment to the unification treaty was passed in Parliament on March 29, 1991.

This so-called speed-up law (Enthemmungsgesetz: 'Gesetz zur Beseitigung von Hemmnissen bei der Privatisierung von Unternehmen und zur Förderung von Investitionen in den neuen Ländern'), which modified 11 existing laws and 130 regulations, and introduced a new law and 62 new regulations, maintained the principle of 'restitution first', but at the same time aimed to encourage new investors. An absolute priority for new investment was given by providing for an investment competition between old owners and potential new investors. As a consequence, if an investor was found who was willing to take over an existing enterprise and to invest substantially, he had priority over the claims of a previous owner who was not willing to undertake a similar size investment and maintain or create an equally large employment level. The individual districts had to issue these investment permits, as a result of which previous owners would eventually be compensated in line with the policy 'job creation and job savings before restitution'.

This is of course a fairly complicated procedure. But to some extent as a result of this procedure and the major efforts to upgrade the property registration offices, privatization began to proceed quite rapidly (20–25 enterprises per day) so that by the end of 1991 a significant part of the old state-owned enterprises had been privatized and a fair number closed down and their assets, i.e. buildings, machinery, etc. privatized. As of July 1991, 632 firms (with about 125,000 jobs) had been privatized through liquidation, with up to one-third of these jobs maintained by the new owners. But given the administrative complexities, and the political difficulty of closing down loss-making enterprises quickly, the privatization process will go on several more years.

6 Position of private firms in the overall economy

We have mentioned above the four methods by which private firms can be created:

- growth of old private firms,
- entry of old private firms,
- entry through creating a new firm,
- restitution,
- restructuring through privatization or through management buy-out/ buy-in.

Growth:
There were only about 600 firms in the manufacturing sector which had less than 100 employees in 1989.

Entry:
The most important of these forms of private activity (at least on paper) has been entry through creating new firms. The number of registrations for new enterprises in 1990, 281 000, indicates the potential. Many of these are in the service sector, but few are in the manufacturing sector. The number of new

enterprises registered, running just below 30,000 per month in late 1990, was still about 22,000 in June 1991, while those closed rose from 4,000 to about 7,000 per month during the same period.

Restitution:
A great number of the 3,000 private enterprises and the 6,700 semi-state enterprises, as well as the 1,900 cooperatives taken over in 1972, were either given back to their old owners or sold in the form of management buy-outs. By October 1990, 3,000 requests for restitution had been approved; almost 80 per cent were in manufacturing, 34 per cent had more than 50 employees, 10 per cent more than 100, 75 per cent of those returned were maintained by the old owners or their successors.

Restructuring:
The vertical disintegration of firms turned out to be another important factor in entrepreneurial activity. The splitting up of sections of companies is encouraged through the separation law (Entflechtungsgesetz), that was part of the speed-up law of March 1991. Subsections of enterprises may be split up on the initiative of the workers or the management involved, if it is not of crucial interest for the core business. By April 18, 1991, 9 953 firms were created in this way. Most of these are still owned by the Treuhand, but 1 200 have already been sold.

With its programme of management buy-outs/management buy-ins (i.e. MBOs/MBIs), that had been articulated since April 1991, the THA intended to encourage this aspect more. To some extent it is also a counterweight to the 'colonization' that is taking place through the massive inflow of West German capital, because of the comparative lack of capital of much of the East German entrepreneurial class. It is clear that the role of small entrepreneurial firms is not only strengthened through the MBO-MBI-programme of the THA and the quick access to assets of liquidated enterprises, but also by many of the financial subsidies and favourable loan conditions granted in this connection.

By October 1991, almost 900 MBOs/MBI's had already been carried out. While two-thirds of them are in the size class up to 50 employees, a fair number are also in the larger size class. But it will take a long time to eliminate the socialist hole in the size distribution of firms. Much will also depend on the extent to which independent key manufacturing activities can be maintained as a nucleus of economic activity in East Germany. If many of the firms taken over by West German and other European companies are only used as extended workbenches, then the potential for an entrepreneurial class, as we observe it in West Germany in such companies as Daimler, Benz, Siemens, Mannesmann, MAN, Volkswagen, etc., will be significantly reduced.

7 The role of the THA

The THA affects the markets in two ways:

- reorganization and monitoring activities
- its privatization activities (which mostly result in horizontal mergers with Western companies).

The THA in essence acts as a holding, controlling and sales agency. The necessary restructuring of the firms – to reduce the degree of vertical integration and bringing the companies back to their 'core' activity and the need for closing down unprofitable enterprises is therefore carried out in a decentralized way. The old 'Kombinate' which have been formed into joint stock companies will first get an Advisory Board (Aufsichtsrat) who will then appoint or reappoint company directors and monitor their performance. The large majority of the members of the Advisory Board come from West German companies, the banking sector or often from related industries. This helps to encourage technology and management transfer. But it also has some competitive implications. Sometimes the Board members come from companies active in the same field or from banks who have as their major clients companies in the same field. As a consequence, the links to West German industries are already obvious. For example, the Advisory Board of Zeiss-Jena had two members from the Board of the Zeiss Group from West Germany. Thus any reorganization would reflect decisions in the interests of its major competitor in West Germany.

The second influence comes from the so-called 'one dollar' 'one D-Mark' people who helped to boost the staff of the THA immediately after unification. Many of these were also borrowed from major West German enterprises and, of course, made sure that in the restructuring potential competition and entry by foreigners were to some extent made more difficult. The THA has meanwhile recognized this and has gone out of its way to avoid such conflicts of interest and to open the selling process more actively to foreigners.

In its privatization activities the THA must also keep the antitrust implications in mind, as is evidenced, for example, by its sale of the East German regional newspapers in 1991. In some instances, such as in the energy and the insurance markets, some of these mergers had already taken place before unification, at a time when only the East German antitrust laws were relevant.

However, one must always keep in mind that the old East German antitrust laws and the West German antitrust laws only become relevant after a certain size threshold. Below that the THA is free to restructure and sell on its own initiative and thereby has an important effect on the emerging competitive industry structure in East Germany.

8   The role of the antitrust authorities

8.1   The East German antitrust authorities

After the passage of the law on joint ventures of January 25, 1990, the possibility for East/West joint venture activities emerged. The new East German government also created an antitrust authority (AfW) whose initial aim was to control the abuse of dominant power (given the monopolized structure and the expected liberalization of price). Pressure from the West German antitrust authorities (the Bundeskatelamt, BKartA) enlarged its responsibility to cover in addition scrutiny of the emerging joint venture activities (AfW, Amt für Wettbewerbschutz IFA). A special law on antitrust policy was passed in June 1990 which gave additional powers to the AfW. This antitrust law came into effect on July 1, 1990, at the time of the currency union, but could be applied retroactively to mergers that had followed the joint venture law. Mergers had to be approved within two months. This new law was mainly aimed at speeding the flow of capital and know-how for mergers and joint ventures. Since the AfW was not legally obliged to prohibit certain mergers, a host of market power-enhancing mergers took place in those last days of the East German government (i.e., in the insurance market, the retail market, the electricity market, the gas market, etc.). The AfW ceased to exist after October 1990. Part of its personnel was taken over by the West German antitrust administration. Its old decisions still apply, however.

8.2   The West German antitrust law

After unification, the Federal Cartel Office was responsible for all of Germany. Any mergers which had not been notified through the AfW could still be checked by the West German office. The BKartA also continued a number of cases which were not finished by the AfW (118 cases, i.e., 42 per cent of AfW's total notifications). In the other 103 cases, both the AfW and the BKartA did separate parallel investigations. Only 46 cases were exclusively processed by AfW. None were opposed, not even the *de facto* wholesale takeover of the East German insurance market by Alliant. Any opposition to these mergers therefore came from the West German side, either because of the parallel process (where both markets were affected) or because of the shift of responsibilities to the West German side.

By the end of June 1991 the West German authorities had registered 816 mergers with East German companies. Some 402 had not yet concluded their mergers, while the other 414 had been legally concluded. Of these, 63 later did not have to be registered, included six cases where the merger proposal was not carried out (for example, the intended merger between Lufthansa and Interflug), only one merger was stopped, and six were modified.

In summary, it must be said that given the enormous pressure on the West German authorities these verifications proceeded rather quickly, i.e., out of the 313 mergers analysed 262 were released within one month. Only for the rest did the Federal Cartel Office exploit the four months period, but often not to the full extent.

9 Analysis of mergers

Merger activity really started picking up after the Currency Union, i.e., after July 1, 1990. The actual number of mergers started to increase as the sales activities by the THA increased. Most mergers took place in the retail sector (essentially non-tradeables) and in the building supply sector, to be followed by machine tools, services and the chemical and electro technical industry. Only 10 per cent of these mergers were by foreigners. Intra-German mergers were very dominant.

Merger activity was of course concentrated in the small-size class (including the takeover of newly separated or created firms) with very little in the very large-size class. This has to do with the difficulty of restructuring some of the very large 'Kombinate' although there was some restructuring before the mergers.

The acquiring companies dominate the size class above $2 billion sales, almost one-quarter were above DM12 billion. Thus a fair amount of mergers in the lower-size class related to small and medium firms (up to the size class of DM500 million sales).

10 The form of mergers

The form of mergers changed over time. Initially only joint ventures were possible, and, of course, they dominated until unification. But even later joint ventures were a very prominent form of merger because this allowed the buyer to take out the most attractive part of the East German company and to link it to the West German partner.

From the sample of mergers analysed by the Federal Cartel Office, 44 per cent of the 350 mergers concluded were a form of joint ventures. The rest were acquired through taking a dominant share (33 per cent) or taking over the whole company (19 per cent). An important role of mergers which may not yet have been concluded but which are quite important (for example, in the energy and public utilities sectors) is the case where a company works under West German management (management contracts) in anticipation of an eventual merger.

One must also see that many of the joint ventures were only a first step before the East German companies were fully taken over. This is not only the result of reducing restrictions on joint ventures (after July 1990 the 49 per cent maximum share rule was discontinued) but also because the West German enterprises wanted to get full control quickly over these subsidiaries in the East. The plans by some East German companies to keep some influence through joint ventures have by now lost almost all significance.

Almost all the 350 mergers were horizontal mergers (95.4 per cent). Only in 23 cases (6.3 per cent) was the area of activity enlarged by the buyer and only 11 cases (3.4 per cent) were vertical mergers. Conglomerate mergers were almost non-existent (only 1.4 per cent).

It seems clear, therefore, that unification has mainly led to a market extension. The West Germans have sought to defend their markets in new regions or to extend their product spectrum slightly. Diversification into companies that were operating in the very difficult macroeconomic environment were therefore of little significance. This, of course, was a policy that facilitated the transfer of know-how to these companies. It is clear that this type of selling approach by the THA ignores the market opening potential that is created through entry and through changing the competitive position of the joint markets.

If one looks at the mergers by sector, it is interesting to recognize that the largest interest was in the non-tradeable sectors. Retailing, newspapers and publishing houses, building materials and machine tools were among the favourite sectors, followed by services. Other sectors were of much less interest to the West German buyers, especially such sectors as metals, shipbuilding, glass, wood, pulp and paper, plastics and rubber, and textiles. All attracted very little interest from potential buyers. On the one hand these are, of course, the sectors which are the most difficult to restructure and with the largest ongoing losses. Because of the revaluation of the currency, their loss of markets was greatest. On the other hand, there is little comparative danger from these markets to the West German suppliers.

If one looks at this in a more systematic fashion, initially entry concentrated on the retailing sector and the associated distribution functions. The manufacturing sector, which continued to be still largely controlled by the THA, only became interesting later, for certain activities. However, as a boom in West Germany, fuelled by a growing demand from the East, started to cause capacity constraints, more enterprises looked for extra capacity in the East. This was encouraged by the increasing subsidies now given in East Germany.

In addition the markets that were most interesting were those which had a regional character and were therefore protected from international competition. Retail trade, services, and the building and construction sectors were important here, but also the acquisition of certain East German trade marks in the beer and tobacco sectors. The interest in the construction sector was related to the reconstruction of the East German infrastructure and expected market volume there.

11 Tentative conclusions

The enormous change in East Germany that was brought about through unification has brought the full market forces of the EC and an integrated international economy fully to bear on East German industry. Given the enormous revaluation and the breakdown of traditional markets, macroeconomic starting conditions were very bad. Given, furthermore, the lack of certain functional management experience necessary to exploit the potential of decentralization (marketing, purchasing, controlling, finance, etc.), mergers with Western companies were an important way in which management, technology and capital transfer could proceed quickly. In effect this has led to a *de facto* colonization of the most interesting and economically profitable activities in the East by the West. The policy of MBOs and MBIs encouraged by the THA was only a small counterweight (a policy which is much less popular in the East).

Mergers are therefore a very important instrument to restructure the economy and to monitor closely the necessary investment and restructuring decisions. Because of the high degree of uncertainty in the region (old market data, meaningless data, non-existent new public data from stock markets and reporting agencies) only a hands-on approach can avoid wrong investment and restructuring decisions (or at least minimize the associated mistakes). Horizontal mergers are therefore the cheapest form in which this takes place. The East German enterprises will obviously have to be reoriented in the product spectrum to a much more competitive domestic market, but also to the West. Since most of these markets are now already dominated by Western products, Western companies have a major advantage in their knowledge of the underlying technology characterizing these markets. Restructuring through mergers is therefore a natural process.

The alternative of trying to stabilize the East German companies through holding companies staffed with Western managers and with the monitoring by the state holding company THA has obvious disadvantages. The problem is not only the lack of sector specific information, but also the much softer budget constraint and the difficulty of monitoring. The THA could also hire West German managers, but has probably less efficient monitoring techniques.

These East/West mergers must therefore be seen not so much as a way of enlarging the sphere of influence and market power of the West German companies, but as an instrument of restructuring. I believe this conclusion also has interesting implications for the restructuring of the rest of Eastern Europe.

Notes

1. Similar problems are facing the newly formed public administration, after the centralized government was replaced by five regional states. Because of the relatively complicated West German legal and institutional arrangements it takes a long time to build up such an administrative structure in the East and to train the administration and the entrepreneurs accordingly.
2. Private firms that had been forced to cooperate with the state.
3. The tax rate for profits of small firms was 90 per cent.
4. In 1989, the East German statistical office estimated its GNP to be 353 bn Marks; the DIW estimate was 290 DM, using W. German prices.

Index

agriculture
  bilateral agreements
    United States and Canada 12
    United States and Mexico 12
  Common Agricultural Policy *see* Common Agricultural Policy
  European Agricultural Guarantee and Guidance Fund (EAGGF), Guidance section 205, 206
  in Greece, impact of EC membership on 102–4
  NAFTA and 12
  numbers employed in 203
Akerlof, G.A., *et al* 273, 276–7
ALADI (Latin American Integration Association) 72
Albert, Michel 172, 182
American National Standards Institute (ANSI) 212
ANDEAN Group 71
Antigua & Barbuda 65, 67, 77, 80
Arestis, Philip 201–8
Aristotle 102
Armstrong, Philip 179
Arrow, K.J. 187, 191–2, 194, 196, 200
  possibility theorem 192, 194
Artis, Michael J. 238
ASEAN countries 71
Atkinson, A. 129

Bahamas 65, 67
Balusn, R. 219n
Bank Accounts Directive 254
Barbados 65, 67, 68, 76, 79
Barre Report 235
Basle Accord 1988 254
beggar-thy-neighbour policies 162, 164, 165
Belgium
  farm incomes 117
  health care expenditure 137, 139
  social expenditure 126
  state enterprises 172

Belize 65, 67, 68, 78
Berendson, B.S.M. 85
Beveridge, Sir William 164
Bhagwati, Jagdish 171
Bliss, C. 186
Bomberg, E. 136
Bortz, Jeffrey 60
Boskin, M.J. 35, 37, 38, 52, 54n
Boyer, Robert 171, 172, 179, 182
Braga de Macedo, J. 186
Bretton Woods 71, 173, 231, 236
British Virgin Islands 65, 67, 68, 77
Brown, C. 115, 116, 117
Buchanan, J. 105
budgetary transfers 98, 100, 112, 113
Bundesbank
  ERM and 245, 246
  quantity-of-money rule 274
  re-unification and 274, 275
  tight monetary policy 245–6
Buse, A. 141n
Bush, George 20, 71, 72

Cameron, Maxwell A. 23–33, 170
Campbell, Bruce 25
Canada
  Canada–US Free Trade Agreement (CUFTA) *see* CUFTA
  fishing industry 177
  job creation 57
  Mexico, trade with *see* NAFTA
  NAFTA and 3–21
    biotechnology inventions, patents for 15
    cultural industries exemption 7, 15
    FTA preferences in US market 7
    Mexico, improved access to 7
    see also NAFTA
  productivity growth 57, 58, 60
  telecommunications 14
  trade dependence of 180, 181
  trade unions 60, 61–2, 63
    Canadian Labour Congress 61, 62

297

transportation 14
unemployment 177, 181
United States and 175–6
   agriculture, bilateral agreements on 12
   manufacturing industries compared, competitiveness and productivity 35–54
   see also CUFTA
   see also North American Bloc (NAB)
CAP *see* Common Agricultural Policy (CAP)
capital mobility 24, 63
   unfettered, effect on trade unions 30
Cárdenas, Cuauhtémoc 33
Caribbean Basin Initiative (CBI) 71–2
Caribbean Common Market (CARICOM) 65–80
   achievements of 69
   areas of activity 66
   case for integration 68–9
   common currency 74, 75
   constraints of small size, overcoming 68–9
   coordinated actions 66
   cultural identity 69
   current mood and situation 70–72
   decision making in 69–70
   deepening of 72–80
      economic strategies 73–4
      economic integration 66, 73–4
         cooperation in production approach 73, 74
         market liberalization approach 73–4
      political economy of 75
      unequal partners 76–8
   foreign policies of member states, coordination of 66
   functional cooperation 66, 69
   Grand Anse Declaration 70
   IMF/World Bank trusteeship 71
   joint actions 66
      in extra-regional trade 66
   Kingston Declaration 70
   Lesser Developed Countries (LDCs)
      see Lesser Developed Countries
   market integration 66
   monetary integration 75
   performance capacity 73
   regional integration 69
   rules of origin 69
   shortcomings of 69
   Single Market 74
   statistical profile 66–8
   textile and apparel exports 11
   Venezuela, agreement with 80n
   West Indian Commission 70, 73, 74
   widening of 78
Caribbean Free Trade Association (CARIFTA) 65
Caribbean Investment Fund 74
CE (Communauté Européenne) mark 213
Ceccini, P. 219n
CEN (European Committee for Standardization) 211
CENELEC (European Committee for Electrotechnical Standardization) 211
Central American Common Market 71
central banks
   Committee of Governors of the Central Banks 235, 237
   Eastern Caribbean Central Bank 76
   EMU 246
   European System of Central Banks (ESCB) 237
Charnovitz, Steve 22n
China 71
Claessens, Evrard 83–95
Clinton, Bill 16, 20, 21, 22n, 28, 30
Cobb–Douglas function 37
Coffey, Peter 238
Cold War
   end of 61
   free trade and 171–3
collective bargaining 179, 201
collective preferences 191, 192, 196
Common Agricultural Policy (CAP) 31, 101, 102, 106, 236
   EC convergence policies and 205
   exchange rate mechanism, the *snake* 236
   expenditure under 111
   externalization of cost 113–14
   farm incomes, support of 114–15
   farm type and size 115–17
   'green' conversion rates 112, 120
   law of one price (LOP) 119

milk quotas 114
Monetary Compensatory Amounts (MCAs) 112–13, 119–20
  origin and outcomes 110–12
  political integration and 112–14
  price policy 110, 117–18
  quotas 114, 119
  revenue under 111
  sanitary and phytosanitary barriers to trade 119
  social policy and income convergence 114–18
  spatial market integration and 118–20
  stabilizers 114
  variable import protection 110
Community Support Framework (CSF) 206
comparative advantage principle 7, 162, 163, 172
comparative cost 161, 163–4
Consolidated Supervision Directive 254
Constantopoulos, M. 101, 108n
copyright, NAFTA and 15
cost-push inflation, Greece 101, 106
CUFTA (Canada-US Free Trade Agreement) 70, 176
  Canada
    cultural industries 7
    unemployment 177
    US trade-remedy laws, effect of 24, 28
  dispute settlement provisions 20
  neo-conservative agenda 25
  public policy and 25
  transnational corporations (TNCs) and 23–4, 27
Curme, Michael 62
Currie, D. 250

de Carmoy, Hervé 178
De Grauwe, P. 134
de la Torre, Augusto 183n
Delors, Jacques 236
Delors Plan 236
Delors Report 237
'Delors II' 116
Demas, William 79
Denmark
  farm incomes 117

health care
  expenditure 137, 139
  financing 136
  state enterprises 172
  taxation of savings 232
  trade balance 94
Deravi, M. Keivan 238
deregulation measures 179
Dillon, John 28
direct transfers through trade 98, 100
Divinney, T. 219n
Dominica 65, 67, 77
Drache, Daniel 28, 170–84

EAGGF, (European Agricultural Guarantee and Guidance Fund), Guidance section 205, 206
East Caribbean Common Market (ECCM) 65
East Germany see Germany
Eastern Caribbean Central Bank 76
economic integration
  cooperation in production approach 73, 74
  gradualism v. acceleration 76
  institutuionalized 28
  market liberalization approach 73–4
  political economy of 75
  political union and 187–91
  social democratic perspective 28–33
  societal needs and 28–33
  trade unions and 180
  see also trade unions
  see also trade blocs
Economic and Monetary Union (EMU) 110, 208
  regional imbalance and social protection and 122–34
  see also European Monetary Union
Eichengreen, B. 247, 248, 250n
El-Agraa, A.M. 186
Emerson, Michael 176, 179, 180, 239, 240
EMS see European Monetary System
EMU see European Monetary Union
Englander, Steven 156n
Enterprise for Americas Initiative (EAI) 71, 72
environment
  EC standards 33

free trade, effect of 24
NAFTA and 8, 15–16, 27
North American Commission for the Environment (NACE), proposed 16
trade policy and 27
Esping-Andersen, Gösta 179, 182
ETSI (European Telecommunications Standards Institute) 211
European Agricultural Guarantee and Guidance Fund (EAGGF), Guidance section 205, 206
European Commission 32
European Committee for Electrotechnical Standardization (CENELEC) 211
European Committee for Standardization (CEN) 211
European Community (EC) 27, 161, 166–8, 170, 188
  banking 230, 253–5
    'Banking 1992', definition 253
    directives on 254–5
      Second Banking Directive 210, 215, 218
  budgetary transfers 98, 100, 112, 113
  Cohesion Fund 141, 206
  Committee of Governors of the Central Banks 235, 237
  Common Agricultural Policy *see* Common Agricultural Policy
  communitarization 84
  compensatory arrangements 33
  Consolidated Supervision Directive 254
  de-mineralization 84
  decentralization 33
  democracy as condition of membership 30
  direct transfers through trade 98, 100
  EC–92 programme 210–19, 252
  economic cohesion 122
  economic welfare 190–91
  electronics production 214
  EMU *see* Economic and Monetary Union; European Monetary Union
  Exchange Rate Mechanism (ERM) *see* Exchange Rate Mechanism
  'Excluded Sectors' Directive 215

externalization of trade 83–95
farm income 100, 114–15, 117
FEOGA 100
financial integration 223–34
  banks 230
  company taxation 233–4
  conceptual framework 226–8
  direct credit controls 230
  economic agents
    enterprises 229
    households 229
  exchange controls 226
  exchange rate stability 227, 231–2
  financial intermediaries 230
  fiscal dimension 232–4
  freedom of establishment 226, 254
  government budgets, financing of 230–31
  insurance companies 230
  main directives 228
  monetary policy 230
  money laundering 228
  potential for financial development 224–6
  programme of 226
  prudential and regulatory systems, harmonization of 226–7
  public deficit, financing of 230–31
  reserve requirements on bank deposits 230
  restructuring of financial systems of member states 229
  stock market capitalization 224–5
  taxation of interest income 227, 232–4
financial sector 215–16
First Banking Coordination Directive 254
'Fortress Europe' 86, 210, 216
Free Capital Movements Directive 255
freedom of establishment 226, 254
'green' conversion rates 112, 120
health care in members states 135–8
  expenditure 137–8
  determinants of 138–41
  financing 136
home country supervision 227
import and trade volumes 84
income transfers 98–100

internalization of trade 83–95
Japan and 216
labour mobility 33, 247
law of one price (LOP) 119
local content 214–15
Lomé Convention 72
market liberalization principles 74
Monetary Compensatory Amounts (MCAs) 112–13, 119–20
monetary integration
  EMS and 238–9
  history of 236–8
  Maastricht Treaty and 239, 243
  see also Economic and Monetary Union; European Monetary Union
mutual recognition, principle of 215, 227
NAFTA compared 28–33
Own Funds Directive 254
peripheral countries of 203–5
  EC policies and 205–8
  education and training 207–8
  foreign direct investment (FDI) 206
  manufacturing sector 206–7, 208
  small to medium enterprises (SMEs) 207, 208
  see also Southern Europe *below*
political integration 112–14, 189–90, 196–9
public procurement 214–15
quotas 114, 119
reciprocity 255
  mirror image 210, 216
  national treatment 210, 216
regional cohesion 122–34
rules of origin 214–15
Second Banking Coordination Directive 254
Second Banking Directive 210, 215, 218
single licence 215, 227
Single Market *see* Single European Market
social, labour and environmental standards 33
social protection 122–34
  meaning 122
Solvency Ratios Directive 255
Southern Europe 186–200, 241

  see also peripheral countries of *above*
standards, harmonization of 210–12, 213
  European Committee for Electrotechnical Standardization (CENELEC) 211
  European Committee for Standardization (CEN) 211
  European Telecommunications Standards Institute (ETSI) 211
  'New Approach' 211–12
Structural Funds 205, 206, 241
subsidiarity 30, 33, 190
supranational institutions 33
testing and certification 212–14
  CE (Communauté Européenne) 213
trade balances 93–5
trade creation effect 204–5
trade diversion effect 204
trade unions, effect on 30–31
unemployment 56, 98, 177, 204, 206
United States and *see* United States
European Court of Justice 70
European Currency Unit (ECU) 236, 237
European Financial Area 223
European Monetary Institute (EMI) 237
European Monetary System (EMS) 223, 231, 236
  exchange rate mechanism of 237
  monetary integration and 238–9
European Monetary Union (EMU) 235–42, 243–50
  budget deficit and 237
  currency devaluations and 237
  future of 239–42
  inflation rate and 237
  interest rate and 237
  macroeconomics and 244–5
  microeconomics and 246–8
  monetary policy 245–6
  policy options 248–50
  transactions costs 239–40
  see also Economic and Monetary Union
European Parliament 32, 70
European Regional Development Fund (ERDF) 205, 206
European Social Fund (ESF) 205, 206

European System of Central Banks
    (ESCB) 237
European Telecommunications Standards Institute (ETSI) 211
Exchange Rate Mechanism (ERM) 120, 231–2
  Bundesbank and 245
  currency crisis (1992) 243
  currency devaluations 237
  monetary integration and 238–9
  'soft' 249, 250
'Excluded Sectors' Directive 215

Farrell, Terrence 76, 80n
Faux, Jeff 27
FEOGA 100
Filatotchev, J.V. 278
First Banking Coordination Directive 254
Fordism 201–3
  crisis in 201–2
  Peripheral Fordism 202–3
'Fortress Europe' 86, 210, 216
France
  EAGGF, contributions from 205
  education and training 207–8
  farm incomes 117
  health care expenditure 137, 139
  labour force, increase in 56
  labour productivity, growth of 151–2
  state enterprises 172
  trade balance 94
  trade dependence of 180, 181
Frankel, J.A. 245
Free Capital Movements Directive 255
free trade
  benefits of 24, 162
  blocs *see* trade blocs
  capital mobility, increased 24
  Cold War and 171–3
  econometric models 23, 24
  effects of 24–5
  gains from trade 23, 162
  global, full employment and 179–80
  human capital, role of 24
  income distribution, changes in 24
  institutional, social and political
    structures 24
  intrafirm trade and 23, 24
  neoclassical trade theory 24

public services, provision of 25
  as restructuring programme 23–5
  role of governments 24
  terms of trade under 164–6
  trade unionism, effect on 24
  zones *see* trade blocs
free trade agreements (FTAs) 75
  see also CUFTA; NAFTA
free trade blocs *see* trade blocs
Freedman, A. 35
Freedom of Establishing Directive 254
Friedman, George 171, 183n
full employment 179–80

G–7 236
GATT (General Agreement on Trade
    and Tariffs) 15, 112, 161, 172–3, 174
  dispute settlement 16, 172–3
  EC-92 and 218
  principles of 165
  rules of origin and 214
  trade disputes, settlement of 172–3
  US and 25
Georgakopoulos, Theodore 98–108, 168
Germany
  antitrust law 291–2
  Bundesbank 245, 246, 274, 275
  CAP and 112
  coal industry 177
  education and training 207–8
  farm incomes 117
  health care expenditure 137, 139
  industrial strategy 172
  labour force, increase in 56
  labour productivity, growth of 151–2
  mergers 291–3
  re-unification 247
    Bundesbank's quantity-of-money
      rule 274
    conversion rate for money assets 275
    Currency Union 292
    East Germany
      antitrust authorities, role of 291–2
      currency reform 285
      economic structure 283–4
      industrial structure 283–4
      initial reforms 284–5
      labour market conditions 277–8

private firms, position of 288–9
privatization *see* Treuhandanstalt *below*
restructuring economy of 282–95
firms, ability to bear investment risks 275–6
flow problem 274, 276
German Monetary Union (GMU) 274–6
inflation resulting from 239
integrated labour market 273–4
joint-ventures 291, 292
mergers
  analysis of 292, 294
  form of 292–3
  importance of 294
money overhang 274
sequence of 273–4
stock problem 274
trade unions 276
Treuhandanstalt (THA) 279–80, 282, 284
  initial progress 286–8
  management buy-outs/management buy-ins (MBOs/MBIs) 280, 289
  privatization
    initial progress 286–8
    means of 280
    stimulating private enterprise 285–6
  role of 285–6, 290
  subsidization 280
unemployment 276–7
Unity Fund 274
wage policy 276–8
trade balance 94
trade dependence of 180, 181
Gertler, Meric 170, 175
Giannitsis, T. 108n
Gibson, D.H. 186
Glasbeek, Harry 179
Golke, Rainer 287
Gos, Erik 122–34
Greece
cost-push inflation 101, 106
EC membership 143–56, 162, 168
  agriculture
    Common Agricultural Policy (CAP) 101, 102, 106, 112
    EAGGF, contributions from 205
    employment in 203
    farm incomes 116, 117
    farmers, income support for 100
    impact on 102–4
  exchange rate changes 101, 106
  exports to EC 100, 101
  farmers, income support for 100
  food prices, increase in 106
  imports from EC 100, 101
  industrial production 98
  inflation rate 98, 101, 106, 238
  inter-country income transfers 98–100
  macroeconomic aspects 106
  manufacturing, impact on 104–5
  national currency, depreciation of 106
  public sector, impact on 105
  trade and welfare effects of 100–102
  unemployment 98, 177
education and training 207–8
EMU and 240, 241
financial system 255–8
  Athens Stock Exchange (ASE) 253, 256, 258
    market efficiency 260
  banking system 255–6
    Bank of Greece 255, 257
    commercial banks 257
      restrictions on portfolio of 257
    and credit policy 256–7
    regulation of 257–8
      effectiveness of 258
      monetary control 257–8
      prudential control 257
    selective credit policies 258
    specialized credit institutions 257
  capital market 256
  competition versus solvency 261
  conflict of interest 262
  efficiency 259–61
    allocational efficiency 259
    informational efficiency 260
    operational or transactional efficiency 261–2
  fairness 261
  financial innovation 263–4
    average rate caps 267–8

floors and collars 267
interest rate caps 267
options 264–5
  arbitrageurs 265
  hedgers 265
  payoffs 264–5
  speculators 265
securitization 268
swaps 265–6
  interest rate swaps 266–7
  swaptions 268
freedom of entry 261
full disclosure 261
market integration and industry consolidation 262–3
  mergers and acquisitions 262–3
  strategic alliances 263
securities market 256
health care
  expenditure 137, 138, 139
  financing 136
investment, levels of 204
labour productivity, growth of 151–2
trade balance 94
unemployment 98, 177
'green' conversion rates 112, 120
Grenada 65, 67, 77, 79
Grinspun, Ricardo 23–33, 170
Guyana 65, 67, 68, 70, 76, 78, 79
  balance of payments crisis 69

Hallock 61, 62, 63
Harris, Rick 176
Hart, M. 25
Haspeslagh, Ph. 92
Hayami, Y. 37
Hayashi, Fumio 166
Hecker 61, 62, 63
Helleiner, Gerald 27
Hightower, W. 219n
Hitiris, Theo 83, 135–41
Hong Kong 71
Hufbauer, Gary 3–22, 60, 80n, 170, 175, 176
Huhne, Christopher 176, 239, 240

Ilzkovitz, Fabinne 156n
Imaz, Carlos 62
IMF (International Monetary Fund) 71, 77, 78, 80

income transfers
  budgetary transfers 98, 100, 112, 113
  direct transfers through trade 98, 100
individual preferences 191–6
intellectual property rights, NAFTA and 15
International (Bretton Woods) Development Agencies Trusteeship 71
international credit economy 202
International Standards Organization (ISO) 212
international trade
  beggar-thy-neighbour policies 162, 164, 165
  comparative cost as basis for 161, 163–4
  comparative advantage principle 162, 163
  government intervention and 24
  neo-mercantilism 164, 165
  neoclassical theory 24
  tariffs and quotas 164, 165
  terms of trade 162, 164–6
intrafirm trade 23, 24
  see also transnational corporations
Ireland
  agriculture
    CAP and 112, 115
    EAGGF, contributions from 205
    employment in 203
    farm incomes 116
  currency devaluation 243
  education and training 207–8
  EMU and 240
  ERM and 243
  health care expenditure 137, 139
  investment
    foreign direct investment (FDI) 206
    levels of 204
  taxation of savings 232
  trade balance 94
  unemployment 204, 206
Isard, W. 85
Island developing communities (IDCs) 68
Italy
  ERM and 238, 243
  farm incomes 116
  health care
    expenditure 137, 139

financing 136
labour force, increase in 56
state enterprises 172
taxation of savings 232
trade balance 94
trade dependence of 181

Jamaica 65, 66, 67, 68, 70, 76, 79
    balance of payments crisis 69
Japan 27, 167
    EC and 216
    export-substituting investment 216
    labour force, increase in 56
    Pacific Rim agreement 71
    savings rate 166
    trade dependence of 181
    unemployment 56–7
    US, relationship with 216
'Jean Monnet' project 85
Jemison, D. 92
Jenkins, Roy 236

Katseli, L. 203
Keeble, D., *et al* 201
Kelly, Margaret R. 183n
Kenen, P. 246
Keynes, John Maynard 164, 165, 190, 246
Kintis, A.A. 156n
Koester, U. 112
Kohl, Helmut 284
Kollias, Sotirios 223–34
Kondonassis, A.J. 235–42
Kopinak, Kathryn 26
Kreklewich, Robert 27
Krugman, P.R. 33n

labour mobility, in EC 33, 247
labour relations, NAFTA and 56, 61
Larre, B. 186
Latin American Integration Association (ALADI) 72
Lau, L.J. 35, 37, 38, 52, 54n
law of one price (LOP) 119
Lawrence, Robert Z. 172
Le Grand, J. 125
Leaner, Dick 181
Lebard, Meredith 171, 183n
Lee, Thea 27
Leeward Islands 65, 68

Leeward Islands Federation 65
Lesser Developed Countries (LDCs) 76, 79–80, 167
    CARICOM treaty concessionary regime 66, 68, 77–8
    characteristics of 77
    harmonization of tariffs 69
Lipietz, A. 202
Lipsey, R. 219
Litan, Robert E. 172
local content requirement
    in EC 214–15
    NAFTA and 8
Luxembourg
    farm incomes 117
    health care expenditure 137, 138

Ma, B.K. 38, 52
Maastricht Treaty 122, 175, 206, 235
    convergence, aim of 205, 208
    economic and social objectives of EC 189–90
    EMU and 246
    health protection 135, 136
    monetary integration and 239, 243
    social charter 30
McKinnon, R.I. 277
Malaysia 71
Malliaris, A.G. 235–42
Malthus, Thomas 164
markets
    domestic, role of 24
    imperfectly competitive 23
    open, unemployment and 173
    organization of, trade blocs and 188–9
    segmented 174
    structure of, government intervention and 24
Maroulis, D. 108n
MDCs 76–7, 78
    external debt problems 76
mergers
    in Germany 292–4
    in Greece 262–3
    proposed directive on 233
    taxation on gains arising from 233
Metghalchi, Massoud 238
Mexico
    automobile industry 10
    Canada, trade with *see* NAFTA

energy resources 8, 27–8
foreign investment 14
indebtedness of 25, 26, 29
labour force expansion 58
maquiladora industry 26, 27
NAFTA and 3–21
  capital inflows 3, 25–6
  human capital, effects on 26
  job creation 26
  real wages and income inequality 26
  reform process 3, 6
    legal and judicial reforms 21
  trade unions 26
  transnational corporations (TNCs) 26
  see also NAFTA
oil 8, 27–8
productivity 57–8
telecommunications market 14
trade unions 26, 30, 60, 61, 62
transportation 12, 14
United States and
  agriculture, bilateral agreements on 12, 13
  Binational Commission 20
  'Border Plan' 16
  emigration 6–7, 58, 59–60, 61
  trade with 5, 6, 7, 176
  see also NAFTA
see also North American Bloc (NAB)
Mill, John Stuart 83
Miller, M. 249
Mittelstadt, Axel 156n
Molle, W. 186
monetarist policies 24
Monetary Compensatory Amounts (MCAs) 112–13, 119–20
monetary integration
  CARICOM and 75
  EMS and 238–9
  ERM and 238–9
  European, history of 236–8
  Maastricht Treaty and 239, 243
  see also Economic and Monetary Union; European Monetary Union
Monnet index 85–8, 90, 91
Montserrat 65, 67, 77
multinational enterprises (MNEs) 204, 206–7

Müller, Jürgen 282–95
Mundell, R. 246
Mutual Recognition Agreements (MRAs) 218

NAFTA (North American Free Trade Agreement) 70, 161, 170, 175, 178, 188, 252
  accession to 21
  agriculture 12
  aims of 61
  apparel 10–11
  asymmetries of power 27–8
  automobiles 8–10
  backgrounds to 3–7
  Committee on Standards-Related Measures 15
  dispute settlement procedures 8, 15–16, 20–21, 32
  economic development and 25–7]
  efficiency benefits 7
  employment, impact on 16–20
  energy 8
  environment 8, 15–16, 27
    Committee on Sanitary and Phytosanitary Measures 15
  European Community (EC) compared 28–33
  financial sector, growth of employment in 61
  financial services 12
  gains from trade 23
  growth stimulus 7
  implications for members 3–7
  information sector, growth of employment in 61
  intellectual property rights 15
  investment 14–15
  job creation 26, 57
  labour adjustment 16–20
  labour relations and 56, 61
  manufacturing jobs, decline in 61
  Mexico and *see* Mexico
  most-favoured-nation (MFN) obligation 14
  North American Free Trade Commission 20
  provisions of 7–21
  public policy and 31
  rule of origin 11

service sector, growth of employment in 61
telecommunications 14
textiles 10–11
trade unions and 26, 31, 61–3
transnational corporations (TNCs) and 23–4, 27, 30
transportation 12, 14
US trade-remedy laws and 24
see also Canada; Mexico; United States
Nelson, Douglas 172
neoclassical trade theory 23, 24
Netherlands
EAGGF, contributions from 205
farm incomes 117
health care expenditure 137, 139
labour force, increase in 56
state enterprises 172
taxation of savings 232
trade balance 94
Nevin, E. 186
North American Bloc (NAB)
capital accumulation 61
employment in 56–7
labour force, growth of 56
productivity 57–8
unemployment 56–7, 61
working class in 58–61
see also Canada; Mexico; United States
North American Commission for the Environment (NACE), proposed 16
North American Free Trade Agreement *see* NAFTA
North Korea 71

Obstfeld, M. 33n
Ohmae, Kenichi 178
oil crisis (1973) 83
oil crisis (1979) 84
oligopoly 167, 261
Organization of Eastern Caribbean States (OECS) 65, 73, 76, 77, 79
Osberg, L. 131
O'Shea, Eamon 134n
Own Funds Directive 254

Pacific Rim agreement 71, 161, 188, 252
Pacolet, Jozef 122–34

Padoa-Schioppa, T. 243
Paliginis, Eleni 201–8
Pantos, Themis D. 252–69
Paraskevopoulos, Christos C. 35–54, 252–69
Paschakis, J. 245
Paschos, P. 100, 103
patents, NAFTA and 15
Peripheral Fordism 202–3
Peterson, J. 136
Pigou, A.C. 165
political integration
CAP and 112–14
in EC 112–14, 189–90, 196–9
economic integration and 187–91
Porter, Michael 93, 175
Portugal
agriculture
EAGGF, contributions from 205
employment in 203
farm incomes 116
currency devaluation 243
education and training 207–8
EMU and 240, 241
ERM and 238, 243
health care
expenditure 137
financing 136
inflation 238
investment
foreign direct investment (FDI) 206
levels of 203–4
trade balance 94
trade dependence of 180, 181
Posnett, J. 140, 141n
Pournarakis, Mike 210–19
Pradilla Cobos, Enrique 62
preferences 191
collective 191, 192, 196
individual 191–6
social 191–6
price theory 166–7
privatization 25, 179
in Eastern Europe 278–9
in Germany 279–80
public procurement 214–15
public services, provision of, free trade and 25

Quirk, J. 194

Reagan, Ronald 71
Ricardo, David 161, 162, 163, 273
    comparative advantage principal 162, 163
    comparative cost, law of 161, 163–4
Rima, Ingrid H. 161–9
Rohwedder, Detlev 287
Ruggie, John Gerard 172
rules of origin 174
    CARICOM and 69
    definition 174
    EC and 214–15
    NAFTA and 11
Ruttan, V.W. 37

St. Kitts & Nevis 65, 67, 77
St. Lucia 65, 67, 77, 80
St. Vincent & Grenadines 65, 67, 77, 80
Salinas, Samuel 62
Salvatore, Dominick 165
Saposnik, R. 194
Sbragia, Alberta M. 175, 183n
Schott, Jeffrey J. 16, 60, 80n, 175, 176
Second Banking Coordination Directive 254
Second Banking Directive 210, 215, 218
segmented markets 174
Sehwok, R. 219n
Sharpe, Andrew 181
Shrybman, Steven 27
Sinclair, S. 24
Singapore 71
Single European Act 83, 175, 178, 210, 228, 236, 253
Single European Market 206, 208, 210, 212, 216, 218, 253
    financial dimension of 223–4
Sinn, G. 278
Sinn, H.-W. 273, 278
small to medium enterprises (SMEs) 207, 208
    transactions costs and 240
Smithin, John N. 243–50
Smithsonian Accord 236
Smoot–Hawley Tariff 165
social choice 187
social dumping 24, 30
Social Fund, European *see* European Social Fund
social preferences 191–6

Solow, R.M. 35, 36, 144
Solvency Ratios Directive 255
South Korea 71, 167
Southern Cone Common Market 71
Spain
    agriculture
        EAGGF, contributions from 205
        employment in 203
        farm incomes 116
    currency devaluation 243
    EC membership 162
    education and training 207–8
    EMU and 240, 241
    ERM and 238, 239, 243
    health care
        expenditure 137, 139
        financing 136
    investment
        foreign direct investment (FDI) 206
        levels of 203–4
    trade balance 94
    trade dependence of 181
    unemployment 204
Spero, Joan 178
Strange, Susan 178
subsidiarity 30, 33, 190
Sweden, trade unions in 182

Taiwan 71, 167
Taylorism 208
technological change
    biased 35
    disembodied 35, 36
    role of 24
Teichman, Judith 25
Thailand 71
Todd, D. 156n
Tomann, Horst 273–81
Torres, R. 186
Tovias, Alfred 171
trade blocs
    access to 171
        artificially enhanced 176–7
    adjustment to 171, 175
    asymmetry between member states 171, 175–6
    Cold War and 171–3
    domination by single nation 175–6
    full employment and 179–80
    market organization and 188–9

social welfare, corporate efficiency of 178–9
trade regimes 170–71
see also economic integration
trade dependence 180, 181
trade regimes 170–71, 178
trade unions
  in Canada 60, 61–2, 63
  EC membership, effect of 30–31
  economic integration and 180
  free trade, effect of 24
  Germany 276
  in Mexico 26, 30, 60, 61, 62
  NAFTA and 26, 31, 61–3
  in Sweden 182
  unfettered capital mobility, effect of 30
  in US 61, 62
  wages and 179–80
    see also wages
  weakening of by free trade 24
Trade-Related Investment Measures (TRIMS) 15, 218
trademarks, NAFTA and 15
transnational corporations (TNCs) 23, 25, 178–9, 217–18
  CUFTA and 23–4, 27
  Mexico and 26
  NAFTA and 23–4, 27, 30
Treaty of Basseterre 65
Treaty of Chaguaramas 65, 69, 74
Treaty of European Union *see* Maastricht Treaty
Trinidad and Tobago 65, 67, 68, 70, 76, 79
Tsakatos, E. 186

Uimonen, Peter 22n
unemployment
  Canada 177, 181
  in EC 98, 177, 204, 206, 207
  education levels and 207
  European Community 56, 98, 177, 204, 206
  European Community (EC) 56
  Greece 98, 177
  Ireland 204, 206
  Japan 56–7
  North American Bloc (NAB) 56–7, 61
  open markets and 173
  Spain 204
Ungerer, Horst, *et al* 238
United Kingdom
  CAP and 112
  coal industry 177
  education and training 207–8
  ERM and 238, 239, 243, 245–6
  farm incomes 117
  health care
    expenditure 137, 139
    financing 136
  labour force, increase in 56
  trade balance 94
  trade dependence of 181
United States
  Advancing Skills Through Education and Training (ASETS) 20
  apparel trade 10–11
  Bush administration 15, 16, 20, 71, 72
  Canada and 175–6
    agriculture, bilateral agreements on 12
    manufacturing industries compared, competitiveness and productivity 35–54
    see also CUFTA
  Canada–US Free Trade Agreement (CUFTA) *see* CUFTA
  Clinton Administration 16, 20, 21, 28, 30
  Enterprise for Americas Initiative (EAI) 71, 72
  European Community (EC) and
    EC–92 programme 210–19
    local content 214–15
    public procurement 214–15
    reciprocity
      mirror image 210, 216
      national treatment 210, 216
    rules of origin 214–15
    standards 210–12
      American National Standards Institute (ANSI) 212
      testing and certification 212–14
      National Institute of Standards and Technology (NIST) 214
    trade and investment gains 216–18
  GATT and 25
  Japan, relationship with 216
  job creation 57

labour mobility 247
Mexico and
  agriculture, bilateral agreements on 12, 13
  American workers in 59
  Binational Commission 20
  'Border Plan' 16
  immigrants from 6–7, 58, 59–60, 61
  trade with 5, 6, 7
  NAFTA and 3–21
    foreign policy and 6–7
    industrial reorganization 3
    labour market 16–20
    long-term competitiveness 27
    reforms 3
    see also NAFTA
  North American Commission for the Environment (NACE), proposed 16
  productivity 57–8
  Reagan Administration 71, 216
  telecommunications 14
  textiles and apparel trade 10–11
  trade balance 180, 181
  trade unions 61, 62
  trade-remedy laws 24, 28
  transportation 12, 14
  see also North American Bloc (NAB)

Van der Hoop, J.H. 92
Velasco Arregui, Edur 56–63
Venezuela, CARICOM and 80n

Vinals, J., et al 203
Visser, Jelle 62

wages
  in an open economy 180–82
  collective bargaining 179, 201
  in East Germany 276–8
  'inflation plus' 201
  market forces 179
  NAFTA and 20, 27, 61
  social-wage bargains 182, 201
  trade unions 179–80
  wage rigidity 179
Walcott, Susan 168
Wallace, William 172
Watkins, M. 25
Werner, Pierre 235
Werner Report 236
West Germany see Germany
West Indian Commission 70, 73, 74
West Indies Associated States (WIAS) 65
West Indies Federation 65
Whalley, John 22n
Williamson, J. 245, 249, 250, 250n
Windward Islands 65, 68
Wolf, Bernard M. 243–50
World Bank 71, 77, 78, 80
Wyplosz, C. 248

Zanias, George P. 110–20
Zestos, George K. 143–56